Oscar Wilde on Stage and Screen

Oscar Wilde on Stage and Screen

ROBERT TANITCH

Methuen

Published by Methuen 1999

1 3 5 7 9 10 8 6 4 2

First published in the United Kingdom in 1999 by
Methuen Publishing Limited
215 Vauxhall Bridge Road, London SWlV 1EJ

Peribo Pty Ltd, 58 Beaumont Road, Mount Kuring-Gai
NSW 2080, Australia, ACN 002 273 761
(for Australia and New Zealand)

The cover photograph and all other photographs of Oscar Wilde are from the collection of Merlin Holland, except for the Plays part title photograph which is from the William Andrews Clark Library, Los Angeles.

Methuen Publishing Limited Reg. No. 3543167

A CIP catalogue record for this book is available from the British Library

ISBN 0 413 72610 X

Typeset by MATS, Southend-on-Sea, Essex
Printed and bound in Great Britain by
Biddles Ltd, Guildford and King's Lynn

FOR JOHN AND KATE COOPER

Also by Robert Tanitch

A Pictorial Companion to Shakespeare's Plays
Ralph Richardson, A Tribute
Olivier
Leonard Rossiter
Ashcroft
Gielgud
Dirk Bogarde
Guinness
Sean Connery
John Mills
Brando
Clint Eastwood
The Unknown James Dean

Contents

OTHER WORKS

I awoke the imagination of my century so that it created a myth and legend round me. I summed up all systems in a phrase; and all existence in an epigram.

Oscar Wilde

Foreword

Oscar Wilde, the most famous playwright of his day, and the author of the most famous and popular comedy in the English language, died in ignominy in 1900 at the age of forty-six. One hundred years on, his tragedy continues to haunt the imagination, but his rehabilitation is complete and his comedies are more popular than ever.

Wilde wrote domestic comedies, problem plays, pastiche Renaissance dramas, Biblical epics, ghost stories, murder stories, fairy stories, poems, ballads, essays and letters.

This book is a record of his works and life presented on stage and screen from about 1880 (twenty years before his death) to the present day. It covers theatre, film, opera, musicals, ballet, television, one-man shows, revues and documentaries.

His plays and novels are critiques and satires at the expense of the vacuous, self-indulgent, snobbish, avaricious and hypocritical high society of late-Victorian England. Their subject matter is sexual morality, sexual indiscretion, scandal and public disgrace, and they offer a mirror to his own life.

The critics have always complained that Wilde's characters are indiscriminate mouthpieces for a superfluity of wit and that his plots creak with old-fashioned contrivances. But the public have always ignored the critics; the epigrams and the melodrama are the very reason for the plays' continuing success at the box office.

Wilde is continually revived world-wide. It would be difficult to find a theatre which has not produced *The Importance of Being Earnest*. His novels and short stories are regularly adapted. Biographies and essays about him continue to be published. Statues are raised and plaques are unveiled. His life, more than any other author's life, is constantly being dramatised.

When Oscar came down from Oxford in 1878 he said he would be famous; and if he couldn't be famous, he would be notorious. His fame and notoriety are inseparable. The pages which follow are a record of that fame and that notoriety.

Would you like to know the great drama of my life? It is that I have put my genius into my life – I have only put my talent into my works.

Oscar Wilde

LIFE

Oscar Wilde at Oxford in April, 1876.
Photograph: Hills and Saunders.

Oscar Fingal O'Flahertie Wills Wilde Chronology

1854	16 October: Birth in Dublin, at 21 Westland Row, the son of Sir William and Lady Jane Francesca Wilde. His father became a famous eye-specialist. His mother, under the pen-name of 'Speranza', wrote patriotic verse.
1864–71	Portora Royal School, Enniskillen.
1870	Birth of Lord Alfred Douglas, son of the Eighth Marquis of Queensberry.
1871	Portora Gold Medal: Best classical scholar.
1871–74	Trinity College, Dublin.
1872	Top of his year in Classics.
1874	Berkeley Gold Medal for Greek.
1874–78	Scholar at Magdalen College, Oxford.
1875	Travels in Italy.
1876	Death of Wilde's father. First-class degree in Classical Moderations.
1877	Visits Greece and Rome.
1878	Wins Newdigate Prize with his poem, 'Ravenna'. First-class Bachelor of Arts degree in Litterae humaniores.
1879	Moves to London.
1881	First collected edition of *Poems* published by Bogue. Appears in W P Frith's painting, *The Private View of the Royal Academy*.
1882	Lectures in USA and Canada.
1883	*Vera* premiered in New York. Lecture tour in England. Becomes engaged to Constance Mary Lloyd.
1884	Marries Constance Mary Lloyd. Honeymoon in Paris.

1885	Birth of his first child, Cyril.
1886	Meets Robert Ross. Birth of second son, Vyvyan.
1887	Editor of *Woman's World* magazine. *The Canterville Ghost* published.
1888	*The Happy Prince and Other Tales* published.
1889	*The Birthday of the Infanta* published in Paris. *The Portrait of Mr W H* published.
1890	*The Picture of Dorian Gray* published in *Lippincott's Monthly Magazine.*
1891	Meets Lord Alfred Douglas. *The Duchess of Padua* premiered anonymously in New York. *The Soul of Man Under Socialism* published. *The Picture of Dorian Gray* published in book form. *Intentions* published. *Lord Arthur Savile's Crime* published. *A House of Pomegranates* published.
1892	*Lady Windermere's Fan* premiered in London. Limited edition of *Poems* published. *Salomé* banned by the Lord Chamberlain.
1893	*Salomé* published in French. *A Woman of No Importance* premiered in London.
1894	*Salomé* published in English. *The Sphinx* published.
1895	*An Ideal Husband* premiered in London. Visits Algiers. *The Importance of Being Earnest* premiered in London. Takes Queensberry to court for libel. Arrested for gross indecency. Stands trial. Sentenced to two years' hard labour. Adjudicated bankrupt.
1896	Death of Wilde's mother. *Salomé* premiered in Paris.
1896–7	Writes *De Profundis* in prison.

1897	Released from Reading Gaol. Travels in France. Visits Naples, Capri and Sicily.
1898	Resides in Paris. *The Ballad of Reading Gaol* published. Death of Constance Wilde.
1899	Travels in France and Switzerland.
1900	Received into the Roman Catholic Church. Death in Paris on 30 November. Buried at Bagneux Cemetery, Paris.
1905	*De Profundis* (heavily expurgated) published.
1906	Bankruptcy discharged.
1908	First collected edition of works published by Methuen.
1909	Reinterred in the French National Cemetery at Père-Lachaise. The sculpture on the tomb is by Epstein.
1915	Cyril Wilde is killed in action at Neuve Chapelle in World War One.
1918	Death of Robert Ross.
1945	Death of Lord Alfred Douglas.
1949	*De Profundis* (the unexpurgated version) published.
1954	Celebrations of centenary of Wilde's birth in Dublin, London and Paris. Commemorative plaques at: 21 Westland Row, Dublin 1 Marrion Square, Dublin 1 Tite Street, Chelsea, London Hôtel d'Alcase, Paris Ceremony at Père-Lachaise Cemetery, Paris, attended by French writer and autobiographer, André Maurois, Minister of Culture. Lunch at Savoy Hotel London, attended by T S Eliot, Augustus John and Edith Evans.
1956	Four-act version of *The Importance of Being Earnest* published.
1962	Collected letters published.

1967	Death of Vyvyan Wilde.
1984	Wilde Theatre opens in Bracknell, Berkshire.
1992	Peter Tatchell lobbies the Metropolitan Police, the Home Office, English Heritage and Westminster Council to turn the soon-to-be-vacated Bow Street Police Station into a Wilde Museum and a Lesbian and Gay History Museum.
1994	Outrage, a gay rights group, seeks posthumous royal pardon for Wilde.
1995	Dedication of memorial stained-glass window in Poets' Corner at Westminster Abbey, London. Seamus Heaney gives the address. John Gielgud reads from *De Profundis*. Commemorative plaque at Theatre Royal, Haymarket, London, unveiled by John Gielgud. Judi Dench and Michael Denison act the interview scene from *The Importance of Being Earnest*.
1997	Statue by Danny Osborne erected in Marrion Square, Dublin.
1998	Statue by Maggie Hambling erected in Adelaide Street, off The Strand, London, unveiled by Lucien Holland, great grandson of Oscar Wilde. Judi Dench and Nigel Hawthorne read the final scene of Act One of *A Woman of No Importance*.

Scandal

The latter part of the Victorian age, like any other age, had its fair share of public scandals. Some of the more notorious are listed below:

1864 Lady Wilde (Oscar's mother) was sued for libel when she accused Mary Travers of making unfounded allegations against Sir William Wilde (Oscar's father). Travers claimed he chloroformed her and then raped her.

1870 The Prince of Wales was subpoenaed as a respondent in the divorce proceedings of Sir Charles and Lady Mordaunt.

1875 Colonel Valentine Bakes was found guilty of molesting a respectable girl in a railway carriage.

1884 Sir Charles Wenworth Dilke was accused of adultery and found guilty.

1885 W T Stead, editor of the *Pall Mall Gazette*, wrote a series of articles on child prostitutes and was imprisoned for three months for assisting in procuring a young girl to prove his point.

In 1885 the Criminal Law Amendment Act was passed, aimed at raising the age of consent from thirteen to sixteen. This was in response to Stead's exposé of the London traffic in prostitution in his magazine, the *Pall Mall Gazette*. On its way through committee the Bill picked up an extra clause, which provided for any act of gross indecency between males. There was no mention of acts between females because Queen Victoria said it was an impossibility and Prime Minister Gladstone did not feel able to correct her.

1889 The Cleveland Street Scandal. Postboys were supplementing their income as male prostitutes. Members of the aristocracy who had visited the brothel felt it wise to leave the country; some never returned.

Archduke Rudolf and Baroness Marie Vetsera committed suicide at a hunting lodge in Mayerling.

Lt Colonel Sir William Gordon-Cummings was accused of cheating at cards at Tranby Croft and the Prince of Wales gave evidence.

1890 Charles Stewart Parnell, following his affair with Katharine O'Shea, is cited as co-respondent in a divorce case and is forced to retire as leader of the Irish Nationalists Party.

1895 The Oscar Wilde trial.

1898 Captain Alfred Dreyfus, on the French Army General Staff, was wrongly accused of passing military documents to the German military attaché in Paris. Dreyfus was not exonerated for another eight years.

Trials of Oscar Wilde

On 28 February 1895, the Marquis of Queensberry left a card at Wilde's club which read 'To Oscar Wilde posing as a somdomite'. (Spelling was not Queensberry's strong point.) Wilde felt he had no option but to start libel proceedings. The result was as follows:

1 Mar Queensberry is arrested.

3 Apr The Queensberry trial opens at the Old Bailey before Mr Justice Collins. Sir Edward Clarke is Counsel for the Prosecution. Mr Edward Carson is Counsel for the Defendant.

5 Apr Wilde withdraws his prosecution and is arrested, charged with gross indecency. Bail is refused. He could

have left the country. The legal establishment gave him ample opportunity to catch the last train to Paris, but he chose to remain and face the music.

26 Apr – 7 May	Wilde is tried jointly with Alfred Taylor on charges of homosexuality before Mr Justice Charles. Sir Edward Clark is Counsel for the Defence. Mr Charles Frederick Gill is Counsel for the Crown. The jury fails to agree and the trial ends without a verdict. Wilde is released on bail of £5,000.
20 – 25 May	Wilde is retried before Mr Justice Wills, found guilty, and sentenced to two years' hard labour. Wilde's name is removed from all theatre posters and programmes.
4 July	Wilde is transferred from Pentonville Prison to Wandsworth Prison.
26 July	Wilde is adjudicated bankrupt.
20 Nov	Wilde is transferred from Wandsworth Prison to Reading Gaol. From two o'clock till half-past two he has to stand on the centre platform of Clapham Junction Railway Station in convict dress and handcuffed, surrounded by a jeering mob.

Oscar Wilde was arrested on a charge of gross indecency. During the second trial he was questioned about a poem. 'Two Loves' (not written by him) which had appeared in the Oxford magazine *The Chameleon*, which ended with the two lines:

> Then sighing said the other, 'Have thy will
> I am the Love that dare not speak its name.'

Wilde was asked by the Counsel for the Crown, Charles Frederick Gill, what 'the Love that dare not speak its name' was. Wilde replied:

> 'The Love that dare not speak its name' in this century is such great affection of an elder for a younger man as there was between David and Jonathan, such as Plato made the very basis of his philosophy, and such as you find in the sonnets of Michelangelo and Shakespeare. It is that deep, spiritual affection that is as pure as it is perfect. It dictates and pervades great works of art like those

> of Shakespeare and Michelangelo, and those two letters of mine, such as they are. It is in this century misunderstood, so much misunderstood that it may be described as the 'Love that dare not speak its name', and on account of it, I am placed where I am now. It is beautiful, it is fine, it is the noblest form of affection. There is nothing unnatural about it. It is intellectual, and it repeatedly exists between an elder and a younger man. When the elder man has intellect, and the younger man has all the joy, hope, and glamour of life before him. That it should be so the world does not understand. The world mocks at it and sometimes puts one in the pillory for it.'

There was loud applause and some hisses. The Judge threatened that if there were any more manifestations of feeling, he would clear the court.

Presentiments

The extraordinary thing about the plays and the novels is how remarkably prophetic they are. They vividly anticipate Wilde's downfall. At times, it sounds (with hindsight) as if he is expressing his own worst fears. A selection of quotes follows:

The Picture of Dorian Gray (1890)

> You seem to forget that I am married, and the one charm of marriage is that it makes a life of deception absolutely necessary for both parties.

> I was on the verge of a terrible crisis in my life. I had a strange feeling that Fate had in store for me exquisite joys and exquisite sorrows.

> A man cannot be too careful in the choice of his enemies.

> The mere danger gave me a sense of delight.

One could never pay too high a price for sensation.

Yet these whispered scandals only increased, in the eyes of many, his strange and dangerous charm . . . Society, civilised society at least, is never very ready to believe anything to the detriment of those who are both rich and fascinating. It feels instinctively that manners are of more importance than morals.

I think it right you should know that the most dreadful things are being said against you in London . . . Why is it, Dorian, that a man like the Duke of Berwick leaves the room of a club when you enter it? Why is it that so many gentlemen in London will neither go to your house nor invite you to theirs? . . . Why is your friendship so fatal to young men? There was that wretched boy in the Guards who committed suicide. You were his great friend. There was Sir Henry Ashton, who had to leave England, with a tarnished name. You and he were inseparable. What about Adrian Singleton, and his dreadful end? What about Lord Kent's only son, and his career? . . .

And what sort of lives do these people, who pose as being moral, lead themselves? My dear fellow, you forget that we are in the native land of the hypocrite.

He felt as if an iron ring was being slowly tightened round his forehead, as if the disgrace with which he was threatened had already come upon him.

Lord Arthur Savile's Crime (1891)

The proper basis for marriage is mutual misunderstanding.

The same feeling of dread over him, the same sickening sense of coming evil.

For the first time he became conscious of the terrible mystery of destiny, the awful meaning of Doom.

Was there no escape possible?

He felt that some tragedy was hanging over him, and that he had been suddenly called upon to bear an intolerable burden.

Perhaps, some day, his own name might be placarded on the walls of London. Some day, perhaps, a price would be set on his head also. The thought made him sick with horror.

He hated the idea of being lionised at Lady Windermere's, or seeing his name figuring in the paragraphs of vulgar society-newspapers.

Lady Windermere's Fan (1892)

Mrs Erlynne was once honoured, loved, respected. She was well born, she had position – she lost everything – threw it away, if you like. That makes it all the more bitter. Misfortunes one can endure – they come from outside, they are accidents. But to suffer from one's own faults – ah! that is the sting of life.

We have been too lax. We must make an example.

But there are moments when one has to choose between living one's own life, fully, entirely, completely – or dragging out some false, shallow, degrading existence that the world in its hypocrisy demands.

He shall have a scandal. He shall have the worst scandal there has been in London for years. He shall see his name in every vile paper, mine on every placard.

You don't know what it is to fall in the pit, to be despised, mocked, abandoned, sneered at – to be an outcast! to find the door shut against one, to have to creep in by hideous byways, afraid every moment lest the mask be stripped from one's face, and all the while to hear the laughter, the horrible laughter of the world, a thing more tragic than all the tears the world has ever shed. One pays for one's sins, and then one pays again, and all one's life one pays.

WINDERMERE: What is the difference between scandal and gossip?

CECIL GRAHAM: Oh! gossip is charming! History is merely gossip. But scandal is gossip made tedious by morality. Now, I never moralise. A man who moralises is usually a hypocrite, and a woman who moralises is invariably plain.

We are all in the gutter, but some of us are looking at the stars.

A Woman of No Importance (1893)

Children begin by loving their parents. After a time they judge them. Rarely, if ever, do they forgive them.

The basis of every scandal is an absolute immoral certainty.

Everyone is born a king, and most people die in exile, like most kings.

There are other countries than England. Oh! other countries over sea, better, wiser and less unjust lands. The world is wide and very big . . . We shall somewhere find green valleys and fresh waters, and if we weep, well, we shall weep together.

I have lied to the world. For twenty years I have lied to the world. I could not tell the world the truth. Who can ever?

Nothing succeeds like excess.

It is perfectly monstrous the way people go about, nowadays, saying things against one behind one's back that are absolutely and entirely true.

HESTER: A woman who has sinned should be punished, shouldn't she?
MRS ARBUTHNOT: Yes.
HESTER: She shouldn't be allowed to come into the society of good men and women?
MRS ARBUTHNOT: She should not.
HESTER: And the man should be punished in the same way?
MRS ARBUTHNOT: In the same way.
HESTER: And the children, if there are children, in the same way also?
MRS ARBUTHNOT: Yes, it is right that the sins of the parents should be visited on the children. It is a just law. It is God's law.

An Ideal Husband (1895)

Nowadays, with our modern mania for morality, everyone has to pose as a paragon of purity, incorruptibility, and all the other seven deadly virtues – and what is the result? You all go over like ninepins – one after another. Not a year passes in England without somebody disappearing. Scandals used to lend charm, or at least interest, to a man – now they crush him. And yours is a very nasty scandal. You couldn't survive it.

You know what your English papers are like . . . Think of their loathsome joy, of the delight they would have in dragging you down, of the mud and the mire they would plunge you in. Think of the hypocrite with his greasy smile penning his leading article, and arranging the foulness of the public placard.

I tell you that there are terrible temptations that it requires strength, strength and courage, to yield to. To stake all one's life on a single moment, to risk everything on one throw, whether the stake be power or pleasure, I care not – there is no weakness in that. There is a horrible, a terrible courage.

I feel that public disgrace is in store for me. I feel certain of it. I never knew what terror was before. I know it now. It is as if a hand of ice were laid upon one's heart. It is as if one's heart were beating itself to death in some empty hollow.

And now what is there before me but public disgrace, ruin, terrible shame, the mockery of the world, a lonely dishonoured life, a lonely dishonoured death, it may be, some day?

Sooner or later we have all to pay for what we do.

The Importance of Being Earnest (1895)

My duty as a gentleman has never interfered with my pleasure in the smallest degree.

If I ever get married I'll try to forget the fact.

I hope you have not been leading a double life, pretending to be wicked and being really good all the time. That would be hypocrisy.

JACK: He seems to have expressed a desire to be buried in Paris.
CHASUBLE: In Paris! I fear that hardly points to any very serious state of mind at the last.

We have to be at Holloway no later than four o'clock otherwise it is difficult to obtain admission. The rules are very strict.

Come dear, we already have missed five, if not six trains. To miss any more might expose us to comment on the platform.

Wilde and the Aesthetic Movement

The Aesthetic Movement, cultivated by the pre-Raphaelites, flourished in the 1870s and 1880s. Key figures in the movement were Oscar Wilde, James McNeill Whistler, and Aubrey Beardsley.

The Aesthetes believed that art was self-sufficient and need have no ulterior motive, neither moral, nor political, nor religious. Essayist and critic Walter Pater wrote in his *Studies in the History of the Renaissance* (1873) that 'The most precious moment of life is the pursuit of sensations raised to a pitch of poetic passion, the desire of beauty, the love of art for art's sake.'

Wilde had met Pater while he was up at Oxford and became his leading disciple and advocate spreading the gospel on his lecture tours in America.

Wilde was regularly caricatured in the cartoons of George du Maurier in *Punch*, appearing as Maudle the Painter and Jellaby Postlethwaite, the poet. Or so it was generally believed. Du Maurier himself categorically denied that Postlethwaite was Wilde, saying that the character was founded not on any one person but on a whole school of Aestheticism.

Postlethwaite, bearded and thin, doesn't look anything like Wilde, while Maudle only really looks like Wilde in *The Choice of Profession* (12 February 1881) and *A Discussion on Women's Rights* (31 December 1881).

Wilde is more readily recognisable in *The Six Mark Teapot* (30 October 1880) where this exchange takes place:

Aesthetic Bridegroom: It is quite consummate, is it not?
Intense Bride: It is, indeed! Oh, Algernon, let us live up to it.

The dialogue was based on a remark made by Wilde when he was up at Oxford University to the effect that he found it very hard to live up to his blue china. The remark was roundly condemned by Dean Burgess from the pulpit of St Mary's Church in terms which would not have disgraced Lady Bracknell: 'When a young man says not in polished banter, but in sober earnestness, that he finds it difficult to live up to the level of his blue china, there has crept into these cloistered shades a form of heathenism which it is our bounden duty to fight against and to crush out, if possible.'

Wilde was also caricatured in a number of plays and musicals:

1877 *The Grasshopper*

Premiere: Grosvenor Gallery.

To celebrate the opening of the gallery, a dance burlesque was performed by a trio imitating Wilde, James McNeill Whistler, the US-born painter and graphic artist, and Frank Miles, the artist with whom Wilde shared rooms when he first came to London.

1880 *Where's the Cat?*
A play by James Aubrey.

Premiere: Criterion Theatre, London.

Herbert Beerbohm Tree, who made his reputation in farce and became one of Britain's leading actor-managers, was cast as Scott Ramsay, an author and aesthete. The role was a lampoon of Wilde and he adopted Wilde's mannerisms. In 1882 Tree wrote a parody of Wilde's affectations for *Punch*. In 1893 he produced the premiere of *A Woman of No Importance* and created Lord Illingworth.

1881 *The Colonel*
A play by F C Burnand.

Premiere: Prince of Wales Theatre, London.

Burnand was the editor of *Punch*. His comedy, an adaptation of a French farce, was a joke at the expense of aesthetes and their lilies, peacock feathers, sunflowers, circular Venetian fans, and blue white jars. One of the play's main characters was Lambert Streyke, an art imposter. James Fernandez, who played him (and looked more like an elderly schoolmaster than an art professor) affected Wilde's mannerisms.

The anonymous drama critic of the *Illustrated Sporting and Dramatic News* made the following observation in his review:

> The modern Aesthete is rather a gorgeous creature; and as a well-known, amiable, and very long-haired Aesthete observed on the first night, had he been called in he could have given the management some valuable hints as to how aestheticism might be corporeally burlesqued.

Queen Victoria attended a Royal Command performance at Albergeldie Castle in Scotland and was (according to her diary) 'very much amused'.

1881 *Patience (or Bunthorne's Bride)*
An entirely new and original Aesthetic Opera by W S Gilbert and Arthur Sullivan.

Premiere: Opera Comique, London.
Transferred: Savoy Theatre, London.

Patience, the most enduring satire on the Aesthetic Movement, perpetuates the philistine idea that the pursuit of the Arts is a painfully effeminate activity between consenting adults in public. But, as Gilbert said, 'Don't be frightened – it's only poetry!'

The story revolves round the rivalry of Reginald Bunthorne (a fleshly poet) and Archibald Grosvenor (an idyllic poet) and the attraction the two men have for twenty love-sick maidens. 'Cling to one another,' Bunthorne advises the swooning ladies, 'and think of faint lilies.' Both poets were dressed in velvet suits and knee breeches of the kind Wilde wore on his lecture tours.

The Fleshly School was the name Robert Buchanan had given to a pamphlet he had written in 1871 attacking Dante Gabriel Rossetti and Algernon Swinburne.

Bunthorne is (on his own admission) an aesthetic sham and poseur, who has taken up the cult merely to attract the worship of women. It is obvious from the cartoons and stage photographs of the day that George Grossmith (the singer who created Bunthorne) was made up to look like the painter James McNeill Whistler. He had Whistler's moustache, black curls, white lock of hair and eye glass. He also had Whistler's vocal mannerisms.

Devotees of Gilbert and Sullivan operas, nevertheless, have always identified the effeminate, petulant and posturing Bunthorne with Wilde; and indeed, as a direct result of the success of *Patience* in America in 1882, Wilde was invited to lecture in the United States. The promoters, no doubt, hoped he might be persuaded to advertise the show by walking down Broadway with either a poppy or a lily in his medieval hand.

When Wilde arrived in New York (having been disappointed with the Atlantic) he was asked by a customs official if he had anything to declare. 'I have nothing to declare,' he replied, 'except my genius.' Later, attending a performance of *Patience* at Standard Theatre, he discovered that J H Ridley (the American actor who played Bunthorne) had made up to look like him.

Wilde had his own little joke at the expense of Gilbert and Sullivan fourteen years later in Act III of *The Importance of Being Earnest* when Jack and Algernon enter 'whistling some dreadful popular air from a British Opera'. Actors playing the roles almost invariably whistle out of tune.

The Savoy Theatre was the first London theatre to be lit by electricity. The lights were turned on during a matinee performance of *Patience.*

1884 *The Charlatan*
A play by Robert Buchanan.

Premiere: Theatre Royal, Haymarket, London.

One of the main comic characters in Buchanan's play was Mervyn Darrell, who talked in epigrams and paradoxes, and made a note of all his *bons mots* in a notebook so that he could put them in his autobiography. Frederick Kerr, who was cast as Darrell, modelled his performance on Wilde.

1892 *The Poet and the Puppets*
A travestie of *Lady Windermere's Fan* by Charles Brookfield and music by J M Glover.

Premiere: Comedy Theatre, London.

When Wilde heard that 'a travestie' was to be performed, he appealed to the censor and insisted the authors should read him the text before it was staged.

J M Glover in his autobiography, *Jimmy Glover His Book*, (Methuen, 1911), gave this account of their meeting:

> While cigars were burned, the poet puffed, and punctuated each page as it was read with such phrases as 'Delightful!' 'Charming, my old friends!' (His calling Brookfield 'old friend' was touching.) 'It's exquisite!' etc., etc. As he showed us to the door he just gave us this parting shot: 'I feel, however, that I have been – well – Brookfield, what is the word? – what is the thing you call it in your

> delightfully epigrammatic Stage English? eh? Oh, yes! – delightfully spoofed.

In the event, the only objection Wilde made was to his name being used in the following song:

> They may bubble with jest at the way that I'm dressed,
> They may scoff at the length of my hair,
> They may say I'm vain, overbearing, inane,
> And object to the flowers that I wear,
> They may laugh till they're ill, but the fact remains still
> A fact that I've proclaimed since I was a child.
> That's taken, my dears, nearly two thousand years
> To make Oscar O'Flaherty – Wilde.

The Poet and the Puppets was more about Wilde than it was about *Lady Windermere's Fan*. Charles Brookfield played 'A Moralist' and did a number of impersonations of stage and public personalities. Charles Hawtrey played 'A Poet' and did just the one impersonation.

Not everybody was impressed. One critic observed: 'Mr Hawtrey makes up wonderfully as Mr Wilde, and I dare say reproduces his manner and attitude very well also. I can say no more than that for I have not thought of Mr Wilde of sufficient importance to observe him very closely. I fancy that the bulk of our forty million are much in the same position'.

Three years later Hawtrey and Brookfield would create Lord Goring and his manservant, Phipps, in *An Ideal Husband*. Brookfield would also furnish the police with information which would help to convict Wilde. On the day Wilde was sentenced to two years' hard labour, he and Hawtrey invited Queensberry to a celebratory dinner. Such was Wilde's disgrace and ostracism that it would be another forty years before he would be portrayed on stage, and then only for a private audience.

Twentieth-Century Biography

1936 *Oscar Wilde*
A play by Leslie and Sewell Stokes.

Premiere: Gate Theatre Studio, London.

Director	Norman Marshall
LORD ALFRED DOUGLAS	John Bryning
A PORTER	Charles Dacres
LOUIS DIJON	Patrick Gover
OSCAR WILDE	Robert Morley
EUSTACE	Frith Banbury
FRANK HARRIS	Reginald Beckwith
CHARLIE PARKER	John Carol
A BUTLER	Andrew Cruickshank
ALLEN	Michael Morice
MR JUSTICE COLLINS	Bradley Smith
SIR EDWARD CLARKE	Andrew Cruickshank
MR E H CARSON	Harry Hutchinson
MR JUSTICE WILLS	Bradley Smith
THE SOLICITOR GENERAL	Charles Barrett
A WAITER	Cot D'Ordon

The actor Frank Pettingell and author Leslie Stokes were rehearsing a play about Oscar Wilde by Maurice Rostand (son of Edmund, the author of *Cyrano de Bergerac*) in which they were cast respectively as Wilde and Edward Carson, QC. The production was cancelled at the insistence of Lord Alfred Douglas, who protested that the play was 'a travesty of the truth and a deliberate misrepresentation of well-known and often-recorded facts'. Rostand had based his script on the assumption that Douglas had never seen nor spoken to Wilde after he came out of prison.

Leslie Stokes and his brother, Sewell, then set about writing their own play. Douglas raised no objection to the new script. However, the Lord Chamberlain, who acted as censor of theatre in Britain, refused them a licence. The play had to be produced in a private club theatre. Censorship of plays in Britain was not abolished until 1968.

By the time the Stokes were ready to start rehearsing, Pettingell was committed to appear in Edgar Wallace's thriller, *The Frog*, so they had to find another actor. Gerald Cooper was engaged. Ten days before the production was due to open, he was fired by the director, Norman Marshall, who offered the role to the twenty-eight-year-old Robert Morley. Oscar Wilde was a major turning point in Morley's career, leading directly to his casting in the Hollywood film *Marie Antoinette* (starring Norma Shearer) and an Oscar nomination for his performance as Louis XVI.

The two authors were praised for their sympathetic and impartial handling, although, inevitably, there were some critics who thought the subject matter 'left a slightly unpleasant taste in the mouth'. Nobody thought the Stokes brothers had written a good play; they were said to be at their best when they were quoting Wilde's own words. The most surprising criticism was that the actual trials lacked drama.

Douglas never saw the play. He told the authors it would be too painful an experience for him to attend a performance.

> Mr Robert Morley achieves a remarkable likeness to Wilde's portrait and speaks his lines with acceptable character. But the play is little but a précis of notorious facts which seem to emphasise the sordid at the expense of the significant.
>
> Harold Hobson *Observer*

> The only criticism I have to make of Mr Robert Morley's admirable impersonation of him (which, Mr Stokes said, had been the making of the play) was the absence in it of that temperamental gaiety, the exuberant spirit of irresponsibility combined with astonishing pointfulness of comment, which made him so matchless a companion.
>
> Desmond McCarthy *New Statesman*

1938 The production transferred to Fulton Theatre, New York.

Director	Norman Marshall
LORD ALFRED DOUGLAS	John Buckmaster
LOUIS DIJON	Edward Trevor
ARAB BOY	Richard Charlton
HOTEL WAITER	Kenneth Treseder

OSCAR WILDE	Robert Morley
EUSTACE	Wyman Kane
FRANK HARRIS	Harold Young
CHARLIE PARKER	John Carol
A BUTLER	Colin Hunter
ALLEN	Arthur Gould-Porter
MR JUSTICE COLLINS	Frederick Graham
SIR EDWARD CLARKE	J W Austin
MR E H CARSON	Mark Dignam
MR JUSTICE WILLS	Oswald Yorke
SOLICITOR GENERAL	Gordon Richards
CLERK OF COURT	Lewis Dayton
A WAITER	Reginald Malcolm
JULES	Jean Del Val

Robert Morley's performance was hailed as one of the most brilliant of the New York season and praised for being 'remarkably plausible' and 'witty and humorous as well as strangely touching'.

> As no actor I have ever seen in any revival of one of Oscar's plays has been able to do, Mr Morley gives point and charm and naturalness to Oscar's epigrams. He purrs with pleasure, as with seeming spontaneity, he rolls them out . . . At first he is the arrogant flâneur; then the amoral decadent; next the witness, witty in his self-defence; then the cornered wretch in a state of sad collapse; and finally the bloated ruin of the last years in Paris. Let there be no mistake about it: Mr Morley's Oscar is an extraordinary performance which, if you are wise, will command your immediate attention.
>
> John Mason Brown *New York Times*

> Oscar Wilde is treated frankly, honestly and with no attempt at sensationalism, and it would be the rankest kind of hypocrisy to protest against its presentation.
>
> George Jean Nathan *Saturday Review*

1938 Revived: Arts Theatre, London.

Director	Ronald Adam
LORD ALFRED DOUGLAS	Peter Osborn

A PORTER	Roy Purcell
LOUIS DIJON	Francis James
OSCAR WILDE	Francis L Sullivan
EUSTACE	John Penrose
A WAITER	Anthony Sagar
FRANK HARRIS	Alan Wheatley
CHARLIE PARKER	Leonard Coppins
A BUTLER	Gerald Welch
ALLEN	Julian Somers
MR JUSTICE COLLINS	Brian Carey
SIR EDWARD CLARKE	Bernard Merefield
MR E H CARSON	Earle Grey
MR JUSTICE WILLS	Julian Somers
THE SOLICITOR GENERAL	Charles Mortimer
A WAITER	Cot D'Ordon

Leslie and Sewell Stokes's play was revived at a club theatre, but they, not wishing to be associated with the interpretation of this particular production, asked for their names to be withdrawn from the programme and all advertisements.

> The evening is saved from unrelieved morbidity by the beautiful playing of Mr Francis L Sullivan as the central character. Mr Sullivan gives to Wilde all the surface glitter which Mr Robert Morley conveyed in the same part. And he is far more successful than Mr Morley in suggesting the human tragedy behind the brilliant façade.
>
> *Sunday Times*

> Mr Francis L Sullivan gives one of his finest performances. He is a little too unctuous perhaps; but for all that he is a superbly flamboyant figure of the Wilde of the days of triumph; he makes a subtle transition from the flippancies of the early stages of the trial to a sincere and eloquent defence of 'the love that dare not speak its name'.
>
> *The Times*

> A great pity that Francis L Sullivan's brilliant performance cannot be seen by a wider public.
>
> *Sunday Dispatch*

1948 Revived: Boltons Theatre, London.

Director	Leslie Stokes
LORD ALFRED DOUGLAS	Peter Reynolds
A PORTER	Lempriere Hammond
LOUIS DIJON	Alan Adair
OSCAR WILDE	Frank Pettingell
A WAITER	Anthony Cundell
EUSTACE	Anthony Walman
FRANK HARRIS	Julian Somers
CHARLIE PARKER	Edward Judd
A BUTLER	Anthony Cundell
ALLEN	Dennis Harkin
MR JUSTICE COLLINS	Lempriere Hammond
SIR EDWARD CLARKE	Thomas Hutchinson
MR E H CARSON	John Probert
MR JUSTICE WILLS	Stanley Lathbury
THE SOLICITOR GENERAL	Anthony Nicholls
A WAITER	Peter Raymonde

Frank Pettingell, who was to have been in the original 1936 production, finally got to play Wilde.

> Frank Pettingell achieved a remarkable physical resemblance to Wilde. In the early scenes his delivery of the wit seemed not spontaneous enough. At the trial however, he was excellent and the subsequent dissolution was portrayed with true pathos and most moving restraint.
>
> *Daily Telegraph*

It was hoped that this time the production, its third at a club theatre, would be able to transfer to the West End. The Lord Chamberlain came twice to see the play, but still felt he could not lift the ban on public performance.

Oscar Wilde was revived in Los Angeles in 1977 when Leon Charles played Wilde.

1960 *The Importance of Being Oscar*
One-man show by Micheál Mac Liammóir.

Premiere: International Theatre Festival, Dublin.
Transferred: Apollo Theatre, London.

Actor	Micheál Mac Liammóir
Director	Hilton Edwards

The setting was simple: a bare stage, a Regency sofa, a floral plinth, a table, and a chair. The performance (described by the performer as 'a tribute from one Irishman to another') was elegant and eloquent.

Micheál Mac Liammóir, wearing a green carnation, bore a strong physical resemblance to Wilde but he did not so much impersonate Wilde as conjure up his personality. When he stressed that the shame and scandal (for which Wilde would seem to be primarily remembered) should be seen in their right perspective there was a cry of 'Bravo!' from the stalls followed by some applause.

The programme was divided in two halves: before and after the trials. The first half was a recital in much the same vein as John Gielgud's performance in George Ryland's Shakespeare anthology, *Ages of Man*, and Emlyn Williams's recreation of Charles Dickens's readings and his portrait of Dylan Thomas.

There was rather too much from *The Picture of Dorian Gray*; and Lady Bracknell's interview of John Worthing in *The Importance of Being Earnest* was, perhaps, too familiar for inclusion in the programme. Much more interesting, for its rarity, was the extract from *Salomé*, which he performed in French.

The second half of the evening was the better half and captured most movingly Wilde's fall. Mac Liammóir acted a long extract from *De Profundis* superbly. Wilde's conversation with his prison warder was a delightful comic interlude.

> It is theatre, in the first and supreme place, because Mr Mac Liammóir is a great actor.
>
> Bernard Levin *Daily Express*

> Mr Mac Liammóir is magnificently touching and magnificently funny, and always utterly engrossing.
>
> Robert Muller *Daily Mail*

In 1961 Mac Liammóir appeared at the Royal Court Theatre, London, on British television in a half-hour version, and at Lyceum Theatre, New York. He followed this with a tour of the USA and performances at the Paris Festival.

The *New York Times* hailed *The Importance of Being Oscar* as 'a vivid and memorable evening'. The *New York Herald-Tribune* said it was 'overwhelmingly well done'.

> Being a brilliant writer himself, as well as a perceptive critic, Mr Mac Liammóir's observations on Wilde's life, character and work are eloquent, appreciative, dramatic and compassionate, and they are too witty to fall into any excess of hero-worship.
>
> Richard Watts, Jr *New York Post*

The Importance of Being Oscar also played at the Dublin Festival (1962), Aldwych Theatre, London (1963), on tour in Australia and New Zealand (1964) and at the Theatre Royal, Haymarket, London (1966).

In 1963 Mac Liammóir devised another anthology, *I Must Be Talking to My Friends*, which he alternated with *The Importance of Being Oscar*, and in which there was 'more about Wilde'.

1960 British television: *On Trial: Oscar Wilde*

Script	Peter Lambda
Director	Silvio Narizzano
Narrator	Andrew Faulds
Commentator	J B Priestley
MR JUSTICE CHARLES	Harold Scott
USHER	Lewis Wilson
CLERK OF ARRAIGNS	Deering Wells
OSCAR WILDE	Micheál Mac Liammóir
ALFRED TAYLOR	Alan Browning
MR C F GILL	Derek Sydney
SIR EDWARD CLARKE	André Morrell
EDWARD CARSON	Martin Benson
CHARLES PARKER	Brian Alexis
FREDERICK ATKINS	Clive Colin Bowler
EDWARD SHELLEY	Michael Caridia

FOREMAN OF THE JURY	Beresford Williams
MARQUIS OF QUEENSBERRY	Tudor Evans
LORD ALFRED DOUGLAS	Michael Bangerter

Granada Television's *On Trial* series had already included programmes on Sir Roger Casement (Irish Republicanism), Sir Charles Dilke (divorce), the Baccarat Scandal (cheating at cards and slander), W T Steed (abduction), Spencer Cowper (murder), Admiral Byng (cowardice), Horatio Bottomley (fraud), and Governor Joseph Wall (murder).

Oscar Wilde was on trial for gross indecency. The trial was a faithful reconstruction; nothing was added, though a great deal, inevitably, was left out. Micheál Mac Liammóir's performance as Wilde was beautifully understated.

'Did you ever kiss him?' asked Edward Carson, QC, referring to the sixteen-year-old Walter Grainger, a servant who had waited at Wilde's table.

'Oh, dear no,' replied Wilde. 'He was a peculiarly plain boy. He was, unfortunately, extremely ugly. I pitied him for it'.

The case, and Wilde's reputation, were lost for this foolish quip. Carson pounced. 'Why did you mention his ugliness? Why? Why? Why?' Martin Benson (playing Carson) growled the 'why's'.

In the second trial, the blackmailing rent boys, Charles Parker and Frederick Atkins, and the pathetic, blubbing Edward Shelley (who said he had been deeply shocked by Wilde's advances) took centre stage, and, largely, because of the way the actors had been encouraged to 'act' their parts, the production became more of a play than a documentary.

The programme ended with a statement to the effect that the government had wanted a verdict of guilty. J B Priestley thought the judge's harsh sentence of two years' hard labour was totally characteristic of a hypocritical nation that hated merriment.

1960 British film: *Oscar Wilde*

Director	Gregory Ratoff
Screenplay	Jo Eisinger

OSCAR WILDE	Robert Morley
CONSTANCE WILDE	Phyllis Calvert

LORD ALFRED DOUGLAS	John Neville
SIR EDWARD CARSON	Ralph Richardson
ROBERT ROSS	Dennis Price
MARQUIS OF QUEENSBERRY	Edward Chapman
GEORGE ALEXANDER	Martin Benson
JUSTICE HENN COLLINS	Robert Harris
JUSTICE WILLS	Henry Oscar
SOLICITOR GENERAL	William Devlin
COBBHAM	Stephen Dartnell
LIONEL JOHNSON	Ronald Leigh-Hunt
INSPECTOR RICHARDS	Martin Boddey
RICHARD LE GALLIENNE	Leonard Sachs
CLERK OF ARRAIGNS	Tom Chatto

In 1960 there were two films about Oscar Wilde: *The Trials of Oscar Wilde* (produced by Warwick, starring Peter Finch) and *Oscar Wilde* (produced by Vantage, starring Robert Morley). Warwick sued Vantage in order to prevent their distribution, alleging infringement of copyright.

'I should have thought two films were better than one. I'd be quite happy to appear in both,' said Morley.

The judge threw out the case. In the race which followed to see who would get to the West End screens first, Vantage passed the post – opening in London in the last week of May – just one week ahead of their rival.

Oscar Wilde was an unpretentious, black-and-white version, quite lacking in style and depth, and directed with such restraint as to give no offence. The pre-credit opening sequence began in the French cemetery of Père-Lachaise where Wilde is buried. A voice-over (from the grave) promised cinemagoers 'the story of my tragedy'. The titles then rolled over Toulouse-Lautrec's portrait of Wilde.

The film proper began with the premiere of *Lady Windermere's Fan* and the speech Wilde had made on the occasion. The scriptwriter obviously thought the premiere was a good place for Wilde to meet Lord Alfred Douglas. In reality, they had met the previous year in Wilde's home.

'Theirs was a relationship the world could not, *would* not tolerate,' shrieked the film posters. Gregory Ratoff provided a collage of shots to show Victorian society shocked and disapproving but, apart from a glimpse of a rowdy scene in a restaurant, there was nothing on the screen that would have provoked the gossip.

John Neville (idol of the gallery girls at the Old Vic Theatre in London in the 1950s) had the good looks, but at thirty-five he was too mature, too dignified, and too stilted to be playing the twenty-one-year-old Lord Alfred Douglas. He was not helped by the hollow theatrics of two scenes. In the first he had to toast Wilde ('To the Lord of Language and the King of Life') and smash a glass on the floor. In the second he had to blurt out to Constance that his father thought his relationship with Wilde was more than platonic.

Neville's Bosie clearly wanted to compete with Wilde on his home ground: 'Beardsley,' he said, 'has a superb line but he doesn't know when to draw it'. It seemed for one moment as if Wilde were going to say, 'I wish I had said that,' and Bosie were going to retort, 'You will, you will Oscar'. The scene where Oscar pretended to be a detective from Scotland Yard and saved him from the hands of a pathetic blackmailer was merely absurd.

Morley, very persuasive – physically, facially, and stylistically – was totally at ease with Wilde's epigrams. Practically everything he said was, in fact, a direct quote, either from *De Profundis* or from the plays.

The final scene found him sitting in a Parisian café, drunk where he was joined by Robbie Ross (played by Dennis Price), who beat a hasty retreat. The scene was an unforgivable slur on Ross, who stood by Wilde while he lived and also after his death, putting his affairs in order and settling his debts. Wilde, in the film, was left all on his own. Morley, laughing hysterically (as he had done in the 1936 production of Leslie and Sewell Stokes play), asked the waiter if he could play something gay on his accordion, 'gay' not having the connotation in 1960 that it has today.

Jo Eisinger's screenplay left a lot out. There was no indication of the volatile relationship between Wilde and Bosie. There was no Wilde standing on Clapham Junction railway station platform in convict's clothes and chains, being jeered at by the crowds. There were no prison scenes. The film, instead, concentrated on the first libel trial and the brilliant cross-examination by Edward Carson, QC.

The court scenes had an almost documentary flavour; the dialogue was lifted straight from the transcripts. Wilde had been stupid enough to begin with a lie about his age (claiming to be thirty-eight, not forty) and Carson thereafter always made a point of stressing the difference between Wilde's age and the ages of his companions (usually between eighteen and twenty) and to ask what he and they had in common and for what services he had been pressing gifts and cigarette cases on them.

Wilde, asked if he had given champagne to the lads, replied, 'What gentleman would stint his guests?' Carson echoed him sarcastically, 'What gentleman would stint the valet and groom?' He had the major advantage of knowing that Wilde was lying and having witnesses to prove it. As the evidence mounted against Wilde, Morley wilted, the energy, confidence and wit visibly draining out of him.

Wilde and Carson had been at Trinity College, Dublin, together. 'No doubt,' Wilde had said before the trial began, 'he will perform the task with all the bitterness of an old friend'. Ralph Richardson, as Carson, was a cruel, merciless, sarcastic, public-school bully, relishing a job well done. The eyes sparkled as he boxed Wilde into a corner.

Edward Chapman gave a superficial, weekly-rep performance as Queensberry. The brawl in the street with Wilde was an invention of the film – Wilde had, in fact, deliberately remained backstage during the premiere of *The Importance of Being Earnest* precisely to avoid such an encounter.

Robert Morley delivers the wit but not the emotion.

Dilys Powell *Sunday Times*

I had forgotten how moving Robert Morley could be.

Isabel Quigley *Spectator*

Morley is too benign to be really Wilde.

Nina Hibbin *Daily Worker*

1960 British film: *The Trials of Oscar Wilde*
US title: *The Man with the Green Carnation.*

Screenplay and director	Ken Hughes
OSCAR	Peter Finch
CONSTANCE	Yvonne Mitchell
EDWARD CARSON	James Mason
SIR EDWARD CLARKE	Nigel Patrick
MARQUIS OF QUEENSBERRY	Lionel Jeffries
LORD ALFRED DOUGLAS	John Fraser
LADY WILDE	Sonia Dresdel
ADA LEVERSON	Maxine Audley

WOOD	James Booth
ROBBIE ROSS	Emrys Jones
CHARLES HUMPHRIES	Lloyd Lamble
FRANK HARRIS	Paul Rogers
ARTHUR	Ian Fleming
PRINCE OF WALES	Laurence Naismith
LILLIE LANGTRY	Naomi Chance
AUCTIONEER	Meredith Edwards
FIRST CLERK	Anthony Newlands
SECOND CLERK	Robert Perceval
CHARLES GILL	Michael Goodliffe
WILLIE WILDE	Liam Gaffney
LORD ASHFORD	William Kendall
LORD SONNING	Ronald Cardew
LADY QUEENSBERRY	Cecily Paget-Bowman
LORD PERCY DOUGLAS	Derek Aylward
INSPECTOR	Campbell Singer
CONSTABLE	Victor Brooks
REPORTER	Alfred Burke
JUSTICE COLLINS	A J Brown
JUSTICE CHARLES	Charles Carson
JUSTICE WILLS	David Ensor
SYDNEY	Edward Evans
COURT USHER	Howard Lang
LANDLADY	Gladys Henson
CAFÉ ROYAL MANAGER	John Welsh

In the race to get to the West End first in 1960 ('the battle of the Oscars', as it was known), *Oscar Wilde* won by a neck, but *The Trials of Oscar Wilde* was the better film, more authentic in its recreation of the period, more money having been spent on it.

Ken Hughes's screenplay was based on two books, *The Trials of Oscar Wilde* by Montgomery Hyde, and *The Springed Lute* by John Furnell.

The opening scene, at the premiere of *Lady Windermere's Fan*, quickly established that Wilde's homosexuality was common gossip in fashionable society. The second scene, set in the Café Royal, established Wilde as the brilliant conversationalist, entertaining the Gentlemen of the Press and keeping the table aroar with his wit. The third scene showed Wilde, the father, reading *The Happy Prince* to his two boys at bedtime.

In the fourth scene the blackmailer, Alfred Wood, arrived with a love poem Wilde had written to Lord Alfred Douglas in which he had said that 'his rose-red lips were made for song and kisses' and likened him to 'Hyacinthus whom Apollo had adored so madly'. Wood was such a half-hearted blackmailer that Wilde took him off to dinner and bed. The poem would be later copied and sent all over London, finally ending up in court where it formed part of the criminal charges brought against him for corrupting youth.

Peter Finch – not, perhaps, the most obvious casting – brought to Wilde a greater depth than Robert Morley had done. The performance, sensitive, sympathetic, credible, had both stature and dignity.

John Fraser was much closer to Lord Alfred Douglas's age than John Neville had been; he was also much more believable as the neurotic, self-indulgent, arrogant young man, insatiable in his extravagances, who 'demanded without grace and received without thanks'. Bosie had thought it was his God-given right to live at Wilde's expense.

There was a vicious scene when he visited Wilde, sick in bed in a small house in Worthing screaming, taunting and threatening him with a knife. There was an equally hysterical confrontation with his father at the funeral of his brother, Viscount Drumlanrig, who had committed suicide. He had been having an affair with the Prime Minister, Lord Rosebery. For Queensberry to have one son who was homosexual was a misfortune; to have two sons who were homosexuals looked like carelessness. He threatened to kill Bosie and to put Wilde behind bars.

Queensberry was played by Lionel Jeffries with manic intensity, as an apoplectic stage villain straight out of a Victorian melodrama. The Marquis was quite clearly mad. He made a scene at the premiere of *Lady Windermere's Fan*; he burst into Wilde's home, accompanied by a pugilist (whom Wilde took by the scruff of the neck and chucked out); finally, he presented him with a bouquet of cabbages at the premiere of *The Importance of Being Earnest*.

'Thank you, my dear fellow,' said Wilde, 'every time I smell it I shall be reminded of you'. The whole foyer roared with laughter at Queensberry's humiliation.

But this last incident was sheer fiction. The real Queensberry tried to deliver a bouquet of vegetables, and failed. Detectives from Scotland Yard, forewarned, had had him barred from the theatre. He went straight to the Albermarle Club to personally deliver his infamous card: 'To Oscar Wilde, posing as a somdomite'. (Ken Hughes corrected his spelling, as Gregory Ratoff had also done in his film.)

Queensberry had continued to hound Wilde (almost literally) after his arrest and when he was on bail. In the film he was seen pursuing him in a hansom cab, as if he were fox hunting – the unspeakable in full pursuit of the uneatable.

Wilde (aided by Bosie and also his own mother – seen briefly on the staircase of her home) seemed determined to bring about his own destruction; he refused to leave for the Continent.

The court scenes worked well, though not as well as they had done in the Robert Morley film, where Ralph Richardson had played Carson. James Mason's QC assumed an Irish accent and carried out his lethal interrogation in a very quiet manner, occasionally betraying his irritation at Wilde's 'clever' replies. The trial moved to its dramatic climax when Carson asked Wilde if he had kissed the sixteen-year-old waiter, Grainger.

When Carson said he would produce a number of rent boys to back up the Defence's case, Wilde withdrew his charges against Queensberry. But it was too late. There were two more trials. Wilde would make another fatal *faux pas* in the second trial: 'I am a lover of youth,' he said, and the admission, as played by Finch, hung in the air for what seemed an eternity before anybody spoke. (This being 1960, the film did not put the rent boys in the dock and allow cinemagoers to hear their evidence.) The Finch film spent less time on the trials than the Morley film had done; they should have swapped titles.

Nigel Patrick (in his role of Edward Clarke) was given a scene with his clerk in which he made it clear that although he personally found homosexuality 'loathsome, degenerate and unnatural'. He condemned the witch-hunt and expressed his contempt that Wilde should be 'crucified by common criminals, blackmailers and paid informers'. Wilde, he said, was a victim of national prejudice and hysteria. The press and public had prejudged him guilty. All Wilde could hope for 'was a glimmer of Christian charity and forgiveness,' and there did not seem much chance of that.

Yvonne Mitchell (as Constance Wilde) suffered in silence; yet, in her quiet way she was just as lethal as Patrick's Carson, denying Oscar access to his children and threatening to cut his allowance if he ever saw Bosie again.

Wilde's time in Reading Gaol was quickly passed over. The film ended with his release and departure for the Continent. Bosie turned up at the station, a big smile on his face, only to find himself totally ignored. The snub made for a good, old-fashioned theatrical 'curtain', but the whole scene was, of course, an absolute fiction, a sop to the cinemagoing public.

> Finch's Oscar is a loser all the way.
>
> Fred Majdalany *Daily Mail* (headline)

> Finch wins hands down.
>
> Margaret Hinxman *Daily Herald* (headline)

> He (Peter Finch) has nothing of the grotesque in his playing – nothing of Morley's beamish boy popping with epigram.
>
> Alexander Walker *Evening Standard*

> Peter Finch's Wilde is one of the most complete screen creations I can recall in a British film.
>
> David Robinson *Financial Times*

1960 *A Wilde Evening with Shaw*

Premiere: Forty-First Street Theatre, New York.

Co-director	Cedric Hardwicke
CAST	Richard Gray Mayo Loiseau

The evening was a dramatisation of the lives and wit of Oscar Wilde and Bernard Shaw. There were excerpts from *The Critic as Artist, An Ideal Husband, The Happy Prince, The Decay of Living, The Importance of Being Earnest, De Profundis*, and *The House of Judgement*.

The effort to find a parallel between Wilde and Shaw was forced and the commentary flippant. The two actors, much given to grimacing and gesturing, failed to create, let alone sustain, a mood. The evening was dismissed as 'pretentious and tedious' by the *New York Times*, 'insufferably cute and earnestly ordinary' by the *New York Standard*, and 'a terrible fiasco' by the *Morning Telegraph*.

1963 Ballet: *Country Houses*

Premiere: Gramercy Theatre, New York.

Choreography	Elaine Summers
Sound	Words of Oscar Wilde arranged by Robert Dunn

A woman hung upside down by the proscenium arch reading selected texts by Wilde, while the dancers, dressed in white like ghosts from the country houses of the past, presented *tableaux vivants* of people in conversation.

1965 British television: *Famous Gossips: Oscar Wilde*

Director	Patrick Garland
OSCAR WILDE	Alan Badel
GARCON DE CAFÉ	Peter Bowles

The script was adapted from the letters of Oscar Wilde. Oscar was living on the Continent under the assumed name of Monsieur Sebastien Melmoth, which he had borrowed from the Christian martyr in C R Maturin's novel, *Melmoth the Wanderer*.

Wilde was extremely hard up, often insulted, and alone. He sat in a Parisian café gossiping about Frank Harris (the author and his biographer), Leonard Smithers (his publisher), the Pope, the chastity of Switzerland, photographing cows in Rome, and dying beyond one's means.

As Robert Ross pointed out (after Wilde's death), dying is really a very difficult and expensive luxury for a foreigner.

1967 Promotional film: *We Love You*

Song	Mick Jagger and Keith Richards
Recording	Rolling Stones
Director	Peter Whitehead
CAST	Marianne Faithful Mick Jagger Keith Richards

The film promoted the record *We Love You*, with scenes based on the Ken Hughes film, *The Trials of Oscar Wilde.* The song celebrated Mick Jagger's release from prison. John Lennon and Paul McCartney provided the vocal back-ups. The song was a 'thank you' to all the people (and that included *The Times*) who had supported Jagger after his arrest on a drug charge. The BBC banned the film because of its anti-Establishment nature.

1969 British Film: *The Best House in London*

Screenplay	Denis Norden
Director	Philip Saville
OSCAR WILDE	John De Marco
LORD ALFRED DOUGLAS	George Reynolds

A Victorian cad (David Hemmings) set up a government sponsored brothel on the French system, catering for exotic perversions. Oscar and Bosie were just two of the many Victorians, who made fleeting appearances in this bawdy, hit-and-miss romp.

1971 *Oscar X*
A play by Tudor Gates.

Premiere: Mercury Theatre, London.

An Irish black streetcleaner by the name of Oscar Fingal O'Flaherty Ngko (Derek Griffiths) was falsely accused of abducting a schoolgirl. The police inspector (Norman Wooland) revealed his racial prejudice while interrogating him.

1971 British television: *A Bruisèd Daffodil of Last Night's Sin*

Director	Margaret McCall
Screenplay	Margaret McCall
OSCAR WILDE	Freddie Jones
LEONARD SMITHERS	Wolfe Morris
AUBREY BEARDSLEY	Colin Jeavons
ERNEST DOWSON	David Wood

ARTHUR SYMONS	John Wood
FRENCH POET	Terry Scully

Oscar Wilde, the illustrator Aubrey Beardsley, the poet Ernest Dowson, and a composite French poet, quoted from their own works while publisher Leonard Smithers sat in the Café Royal (next to a very bored *fin de siècle* prostitute who said nothing) and recollected his relationship with the three 'decadents'. All of them died young: Beardsley at twenty-six, Dowson at thirty-three, Wilde at forty-six, and Smithers at forty-eight.

Margaret McCall's script and direction were highly artificial. Freddie Jones, in white tie and tails, and wearing a green carnation, was the most mannered and affected of all the actors. Wilde emerged as an absurd, self-dramatising figure, strutting, posturing, and spouting epigrams to a drum roll, as if he were a circus act. Jones, declaiming Herod very badly, was forced to compete with projected images of Beardsley's drawings from *Salomé* while he spoke. It was a losing battle.

Jones was more subdued (and therefore far more effective) towards the end when Oscar was starving in Paris and remembering the terrible conditions he had suffered in prison. But even here McCall could not leave the actor alone and while he was talking she played a radio recording of Edith Evans and John Gielgud acting the 'interview' scene from *The Importance of Being Earnest* and punctuated it with pre-recorded roars of hollow laughter.

A Bruisèd Daffodil of Last Night's Sin took its title from a poem by Richard Le Gallienne.

> Freddie Jones made a rather touching figure in his decline but spoke the epigrams ('geniuses are born, not paid') in a kind of nasal whinny, something between Charles Laughton as Captain Bligh and a poetry reader on Radio 3.
>
> Peter Black *Daily Mail*

> Freddie Jones's slightly unctuous Wilde would have earned him an Oscar in a hammier age; but so, of course, would Wilde's.
>
> Maurice Wiggin *Sunday Times*

1972 *O W*
A ballet by Joe Layton.

Performed by the Royal Ballet Company.
Premiere: Sadler's Wells Theatre, London.

Music	William Walton
Conductor	John Lanchbery

Part 1: *Masque*

QUEENSBERRY	Kerrison Cooke
SERVANT	Stephen Jefferies
SPHINX	Vyvyan Lorrayne
BUTTERFLIES	Margaret Barbieri
	Nicholas Johnson
OSCAR WILDE	Paul Clarke

Part 2: *De Profundis*

'Pain, unlike pleasure, wears no mask.'

O W	Michael Somes
CONSTANCE	Margaret Barbieri
BOSIE	Nicholas Johnson
SPHINX	Vyvyan Lorrayne
QUEENSBERRY	Kerrison Cooke
YOUNG CHAP	Stephen Jefferies
VOICE	John Gielgud

Joe Layton's ballet (to William Walton's Suite from *The Quest* and the Viola Concerto) was confusing if audiences knew nothing of Wilde's life. He was seen at two flamboyant stages: firstly, as an effeminate youth (Paul Clarke), and then as a corpulent, middle-aged dilettante (Michael Somes).

The opening *Masque* was a mistake, perpetuating Gilbert and Sullivan's cheap and dreary *Patience* caricature with a camped-up burlesque of a homosexual lepidopterist, dressed in green, ensnaring butterfly ballet-boys wearing wings.

The humour was crude. The conflict between Wilde and Queensberry, for instance, was presented as a comic boxing match with Wilde defending himself with a sunflower. The silly fisticuffs gave no idea of Queensberry's mad and dangerous vindictiveness. Kerrison Cooke's Marquis was merely a figure of fun and far too young.

The battle between Bosie and Constance for Wilde was more impressive. Best of all was that moment when Queensberry drove Wilde, like a horse, to his downfall. But in the end it was Wilde's own words from *De Profundis*, pre-recorded by John Gielgud, which produced the sympathy, rather than the choreography.

> It fell a long way short of the dramatic irony, hubris and pathos, of the story.
>
> Philip Hope-Wallace *Guardian*

> Michael Somes's performance is astonishing. Long retired from dancing roles, his body responds with a certain awkwardness to the demands Layton's choreography makes on it. Yet this very ungainliness, combined with the true grace of his bearing, gives the role poignancy. Made up as a monster, he still expresses an ineffable sweetness of nature. Thus the paradox of Wilde's personality is given physical expression on stage.
>
> John Percival *Financial Times*

1972 *Wilde!*
A drama by Frederick Gaines.

Premiere: Theatre de Lys, New York.

Director	John J Desmond
WILDE	Albert Stratton
O'FLAHERTIE	Charles Siebert
WILLS	Barbara Caruso
FINGAL	Carol Williard

The action, romantic and impressionistic, took place in Paris shortly before and during Oscar's death. Oscar, in drag, sat at a dressing-table while figures representing aspects of him and his past appeared.

> The evening belongs to Albert Stratton, who delivers a ripe, dying-swan portrayal as the self-defensive and pathetic Wilde.
>
> Mel Gussow *New York Times*

1973 *The Faggot*
A musical revue by Al Carmines.

Premiere: Astor Palace Theatre, New York.

Director	Al Carmines
OSCAR	David Pursley
BOSIE	Ira Siff

The revue was a series of vignettes of homosexual lives and attitudes in songs and sketches. The Wilde number was particularly successful, stopping the show every night.

1973 *Feasting with Panthers*
A play by Adrian Hall and Richard Cumming.

Premiere: Trinity Square Repertory Company, Providence, Rhode Island, USA.

Director	Adrian Hall
OSCAR WILDE	Richard Kneeland
CAST	George Martin
	David Kennett
	Richard Jenkins
	Robert Black
	Robert J Colonna
	James Eichelberger
	David C Jones
	Richard Kavanagh
	T Richard Mason
	Daniel Von Bargen
	Jobeth Williams
	Timothy Crowe
	William Damkoehler

The production drew on Wilde's work, interspersed with scenes from his life, to create a portrait of Wilde. The action was set in Reading Gaol. The cast played a variety of roles. There was only one woman in the cast; men played both sexes. Salomé was acted entirely in drag. The governor of the prison was suddenly transformed into Lady Bracknell and Wilde into John Worthing. The second act opened with a half-human, half-puppet realisation of *The Fisherman and His Soul*.

> Salomé is portrayed as a certifiable hermaphrodite. Is this out-of-the-closet explicitness for simple-minded shock value or a serious probing of Oscar Wilde as an extension of his characters? You can answer according to personal reactions. To this writer the latter suggestion seems justifiable. For all the affront of being forced to look at a pair of bare, broad-beamed male behinds, for all the costume borrowings from Aubrey Beardsley's more outrageous drawings, a theatrical statement is successfully made.
>
> Edwin Safford *Providence Sunday Journal*

> Richard Kneeland – there can be no doubt about it – is Oscar Wilde. The original, I fully believe, could learn from him. He is affected without being comical, effete without being effeminate, witty without a trace of maliciousness. He has strength, affability, irony and insouciance, and he makes them work together in a superb and fully convincing portrait.
>
> John Heasley *Brown Daily Herald*

1975 *Oscar Remembered*
A one-man show by Maxim Mazumdar.

Premiere: Stratford Festival, Ontario, Canada.

Actor	Maxim Mazumdar
Director	William Hutt

Mazumdar's show was a recollection of Wilde through Alfred Douglas. *Oscar Remembered* also played at The Round House, London, in 1979.

1977 *Diversions and Delights*
A one-man show by John Gay.

Premiere: American Conservatory Theater, San Francisco.
Followed by tour.
Transferred: Eugene O'Neill Theatre in 1978.

Actor	Vincent Price
Director	Joseph Hardy

John Gay's script was based on the conceit that Wilde, in exile in France (after his release from prison) was appearing in a seedy Parisian lecture hall. The first half of the programme was devoted to his over-familiar epigrams. The second half was devoted to his fall.

> Vincent Price's impersonation of Wilde makes up for many of the script's shortcomings. From his striking physical appearance (a boyishly waved hairdo incongruously perched atop a ravaged aristocratic face) to his properly arched delivery, Price's characterisation is remarkable.
>
> Don Shewey *Boston Phoenix*

> He never really lets down his guard; there's no audience empathy or connection on the gags, only a proficient actor's inate sense of how to play a laugh – or a tear-jerker – for its calculated effect.
>
> *Daily Californian*

> Only towards the end, when the Wilde self-pity flows like a flat seltzer, does Price become wearing. The verbal flagellation should be trimmed.
>
> *Variety*

1978 *Mad Oscar*
A play by Sheldon Feldner.

Premiere: Berkeley Repertory Theater, California, USA.

Director	Peter Donat
OSCAR	Michael Leibert
DOUGLAS	Paul Laramore
ROSS	Marc Geiger
TURNER	Dale Elliott
HARRIS	Don West
MELLOR	Troy Evans
SMITHERS	Robert Haswell

> Feldner's script nicely segues between imagined speech and actual Wildean epigrams, but it does need polishing (too many bad puns, old jokes, even some incorrect grammar) and rethinking. Michael Leibert gives us a Wilde that shifts from

> little-boy-lost to consummate genius. It is a rich impersonation. Paul Laramore makes a properly detestable Douglas.
>
> Bernard Weiner *San Francisco Chronicle*

1978 British television: *Lillie*

Director	Peter Walker
LILLIE LANGTRY	Francesca Annis
EDWARD LANGTRY	Anton Rodgers
PRINCE OF WALES	Denis Lill
OSCAR WILDE	Peter Egan

The thirteen one-hour episodes were based on the life and loves of actress Lillie Langtry, the Jersey Girl, mistress to the Prince of Wales, the future King Edward VII. Peter Egan camped it up as Wilde.

> Wilde is played as a swoopy aesthete. The steel of his repartee is quite missing; everything he says is as soft as his wrist.
>
> Clive James *Observer*

1979 *Trials of Oscar Wilde*
Devised and directed by Peter Coe.

Premiere: Citadel Theatre, Edmonton, Alberta, Canada.

1980 *It's Wilde!*
A musical by Burton Wolf and Randy Klein.

Premiere: Theatre East, New York.

Director	Burton Wolf
OSCAR WILDE	Ross Petty
EDWARD CARSON	Allan Stevens
CONSTANCE WILDE	Betsy Jamison
'BOSIE' DOUGLAS	Peter Toran
SPECTATOR	Carol Cass

In prison, Wilde sang 'All the Flowers Turn to Snow'. Carson sang 'Rape Me' to Constance. The show was variously described as banal, idiotic, commonplace, complete drivel, wildly awful, and the 'worst show not only on earth but also in heaven'. The second act took place in heaven. *It's Wilde!* opened on 21 May and closed on 25 May.

> The entire production was overdone with the sort of gloss you might encounter in a Vegas bistro.
>
> *Backstage*

1980 Madrid. Premiere of *The Remarkable Oscar Wilde*, a one-man show written and acted by Denis Rafter.

1981 *Work is the Curse of the Drinking Classes*
Written and performed by Neil Titley.

Premiere: King's Head, London.

> Titley gently balances Wilde's almost dutiful humour with an unsentimental portrayal of his suffering in *Reading Gaol.*
>
> Charles Spencer *Evening Standard*

> It is a good portrait, funny and melancholic, of the face behind *Dorian Gray*.
>
> Ned Chaillet *The Times*

1981 *Feasting with Panthers*
Devised, directed and designed by Peter Coe.

Premiere: Chichester Festival Theatre.

Act I The First Trial: Wilde *v* Queensberry

COUNSEL FOR THE PROSECUTION	Donald Houston
LORD ALFRED DOUGLAS	John Higginson
CLERK TO THE COURT	Peter Glaze
WARDER	David Hitchen
MARQUIS OF QUEENSBERRY	Frank Shelley
COUNSEL FOR THE DEFENCE	Aubrey Woods
JUDGE	Lockwood West
OSCAR WILDE	Tom Baker
FOREMAN OF THE JURY	Richard Evans
ONLOOKERS	Keith Bartlett
	Richard Evans
	Amanda Holmes
	Terry Sheppard

Act II The Second Trial: Regina *v* Wilde

OSCAR WILDE	Tom Baker
WARDER	David Hitchen
CLERK TO THE COURT	Peter Glaze
COUNSEL FOR THE PROSECUTION	Aubrey Woods
COUNSEL FOR THE DEFENCE	Donald Houston
CHARLES PARKER	Johnathon Morris
JANE COTTER	Sue Withers
ALFRED WOOD	Jeremy Anthony
FREDERICK ATKINS	Gary Fairhall
EDWARD SHELLEY	Stephen Bone
JUDGE	Lockwood West
POLICE CONSTABLE 396A	Michael Anthony
LORD ALFRED DOUGLAS	John Higginson
MARQUIS OF QUEENSBERRY	Frank Shelley
FOREMAN OF THE JURY	Richard Evans

> People thought it dreadful of me to have entertained at dinner the evil things of life, and to have found pleasure in their company. But they, from the point of view through which I, as an artist of life, approached them, were delightfully suggestive and stimulating. It was like feasting with panthers. The danger was half the excitement.
>
> Oscar Wilde *De Profundis*

Peter Coe's *Feasting with Panthers* was based on the transcripts of the trials. In the first trial, in which Wilde had brought a charge of libel against the Marquis of Queensberry, he was his confident, witty, public self; and so long as he was allowed to keep to literature, he could score points easily, if ill-advisedly, off Edward Carson, Counsel for the Defence.

The most electrifying moment was when his flippancy betrayed him and he avowed he had not kissed a sixteen-year-old boy: 'Oh dear, no. He was peculiarly plain. He was, unfortunately, extremely ugly'.

Carson was quick to pounce. 'Why? Why? Why did you add that?' He kept repeating the 'whys', not allowing Wilde time to collect his thoughts.

Wilde floundered badly 'You sting me and insult me and try to unnerve me; and at times one says things flippantly when one ought to speak more seriously.'

In the two trials that followed (here condensed into one trial), witty repartee gave way to truth as various young blackmailers took the stand. Johnathon Morris and Jeremy Anthony (as the rent boys, Charles Parker and Alfred Wood), trying to avoid saying what they actually had done with Wilde, offered what were, in effect, comic turns.

The Chichester audience often laughed in exactly the same places that the original courtroom had laughed in 1895 and so it was easy for the judge to admonish them; and indeed at one point, to everybody's delight, Lockwood West (playing the judge) accused the whole theatre of 'morbid curiosity and prurient behaviour'.

Tom Baker's smirking performance was a travesty of the poseur Wilde was accused of being. But his *ex tempore* definition of 'the love that dare not speak its name' was nobly spoken.

Lord Alfred Douglas remained silent throughout.

> For all the portly figure and flowing hair, Tom Baker is not obvious Oscar material, which partly accounts for the success of his performance. He does not play an aesthete, but a man who has adopted the aesthetic mask, believing it will give him a charmed life.
>
> Irving Wardle *The Times*

> Tom Baker labours under the disadvantage of not looking much like Wilde but he expertly catches the contrast between the arrogant poseur, with his glittering eyes and toothy, self-congratulatory grin, and the pathetic victim who suddenly realises that he has lost his case.
>
> Francis King *Sunday Telegraph*

1981 Irish television: *Joyce, Yeats and Wilde*

Director	Sean O'Mordha
CAST	Seamus Heaney
	Richard Ellmann
	Diana Quick
	Stephen Rea

The programme was a tribute to 'three of Ireland's greatest writers'. In the first part, Seamus Heaney and Richard Ellmann strolled through Dublin's literary sites from Howth Head to Trinity College and the Martello Tower to 'explore the unique and universal qualities of these writers' imaginations and their enduring meaning to us'. In the second part, Stephen Rea and Diana Quick performed a patchwork of poems, prose and epigrams of all three writers.

1982 *The Wilde Spirit*
Conceived and performed by Kerry Ashton.

Premiere: Theater Off Park, New York.

1982 *I'm Just Wilde about Oscar*
A musical by Penny Faith and Howard Samuels.

Premiere: King's Head, London.

Director	Roger Haines
CONSTANCE WILDE	Michelle Fine
BOSIE DOUGLAS	Howard Samuels
OSCAR WILDE	Jonathon Stephens
NARRATOR	Simon Lee

The show was an hour-long medley of familiar songs by Irving Berlin, Stephen Sondheim, Noël Coward, Bob Dylan and Paul McCartney, which were used to illustrate Wilde's life. The biography was perfunctory. It was best to forget Wilde and just enjoy the songs. The most relevant were 'Bunthorne's Song' from Gilbert and Sullivan's *Patience*, Coward's 'Mad About the Boy', and Sondheim's 'Could I Leave You'.

1982 *Lord Alfred's Lover*
Written and directed by Eric Bentley.

Premiere: New Vic Theater, New York.

CHARLES PARKER	Christopher Cosani
LORD ROSEBERY	Christopher Cosani
YOUNG LORD ALFRED DOUGLAS	Matthew Colson
QUEENSBERRY	Callan Egan
SIR EDWARD CLARKE	Callan Egan

FREDDY WOOD/CLIBURN	Michael Gnat
CONSTANCE WILDE	Suzanne Hall
ROBBIE ROSS	Mitchell Sugarman
CARSON	Nicholas Haylett
OSCAR WILDE	Maxim Mazumdar
ARTHUR MARLING	David Officer

I did nothing to induce compassion, especially of the skimmed-milk liberal sort. After all, this is a play in which heterosexual society is the enemy; there is no way of fudging that.

Eric Bentley, interviewed by John Hofsess *New York Native*

An aging Lord Alfred Douglas told the story of the trial in a confession to a priest. Like Wilde before him, he had become a Roman Catholic in his old age. He confessed that he and Wilde had never been lovers, only in love. The confession was all fake. He remained 'an unrepentant faggot'.

1985 British television: *Oscar*
US title: *Oscar Wilde*
A trilogy by John Hawkesworth.

Director	Henry Herbert
OSCAR WILDE	Michael Gambon
LORD ALFRED DOUGLAS	Robin Lermitte
CONSTANCE WILDE	Emily Richard
THE MARQUIS OF QUEENSBERRY	Norman Rodway
ROBERT ROSS	John Hudson
GEORGE BERNARD SHAW	Bryan Murray
HUMPHREYS	Neil Cunningham
DOCTOR	David Collings
CLIBBORN	Donald Sumpter
ALFRED TAYLOR	Tim Hardy
FRED ATKINS	Karl Howman
CHARLIE PARKER	Nick Reding
WOOD	Ian Holt
BROOKFIELD	Russell Keith Grant
BEERBOHM TREE	Peter Cellier
MRS TREE	Anne Lambton
GEORGE ALEXANDER	John Repsch
PRINCE OF WALES	James Bree
LADY LONSDALE	Helen Shingler

AMERICAN BEAUTY	Betsy Brantley
LILLIE LANGTRY	Catherine Strauss
MAX BEERBOHM	Robert Burbage
LABOUCHERE	Michael Beint
MEMBER OF PARLIAMENT	Richard Owens
POLICE INSPECTOR	Christopher Saul
CLUB PORTER	Neville Phillips
JEWELLER'S ASSISTANT	Will Knightley
NANNY	Pat Quayle
CYRIL WILDE	Jonty Lovell
VYVYAN WILDE	Jonathan Haley
NARRATOR	Michael Pennington
EDWARD CARSON	Ronald Pickup
SIR EDWARD CLARKE	Nigel Stock
SIR FRANK LOCKWOOD	Jerome Willis
MR JUSTICE WILLS	Bernard Miles
SIR GEORGE LEWIS	William Fox
SIR JOHN BRIDGE	Paul Williamson
INSPECTOR NEWTON	Norman Rutherford
BROCKWELL	Ian Thompson
LITTLECHILID	Ken Sharrock
KEARLEY	Kevin White
FOREMAN OF THE JURY	Harry Walker
CLERK OF ARRAIGN	John Leeson
CLERK IN MAGISTRATE'S COURT	Peter Mackriel
AUCTIONEER	Michael Sadler
MOTHER AT AUCTION	Amanda Garwood
FATHER AT AUCTION	James Coyle
REPORTER	Stephen Warden
PROSTITUTE	Kim Hicks
MAJOR NELSON	Colin Rix
WARDEN MARTIN	Bruce Payne
SOLICITOR	Russell Kilmister
GOVERNOR OF PENTONVILLE	Richard Simpson
HEAD WARDER OF PENTONVILLE	Martyn Read
WARDEN OF PENTONVILLE	Stuart McGugan
PRISON DOCTOR	Michael Gaunt
ENGLISHMAN IN CAFÉ	Noel Johnson
ENGLISHWOMAN IN CAFÉ	Rita Davies
TURNER	David Ballantyne

GIRL WITH BOSIE	Sarah Bullen
MR WILDY	John Baker
MAN AT STATION	James Bryce
POPPINO	Bruno Tonioli
YOUNG FRENCH GIRL	Anoushka Menzies

John Hawkesworth's script was based upon two books by H Montgomery Hyde, his biography of Wilde and *The Aftermath*. In America the title had to be changed because Oscar is a registered trade mark.

The three episodes dealt with the last nine years of Wilde's life. They began with a prelude: the amendment of the law to protect thirteen-year-old girls from being sold into brothels. A new clause was added at the last minute to make gross indecency between male persons in public and private an offence. The clause was immediately recognised as a blackmailer's charter.

The first episode, *Gilded Youth* (which dropped epigrams and names in the most obtrusive manner), opened with Robbie Ross introducing Lord Alfred Douglas to Wilde. As shown in this television version, their affair was strictly platonic, limited to longing looks in a punt, just one kiss, and an occasional line like 'Your twisted lips drove me to distraction'.

Robin Lermitte's beautiful, gild-haired Bosie was an idle, shallow, petulant and ruinously expensive Narcissus, wasting Wilde's time and money. His mad rage, mania and cruelty, though mentioned, were not seen. He did lose his temper with Wilde (when they were quarrelling over his translation of *Salomé*) and suggested he should pick up a dirty little renter. But, though Michael Gambon bore a considerable facial and physical resemblance to Wilde, there was nothing comparable to the 'scenes' between Peter Finch and John Fraser in *The Trials of Oscar Wilde* (1960).

In prison Wilde blamed himself for the biggest mistake of his life, namely letting Douglas turn the 'brilliant comedy' of his life into 'a revolting and repellent tragedy'.

The first episode showed Wilde as the loving father, telling his children the story of *The Happy Prince*, and as the successful playwright, attending the first night of *The Importance of Being Earnest* where he delivered a speech Wilde had actually delivered at the first night of *Lady Windermere's Fan*.

It also showed Wilde 'feasting with panthers', (that is visiting a male brothel). 'The danger,' he explained, 'was half the excitement. I was tired of the heights so I went to the depths for a new sensation'.

The script raised the old lie that he was advised by his doctor to discontinue physical relations with his wife on account of his syphilis. 'Completely?' he asked. 'Oh, yes, completely,' was the reply. He burst into tears.

The best scene was when the blackmailer Clibborn tried to extort money from Wilde with a love letter Wilde had written to Bosie. Wilde dismissed the letter as a prose poem and advised him to sell it. 'I've never been offered £60 for a work of mine,' he said. Clibborn handed over a whole bunch of letters, adding, 'It's no good trying to rent you because all you do is laugh at me'.

The trials were shown as the direct result of Douglas's vendetta against his father, an illiterate and dangerous man, who went round threatening to thrash everybody in sight. 'What a funny little man you are,' said his son. Norman Rodway, who played the Marquis, growled and looked (as Wilde said he did) ape-like.

The first episode ended with the arrest of Queensberry for libel and with Wilde assuring his solicitor, Charles Humphreys, that he had never committed sodomy with male prostitutes.

The second episode dealt with the trials. In the dock Wilde was confident: 'I delight in the company of people much younger than myself . . . I recognise no social distinctions of any kind at all'. His flippancy cost him dear when in answer to Edward Carson's question whether he had kissed a young man, he replied, 'Oh, dear, no, he was peculiarly plain'. Carson was played by Ronald Pickup with icy, piercing coldness.

When Carson threatened to put a whole series of young men in the witness box, Humphreys advised Wilde to leave the country. The legal Establishment gave him every opportunity to do so by delaying the issue of the warrant for his arrest. But Wilde refused to take it. 'I don't think I could bear life if I were to flee,' he said. 'I can't see myself slinking about the Continent, a fugitive from justice'. Mesmerised by Bosie, he refused to listen to good advice.

Nigel Stock (as Sir Edward Clarke for the Defence) was most moving in his final plea when he begged the jury to clear Wilde and 'clean society of this dreadful stain'. The jury found Wilde guilty and the judge sentenced him to two years' hard labour.

The final episode, entitled *De Profundis*, opened with Wilde in prison, degraded and humiliated. There was far too much voice-over and certainly far too much illustration of *The Ballad of Reading Goal* when the script should have been getting on with Wilde's own story. There were endless flashbacks to the previous episodes, plus a scene with a rent boy, Charlie Parker, which Nick Reding played in the nude. The trilogy ended with Wilde, a ruined man, living the life of an outcast in France.

> The series was a missed opportunity then particularly because it concentrated in a conventional manner upon Wilde's 'fall' and did nothing to illuminate the fact that he was the greatest artist of his period, in his critical writings no less than in his more notorious drama.
>
> Peter Ackroyd *The Times*

> Gambon's performance overall, historically accurate or not, has its own logic and was a lot better and more subtle than the crude text deserved.
>
> Hugh Herbert *Guardian*

1986 Irish television: *Oscar Wilde – Spendthrift of Genius*

Script	Richard Ellmann
Director	Sean O'Mordha
NARRATOR	Denys Hawthorne
CAST	Alan Stanford
	Barbara Brennan
	Seamus Forde
	Aiden Grennell

This documentary focused first on Wilde's rise in social and literary circles and then on his collapse. Wilde was seen in a variety of roles: student, celebrity, dramatist, convict, and exile.

1987 *Love, Oscar*
A one-man show by Stephen Holt.

Premiere: Theater for the New City, New York.

Wilde's letters were adapted and performed by Stephen Holt.

> It is difficult to sustain an audience's interest (particularly for two acts) in a person's love, no matter how volatile and laudatory the lover, for a talentless, egocentric nonentity. Holt, who also plays Wilde, cannot overcome this obstacle, making Wilde more campy than necessary, mitigating the tragedy.
>
> G B Lasdun *New York Native*

1988 *A Trinity of Two*
A play by Ulick O'Connor.

Premiere: Abbey Theatre at the Peacock Theatre, Dublin.

Director	Thomas MacAnna
EDWARD CARSON	Clive Geraghty
OSCAR WILDE	Des Cave

> It was two Irishmen fighting about nothing . . . and I was only a puppet and so was Ulster and so was Ireland.
>
> Edward Carson

Oscar Wilde and Edward Carson were students together at Trinity College, Dublin. Ulick O'Connor's play, set in Carson's London Club and the Calisaya Café, Paris, was a series of monologues and biographical snippets which explored the relationship between the brilliant writer and the brilliant barrister inside and outside the courtroom. The two men – one with a tongue like a silver razor, the other with a tongue like a hatchet – had more in common than they might have suspected. The script became an examination of the relationship of the Protestant Irish to the British Establishment.

> Desmond Cave's Wilde and Clive Geraghty's Carson are marvellously contrasted in quietly splendid performances.
>
> Desmond Rushe *Irish Independent*

1989 *Oscar*
A ballet by Domy Reiter-Soffer.
Performed by the Irish National Ballet.

Premiere: Cork, Ireland.

Music	Arnold Bax
OSCAR	Cornel Crabtree
ROSS	Armando Luna
OTHER SELF	Daire O Dunlaing
BOSIE	Pieter-Paul Blok
ADA LEVERSON	Denise Roberts
LADY WILDE	Michele Szymanski
VOICE	John Kavanagh

The ballet traced Wilde's awakening sexuality. Since homosexuality was still an offence in the Republic of Ireland in 1989, the subject matter was a brave choice. The choreography was notable for a dream sequence in which Wilde's mother appeared as Brunhilde, his wife as Salomé, and Queensberry as a pursuing fate.

Oscar was the Irish National Ballet's last production. Always financially in a parlous state, they had to disband when the Irish Arts Council refused to fund them any more.

> Unquestionably the finest moments are the beautifully crafted and sculptured duets between the two men which completely avoid the slightest sign of camp.
>
> Sally Whyte *Dance and Dancers*

1989 *Saint Oscar*
A play by Terry Eagleton.

Premiere: Guildhall, Derry, Ireland.

Director	Trevor Griffiths
OSCAR WILDE	Stephen Rea
LADY WILDE	Ellen Pollock
RICHARD WALLACE	Seamus Moran
LORD ALFRED DOUGLAS	Peter Hanly
EDWARD CARSON	Stanley Townsend
JUDGE	Jim Queally
JAMIE	Aidan McCann

Saint Oscar, subtitled 'An irreverent musical biography', was performed by the Field Day Theatre Company. Terry Eagleton's Wilde was a victim of colonial rule, a symbol of Anglo-Irish disunity, and also a symbol of the oppression that the Irish suffer. His homosexuality was presented as a protest against British colonisation and her subjugation of Ireland.

'I have never understood the meaning of the term morality,' said Eagleton's Wilde, 'other than as a ploy for oppressing others'. He spoke in epigrams (though only one of them was actually by Wilde) and his long monologues were broken by one-to-one didactic confrontations.

Firstly, there was his mother, Lady Wilde, feminist patriot, who represented nationalism. She castigated him for his lack of interest in politics and for abandoning Ireland. Then there was Richard Wallace (a fictitious activist friend), who berated him for ignoring the working classes and wanted him to be a militant socialist.

WALLACE: What have you ever done for your country?
WILDE: I got out.

Thirdly, there was Edward Carson, QC:

CARSON: You are a bugger, Mr Wilde, are you not?
WILDE: Certainly not, sir, I'm Irish. There are no buggers in Ireland. The Church would not allow it. We are a God-fearing people, pious to a fault . . . Homosexual behaviour is as English as Morris dancing, if somewhat less tedious.

In *Saint Oscar*, Wilde objected to his trial on the grounds that no Irishman would receive a fair hearing. He wanted to be defended by metaphysicians rather than by lawyers and he wanted to have a jury composed of his peers: 'poets, perverts, vagrants, and geniuses'.

Eagleton suggested Wilde had been destroyed by the British to divert public attention from Prime Minister Lord Rosebery's affair with Queensberry's eldest son, Viscount Drumlanrig. 'Homosexuality among the upper classes is,' said Wilde, 'as habitual as high tea.'

Lord Alfred Douglas (described as the most brutal and intolerable of egoists) visited him in prison and was his usual charming self: 'Do you think I am going to spend the rest of my life with you?' he screamed.

The action was interrupted every so often by ribald ballads sung by a chorus of lewd Irish boys:

If you're queer and you're Irish and wear a daft hat
Don't screw the son of an aristocrat

If you can't find a job
Find yourself a nob

Bend over for the gentry
So they can make an entry

Trevor Griffith's production was surreal. The first act was dominated by a huge plastercast of Saint Sebastian with two arrows stuck in him. In the second act a judge sat atop a ladder, a towering figure in scarlet, his enormous robes covering not only the ladder but the floor as well.

Saint Oscar was essentially a one-man show for Stephen Rea. His performance was quite extraordinary, totally unlike anything he had done previously or has done since. He acted Wilde ('a man with a great future behind him') as a vain, arrogant, raving queen with purple lips and eye-shadow.

'I was born queer,' he confessed. 'I'm superficial. There's nothing skin-deep about my superficiality . . . My whole life has been one long unnatural practice'.

Rea wore all his costumes at the same time. He began by shedding his hat, cloak and dressing-gown (which came down to his feet) to reveal a purple velvet suit and orange waistcoat. He then removed them to reveal a green suit and a green carnation. From there it was but a short step to prison grey uniform and bucket and chains. He ended up half-naked, with two arrows stuck in him, and adopted a Saint-Sebastian pose.

> To complain that the historical Oscar Wilde was a much more entertaining and compelling figure than this cardboard character, is no doubt beside the point.
>
> Anthony Curtis *Financial Times*

> It is wishful thinking to see Wilde as a conscious or committed political creature and sheer sophistry to imply sleeping with boys is evidence of radicalism.
>
> Benedict Nightingale *The Times*

> Eagleton's Oscar is made to utter not only drivel but also a great amount of cheaply coarse obscenity. Far from canonising Wilde, the play trivialises and cheapens him.
>
> Charles Osborne *Daily Telegraph*

The production transferred to Hampstead Theatre Club, London, in 1990 and was also seen on Channel 4 television. The cast was the same on television as it had been at Derry and Hampstead, except that Brendan Gleeson played Edward Carson.

1990 *Diversions and Delights*
A one-man show by John Gay.

Revived: Playhouse, London.

Actor	Donald Sinden
Director	Frank Dunlop

Donald Sinden looked as if he had stepped out of one of Wilde's old photographs and occasionally there was a glimpse of what he might have done with the part had he been given a less inept script and the production had been less camp.

> Sinden looks like an overblown Cupid wearing lipstick or an overgrown Fauntleroy in a purple cravat. Sinden's familiar fruity boom is just a bit too robustly in place. This is Oscar reinvented by a latter-day Henry Irving; not the author of *De Profundis*.
>
> Benedict Nightingale *The Times*

1990 *Oscar*

A musical by James Clutton and Damian Landi.

Premiere: Intimate Theatre, Palmers Green, London.

Director	Neil Rutherford
OSCAR	Robert Bastian
CONSTANCE	Vanessa Barrett
BOSIE	Leighton Carter
WHISTLER	Pete Graham
QUEENSBERRY	John McSpadyen
SPERANZA	Jayne Moore
ROBERT ROSS	Richard Leggott
EDWARD CARSON	Andy Hall
LILLIE LANGTRY	Gemma Germaine Gardner

1991 *Oscar*

Book, music and lyrics by Mike Read.

Premiere: Chilston Park, Kent.

Director	Christopher G Stanford
OSCAR WILDE	Don Gallagher
CONSTANCE WILDE	Janet Dibley
BOSIE	Philip Day
QUEENSBERRY	Alvin Stardust

1992 Mike Read's musical was revived at the Old Fire Station, Oxford, with the following cast:

OSCAR WILDE	Alex Hanson
CONSTANCE WILDE	Lorna Dallas
BOSIE	Patrick Jamieson
QUEENSBERRY	Chris Corcoran

1992 British television: *The Blackheath Poisonings*
Adapted by Simon Raven from the novel by Julian Symons.

Director	Stuart Orme
OSCAR WILDE	Richard Strange

The Blackheath Poisonings was a three-part Victorian murder mystery. Wilde appeared in two out of three episodes.

1992 James Clutton and Damian Landi's musical was revived at the Buxton Festival and the Tricycle Theatre, Kilburn, London.

1993 *Stephen & Mr Wilde*
A play by Jim Bartley.

Premiere: Persephone Theatre, Saskatoon, Canada.

Director	Bill Glassco
WILDE	Donald Carrier
STEPHEN	Philip Atkin
HAWTHORNE	John Ralston
LOUISE	Shannon Lawson
SWEET	Alphonse Gaudet
NANCY	Sara Gordon

Jim Bartley based his play on Kevin O'Brien's *Oscar Wilde in Canada*. Stephen Davenport was a black American and Wilde's personal valet for several months of his North American lecture tour in 1882. Wilde was twenty-seven and Stephen was thirty-nine.

Jim Bartley, in his introduction to the published play, said that 'The play blends history with fiction on the theory that they are hopelessly blended anyway and that the truth lies somewhere in the middle, between experience and imagination'.

1994 *Oscar*
A monologue by David Norris.

Premiere : Dublin Festival.

OSCAR	Kevin McHugh

1994 *Wilde about Oscar*
A play by James T Meredith.

Premiere: Brighton Festival.
Transferred: Duke's Head, London.

Director	David Alexander
OSCAR WILDE	James T Meredith
BOSIE	Adrian Sharp

The play, presented by the Green Carnation Company, was a mixture of extracts from Wilde's letters and plays, and biographical material.

> Meredith is quite touching as Wilde; he is especially good at portraying the martyred wanderer's final years of raddled disgrace and is well matched by Adrian Sharp as Bosie, a perfumed object of desire with the mind of a callous bitch.
>
> Roger Foss *What's On*

1994 *Oscar*
Book, music and lyrics by Mike Read.

Revived: King's Head Theatre, London.

OSCAR WILDE	Nigel Williams
CONSTANCE WILDE	Prue Clarke
BOSIE	Daniel Goode
QUEENSBERRY	Bill Homewood

In musicalising Wilde it trivialises him and, worse, makes him a bore.

Nick Curtis *Evening Standard*

Artlessly shallow; lugubriously sentimental and nauseous saccharine Mike Read's show is liable to do very well – even if it doesn't find the West End transfer that it appears to be seeking.

Patrick Marmion *What's On*

1994 *The Love that Dare not Speak its Name*

Premiere: Her Majesty's Prison, Blundeston, Suffolk.

The Love that Dare not Speak its Name described a meeting between Wilde, Bosie Douglas and Constance Wilde in Holloway Prison in 1895. The script was written by the prisoners with the help of Lady Alice Douglas, a descendent of the Douglas family.

1995 *C.33*
A play by Robert Badinter.

Premiere: Théâtre National de la Colline, Paris.

Director	Jorge Lavelli
OSCAR WILDE	Roland Bertin
ROBERT ROSS	Jean-Loup Wolff
ALFRED DAY	Luc-Antoine Diquero
QUEENSBERRY	Bernard Spiegel
SIR EDWARD CLARKE	Frédéric Norbert
CONSTANCE WILDE	Dolores Torres

1995 *Le Procès d'Oscar Wilde*
Adapted and directed by Bernard Mouffe.

Premiere: Palais de Justice, Brussels.

The trials of Oscar Wilde, based on the actual transcripts, were acted by a cast of lawyers and actors.

1995 *A Trinity of Two*
A play by Ulick O'Connor.

Revived: Abbey Theatre at Peacock Theatre, Dublin.

Director	Thomas MacAnna
EDWARD CARSON	Des Cave
OSCAR WILDE	Stanley Townsend

> The two actors are channelled by the script into a kind of pastiche, in which neither is enabled to develop a character from within, but required to sustain a single note from start to finish – which they do with considerable skill.
>
> Gerry Colgan *Irish Times*

> Stanley Townsend's performance gives Wilde's character great depth, looking beyond his superficial wit. In many ways his main failing was the same as Carson's – he was unwilling to be a hypocrite.
>
> Kevin Burns *Sunday Express* (Eire)

1995 British television: *Wilde Night*

To mark the centenary of his trial, BBC2 paid tribute to Wilde's memory with six programmes:

10.50 am. *The Importance of Being Earnest*
A screening of the 1952 film, starring Michael Redgrave, Michael Denison and Edith Evans.

8.20 pm. *A Fear to Appear Queer, Oscar Dear*
The theme of this 'Open House Special' was that Wilde's legacy as a martyr had not helped twentieth-century gays. The discussion was led by the academic Alan Sinfield, author of *The Wilde Century*. There were contributions from the comedian Julian Clary, drag artist Dave Lynn, and MP Chris Smith.

8.50 pm. *Oscar and Me*
Simon Callow explained his obsession since childhood with Wilde and his writings.

9 pm. *The Life and Loves of Oscar Wilde*
The *Timewatch* programme presented a portrait of Wilde. There were contributions by his grandson Merlin Holland and by Lady

Alice Douglas, who was observed teaching *The Ballad of Reading Goal* to lifers in one of Her Majesty's prisons. Lady Alice said her work was an expiation of family guilt.

Peter Hall described what English society had done to Wilde as 'sexual ethnic cleansing of the most disgusting kind'. John Gielgud read *De Profundis* in Westminster Abbey.

There was also a recording of *The Ballad of Reading Goal*, which was purported to be by Wilde.

10 pm. *The Trials of Oscar Wilde*
A screening of the 1960 film, starring Peter Finch and John Fraser.

12 midnight *The Picture of Dorian Gray*
A screening of the 1945 film, starring Hurd Hatfield and George Sanders.

1995 Advertisement. Perrier-Jouet used Wilde's picture and name in their posters in their campaign. The copy was crass: 'Exquisite, decadent, sensual and frivolous. Like Oscar Wilde, Perrier-Jouet is all these things'.

1995 British film: *A Man of No Importance*

Director	Suri Krishnamma
Screenplay	Barry Devlin
ALFIE BYRNE	Albert Finney
LILLY BYRNE	Brenda Fricker
CARNEY	Michael Gambon
ADELE RICE	Tara Fitzgerald
ROBBIE FAY	Rufus Sewell
MRS GRACE	Anna Manahan
ERNIE LALLY	Joe Pilkington
RASHER FLYNN	Brendan Conroy
PHIL CURRAN	Pat Killalea
JACK CURRAN	John Killalea
MRS CROWE	Joan O'Hara
MRS ROCK	Eileen Reid
BALDY	David Kelly
FR KENNY	Mick Lally
JOHN	Stuart Dunne
BRETON-BERET	Joe Savino

KITTY	Paudge Behan
CARSON	Patrick Malahide
LANDLADY'S SON	Dylan Tighe
GARDA	Enda Dates
FIRST YOUNGMAN	Jonathan Rhys-Myers
TREASURER	Jimmy Keogh
WOMAN AT CANAL	Catherine Byrne
SECOND YOUNGMAN	Vincent Walsh
THIRD YOUNGMAN	Seamus Flavin

Barry Devlin's screenplay, based on incidents in Wilde's life, was set in Dublin and updated to 1963, the year of the John Profumo and Christine Keeler sex and spy scandal, which had brought down the Conservative government.

The film, whimsical and sentimental, opened with Alfie Byrne (a bus conductor, played by Albert Finney) walking to work reciting lines from *The Ballad of Reading Gaol* while Cole Porter's '*Let's Do It*' played on the soundtrack.

Byrne regaled his passengers with '*The Harlot's House*' and other poems. He had a passion for Wilde and had already produced *The Importance of Being Earnest* at the drama club he ran in a local church hall. He now wanted to stage *Salomé*.

Byrne was a repressed homosexual and the most moving moment was when he confessed to his sister (Brenda Fricker) that he had never made love to anybody. He was in love with his young but straight bus driver, Robbie Fay (Rufus Sewell), whom he nicknamed Bosie. 'I'm going to find out who this Bosie is,' said Robbie Fay. 'Better be a bloke, regular guy, know what I mean'.

Sitting in front of a mirror, Byrne quoted from *De Profundis*: 'If I can produce only one beautiful work of art, I shall be able to rob malice of its venom, cowardice of its sneer, and pluck out the tongue of scorn by its roots. If life be, as it surely is, a problem to me, I am no less a problem to life'.

Shattered by his discovery that the nice girl (Tara Fitzgerald) he had cast as Salomé was not a virgin and that Fay had a girlfriend, Byrne decided to come out of the closet. ('The only way to get rid of a temptation is to yield to it'.) Donning rouge, eye make-up, a green carnation, a cape, and a floppy hat, he looked exactly like Wilde did in the Napoleon Sarony photographs. He cruised a gay pub, got beaten up by the local lads, and ended up in the gutter looking up at the stars.

Later, he tried to commit suicide by jumping into a river; the water came up to his knees. 'What a silly little man you are,' he said to himself. One of the pleasures of the script was recognising the quotes.

The butcher (Michael Gambon), who was to have played Herod, took on Queensberry's role instead, and hounded Byrne, making certain the parish council banned *Salomé*. The vindictive bus inspector (Patrick Malahide), who revelled in Byrne's disgrace and transferred Fay (against his will) to another bus, was called Carson.

It was to Carson, of course, that Byrne addressed his 'The love that dare not speak its name' speech: 'There is nothing unnatural about it. It is intellectual, and it repeatedly exists between an elder and a younger man, when the elder man has intellect, and the younger man has all the joy, hope and glamour of life before him'.

The passengers stood by Byrne. So did Robbie Fay (as Robbie Ross had done): 'I don't care what you've done. I like you'. The upbeat ending was true neither to Alfie Byrne, nor to Wilde, nor, in fact, to the performance Albert Finney had built up.

1996 *Wilde at Heart*
Devised and directed by Patrick Marley.

Premiere: Lyric Studio Hammersmith, London.

CAST	Patrick Marley
	Virginia Lester

A programme on the life and works of Oscar Wilde.

1996 British television: *Indecent Acts*

Director	William Parry
Narrator	John Sessions
Reader	Corin Redgrave

The programme traced Wilde's experiences and examined the social and sexual legacies. There were also readings from his works.

1997 *The Importance of Being Oscar*
by Micheál Mac Liammóir

Revived: Savoy Theatre, London.

Actor	Simon Callow
Director	Patrick Garland

Simon Callow (who had been Mac Liammóir's dresser before he went up to university) did not pretend to be Wilde. Nor did he pretend to be Mac Liammóir. He was unexpectedly subdued and the only green carnations in sight were those worn by the first-night audience.

The first half of the programme told the story of Wilde's unlikely encounter with the miners of Colorado and included two witty observations which ought to be much better known than they are. The first was on London fog: 'an amateur attempt to imitate the French Impressionists'. The second was on sentimentality: 'merely the bank holiday of cynics'.

The extract from *An Ideal Husband* didn't work because in order to differentiate between Lord Goring and his manservant, Phipps, Callow had to make Phipps ridiculously old. Much more successful were his portraits of Lord Caversham (a role to which he could obviously return in his old age), and of Herod (which he acted in French).

The long extract from *The Picture of Dorian Gray* was of historical interest because in it Basil Hallward, the painter, asked Dorian the very same questions London society had begun to ask about Wilde: 'Why is it, Dorian, that a man like the Duke of Berwick leaves the room of a club when you enter? Why is it that so many gentlemen in London will neither go to your house nor invite you to theirs? . . . Why is your friendship so fatal to young men?'

The second half started with the judge's harsh sentence (two years' hard labour) and then went on to include Ada Leverson's account of Wilde's release from prison. There was an extract from *The Ballad of Reading Gaol*, and, in a lighter vein, a very funny, if somewhat patronising, conversation on literature between Wilde and his prison warder.

The high spot of Callow's performance was a long passage from *De Profundis*. The pain, the anger and the bitterness were deeply felt and expressed without resource to histrionics.

> It makes for a sympathetic evening, but it also leaves you reflecting that an encounter with Wilde himself would have been a rather more startling experience.
>
> John Gross *Sunday Telegraph*

It might have been more interesting if Callow had made a dramatic point of the fact that it was Mac Liammóir's portrait of Wilde, thus bringing out the fascinating parallels between the two men and accounting for the performer's obsessive identification.

Paul Taylor *Independent*

I cannot think of a better actor than Callow to convey genius and the lunatic self-destruction of the poet and the playwright.

Sheridan Morley *Spectator*

1997 *Gross Indecency – The Three Trials of Oscar Wilde*
A play written and directed by Moisés Kaufman.

Premiere: Greenwich House, New York.
Transferred: Minetta Lane Theater, New York.

OSCAR WILDE	Michael Emerson
LORD ALFRED DOUGLAS	Bill Dawes
QUEENSBERRY, GILL, LOCKOOD	Robert Blumenfeld
CLARKE, OTHERS	Trevor Anthony
CARSON, NARRATOR	John McAdams
NARRATOR, ATKINS, JUDGE, OTHERS	Andy Paris
NARRATOR, WOOD, SHAW, OTHERS	Greg Pierotti
NARRATOR, PARKER, HARRIS, OTHERS	Troy Sostillio
NARRATOR, MAVOR, TAYLOR, OTHERS	Greg Steinbruner

The truth,' said Wilde, 'is rarely pure and never simple.' Moisés Kaufman's script – sharp, intelligent and dramatic – drew on the original trial transcripts, letters, newspapers, biographies and epigrams written by Wilde and such contemporaries as Sir Edward Clarke (his Counsel during the trials), Frank Harris (his biographer), Lord Alfred Douglas, and Bernard Shaw. Kaufman also included lines cut from *Lady Windermere's Fan* and introduced a satirical revue sketch raising laughter at the expense of a latter-day critic, a facile but engaging joke.

The judge, in his summing-up, outdid himself. 'I would rather,' he said, 'try the most shocking murder case that it has ever fallen to my lot to try than to be engaged in a case of this description'. In passing sentence, he declared that Wilde had been at the centre of a circle of extensive corruption of the most hideous kind among young men and that, under the circumstances, he would be expected to pass the severest sentence that the law allowed, two years' hard labour. 'In my judgement,' he added, 'it is totally inadequate for such a case as this'.

The production had a physical simplicity. A nine-man ensemble faced the audience in two rows. In the back row, either side of a lectern (which stood for the dock) sat Bosie with Wilde's counsel on the left and Queensberry with his counsel on the right. In the front row at a long table, surrounded by books and papers, sat four young narrators, who played a variety of roles: lawyers, journalists, auctioneers, Queen Victoria, and so on. For the most part the actors addressed the audience directly.

Gross Indecency was part courtroom drama, part morality play, part history lesson, part social commentary, part gossip column. The drama focused on Wilde, the artist, prosecuted as much for his art and radical opinions as for his homosexuality. Wilde's infatuation with Bosie was expressed through Hallward's idolatry of Dorian in *The Picture of Dorian Gray*.

The off-the-cuff defence of 'the love that dare not speak its name' was remarkable; but Wilde's affairs with male prostitutes were hardly platonic and Kaufman underlined this by the appearance of four working-class hustlers in Victorian underwear.

Wilde was betrayed by his wit and arrogance. He made the fatal slip. Asked by Clarke if he had ever kissed a certain young man, he glibly replied, 'Oh, dear no. He was a peculiarly plain boy. He was unfortunately, extremely ugly. I pitied him for it'. Carson was quick to move in for the kill. Trapped, unnerved, Wilde became inarticulate.

Michael Emerson, slim and sensitive, bore no physical resemblance to Wilde whatsoever. The characterisation was all in the language, attitude, vocal mannerisms and affectation. Emerson's Wilde was what Queensberry said Wilde was: a poseur, and smug with it.

> This is a dazzling and thought-provoking piece, with a wit and ingenuity that are specifically of the theater, which is where poor Wilde shone and ought to have stayed.
>
> David Lyons *Wall Street Journal*

Mr Emerson's performance also does what productions of Wilde's plays do all too seldom. It gets under the skin of the wit; shows us the man in his emotional vulnerability, as well as his aphoristic glory.

Margo Jefferson *New York Times*

1997 *The Secret Fall of Constance Wilde*
A play by Thomas Kilroy.

Premiere: Abbey Theatre, Dublin.

Director	Patrick Mason
Designer	Joe Vanek
CONSTANCE	Jane Brennan
OSCAR WILDE	Robert O'Mahoney
ALFRED DOUGLAS	Andrew Scott
ATTENDANTS	Jonathan Shankey
	Muirne Bloomer
	Eric Lacey
	Jack Walsh
	Ciara O'Callaghan
	Kevin Murphy

It makes me feel sometimes as if you yourself had been merely a puppet worked by some secret and unseen hand to bring events to a terrible issue. But puppets themselves have passions. They will bring a new plot into what they are presenting, and twist the ordered issue of vicissitude to suit some whim or appetite of their own.

Oscar Wilde *De Profundis*

Constance married Oscar in 1884. They had two sons, Cyril and Vyvyan. When the bailiffs moved into their home two days before the second trial opened, Constance fled to the Continent taking the children with her, and returned only to break the news to him of his mother's death. They were not reconciled.

'Some dramas rise to the heights of the Aristotelian, others descend to the depths of realism,' said Wilde; 'mine lies somewhere in between'.

Thomas Kilroy's haunting and absorbing play was a factual/ fictional examination of the relationship between Constance, Oscar and Bosie. The title was a pun, referring both to a real fall she had had down the stairs in 1895 which hastened her death at the early age of forty in 1898, and to the fall of self-destruction.

Neither Constance nor Oscar was presented realistically. Constance was portrayed as a victim of parental abuse. Bosie was his familiar self: petulant, manipulative, selfish, coquettish and sadistic.

Patrick Mason's abstract, stylised production, designed by Joe Vanek, was visually striking. Oscar's children were played by puppets; the puppeteers were dressed in black and (in the Banraku manner) remained on stage.

The play was praised for its intellectual and emotional depth.

> Jane Brennan memorably presents an intellectually adept yet vulnerable Constance of extraordinary mental fortitude and sympathy. Her configuration of a stoical, neglected woman with a latent, untapped desire is delivered with a meticulous balance of that mixture of austerity, motherliness and tolerance which was the lot of the Victorian wife . . . Ultimately, though, the lack of risk-taking in Kilroy's text gives us cardboard cut-out and clichéd figures. This is still theatre of a very high quality but adherence to the parameters of ordinary characterisation makes *The Secret Fall of Constance Wilde* beautiful to look at but hollow on the inside.
>
> *Examiner*

1997 British television: *Omnibus*

Script	Michael Bracewell
Director	Hugh Thompson
PRESENTER	Michael Bracewell
CONTRIBUTORS	Neil Tennant
	Tom Stoppard
	Stephen Fry
	Philip Hoare
	Ulick O'Connor

Michael Bracewell, in his documentary in the *Omnibus* series to mark the one hundredth anniversary of Wilde's release from prison, looked at his life and legacy.

The programme opened with three quotes from Wilde. The first was delivered by Stephen Fry: 'All art is quite useless.' The second by Tom Stoppard: 'It is through disobedience that progress has been made, through disobedience and rebellion.' The third by Neil Tennant: 'If one tells the truth one is sure sooner or later to be found out.'

Other familiar quotes were delivered, somewhat self-consciously, by a barman, a drunk, undergraduates, prison inmates, and a down-and-out. There were brief extracts from the 1988 BBC television production of *The Importance of Being Earnest* and Albert Lewin's 1945 film of *The Picture of Dorian Gray*.

Bracewell drove round the West End and Soho. He visited Reading Goal. He descended the steps of one of London's deepest Underground stations. The latter locale was used absurdly to make the observation that 'Perhaps one of the reasons that Oscar has endured is that he is the Virgil to guide us down to our personal infernos. He showed by example the universality of temptation.'

Bracewell wondered if people were trying to make Oscar too respectable. He saw Oscar as the century's first pop celebrity/prophet and related him to the pop stars of the 1950s and 1960s. 'Oscar was an aesthete with attitude,' he said, who 'would treat London as an art gallery with himself as the principle exhibit.'

Stoppard made two points: firstly, that Wilde 'had perfect pitch, perfect touch, a musician's sense of a sentence,' and, secondly, that it did Wilde a gross disservice to treat him as a gay hero.

The programme ended with Bracewell in Paris, sitting on the bed in which Oscar had died, and quoting from *De Profundis*: 'I treated art as the supreme reality and life as a mere mode of fiction. I awoke the imagination of my century so that it created myth and legend around me.'

1997 *The Invention of Love*
A play by Tom Stoppard.

Premiere: Royal National Theatre, London.

A E Housman, author of *A Shropshire Lad*, had three passions in his life: Moses Jackson (an Oxford undergraduate), poetry, and classical scholarship. 'I would have died for you,' he said of Jackson, 'but I never had the luck.'

Towards the end of the play there was an imagined meeting

between Housman (John Wood) and Oscar Wilde (Michael Fitzgerald). They had never met in real life.

Stoppard's text, a mixture of what Wilde actually said and pastiche Wilde, captured his conversational style brilliantly, and for one brief scene Oscar took over the play.

Wilde argued that 'The betrayal of one's friends is a bagatelle in the stakes of love. But the betrayal of oneself is a lifelong regret . . . Better a fallen rocket than never a burst of light . . . I made my life into my art and it was an unqualified success . . . I had genius, brilliance, daring'.

The contrast between the two men was emphasised. On the one hand, there was Wilde, the extrovert, who knew everybody and had lots of friends. On the other, there was Housman, the introvert, who knew nobody and had only colleagues. Wilde ended up with two years' hard labour. Housman ended up with half a life.

1997 British film: *Wilde*

Director	Brian Gilbert
Screenplay	Julian Mitchell
OSCAR WILDE	Stephen Fry
LORD ALFRED DOUGLAS	Jude Law
LADY 'SPERANZA' WILDE	Vanessa Redgrave
CONSTANCE WILDE	Jennifer Ehle
LADY QUEENSBERRY	Gemma Jones
LADY MOUNT-TEMPLE	Judy Parfitt
ROBERT ROSS	Michael Sheen
ADA LEVERSON	Zoë Wanamaker
THE MARQUIS OF QUEENSBERRY	Tom Wilkinson
JOHN GRAY	Ioan Gruffudd
LIONEL JOHNSON	Matthew Mills
ERNEST DOWSON	Jason Morell
CHARLES GILL	Peter Barkworth
C O HUMPHREYS	Robert Lang
JUDGE	Philip Locke
EDWARD CARSON	David Westhead
CYRIL WILDE	Jack Knight
CYRIL WILDE, AGE 4	Jackson Leach
VYVYAN WILDE	Laurence Owen
ALFRED WOOD	Benedict Sandiford

CHARLES PARKER	Mark Letheren
ALFRED TAYLOR	Michael Fitzgerald
RENT BOY	Orlando Bloom
MINE OWNER	Bob Sessions
FIRST MINER	Joseph May
GEORGE ALEXANDER	Robin Kermode
HOTEL MANAGER	James Vaughan
WARDER	John Bleasdale
DETECTIVE	Peter Forbes

The film opened in a totally unexpected and witty manner, and possibly might have, just momentarily, worried cinemagoers that they were in the wrong cinema and about to watch a Western. Wilde was seen on a lecture tour in Colorado visiting a mine (a symbolic descent into hell?) to address the beautiful, semi-naked miners on art.

One of the dangers of writing about Wilde is that Oscar is liable to spend most of his time spouting familiar epigrams. Julian Mitchell's screenplay went to the other extreme and there was only the occasional evidence of his wit. ('Stay and look after nanny,' he said to his children at the seaside.)

Mitchell paid more attention to Wilde in his role as a loving and caring father than most screenwriters had in the past, but he still spent a disproportionate amount of time on Wilde, the gay icon in bed with young men. Brian Gilbert's production was notable for its sexual explicitness, though there was no full-frontal nudity. The actors took care to cover themselves discreetly with sheets and clothing. The scene with Wilde watching Bosie buggering a rent boy was gratuitous and without foundation.

Wilde handled his blackmailers with style. When they told him they had been offered £60 for one of his love letters he advised them to accept: 'I've never received so large a sum for a prose poem of that length in all my life. Tell your friend I am delighted someone in England values my work so highly'.

The film concentrated on the love affair with Lord Alfred Douglas. Strictly speaking, *Wilde* should have been called *Oscar and Bosie*. The story was inevitably compressed. The trials were dealt with in the most perfunctory manner.

Inexplicably, unforgivably, the fatal moment, which decided Wilde's fate – Edward Carson asking him if he had ever kissed a young man – was left out completely. Why?

Stephen Fry had a physical similarity to Wilde but not the

emotional range as an actor to manage the hubris at the end. He toned Wilde down. There was no flamboyance, no energy, no sparkle. He was gentle, shy and softly spoken, a sad, somewhat detached Oscar, who identified with *The Selfish Giant*. The most striking visual image was of him in the Inns of Court when, symbolically, he walked right through the legal fraternity.

Jude Law (a splendid performance) had Lord Alfred Douglas's beauty, breeding, youth, arrogance, cruelty, and danger. When it came to blazing rows, Bosie was very much his father's son. There was a superb loss of temper when Wilde was in bed with flu and Bosie accused him of being mean, penny-pinching and middle-class. ' When you are not at your best, you're no use!' he screamed.

Tom Wilkinson's Queensberry, a whiskered, vindictive, infamous brute, was momentarily charmed by Wilde's flattering manners. Vanessa Redgrave, as Oscar's eccentric mother (played as Old Mother Riley with umbrella) was observed persuading or rather blackmailing her son to stay in England and face his martyrdom: 'If you go, I will never speak to you again'.

A bright-eyed Michael Sheen was well cast as Robert Ross, the young man who first seduced Oscar. ('There has to be a first time for everything, Oscar. Even for you'.) The screenplay rightly included that moving moment when Ross waited in the corridors of the Old Bailey after Wilde had been sentenced to two years' hard labour so that he could raise his hat to him in loyalty.

There was no distressing death scene. Instead the film ended on an upbeat note with Wilde and Bosie reunited abroad after Wilde's release from prison. A written coda did inform cinemagoers that the affair had not lasted.

> For all its sexual frankness, *Wilde* is a discreet work that amuses and moves us, but never shocks or disturbs.
>
> Philip French *Observer*

1998 *The Judas Kiss*
A play by David Hare.

Premiere: Playhouse, London.
Transferred: Broadhurst Theater, New York.

Director	Richard Eyre
PHOEBE CANE	Stina Nielsen

ARTHUR WELLESLEY	Alex Walkinshaw
SANDY MOFFATT	Richard Clarke
ROBERT ROSS	Peter Capaldi
LORD ALFRED DOUGLAS	Tom Hollander
OSCAR WILDE	Liam Neeson
GALILEO MASCONI	Daniel Serafini-Sauli

> He was an unfinished sketch of a great man and showed great courage and manhood at the collapse of his fortunes. I have never doubted even for an instant that he made the right decision and that he owed to that decision half of his renown.
>
> W B Yeats *Autobiography* (New York, 1965)

The Judas Kiss opened in an elegantly draped bedroom. Two people were having sex. It was not, as the audience might have expected, Oscar and Bosie. Nor was it Oscar and a rent boy; and neither was it Bosie and a rent boy. It was a waiter and a maid. They were interrupted by the butler who informed the waiter he would have to reprimand him in person after work. The form the reprimand would take was not too difficult to guess.

David Hare set the play at two key moments in Wilde's life. The first act took place in the Cadogan Hotel. Wilde's libel action against the Marquis of Queensberry had just collapsed and if he didn't catch the last train to Paris he would be arrested on a charge of gross indecency. Robert Ross begged him to flee. (Everybody else was leaving. It was rumoured that six hundred men caught the train that night.) Bosie wanted him to stay and fight it out.

The second act opened with more gratuitous nudity, which was severely cut when the production went to New York. The scene was set in exile and poverty in Naples following Wilde's release from prison. Bosie continued to live at Oscar's expense. Robbie tried to persuade Oscar to give Bosie up, pointing out that if he did not, he would lose Constance's allowance. But Oscar couldn't give up Bosie. The irony was that Bosie had already decided to give him up.

Why did Wilde stay in England to stand trial? Was it courageous or foolhardy? Hare suggested that Wilde didn't flee because he had no choice but to act out his tragedy. His reputation was destroyed and the action foredoomed. The first act worked precisely, as in Greek tragedy, because the audience knew the outcome.

Had Wilde fled, the story would have been incomplete. There

would have been no further trials, no sentence, no two years' hard labour, no exile, no lasting notoriety, certainly no bandwagon one hundred years later, and, presumably, no play by David Hare. Wilde had predicted his future when he came down from Oxford: 'I'll be a poet, a writer, a dramatist. Somehow or other I'll be famous, and if not famous, I'll be notorious.'

Wilde didn't want to give the English the pleasure of knowing they had driven him away. Had he run away it would have been tantamount to admitting he was guilty. Similarly, in exile, he didn't alter his lifestyle for to have done so would have been to admit that he thought homosexuality was wrong. But he had no desire to speak out and become a gay icon defending his conduct. 'I have nothing to confess,' he said. He did not seek society's approval.

'The truth of a person is only visible through love. Love is not an illusion,' said Wilde, 'life is.' His actions were governed by his infatuation for Bosie, which he described as 'the purest I have known in my life'.

The Judas of the title is Bosie. Hare has said that the true subject of his play is not Wilde but love, not Bosie but betrayal. Wilde said that it would have been artistically truer if Christ had been betrayed by the disciple John because John had loved him most.

Wilde was a big man. Liam Neeson, bear- like in a fur-lined coat, dwarfed everybody, even when he was slumped in a chair. Tom Hollander, as Bosie, was a bit on the small size to be acting opposite such a towering and powerful presence, and had to stand on tip-toe to reach his lips.

Hollander acted Bosie for a shallow, feckless, selfish, petulant and repellent little boy, who saw himself as much a victim as Oscar and even claimed his suffering had been the greater. 'I am not an invert,' he whined. 'I am not disposed, as you are, to love my own sex. For me, as you know, it has been only a phase.' He said this, having just spent his night being buggered by an Italian fisherman. Bosie emerged as a major comic character.

Hare was unfair on Robbie, friend of friends, the voice of reason, *l'honnête homme*, always doing his best to help, acting as go-between between Oscar and Constance, constantly seeking reconciliation. 'Anybody can play the third party,' moaned Bosie. 'It requires no talent.' Bosie felt like an actor himself but one who has been cast in the wrong part.

The major surprise about the script was that it was epigram-free. The wit was largely in Bosie's character and Wilde's irony at Bosie's expense, though there was a moment of self-mockery when he likened his own appearance to a senior pederastic Anglican bishop who had been locked all night in a distillery.

The Judas Kiss ended with an extended quote from *De Profundis*.

> He [Liam Neeson] eschews all camp and he combines authority with relaxation. He has warmth and charm. But in both voice and gesture he has less theatricality than the lines he speaks; and he seems altogether more ordinary than the tragic Romantic and witty poseur Wilde elected to be.
>
> Alistair Macaulay *Financial Times*

> Both Hare's writing and Neeson's performance deny the dangerous moral and aesthetic ambiguity that was so essential to Wilde's writing and personality. Neeson's voice has a limited range; it lacks those insinuating colours that caress and unsettle people. His presence suggests a heterosexuality so relaxed as to be unaware of itself. He is not the icon of dangerous, ambiguous glamour that Wilde was to his contemporaries; he is a lion king with hyenas snapping at his heels.
>
> John Peter *Sunday Times*

> Liam Neeson gives a good, actorly performance in a role that never quite fits. He bites his lines effectively, if to no great point. He is a big, forbidding storm cloud of a presence, but the play never comes alive with the anticipated thunder and lightning.
>
> Vincent Canby *New York Times*

1998 *Gross Indecency – The Three Trials of Oscar Wilde*
A play written and directed by Moisés Kaufman.

Revival: Theatre Royal, Plymouth.

OSCAR WILDE	Corin Redgrave
CARSON, NARRATOR 5	William Hoyland
CLARKE, OTHERS, NARRATOR 6	Brian Protheroe
QUEENSBERRY, GILL, LOCKWOOD NARRATOR 8	James Aubrey
LORD ALFRED DOUGLAS, NARRATOR	Nick Waring

NARRATOR 1, WOOD, SHAW, OTHERS	Barney Craig
NARRATOR 3, PARKER, HARRIS, OTHERS	Mason Phillips
NARRATOR 2, MAVOR, MARVIN, TAYLOR, OTHERS	Christopher Staines
NARRATOR 4, ATKINS, WRIGHT, OTHERS	Andrew Bone

Redgrave's performance is startling and beautifully understated. He is ably supported by the eight other actors, who also deliver faultless characterisations. Of these, mention must be made of James Aubrey's frighteningly horrendous portrayal of the Marquess of Queensberry and later, in a change of character, the QC prosecuting Wilde. Nick Waring brings to life Wilde's boyfriend, Lord Alfred Douglas.

Keith Saunders *Evening Herald*

1999 *Gross Indecency – The Three Trials of Oscar Wilde*
A play written and directed by Moisés Kaufman.

Revival: Gielgud Theatre, London.

OSCAR WILDE	Michael Pennington
CARSON, NARRATOR 5	William Hoyland
CLARKE, OTHERS, NARRATOR 6	Clive Francis
QUEENSBERRY, GILL, LOCKWOOD NARRATOR 8	James Aubrey
LORD ALFRED DOUGLAS, NARRATOR	Nick Waring
NARRATOR 1, WOOD, SHAW, OTHERS	Barney Craig
NARRATOR 3, PARKER, HARRIS, OTHERS	Mason Phillips
NARRATOR 2, MAVOR, MARVIN, TAYLOR, OTHERS	Christopher Staines
NARRATOR 4, ATKINS, WRIGHT, OTHERS	Stephan Noonan

I never write plays for anyone. I write plays to amuse myself. Later, if anyone wants to act in them, I sometimes allow them to do so.

Oscar Wilde

PLAYS

Oscar Wilde in Bournemouth in about 1887.
Photograph: Debenham and Gould.

Theatrical Premieres: 1883–1896

1883

Vera by Oscar Wilde. New York
Ghosts by Henrik Ibsen. Helsinborg

1884

Prince Ida by Gilbert and Sullivan. London

1885

The Wild Duck by Henrik Ibsen. Christiania (Oslo)
The Magistrate by Arthur Wing Pinero. London
The Mikado by Gilbert and Sullivan. London

1886

The Schoolmistress by Arthur Wing Pinero. London

1887

Rosmersholm by Henrik Ibsen. Bergen
The Father by August Strindberg. Copenhagen
Dandy Dick by Arthur Wing Pinero. London
La Tosca by Victorien Sardou. Paris
Otello by Giuseppe Verdi. Milan

1888

The Yeomen of the Guard by Gilbert and Sullivan. London

1889

Miss Julie by August Strindberg. Copenhagen
The Gondoliers by Gilbert and Sullivan. London

1890

The Queen of Spades by Pyotr Tchaikovsky. St Petersburg
Prince Igor by Alexander Borodin. St Petersburg
Cavalleria Rusticana by Pietro Mascagni. Rome

1891

Hedda Gabler by Henrik Ibsen. Munich

1892

Lady Windermere's Fan by Oscar Wilde. London

Monsieur Chasse by Georges Feydeau. Paris
Widowers' Houses by George Bernard Shaw. London
Charley's Aunt by Brandon Thomas. London
Pagliacci by Ruggiero Leoncavallo. Milan
The Nutcracker. Choreography by Lev Ivanov, music by Pyotr Tchaikovsky. St Petersburg

1893

A Woman of No Importance by Oscar Wilde. London
The Second Mrs Tanqueray by Arthur Wing Pinero. London
The Master Builder by Henrik Ibsen. Berlin
The Anatol Cycle by Arthur Schnitzler begins. Vienna
Pelléas et Mélisande by Maurice Maeterlinck. Paris
Madame Sans Gêne by Victorien Sardou. Paris
Hansel und Gretel by Engelbert Humperdinck. Weimar
Falstaff by Giuseppe Verdi. Milan
Manon Lescaut by Giacomo Puccini. Turin
The Weavers by Gerhart Hauptmann. Berlin

1894

Un Fil à la Patte by Georges Feydeau. Paris
The Professor's Love Story by James Barrie. London
Arms and the Man by George Bernard Shaw. London
Thaïs by Jules Massenet. Paris

1895

An Ideal Husband by Oscar Wilde. London
The Importance of Being Earnest by Oscar Wilde. London
Candida by George Bernard Shaw. South Shields
Liebelei by Arthur Schnitzler. Vienna
Swan Lake. Choreography by Marius Petipa and Lev Ivanov, music by Pyotr Tchaikovsky. St Petersburg
The first film show. Paris

1896

Salomé by Oscar Wilde. Paris
The Seagull by Anton Chekhov. St Petersburg
Le Dindon by Georges Feydeau. Paris
Hôtel du Libre Échange by Georges Feydeau. Paris
Ubu Roi by Alfred Jarry. Paris
La Bohème by Giacomo Puccini. Turin

Vera or The Nihilists (1883)

A Drama in a Prologue and Four Acts

Characters in the prologue:
PETER SABOUROFF, an Innkeeper
VERA SABOUROFF, his Daughter
MICHAEL, a Peasant
DMITRI SABOUROFF
NICOLAS, a child
COLONEL KOTEMKIN

Characters in the play:
IVAN THE CZAR
PRINCE PAUL MARALOFFSKI, Prime Minister of Russia
PRINCE PETROVITCH
COUNT ROUVALOFF
MARQUIS DE POIVRARD
BARON RAFF
GENERAL KOTEMKIN
A PAGE
COLONEL OF THE GUARD

Nihilists:
PETER TCHERNAVITCH, President of the Nihilists
MICHAEL
ALEXIS IVANACIEVITCH, known as a Student of Medicine
PROFESSOR MARFA
VERA SABOUROFF
SOLDIERS, CONSPIRATORS, etc.

The scenes of the play:
Prologue A Russian Inn.
Act I 99 Tchernavaya, Moscow. A large garret.
Act II Council Chamber in the Emperor's Palace.
Act III As in Act I.
Act IV Antechamber of the Czar's private room.

The Plot

PROLOGUE Peter Sabouroff has heard nothing from his son, Dmitri, for six months. Dmitri arrives shortly afterwards in chains on his way to Siberia, having been arrested for being a Nihilist. He manages to give his sister, Vera, a secret address in Moscow.

ACT I In Moscow the conspirators recite their oath while waiting for Vera to return from the Grand Duke's ball. She enters in full ball dress to announce that martial law is going to be proclaimed all over Russia. The conspirators, in danger of being arrested, are saved by one of their number, a medical student, Alexis, who reveals himself to be the Czarevitch and passes them off as strolling players.

ACT II The paranoid Czar Ivan is determined to crush the Nihilists. His son reveals he is a Nihilist and pleads for the people. He is arrested. The Czar goes out on the balcony and is shot.

ACT III Prince Paul, banished by Alexis from the court, joins the Nihilists. The Nihilist are convinced that Alexis, the new Czar, is a traitor and that he must be killed. They draw lots and Vera (who is in love with Alexis) draws the lot.

ACT IV Alexis is calling for an amnesty for all political prisoners, implementing new tax reforms, and banishing his father's former ministers and confiscating their estates. He takes a nap and wakes to find Vera about to stab him. He offers her marriage and to be Empress of Russia. 'I am a Nihilist!' she cries. 'I cannot wear a crown.' There is only one thing to do. Vera stabs herself so that he may live and save Russia.

The Characters

VERA SABOUROFF declares that she 'would fan the flames of this revolution into such a blaze that the eyes of all kings in Europe shall be blinded.' Twenty thousand roubles are on her head. Vera draws the lot to kill Czar Alexis.

PRINCE PAUL MARALOFFSKI, the Prime Minister, is responsible for having turned the Czar into a tyrant, and is the most hated man in Russia. He is the first of Wilde's stage dandies, a witty villain, who, according to the Czar, 'would stab his best friend for the sake of writing an epigram on his tombstone':

> It is so exhausting not to talk.
>
> Experience, the name men give to their mistakes.
>
> Culture depends on cookery. For myself, the only immortality I desire is to invent a new sauce.
>
> Life is much too important a thing ever to talk seriously about.

When he is no longer Prime Minister (having been sacked by the new Czar), he turns Nihilist, there being (he says) no alternative; though he 'would much sooner talk scandal in a drawing-room than treason in a cellar.'

IVAN THE CZAR is convinced he is surrounded by murderers and spies. His paranoia is both comic and frightening. 'There shall be a spy in every man's house,' he decrees, 'a traitor on every hearth, a hangman in every village, a gibbet in every square. Plague, leprosy, or fever shall be less deadly than my wrath; I will make every frontier a graveyard, every province a lazar-house, and cure the sick by the sword.'

ALEXIS IVANACIEVITCH, the Czar's son, is a naive young man with a pretty face, curled hair and soft white hands. He loves the people and is intent on reform. Prince Paul takes a cynical view of him: 'He pretends to be devoted to the people, and lives in a palace; preaches socialism, and draws a salary that would support a province.'

THE CONSPIRATORS have a blood-curdling oath: 'To strangle whatever nature is in us; neither to love nor to be loved, neither to pity nor to be pitied, nor to be given in marriage, till the end is come; to stab secretly by night; to drop poison in the glass; to set father against son, husband against wife; without fear, without hope, without future, to suffer, to annihilate, to revenge.'

Vera, Oscar Wilde's first play, was originally printed at his own expense in 1880 and copies were sent to a number of actresses, including Ellen Terry and Geneviève Ward.

Mrs Bernard Beere was to have acted the title role at the Adelphi Theatre on 17 December 1881. The production was withdrawn at the last moment. Nobody is quite certain why. Wilde blamed the cast. But it is generally thought that the play was a bit too topical for comfort and that pressure had been brought on the management. Czar Alexander II had been assassinated earlier in the year.

Vera was produced two years later in New York by the American actress Mary Prescott. Presumably, the assassination of President Garfield six months previously no longer worried the American censor.

Prescott (who said she had been charmed by the play's mournfulness) asked for rewrites. 'Who am I to tamper with a masterpiece?' replied Wilde, and refused to cut the comedy. 'Never be afraid that by raising a laugh you destroy tragedy,' he told her. 'On the contrary, you intensify it.'

Concerned that costumes and scenery might not be up to standard, he designed the scenery and costumes himself, insisting they should be not merely true, but that they should be beautiful as well. He wanted the council chamber to be in yellow satin and Vera to wear a flaming vermilion gown.

The original letter Wilde had written to Prescott on 12 August 1883 was reprinted in the *New York Herald* just before the play opened:

> I have tried to express within the limits of art that Titan cry of the people for liberty, which in the Europe of our day is threatening thrones, and making governments unstable from Spain to Russia, and from north to southern seas. But the play is not of politics but of passion. It deals with no theories of government but with men and women simply.

In an interview with the *World*, Wilde explained that he intended 'to show how far the aspirations of an uncultured people can be made a subject for art. Life under good government is rarely dramatic. Life under a bad government is always so.'

1883 20 August Premiere: Union Square Theatre, New York.

THE CZAR	G C Boniface
PRIME MINISTER	Edward Lamb
BARON RAFF	James Wright
PRINCE PETROVITCH	William Wilson
COUNT ROUVALOFF	J F De Gez
MARQUIS DE POIVRARD	Charles Day
GENERAL KOTEMKIN	George S Paxton
COLONEL OF THE GUARD	Thomas Branick
A PAGE	Lewis Mann
PETER SABOUROFF	Julius Kahn
DMITRI SABOUROFF	Fred Lotto
VERA SABOUROFF	Marie Prescott
MICHAEL	B W Turner
ALEXIS IVANACIEVITCH	Lewis Morrison
NICOLAS	Little Frankie Furlong
PRESIDENT OF THE NIHILISTS	J R Furlong
PROFESSOR MARFA	Edward Harding

The evening was a fiasco. The gallery called for Wilde derisively at the end of each act. Vera's flaming vermilion gown was received with catcalls. Marie Prescott was described by the *Boston Pilot* as 'an inferior actress who can only scold on the stage and off it.' Most of the critics dismissed the play as an immature, worthless and amateur melodrama. Only the *New York Sun* thought it a masterpiece.

> The piece poorly rewarded the public curiosity, however, by a display of several queer scenes, picturesque at points, but mostly ugly, and, by the exposition of a fanciful foolish, highly peppered story of love, intrigue and politics, invested with the Russian accessories of fur and dark lanterns, and overlaid with bantam gabble about freedom and the people.
>
> *New York Daily Tribune*

> The Nihilism which is presented in *Vera* is a stupid and tiresome element of the work. These rapid fellows who talk like lunatics, swear the most preposterous oaths, and act like children give no dramatic force to the play . . . The monotony of the second and fourth act is simply depressing . . . His play is unreal, long-winded and wearisome. It comes as near failure as an ingenious

> and able writer can bring it. We do not think such a play can be popular . . . [*Vera*] is oppressively pedantic and Miss Prescott acted it with a sort of pulpit eloquence. She preached it and that is about all one need say of her performance. She is a conscientious and ambitious actress, who is unable it seems to discriminate between the expression of feeling and declamatory noise.
>
> *New York Times*

> It is long drawn, dramatic rot, a series of disconnected essays and sickening rant, with a coarse and common kind of cleverness.
>
> *New York Herald*

> There was great surprise in store for the people who gathered at the Union Square Theatre on Monday night. They had come to laugh. They remained to applaud. If Oscar Wilde desired any vindication for the abuse, ridicule, and contempt with which he was met on his first visit to this country, it was handsomely secured to him by the triumph of his play.
>
> *New York Mirror*

Vera ran but a week. *Punch* said the play was 'vera bad'. Prescott invited Wilde to play Prince Paul. He declined and returned to England. Prescott went ahead and revived the production in Detroit.

Vera has not been seen since, except for a production by the Jean Cocteau Repertory Company at the Bouverie Lane Theatre, New York, an Off-Off-Broadway theatre, in 1976. It was revived the following year.

The Duchess of Padua (1891)

Characters:
SIMONE GESSO, Duke of Padua
BEATRICE, his Wife
ANDREAS POLLAJUOLO, Cardinal of Padua
MAFFIO PETRUCCI, JEPPO VITELLOZZO, TADDEO BARDI — Gentlemen of the Duke's Household
GUIDO FERRANTI, a Young Man
ASCANIO CRISTOFANO, his Friend
COUNT MORANZONE, an Old Man
BERNARDO CAVALCANTI, Lord Justice of Padua
HUGO, the Headsman
LUCY, a Tire Woman
SERVANTS, CITIZENS, SOLDIERS, MONKS, FALCONERS with their hawks and dogs, etc.

The scenes of the play:
Act I The Market Place of Padua at noon.
Act II A state room in the Ducal Palace.
Act III A large corridor in the Ducal Palace.
Act IV The Court of Justice.
Act V A dungeon in the public prison of Padua.

The action takes place in the latter half of the sixteenth century.

The Plot

ACT I Guido Ferranti arrives in Padua to learn the secret of his birth. Count Moranzone tells him that his father was Duke Lorenzo and that he was murdered by the present Duke of Padua. Moranzone insists Guido give up his friends and revenge his father's death.

ACT II The Duke is a tyrant, indifferent to the suffering of the poor. Learning that the water supply has broken down, he replies in the manner of Marie Antoinette, 'They should drink wine.' The Duchess, on the other hand, is very much a people's Duchess, loved by all. The Duchess and Guido fall in love.

ACT III Guido tells Moranzone that he won't kill the Duke but that he will leave a dagger and a letter on the Duke's pillow while he is asleep to prove he could have killed him if he had wanted. He is just about to do this when the Duchess enters and tells him she has murdered the Duke. 'I did it for you!' Guido instantly falls out of love. The Duchess accuses him of murdering her husband.

ACT IV During the trial, the Duchess tries to stop the truth coming out by denying Guido his right to speak in his defence. When the court finally allows him to speak, he says he is the murderer.

ACT V The Duchess determines to help Guido escape from prison with the aid of her cloak and vizard. He refuses her offer. They kiss. She takes poison 'and then suddenly she leaps up in the dreadful spasm of death, tears in agony at her dress, and finally, with face twisted and distorted with pain, falls back dead in a chair.' This is a hard act to follow and Guido merely seizes her dagger and stabs himself.

'I have no hesitation in saying that it is the masterpiece of all my literary work, the *chef d'oeuvre* of my youth,' Wilde wrote to Mary Anderson, the American actress, who was going to produce the play. She finally rejected it, saying that she didn' t think in its present form it would appeal to the public any more than *Venice Preserv'd* and *Lucretia Borgia* would.

The *Duchess of Padua*, written in blank verse, reads like a pastiche of Shakespeare, Tourneur and Webster, and part of the enjoyment is recognising the quotations and sources: a trial scene out of *The Merchant of Venice*, a death scene out of *Romeo and Juliet*, the odd phrases from *Richard III*, *Hamlet* and *Macbeth*. It seems as if at any moment Beatrice will say, 'I am the Duchess of Padua still.' There are some fine speeches, notably Guido's definition of love and Beatrice's lines beginning, 'I got no mercy and I give it not,' but, on the whole, the best thing about the play is probably the scenery.

The Duchess of Padua was described as a New Italian Love Tragedy and produced anonymously under the title of *Guido Ferranti*. It was produced anonymously (Wilde said) in order that it could be judged entirely on its own merits. But everybody – certainly the critics – knew it was by him.

The play ran for only twenty-one performances. It was 'a gloomy tragedy,' George C D Odell wrote in *Annals of the New York Stage*, 'a little too morbid for playgoers in 1891.' Years later, when he was in exile in France, Wilde didn't think it was worth publishing. 'It is not worthy of me,' he said.

1891 26 January Premiere: Broadway Theatre, New York.

Director	Lawrence Birkett
SIMONE	Frederic Vroom
BEATRICE	Minna K Gale
MAFFIO PETRUCCI	Rankin Duvall
JEPPO VITELLOZZO	George Hazelton
GUIDO	Lawrence Barrett
ASCANIO CRISTOFANO	Lawrence Hanley
COUNT MORANZONE	John Lane
BERNARDO CAVALCANTI	Beaumont Smith
GREGORY	F Lodge
HUGO	Charles Wilson
CAPTAIN OF GUARD	Albert Bruning
SOLDIERS	W R S Morris
	Herbert Pattee
	G McCulla

The new play is deftly constructed in five short acts, and is written in a strain of blank verse that is always melodious, often eloquent, and sometimes freighted with fanciful figures of rare beauty. It is less a tragedy, however, than a melodrama – by which is meant a drama of situation. To their ingredient everything is moulded and sacrificed. The inevitable consequence ensues. The radical defect of the work is insincerity. No one is natural.

New York Daily Tribune

1891 Harlem Opera House, New York. Lawrence Birkett's production was revived under the title *The Duchess of Padua*.

1904 Hamburg. German premiere in a translation by Max Meyerfeld.

1906 Berlin. The actor playing the Cardinal went mad.

1907 St James's Theatre, London. One performance for copyright purposes.

1914 *Guido Ferranti*
An opera by Jane van Etten Andrews.

Premiere: Chicago.

BEATRICE	Hazel Eden
GUIDO	Worthe Faulkner

Lady Windermere's Fan (1892)

A New and Original Play in four Acts

'To the dear memory of Robert Earl of Lytton
in affection and admiration'

LORD WINDERMERE
LORD DARLINGTON
LORD AUGUSTUS LORTON
MR DUMBY
MR CECIL GRAHAM
MR HOPPER
PARKER, A BUTLER
LADY WINDERMERE
THE DUCHESS OF BERWICK
LADY AGATHA CARLISLE
LADY PLYMDALE
LADY STUTFIELD
LADY JEDBURGH
MRS COWPER-COWPER
MRS ERLYNNE
ROSALIE, A MAID

The scenes of the play:

Act I Morning-room in Lord Windermere's house in Carlton House Terrace.
Act II Drawing-room in Lord Windermere's house.
Act III Lord Darlington's rooms.
Act IV Same as in Act I.

Time: The Present *Place:* London

The action takes place within twenty-four hours, beginning on a Tuesday afternoon at five o'clock, and ending the next day at 1.30 p.m.

The Plot

ACT I Lady Windermere is celebrating her twenty-first birthday. Lord Darlington hints that her husband is having an affair and that infidelity should be paid back in kind. When the Duchess of Berwick confirms what Darlington has said to be true, Lady Windermere searches her husband's bureau for proof and finds cheque counterfoils for large sums of money made out to a Mrs Erlynne. She confronts her husband, who, to her amazement, insists she invite Mrs Erlynne to the ball that night. She refuses, saying that if Mrs Erlynne comes she will strike her across the face with her fan. Windermere dares not tell his wife who the woman is, feeling the shame would kill her – the woman is, in fact, her mother whom she believed died when she was a child.

ACT II Mrs Erlynne comes to the ball but Lady Windermere does not strike her. Darlington seizes the moment to declare his love for Lady Windermere and begs her to come away with him. She says she hasn't the courage but when she overhears Mrs Erlynne asking her husband for a regular allowance, she decides to accept Darlington's invitation. She leaves her husband a letter, which Mrs Erlynne intercepts and opens, to discover that her daughter is about to make the same mistake she made twenty years ago. She determines to stop her before Windermere finds out.

ACT III While Lady Windermere is sitting in Darlington's rooms, waiting for his return, Mrs Erlynne arrives and pleads with her to return to her husband. Presuming Mrs Erlynne wants her to accept a *ménage à trois*, she is outraged and refuses. She is finally persuaded to return for the sake of her two-month-old baby. Just as they are about to leave, Darlington returns, accompanied by Windermere and three friends. The two women hide. Windermere discovers his wife's fan and insists he be allowed to search the rooms. Mrs Erlynne, sacrificing her reputation, enters, saying she took the fan by mistake. In the confusion Lady Windermere slips out unseen.

ACT IV Windermere expresses his contempt for Mrs Erlynne. His wife defends her. Mrs Erlynne arrives, saying she has come to return the fan. She asks her daughter for a photograph. While she is out of the room, Windermere lectures Mrs Erlynne on morality. When Lady Windermere returns, Mrs Erlynne persuades her not to tell her husband what had really happened the previous night, and departs for the Continent, never to return.

The Characters

LADY WINDERMERE, rigorously upright, wants to make an example of the notorious Mrs Erlynne, unaware that she is in fact her own mother. ('Good people do a great deal of harm in the world,' says Lord Darlington, 'they make badness of such extraordinary importance.') She has to learn that there are no hard-and-fast rules and that people cannot be divided into good and bad. Her mother gives her an excellent reason for returning to her husband: 'You haven't got the kind of brains that enables a woman to get back. You have neither the wit nor the courage. You couldn't stand dishonour.'

MRS ERLYNNE alienated herself from society by running away with her lover and abandoning her child. 'Repentance is quite out of date,' she says. 'And besides, if a woman really repents, she has to go to a bad dressmaker, otherwise no one believes her.' Her studied amorality hides her true feelings. But though she sacrifices herself for her daughter, she has no ambition to play the part of a mother: the role does not suit her. Lillie Langtry turned down the role, not wishing to play a woman who had a grown-up daughter.

LORD WINDERMERE is devoted to his wife and to spare her distress he allows himself to be blackmailed. He agrees to pay Mrs Erlynne an allowance on the condition that she does not inform his wife who she really is. When he finds Mrs Erlynne in Lord Darlington's rooms, he is convinced she is irretrievably bad and delivers a moral lecture, revealing himself to be a self-satisfied, charmless prig.

LORD DARLINGTON, an amoral dandy, seductive and unscrupulous, is a Restoration rake in Victorian dress. He pretends to be bad to hide his wickedness. ('Why, there are lots of people who say I have never really done anything wrong in the whole course of my life. Of course, they only say it behind my back.') Quick to take advantage of Lady Windermere's unhappiness and innocence, he offers her not friendship but 'passion, worship, love' and begs her to come away with him. Wilde complained to Maurice Barrymore (the American actor who played the role in New York in 1893) that Darlington was not a villain but a man who genuinely believes that Windermere is treating his wife badly. Wilde clearly identified with him:

> I can resist anything except temptation.
>
> I think life is far too important a thing ever to talk seriously about it.

It is absurd to divide people into good or bad. People are either charming or tedious.

We are all in the gutter but some of us are looking at the stars.

A cynic is a man who knows the price of everything and the value of nothing.

THE DUCHESS OF BERWICK, full of mindless chatter, is a deliberate mischief-maker. She married for love and was quickly disillusioned by her philandering husband. She advises Lady Windermere to do what she did: take her husband abroad. Her immediate concern is to marry off her daughter, Agatha, to a rich man. As she says, 'A mother who doesn't part with a daughter every season has no real affection.'

AUGUSTUS 'TUPPY' LORTON is the disreputable brother of the Duchess of Berwick: an obtuse, fat old fool, who is infatuated with Mrs Erlynne, who orders him around, as if they were already married.

LADY AGATHA is described by her mother, the Duchess of Berwick, as a chatterbox. The only thing she says all evening is 'Yes, mama,' thirteen times.

MR HOPPER, a rich young Australian courting Lady Agatha, is one of nature's gentlemen. 'The worst type of gentleman I know,' says Cecil Graham.

MR CECIL GRAHAM thinks like a Tory and talks like a radical. He has a fashionable, casual cynicism. 'My dear fellow, what on earth should we do going about with purity and innocence? A carefully thought-out button-hole is much more effective.' Conceited and excessively trivial, he lets his gossiping tongue run away with him: 'There is nothing like the devotion of a married woman. It's a thing no married man knows anything about.'

MR DUMBY is a camp young man, vacuous, languorous and probably bisexual. 'I am wildly, madly adored,' he boasts. 'It has been an immense nuisance.' He maintains a self-satisfied, catty-witty banter: 'There are only two tragedies. One is not getting what one wants; and the other is getting it. The last is much the worst, the last is the real tragedy.'

LADY PLYMDALE, Dumby's mistress, would like her husband to take an interest in Mrs Erlynne so she can get on with her own affairs without any distraction.

In February 1891 Wilde wrote a letter to George Alexander, actor-manager of the St James's Theatre, admitting that he couldn't get a grip on the play, and that he was going to put it in a bottom drawer and come back to it at a later date. By the autumn the play was finished and called *The Good Woman*. He later changed the title when his mother said it was mawkish and that nobody would care for a good woman. He sent it to the American dramatist and manager, Augustin Daly, hoping that the popular actress Ada Rehan would play Mrs Erlynne.

Alexander, in *Parts I Have Played* (Abbey Press, 1908), describes a meeting with Wilde:

> He sat and talked for a little while, and as he was going he said, 'What about the terms? I'm always in want of money, you know.' I replied that I would give him a thousand pounds for the play. 'That is a very, very large amount,' he said half humourously, half seriously: 'a thousand pounds. It seems almost too good to believe.' He paused for a moment, as if thinking, then he added. 'But knowing you as I do, I have come to the conclusion to take a percentage.' He did, and the play brought him fame and fortune.

Alexander wanted the audience to know at the end of the second act that Mrs Erlynne was Lady Windermere's mother. Wilde didn't want the truth to come out until the last act, arguing that the element of suspense would be lost and there would be no surprise in a mother sacrificing herself for her daughter since the audience would expect her to do so. He also argued that if the audience knew who Mrs Erlynne really was, it would ruin the last act and that his play would require different dialogue and completely different situations.

In his letters to Alexander, Wilde gave detailed instructions about the positioning of the sofa in the fourth act and also instructions about interpretation of lines, articulation, wigs, make-up, costume. He was insistent that Mrs Erlynne was an adventuress and not a cocotte.

1892 20 February Premiere: St James's Theatre, London.

Licensee and Manager	George Alexander
LORD WINDERMERE	George Alexander
LORD DARLINGTON	Nutcombe Gould
LORD AUGUSTUS	H H Vincent
MR DUMBY	A Vane-Tempest
CECIL GRAHAM	Ben Webster
MR HOPPER	Alfred Holles
PARKER	V Sansbury
LADY WINDERMERE	Lily Hanbury
THE DUCHESS OF BERWICK	Fanny Coleman
LADY AGATHA	Laura Graves
LADY PLYMDALE	Miss Granville
LADY STUTFIELD	Madge Girdlestone
LADY JEDBURGH	Miss B Page
MRS COWPER-COWPER	Miss A de Winton
MRS ERLYNNE	Marion Terry
ROSALIE	Winifred Dolan

Ben Webster, who was cast as Cecil Graham, wore a green carnation on stage. So did some members of the audience. People who moved in Parisian homosexual circles would have recognised the signal. (The following year, Robert Hichens would publish a novel called *The Green Carnation* in which he parodied Wilde's literary style and lifestyle.)

The first night was a great success and Wilde, cigarette in hand, took a curtain call:

> Ladies and Gentlemen: I have enjoyed this evening *immensely.* The actors have given us a *charming* rendering of a *delightful* play, and your appreciation has been *most* intelligent. I congratulate you on the *great* success of your performance, which persuades me that you think *almost* as highly of the play as I do myself.

The critics were not amused. Clement Scott in the *Illustrated London News* castigated him for his bad manners. The production ran for 197 performances.

> The supply of these caustic, biting, and epigrammatic utterances is, practically, inexhaustible. They are, if anything, in excess, but

welcome from their undoubted cleverness, and in the serious passages of the play the author shows he can substitute earnestness and feeling for this brilliancy. Whether his play is intended to be a faithful representation of aristocratic life, or is meant to ridicule it, must be left to the playgoer's own decision.

Morning Advertiser

Let justice be done to Mr Oscar Wilde. His play frequently reflects the ideas of others. Some of his scenes are by no means original. Here and there we have incidents which have done duty in comedies for a century or so, but for all that, the general verdict on *Lady Windermere's Fan* is that the play is very clever for an author who had so little experience in writing. For the stage it reveals a spontaneous gift for dramatic composition which may be tuned to good account, and the dialogue, if daring in the last degree, has so much brilliancy, wit and satire as to give great promise for the future when the author's paradoxical fancies are tuned down and he makes his characters speak like living men and women and not like puppets he has been praising recently.

Era

Mr Wilde has the gift of writing witty and memorable dialogue, full of paradoxical surprises, and pregnant with the wisdom of the boudoir and the cynicism of the club smoking room, while under all this there frequently lurk deeper truths of a wider range.

Sunday Times

The play is a bad one, but it will succeed. No faults of construction, no failure in interest, no feebleness in character drawing, no staleness in motive, will weigh in the scale against the insolence of its caricature. Society loves best those who chaff it most, and society will rush to see Lady Windermere, and will cringe to be tickled by her fan. It is the way of the world. When they are sitting in the theatre they will laugh because their enemies are being ridiculed, and when they come home they will ridicule the author. And that is exactly what pleases him most. His appearance addressing society with a deferential tone and a lighted cigarette in his hand was a triumph of a career of humourous audacity!

Daily Telegraph

> George Alexander played Lord Windermere with fine manly feeling and tenderness, and in a style most refined and artistic. There was but one chance of displaying power. That was in the challenge to Lord Darlington, when the husband discovers his wife's fan. This was admirably acted, and in the gentler scenes, Mr Alexander proved that few stage lovers can equal him in expressing chivalrous devotion.
>
> *Morning Post*

> It was a rash experiment to give such a part as that of Lady Windermere to so young an actress as Miss Lily Hanbury, and not successful, for, though she played relatively well, she failed in the two chief scenes to reach the passion of the part. Nor does Mr Nutcombe Gould prove wisely chosen for the part of Darlington: he lacked passion and persuasiveness.
>
> *Graphic*

> One longs for a refreshing breath of sincerity on this barren and dreary waste of epigram. The talk of the characters becomes, in truth, almost as harassing as their actions.
>
> *The Times*

> The part of Mrs Erlynne is superbly played by Miss Marion Terry and is an achievement which that gifted lady may number among her most successful artistic efforts . . . Mr H H Vincent's laughable Lord Augustus deserves a word of special praise; it was just enough of a caricature, without degenerating into buffoonerry.
>
> *Theatre*

> If the fan had a speaking part so that it could tell us all about what was happening while lying in odd corners in a ballroom, it might considerably increase the interest of the play. But this fan has nothing to say at all.
>
> Jingle *Put-Me-Up*

Two days after the first night, in a letter to the Editor of the *St James's Gazette*, Wilde admitted that Alexander had been right about Mrs Erlynne and he had been wrong. He said it wasn't the critics who had made him change his mind but his friends, who had insisted that the psychological interest of the second act would be increased if the audience knew that Mrs Erlynne and Lady Windermere were mother and daughter.

The play was a great success. 'I hear royalty is turned away nightly,' observed Wilde, who had celebrated the premiere by going to bed with Edward Shelley at the Albemarle Hotel. Shelley was an eighteen-year-old clerk at his publishers.

Wilde supervised a revival of *Lady Windermere's Fan* in January 1893 at the Theatre Royal, Torquay. Lily Hanbury and Nutcombe Gould repeated their roles. The rest of the cast, led by the Lady Mayoress, as Mrs Erlynne, was drawn from amateurs. He was unable to attend the opening, the east wind, not knowing who he was (so he said), having given him a cold.

1893 American premiere: Palmer's Theatre, New York.

LORD WINDERMERE	Edward Bell
LORD DARLINGTON	Maurice Barrymore
LORD AUGUSTUS	E M Holland
MR DUMBY	J G Saville
CECIL GRAHAM	Walden Ramsay
MR HOPPER	Edward S Abeles
PARKER	Guido Marburg
LADY WINDERMERE	Julia Arthur
THE DUCHESS OF BERWICK	Mrs D P Bowers
LADY AGATHA	Ann Urhart
LADY PLYMDALE	Fanny Jackson
LADY STUTFIELD	Marie Henderson
LADY JEDBURGH	Emily Seward
MRS COWPER-COWPER	Rose Barrington
MRS ERLYNNE	May Brookyn
ROSALIE	Zenaide Vislaire

It is ingeniously constructed; it is sufficiently supplied with striking situations; it is written in fluent and often pungent dialogue, and it moves steadily and rapidly to a climax. The form of it manifests artistic talent and pleases the sense of symmetry. At that point its worthiness ceases. The substance of it is false and the spirit of it is pert. No such persons exist as populate its scenes nor is there anywhere such a state of society extant as Mr Wilde has suggested . . . It imparts the idea of a clever satirical man who has not yet got over his youth and who wants to create a sensation . . . The talent of Mr Oscar Wilde was long since recognised; nobody disputes it; but a play in order to deserve public sympathy must contain something more than evidence that its writer is a smart person who thinks society to be extremely corrupt. America, at all events, is not just now living in the time of George IV, and second-hand Bulwers are out of date.

New York Daily Tribune

Mr Wilde is generally whimsical and often absurd. Sometimes, in spite of himself, he is just what he would rather not be than anything else in the world – banal . . . the charm of the piece was to be found in the subtle and pervasive atmosphere of polite 'fast' life in the capital of the world at the fag end of the nineteenth century . . . The comedy is richly and tastefully set at Palmer's Theatre and the acting is all careful, direct, and well-intentioned. None of it seemed to be particularly brilliant last night and there was a noticeable lack of tenderness and sympathy in the acting of the two principal women . . . Our admiration for Mr Barrymore never fails altogether, but sometimes it falters, and when he makes love to another gentleman's wife in the manner of a foreman of a fire engine company calling for another line of hose, we do not exactly like him . . . Mrs Bowers, always a justly esteemed actress, seemed to be entirely too vociferous as a gossiping Duchess.

New York Times

George C D Odell wrote in *Annals of the New York Stage* (Columbia University Press, 1949):

Mrs Bowers came to the younger playgoers as a revelation of what the older school could do in the way of crisp, trenchant diction; nothing like her delivery had for years been heard in New York. It is only fair to say the topsy-turvy wit of her speeches and Mr Barrymore's went over the heads of the early audiences; it was a new formula, and one needed to grow used to it.

1901 Coronet Theatre, Notting Hill Gate, London.

LORD WINDERMERE	T B Thalberg
LORD DARLINGTON	J Cooke Beresford
LORD AUGUSTUS	F Owen Baxter
MR DUMBY	Charles Esdale
CECIL GRAHAM	Allen Cunard
MR HOPPER	Charles Grey
PARKER	T G Knott
LADY WINDERMERE	Gertrude Burnett
THE DUCHESS OF BERWICK	Elsie Carew
LADY AGATHA	Isabel Middleton
LADY PLYMDALE	Rosemond Mayne Young
LADY JEDBURGH	Marie Grogan
SIR JAMES ROYSTON	F Herbert
LADY STUTFIELD	Violet Greville
MRS ERLYNNE	Marion Terry
ROSALIE	Maud Vernon

No author's name appeared on the programme.

1902 German premiere : Lobe Theater, Breslau.

1904 St James's Theatre, London.

LORD WINDERMERE	Ben Webster
LORD DARLINGTON	C Aubrey Smith
LORD AUGUSTUS	Sydney Brough
MR DUMBY	A Vane-Tempest
CECIL GRAHAM	Leslie Faber
MR HOPPER	Selwyn Seymour
PARKER	Murray Carrington
LADY WINDERMERE	Lilian Braithwaite
THE DUCHESS OF BERWICK	Fanny Coleman
LADY AGATHA	Corisande Hamilton
LADY PLYMDALE	Pauline French
LADY JEDBURGH	Elinor Aickin
MRS COWPER-COWPER	Eileen Lewis
MRS ERLYNNE	Marion Terry
ROSALIE	Maud Haricourt

'Its brilliant epigrams still scintillate as brightly as ever,' said the *Illustrated London News*. 'Compared with some of our modern pieces *Lady Windermere's Fan* is a fount of purity and freshness,' said the *Era*.

> Nothing could be more delightful than the Mrs Erlynne of Miss Marion Terry – delightful in its 'authority', its sureness of touch, its skilful blending of grave and gay, maternal sacrifice and mundane, not to say semi-mundane, frivolity. Looking as charming as ever and beautifully dressed, Miss Terry was the heroine of the evening and at the fall of the curtain the pit and gallery rang with her name.
>
> *The Times*

> The work itself can scarcely be said to have aged. Its presentation of a world flippant, selfish, mercenary, and unworthy, retains its old vivacity and freshness . . . Mr Webster and Mr Aubrey Smith might with advantage change characters.
>
> *Athenaeum*

1911 St James's Theatre, London.

LORD WINDERMERE	Dawson Milward
LORD DARLINGTON	Norman Trevor
LORD AUGUSTUS	Eric Lewis
MR DUMBY	Ernest Thesiger
CECIL GRAHAM	Owen Nares
MR HOPPER	T N Weguelin
PARKER	G Trevor Roller
LADY WINDERMERE	Lilian Braithwaite
THE DUCHESS OF BERWICK	Mrs G Kemmis
LADY AGATHA	Dorothy Fane
LADY PLYMDALE	Nella Powys
LADY STUTFIELD	Lisa Macready
LADY JEDBURGH	Elizabeth Chesney
MRS COWPER-COWPER	Margaret Chute
MRS ERLYNNE	Marion Terry
ROSALIE	Ernita Lascelles

It is audaciously clever and timidly stupid. Wilde mastered the tricks of the stage in five minutes and never troubled about the rules; and so we get a play that is at once very stagey and clumsy, perfectly planned and feebly constructed . . . These exquisite, high bred things require the neatest and most adroit of handling; and this – on the first night of its revival at any rate – *Lady Windermere's Fan* did not receive from anyone but Miss Marion Terry.

The Times

If these paradoxes now seem rather worn with age – theirs was not the kind of wit which is immortal – yet they call up pleasant recollections of the days when they were young and fresh and seemed good to hear; whilst much of the serious dialogue has a wonderful style.

Illustrated London News

1913 Russian silent film directed by Burenin.

1914 Hudson Theatre, New York.
Transferred: Liberty Theatre, New York.

Director	George Foster Platt
LORD WINDERMERE	Pedro DeCordoba
LORD DARLINGTON	Arthur Byron
LORD AUGUSTUS LORTON	Sydney Greenstreet
MR DUMBY	Wallace Widdecombe
MR CECIL GRAHAM	Norman Tharp
MR HOPPER	Donald Cameron
PARKER	Harry Barfoot
LADY WINDERMERE	Margery Maude
THE DUCHESS OF BERWICK	Sarah Cowell LaMoyne
LADY AGATHA CARLISLE	Margery Card
LADY PLYMDALE	Ruth Holt Boucicault
LADY STUTFIELD	Florence Wollersen
LADY JEDBURGH	Lillian Thurgate
MRS COWPER-COWPER	Sally Williams
MRS ERLYNNE	Margaret Anglin
ROSALIE	Florence Wollersen

> The brilliance of the dialogue still seems undimmed . . . Margaret Anglin plays with a deftness in the lighter parts and with a fine restraint in the emotional scene that makes the success of the splendid third act a personal triumph in every sense.
>
> *New York Times*

1916 British silent film.

Director	Fred Paul
Screenplay	Benedict James
LORD WINDERMERE	Milton Rosmer
LORD DARLINGTON	Arthur Wontner
LORD AUGUSTUS	Nigel Playfair
MR DUMBY	Vivian Reynolds
CECIL GRAHAM	Evan Thomas
MR HOPPER	Sidney Vautier
LADY WINDERMERE	Netta Westcott
THE DUCHESS OF BERWICK	Alice de Winton
LADY AGATHA	Joyce Kerr
MRS ERLYNNE	Irene Rooke

> There is the same world for all of us – and good and evil, sin and innocence, go through it hand in hand. To shut one's eyes to half of life that one might live securely, is as though one blinded oneself that one might walk with more safety in a land of pit and precipice.
>
> Lady Windermere

The film opened with the above legend on the screen. Mrs Erlynne was discovered in bed in Paris with her unpaid bills and English newspaper. Turning to the society pages, she found a picture of her daughter and decided to leave for London immediately. She met her by chance at a dog show and was, as the intertitles worded it, 'flooded with emotions she had suppressed for 20 years'.

Netta Westcott, as Lady Windermere, eyes black-rimmed and bosom heaving, did a lot of silent-screen acting when she had to tear open her husband's paybook and hurl it across the room. Since there were no epigrams, the melodrama was undiluted. Much of the dialogue ('From this moment my life is separate from yours!') was not by Wilde.

In the final scene Mrs Erlynne asked her daughter for the fan (not, as in the play, a photograph) and then, having made her exit, came back to give her a kiss.

The one performance which looked as if it might have worked on stage was Nigel Playfair's Lord Augustus, a very 'Tuppy' fool with a monocle.

1919 American silent film.

> A cold, lifeless thing without a spark of vitality and personal interest in it to comfort the picture 'fan'.
>
> Abel *Variety*

1925 American silent film.

Director	Ernest Lubitsch
Screenplay	Julien Josephson
LORD WINDERMERE	Bert Lytell
LORD DARLINGTON	Ronald Colman
LORD AUGUSTUS	Edward Martindel
LADY WINDERMERE	May McAvoy
GOSSIPY DUCHESSES	Billie Bennett
	Helen Dunbar
THE DUCHESS OF BERWICK	Carrie D'Aumery
MRS ERLYNNE	Irene Rich

The film, which was voted one of the ten best pictures of the year, did not use one epigram by Wilde. Lubitsch said they had no place in a silent film and substituted visual epigrams in their place. A scene at Royal Ascot gave him the opportunity for some social satire. Mrs Erlynne, with the aid of her field glasses, observed the aristocracy rather than the horses. There was also a witty touch when a man's changing relations with a lady were indicated by the manner in which he rang her doorbell.

> Ronald Colman as the heavy plays with fine restraint and Miss McAvoy is most charming and effective as the young wife. Lytell is prone to overact at times . . . Of the men, the one carrying the most conviction was Edward Martindel.
>
> *Variety*

1926 Chinese film: *The Young Lady's Fan*
Adapted and directed by Shen Hung.

1930 Everyman Theatre, London.

Director	Stephen Thomas
LORD WINDERMERE	Cecil Parker/Felix Aylmer
LORD DARLINGTON	Eric Maturin
LORD AUGUSTUS	George Merritt
MR DUMBY	Ernest Thesiger
CECIL GRAHAM	Michael Shepley
MR HOPPER	Eric Lugg
PARKER	John V Trevor
LADY WINDERMERE	Kathleen O'Regan
THE DUCHESS OF BERWICK	Margaret Yarde
LADY AGATHA	Pamela Carme
LADY PLYMDALE	Mary Hinton
LADY JEDBURGH	Nona Hoffe
MRS COWPER-COWPER	Lumena Edwardes/Margery Clayton
MRS ERLYNNE	Kate Cutler
ROSALIE	Madge Snell/Frances Mackenzie

Wilde's characters are puppets of cardboard hung about with sentimental and melodramatic platitudes . . . The chatter is a delight . . . Actors trained in the naturalism of today do not know how to speak it . . . Mary Hinton in a small part gave the best performance of the evening, looking as if she has lived her life in a society that was rigid in its conventions.

The Times

Miss Kate Cutler defies one to say that she is not spectacularly correct as the adventuress by sailing determinedly in and handling the part delightfully . . . We cannot feel for these puppets any more – only laugh at their antics – but the wit with which they are strung will keep them alive for many a revival . . . Mr Ernest Thesiger is the ideal Dumby . . . Mr Eric Maturin makes a tragic villain out of Lord Darlington.

Time and Tide

Was there ever a more brilliantly written act than the third in this play?

James Agate *Sunday Times*

1932 Recital Theatre, New York.

Director	Arthur William Row
LORD WINDERMERE	Richard Stevenson
LORD DARLINGTON	Sherley Oliver
LORD AUGUSTUS	Herbert Standing
MR DUMBY	Arthur William Row
CECIL GRAHAM	Harry Redding
MR HOPPER	Carl Emory
PARKER	Wells Richardson
LADY WINDERMERE	Ellis Baker
THE DUCHESS OF BERWICK	Essex Dane
LADY AGATHA	Florence Williams
LADY PLYMDALE	Marga La Rubin
LADY JEDBURGH	Myra C Brooke
MRS COWPER-COWPER	Jeanne Powers
LADY STUTFIED	Rosamond Carpenter
MRS ERLYNNE	Theresa Maxwell Conover

Never did they suggest the bright artificiality which was Wilde's chief charm even of this more solemn work of his. They played most of it, indeed, on the brink of tears and took their epigrams with emotional seriousness . . . Miss Theresa Maxwell Conover played the mother with baffling awkwardness which left no room for the reality of the stage, let alone the reality of life.

New York Sun

1932 people indulging in eighteen-ninety sentiments and sentimentality are neither believable nor worth paying to listen to.

New York World Telegram

1932 New Yorker Theatre, New York.
Performed in Spanish by La Compañía Dramática Española.

1935 German film: *Lady Windermeres Fächer*

Director	Heinz Hilpert
CAST	Lil Dagover
	Paul Dahlke
	Walter Rilla
	Hanna Waag
	Grethe Weiser

1938 Chinese film: *Shaonainai De Shanzi*

1943 Q Theatre, Kew, Surrey.

Directors	Margaret Yarde
	Ernest Thesiger
LORD WINDERMERE	Peter Copley
LORD DARLINGTON	Graeme Muir
LORD AUGUSTUS	Hamilton Deane
MR DUMBY	Alan Trotter
CECIL GRAHAM	Anthony Bazell
MR HOPPER	Derek Prouse
PARKER	Paul Gane
LADY WINDERMERE	Joyce Howard
THE DUCHESS OF BERWICK	Margaret Yarde
LADY AGATHA	Joan Greenwood
LADY PLYMDALE	Alice Darch
LADY STUTFIELD	Diana Marshall
LADY JEDBURGH	Adrienne Bennet
MRS COWPER-COWPER	Betty Hare
MRS ERLYNNE	Rosemary Scott
ROSALIE	Betty Hare

1944 Mexican film: *El Abanico De Lady Windermere*

1945 Theatre Royal, Haymarket, London.

Director	John Gielgud
Designer	Cecil Beaton
LORD WINDERMERE	Geoffrey Toone
LORD DARLINGTON	Griffith Jones
LORD AUGUSTUS	Michael Shepley
MR DUMBY	Deering Wells
CECIL GRAHAM	Denys Blakelock
MR HOPPER	Hugh Stewart
PARKER	Stuart Bull
LADY WINDERMERE	Dorothy Hyson
THE DUCHESS OF BERWICK	Athene Seyler
LADY AGATHA	Patricia Dickson
LADY PLYMDALE	Gladys Wykeham-Edwards
LADY STUTFIELD	Diana Marshall
LADY JEDBURGH	Phyllis Relph
MRS COWPER-COWPER	Phyllis Thomas/Betty England
MRS ERLYNNE	Isabel Jeans
ROSALIE	Hilda Bruce-Potter
MISS GRAHAM	Anne Bibby/Gillian Raine
SIR JAMES ROYSTON	Raymond Leigh
LADY PAISLEY	Hilda Bruce-Porter
LORD PAISLEY	Thomas Hutcheson
FOOTMEN	Antony Massie/Harry Pease
	Harrop Allin/Victor Albany

In the drab years immediately following the end of World War Two, the magnificence of Cecil Beaton's costumes and scenery made an enormous impact on an audience who still had to have coupons to buy clothes.

> Mr Gielgud's good intentions as a producer are defeated less by individual shortcomings than by the general failure of his company to exploit the rich incidental drollness of the comedy and to live up to the splendour of their surroundings.
>
> Anthony Cookman *Tatler and Bystander*

> Miss Isabel Jeans has the proper sweep and – in the third act – the emotion for Mrs Erlynne, and we shall not readily forget her

last entrance. Thanks to this actress and to the vocal quality that lifts her lines – it is a sort of husky sparkle – Wilde's melodramatics keep an unexpected theatrical effect.

J C Trewin *Punch*

Its pace is too slow and its acting, with one or two conspicuous exceptions, scarcely worthy of its ornate setting. Miss Athene Seyler – a sprite of mischievous scandal in the Duchess's tiara – is a joy whenever she appears.

The Times

1946 Cort Theatre, New York.

Director	Jack Minster
Designer	Cecil Beaton
LORD WINDERMERE	Henry Daniell
LORD DARLINGTON	John Buckmaster
LORD AUGUSTUS	Rex Evans
MR DUMBY	Evan Thomas
CECIL GRAHAM	Cecil Beaton
MR HOPPER	Stanley Bell
PARKER	Thomas Louden
LADY WINDERMERE	Penelope Ward
THE DUCHESS OF BERWICK	Estelle Winwood
LADY AGATHA	Sally Cooper
LADY STUTFIELD	Anne Curson
LADY JEDBURGH	Elizabeth Valentine
MRS COWPER-COWPER	Leonore Elliott
MRS ERLYNNE	Cornelia Otis Skinner
ROSALIE	Marjorie Wood

Cecil Beaton recreated his designs for the New York production and also made his acting début.

Too old to be smart, but not old enough to be a classic.

Brooks Atkinson *New York Times*

The most brilliant comedy in town and the most rewarding . . . Estelle Winwood has a field day.

George Freedley *New York Morning Telegraph*

> The frailties and archaisms of the play are not wholly disguised, but the dramatic virtues are given their full due . . . Cecil Beaton is sheer theatrical magic.
>
> Howard Barnes *New York Herald-Tribune*

1948 Argentinian film: *Historia de una Mala Mujer*
English title: *The Story of a Bad Woman*

Director	Luis Sanlavsky
Screenplay	Pedro Miguel Obligado

LORD WINDERMERE	Alberto Closas
LORD DARLINGTON	Fernando Lamas
LORD ARTHUR	Francisco de Paula
LADY WINDERMERE	Maria Duval
THE DUCHESS OF BERWICK	Amalia S Arino
MRS ERLYNNE	Dolores del Rio

Lord Arthur was the great love of Mrs Erlynne's life, the man she ran away with, deserting husband and child.

> Miss del Rio is moving and understandable in the role of Mrs Erlynne, despite the studied artificiality of some of her poses.
>
> Nid *Variety*

1949 American film: *The Fan*

Director	Otto Preminger
Screenplay	Walter Reisch
	Dorothy Parker
	Ross Evans

LORD WINDERMERE	Richard Greene
LORD DARLINGTON	George Sanders
LORD AUGUSTUS	Hugh Dempster
CECIL GRAHAM	John Sutton
MR HOPPER	Richard Ney
LADY WINDERMERE	Jeanne Crain
THE DUCHESS OF BERWICK	Martita Hunt
LADY AGATHA	Virginia McDowall

MRS ERLYNNE	Madeleine Carroll
ROSALIE	Felippa Rock

Otto Preminger's opulently mounted production was banal and stodgily acted. Much of the dialogue was new. The film opened with a nonagerian Mrs Erlynne telling her story (in flashback) to an aged Lord Darlington during the London Blitz in World War Two. Her memory had been prompted at an auction house, where various articles (including a fan) had been salvaged from bombed buildings and were up for sale.

Jeanne Crain, as Lady Windermere, was winsome and charming, but insignificant. Martita Hunt, as the Duchess of Berwick, had the most elegance and breeding. 'She was,' said *The Graphic*, 'the only person in the picture with real style.'

> *Lady Windermere's Fan* should be a horrible warning to other film makers contemplating a dip into Wildeania.
>
> Milton Shulman *Evening Standard*

> Oh Miss Parker! To add vulgarity to Wilde's egregious ham. How could you?
>
> *Daily Herald*

> This slow, sluggish, incredibly serious piece of pretension, which demonstrates, among other things, the importance of not being over-earnest.
>
> Paul Dehn *Sunday Chronicle*

1954 *After the Ball*
A musical play by Noël Coward, based on *Lady Windermere's Fan.*

Premiere: Globe Theatre, London.

Director	Robert Helpmann
Designer	Doris Zinkeisen

LADY JEDBURGH	Betty Felstead
LADY PAISLEY	Anna Halinka
MRS COWPER-COWPER	Ailsa Gamley
LADY PLYMDALE	Lois Green
LADY STUTFIELD	Pam Marmont

MR DUMBY	Dennis Bowen
LORD PAISLEY	John Morley
MR CECIL GRAHAM	Tom Gill
LADY WINDERMERE	Vanessa Lee
LORD WINDERMERE	Peter Graves
MR HOPPER	Graham Payn
LORD DARLINGTON	Shamus Locke
THE DUCHESS OF BERWICK	Irene Browne
LADY AGATHA CARLISLE	Patricia Cree
PARKER	Leslie Pearson
LORD AUGUSTUS	Donald Scott
MRS ERLYNNE	Mary Ellis
MR GUY BERKELEY	Raymond Savigear
MR RUFFORD	Bill Horsley
LADY RUCKINGE	Silvia Beamish
MISS GRAHAM	Maureen Quinney
MRS HURST-GREEN	Marion Grimaldi
MRS ARTHUR BOWDEN	Margaret Gibson
FOOTMAN	Bill Horsley

> I am forced to admit that the more Coward we can get into the script and the more Wilde we can eliminate the happier we shall be.
>
> Noël Coward *Diaries (Weidenfeld & Nicolson, 1982)*

There were no fanfares for Coward's old-fashioned musical. The songs merely accentuated the bathos of the melodrama. The actual dialogue fell flat. The audience was never certain whether they were meant to be laughing with Wilde or at Wilde. Most critics said they were glad when the ball was over.

Mary Ellis knew how to act Mrs Erlynne but she no longer had the voice to sing Mrs Erlynne. Her songs were taken away from her one by one. The show was billed as an operetta on tour but by the time it reached London it had lost so many songs it had become a musical.

Vanessa Lee knew how to sing Lady Windermere but she was not primarily an actress. There was little of Windermere in Peter Graves, either. Shamus Locke's Lord Darlington handed out his epigrams as if they were visiting cards. Irene Browne, as the Duchess of Berwick, kept the ball rolling by over-acting.

The best lyric was the opening number in Hyde Park, 'Oh What A Century It's Been'. Only twice thereafter did Coward come near to repeating his witty comment on the period: firstly, in a tea-time complaint, 'Why is it the woman who pays? and then in a dandy number for the rakes, 'London at Night'.

Coward turned Mr Hopper and Lady Agatha into hoofers, and Graham Payn and Patricia Cree danced a charming polka in 'May I Have The Pleasure?'

Robert Helpmann, the director, pinpointed what was wrong in his conversation with Charles Castle in *Noël* (Abacus, 1974) when he said: 'Everything that Noël sent up,Wilde was sentimental about, and everything Wilde sent up, Noël was sentimental about. It was two different points of view and it didn't work. It could never have worked.'

> With all its glitter and polish, the show does not – possibly cannot – amount to anything more than a patchwork.
>
> W A Darlington *Daily Telegraph*

> It was champagne in china mugs.
>
> John Barber *Daily Express* (headline)

1955 Théâtre Hébertot, Paris.

Adaptor	Michelle Lahaye
Director	Marcelle Tassencourt

LORD WINDERMERE	Pierre Vaneck
LORD DARLINGTON	François Perrot
LORD AUGUSTUS	Christian Lude
MR DUMBY	Van Doude
CECIL GRAHAM	Marc Doelnitz
MR HOPPER	Georges Vanet
PARKER	Serge Bouillon
LADY WINDERMERE	Marie-France Planeze
THE DUCHESS OF BERWICK	Jeanne Fusier-Gir
LADY AGATHA CARLISLE	Sophie Laurence
LADY PLYMDALE	Marcelle Tassencourt
LADY STUTFIELD	Ludmila Hols
LADY LUXMORE	Denise Bally

MRS ERLYNNE	Michelle Lahaye
ROSALIE	Elyane Valley
MR COWPER-COWPER	Phillipe Hebrard
MR RUFFORD	Roger Pappini

1965 West German television: *Lady Windermeres Fächer*

1966 Phoenix Theatre, London.

Director	Anthony Quayle
Designer	Cecil Beaton

LORD WINDERMERE	John Humphry
LORD DARLINGTON	Ronald Lewis
LORD AUGUSTUS	Wilfrid Hyde White/Douglas Byng
MR DUMBY	Anthony Roye
CECIL GRAHAM	Corin Redgrave
MR HOPPER	Terence Bayler
PARKER	Geoffrey King
LADY WINDERMERE	Juliet Mills
THE DUCHESS OF BERWICK	Isabel Jeans
LADY AGATHA CARLISLE	Carolyn Montagu
LADY PLYMDALE	Jacqueline Lacey
LADY STUTFIELD	Billie Hill
LADY JEDBURGH	Molly Veness
MRS COWPER-COWPER	Anne Sherwin
MRS ERLYNNE	Coral Browne
ROSALIE	Celestine Randall
BISHOP	George Desmond
MISS GRAHAM	Maria Warburg
GUY BERKELEY	Martin Aubrey
SIR JAMES ROYSTON	Peter Jackson
FOOTMAN	Roy Boyd

We play it differently from the way one imagines it must have been done originally. For one thing, we take it quite fast and we guard against a sentimental hearts-and-flowers approach. I think one has to do it in terms of present-day acting methods rather than reconstruct the original style.

Coral Browne, quoted by *The Times*

The serious side of the play proved nearly as funny as the epigrams. The audience had great difficulty taking Lady Windermere's high moral tone seriously. The third act, where mother and daughter found themselves 'on the brink of ruin', played to a great deal of unwanted laughter.

Coral Browne, perfect casting for the handsome, clever Mrs Erlynne, did indeed look like 'an edition de luxe of a wicked French novel meant specially for the English market'. She gave the wit a brittle edge; she was less successful with a mother's belated rush of sentimental feelings.

Isabel Jeans's elegance, authority and comic timing were invaluable. She played down the Duchess of Berwick's essential unpleasantness. Wilfrid Hyde White (as Lord Augustus) was very droll, adding his own lines to Wilde's and then, casually, throwing them all away.

The disadvantage of having these particular actors in two comparatively small roles was that they showed up the other actors. John Humphry's Windermere was a dummy. Juliet Mills, doll-like in looks, doll-like in voice (her vowels all wrong) was hard-pressed to make anything of Lady Windermere.

Ronald Lewis's Lord Darlington was too much the Victorian villain without the saving charm, and Cecil Beaton in his designs emphasised his wickedness by giving him Moorish apartments. The décor throughout was of unfailing vulgarity; Beaton parodied the period rather than heightened it.

Corin Redgrave (sporting a green carnation) was laboured, making Cecil Graham a bore, which, no doubt, he was in real life. Anthony Roye's ridiculously conceited Dumby was much nearer to what Wilde wanted.

> Coral Browne cuts a fine figure as Mrs Erlynne, though here again I missed the genuine note of pathos which the role should certainly strike.
>
> Philip Hope-Wallace *Guardian*

> Anthony Quayle's production's attention to decorative detail is at the expense of dramatic impetus.
>
> *The Times*

1967 British television.

Adaptor	Stanley Miller
Director	Joan Kemp-Welch
LORD WINDERMERE	Ian Ogilvy
LORD DARLINGTON	James Villiers
LORD AUGUSTUS	Richard Vernon
MR DUMBY	John Steiner
MR HOPPER	Elliott Cairnes
PARKER	John Lee
LADY WINDERMERE	Jennie Linden
THE DUCHESS OF BERWICK	Joan Benham
LADY AGATHA	Mia Martin
LADY PLYMDALE	Jennifer Wright
LADY JEDBURGH	Barbara Bolton
MRS ERLYNNE	Barbara Jefford

Barbara Jefford was admirable in this role, suggesting a woman who combined a mind like a cash-register with a heart as big as, say, South Kensington station.

The Times

Barbara Jefford lacked the dazzling glamour necessary to put across Mrs Erlynne as the toast (somewhat burned) of the town but compensated with touches of emotion that made the lady's dilemma plausible.

Variety

James Villiers, who always speaks his lines as if Oscar Wilde had written them, was ideally cast as the cynical but devoted Lord Darlington.

Daily Telegraph

1972 British television.

Director	Rudolph Cartier
LORD WINDERMERE	Ronald Hines
LORD DARLINGTON	Derek Godfrey
LORD AUGUSTUS	Charles Gray

MR DUMBY	Anthony Sharp
CECIL GRAHAM	James Villiers
MR HOPPER	Noel Trevarthen
PARKER	Lee Fox
LADY WINDERMERE	Judy Geeson
THE DUCHESS OF BERWICK	Siân Phillips
LADY AGATHA	Liza Goddard
LADY PLYMDALE	Sheila Brennan
LADY JEDBURGH	Noël Hood
MR COWPER-COWPER	Linda Gray
MRS ERLYNNE	Coral Browne
ROSALIE	Sandra Hall

Elegant, composed, yet somehow pathetic, she [Coral Browne] was everything Wilde could have wished for.

The Times

Mr Villiers with admirable restraint contrived to make it not a portrait of the Artist as Bertie Wooster, gruesomely wisecracking, but something approaching an actual, and occasionally funny, amiable bore.

Peter Fiddick *Guardian*

The only jarring note was Lady Windermere herself, in this case Judy Geeson, who failed to suggest anything more than petulance and seemed out of her dramatic depth, especially amid some very tall company.

Variety

1978 Yvonne Arnaud Theatre, Guildford.
Transferred to Ottawa, Canada.

Director	Val May
LADY WINDERMERE	Ian Hendry
LORD DARLINGTON	Michael Cochrane
LORD AUGUSTUS	Wilfrid Hyde White
MR DUMBY	Robert Tunstall
CECIL GRAHAM	Clive Graham
MR HOPPER	Nicholas Field
PARKER	Paul Ratcliffe

LADY WINDERMERE	Jenny Quayle
THE DUCHESS OF BERWICK	Jessie Matthews
LADY AGATHA	Louise Robertson
LADY JEDBURGH	Daphne Goddard
MRS COWPER-COWPER	Linda Barr
MRS ERLYNNE	Moira Lister
ROSALIE	Linda Barr

1979 Horseshoe Theatre Company (UK tour).

Director	Guy Slater
LORD WINDERMERE	Richard Coleman
LORD DARLINGTON	John Fraser
LORD AUGUSTUS	Raymond Francis
MR DUMBY	Michael Sharvell-Martin
CECIL GRAHAM	Jonathan Cecil
MR HOPPER	Mark Dows
PARKER	Marc Ashley
LADY WINDERMERE	Karen Dotrice
THE DUCHESS OF BERWICK	Betty Marsden
LADY AGATHA CARLISLE	Sheila Felvin
LADY PLYMDALE	Bridget de Courcy
LADY JEDBURGH	Mary Mitchell
MRS COWPER-COWPER	Jane Myerson
MRS ERLYNNE	Hildegard Neil

This revival alternated with *An Ideal Husband.* John Fraser did not disguise the fact that Lord Darlington was a nasty little man and played Act III drunk. What Lady Windermere saw in him was not clear. Karen Dotrice coped remarkably well with the melodrama and was defeated only by the long soliloquy at the beginning of Act II. When she said, 'I have heard such men are brutal, horrible,' she was greeted with one of the biggest laughs of the evening. Betty Marsden was unbelievably common as the Duchess of Berwick. The best performance was by Jonathan Cecil, who played Jonathan Cecil, which suited Cecil Graham perfectly.

1983 Playhouse, Nottingham.

Director	Andrew McKinnon
LORD WINDERMERE	Philip Lowrie
LORD DARLINGTON	Brian Carroll
LORD AUGUSTUS	Vivian Mackerell
MR DUMBY	Benedick Blythe
CECIL GRAHAM	Andy Readman
MR HOPPER	Jonathan Kiley
PARKER	John Gay
LADY WINDERMERE	Julia Swift
THE DUCHESS OF BERWICK	Patricia Kneal
LADY AGATHA	Caroline Swift
LADY PLYMDALE	Dorcas Jones
LADY STUTFIELD	Janet McTeer
LADY JEDBURGH	Diana Olsson
MRS ERLYNNE	Helen Ryan
ROSALIE	Diana Olsson
SIR JAMES ROYSTON	Hugh Grant
FOOTMAN	Hugh Grant

1985 British television.

Director	Tony Smith
LORD WINDERMERE	Tim Woodward
LORD DARLINGTON	Kenneth Cranham
LORD AUGUSTUS	Robert Lang
MR DUMBY	John Clive
CECIL GRAHAM	James Saxon
MR HOPPER	Geoff Morrell
PARKER	Ian Burford
LADY WINDERMERE	Helena Little
THE DUCHESS OF BERWICK	Sara Kestelman
LADY AGATHA	Amanda Royle
LADY PLYMDALE	Veronica Lang
LADY STUTFIELD	Vivien Lloyd
LADY JEDBURGH	Diana Fairfax
MRS COWPER-COWPER	Gloria Connell
MRS ERLYNNE	Stephanie Turner
ROSALIE	Mary Kurowski

There was little evidence of Wilde's sparkling wit in Tony Smith's heavy-going and badly lit production. Kenneth Cranham had no charm whatsoever as Lord Darlington and looked such a monster that it was inconceivable that a Puritan like Lady Windermere would ever have entertained for one moment the idea of running off with him.

Sara Kestelman, ignoring the comedy, played the Duchess of Berwick for a thoroughly unpleasant and malicious woman who knew precisely what she was doing when she told Lady Windermere about Windermere's association with Mrs Erlynne.

> He [Kenneth Cranham] contorted his lips into such fearful grimaces that it's a wonder he did not knock his teeth out. But I can't say I blame him, considering he was stuck with such a stinker of a play. Overheated rubbish like this is enough to make anyone hysterical.
>
> Maureen Paton *Daily Express*

> Helena Little's Lady Windermere was genuinely vexed and her gradual journey towards maturity was done with a still authority that lent this television version an appropriate moral focus.
>
> Andrew Rissick *New Statesman*

> Contemporary members of Equity, with very few exceptions, are not geared to impersonating the Victorian aristocracy. Peers with provincial accents, however immaculately attired in 1890s drag, tax credibility.
>
> *Guardian*

1985 Palace Theatre, Watford.

Director	Prunella Scales
LORD WINDERMERE	Simon Chandler
LORD DARLINGTON	Nicholas Gecks
LORD AUGUSTUS LORTON	Robert McBain
MR DUMBY	Mark Tandy
MR CECIL GRAHAM	Nicholas Hutchinson
MR HOPPER	Geoff Morrell
PARKER	Neal Arden
MR RUFFORD	Mark Cook

SIR JAMES ROYSTON	Don Hanham
LADY WINDERMERE	Joanne Pearce
THE DUCHESS OF BERWICK	Georgine Anderson
LADY AGATHA CARLISLE	Kate Perceval
LADY PLYMDALE	Dawn Keeler
LADY STUTFIELD	Kate Devey
LADY JEDBURGH	Gillian Webb
MISS GRAHAM	Fiona Muir
MRS ERLYNNE	Isla Blair
FOOTMAN	Paul Ibbot

Isla Blair provides much needed dignity, though not much pathos.

Martin Cropper *The Times*

1988 Citizens' Theatre, Glasgow.

Director and designer	Philip Prowse
LORD WINDERMERE	Giles Havergal
LORD DARLINGTON	Robert Gwilym
LORD AUGUSTUS	Robert David MacDonald
MR DUMBY	Jonathan Phillips
CECIL GRAHAM	Laurance Rudic
MR HOPPER	Patrick Hannaway
PARKER	Derwent Watson
LADY WINDERMERE	Carol Brannan
THE DUCHESS OF BERWICK	Fidelis Morgan
LADY AGATHA	Ellis Van Maarseveen
LADY STUTFIELD	Anna Patrick
LADY JEDBURGH	Anne Myatt
MRS ERLYNNE	Angela Chadfield

When Wilde wrote the play, Lady Windermere's relationship to Mrs Erlynne was withheld until the last act; George Alexander persuaded Wilde to change his mind. Philip Prowse returned to Wilde's version by the simple expedient of cutting all Mrs Erlynne's soliloquies.

Windermere was played considerably older than his wife, whom he treated as if she were still a child. The play ended with her slapping his face.

Philip Prowse's production was luxurious, with high ceilings, cream and lace curtains, Louis XVI chairs, and magnificent costumes.

> Prowse has captured superbly an ambiguous social climate of drained but glittering decadence.
>
> Michael Coveney *Financial Times*

1991 Cambridge Theatre Company tour, UK.

Director	Mike Alfreds
Designer	Paul Dart
LORD WINDERMERE	Peter Lindford
LORD DARLINGTON	Nick Dunning
LORD AUGUSTUS	Colin McCormack
MR DUMBY	Robin Hooper
CECIL GRAHAM	Robert Bowman
MR HOPPER	Robert Bowman
PARKER	Robin Hooper
LADY WINDERMERE	Irina Brook
THE DUCHESS OF BERWICK	Maggie Wells
LADY AGATHA	Mary Roscoe
LADY PLYMDALE	Mary Roscoe
MRS ERLYNNE	Lorna Heilbron
ROSALIE	Mary Roscoe

Wilde was acted in tandem with William Wycherley's *The Country Wife*. The two plays (said the flyleaf) exposed the English for what some of them were – a nation of sexual hypocrites, liars and cheats. The Wilde play opened with Lord and Lady Windermere in their underwear being dressed by servants and observed by their guests in masks.

> Poise, elegance and smoothness of movement were decidedly off the menu.
>
> Brian Case *Time Out*

1993 *After the Ball*, Noël Coward's musical version of *Lady Windermere's Fan*, was revived for one performance at Good Shepherd Faith Church, New York.

1993 Rough Magic, Dublin.
Transferred: Tricycle Theatre, Kilburn, London.

Director	Lynne Parker
LADY WINDERMERE	Ali White
PARKER	Mal Whyte
LORD DARLINGTON	Martin Murphy
THE DUCHESS OF BERWICK	Sean Kerns
LADY AGATHA	Miche Doherty
LORD WINDERMERE	Paul Hickey
MR DUMBY	Darragh Kelly
MR HOPPER	Mal Whyte
LORD AUGUSTUS	Sean Kerns
MRS COWPER-COWPER	Miche Doherty
LADY PLYMDALE	Mal Whyte
MRS ERLYNNE	Helen Montague
LADY JEDBURGH	Darragh Kelly

Lynne Parker's production for Rough Magic was a drag act. Wilde was deconstructed and acted for crude knockabout. The male actors played both the male and the female roles, cross-dressing and undressing on stage. 'None of us men do look what we really are. Dammed good thing, too,' said Lord Augustus. The music, provided by a piano and a violin, underlined the sexual ambivalence.

Sean Kerns's Duchess of Berwick was a booming pantomime dame, a grotesque parody of a battle-axe. Helen Montague's Mrs Erlynne was a twentieth-century figure. The last scene was played quite straight.

An uneasy hybrid of two styles never fully reconciled.

Nick Curtis *Evening Standard*

Helen Montague succeeds rather by force than finesse.

Paul Driver *Financial Times*

1994 Albery Theatre, London.

Director and designer	Philip Prowse
LORD WINDERMERE	Rupert Frazer
LORD DARLINGTON	Simon Dutton
LORD AUGUSTUS LORTON	Frank Middlemass
MR DUMBY	Tristram Wymark
CECIL GRAHAM	David Foxxe
MR HOPPER	Michael Onslow
PARKER	Leonard Kavanagh
LADY WINDERMERE	Amanda Elwes
THE DUCHESS OF BERWICK	Jennifer Hilary
LADY AGATHA CARLISLE	Nada Sharp
LADY STUTFIELD	Freya Dominic
LADY JEDBURGH	Marianne Morley
MRS ERLYNNE	Francesca Annis
MISS GRAHAM	Belinda Cawdron
SIR JAMES ROYSTON	Adrian Howells
GUY BERKELEY	David Monteath
MR RUFFORD	Peter Cadden
MISS SAVILE	Janet Wantling
LETITIA SAVILE	Amanda Jenner
SALOME SAVILE	Patti Clare

The West End had not seen such sumptuous sets and such sumptuous costumes since Philip Prowse had directed and designed *A Woman of No Importance* in 1991. The supporting cast were required not only to act; they were also required to model the costumes. The play became a choreographed mannequin parade. Even Lady Windermere was given a whole series of totally unnecessary moves whose sole purpose was to show off her dress.

The production had two original touches. The first was at the ball when Miss Graham (a character without lines and not in Wilde) circled the room continuously. Who was this woman in white, who was ignored by everybody and who was in the action and yet not in it? Presumably, she was Mrs Erlynne's younger self? The second novelty came in the third act when Lady Windermere slipped out of Lord Darlington's room. Normally she makes her escape unseen by anybody in the confusion of the discovery of Mrs Erlynne. In this production Lord Darlington most definitely saw her.

Francesca Annis looked stunning but was unequal to the last act. Simon Dutton had neither Darlington's sexuality nor his charm. The wooden performances elsewhere emphasised the melodrama. The most successful actor was David Foxxe, who wore a green carnation and played Cecil Graham as a nasty caricature of Wilde. Graham was no longer a young dandy but a camp old queen mincing around and eyeing the boys. Foxxe gave the epigrams a homosexual acerbity. Tristram Wymark played Dumby as a pale carbon copy of Graham.

> For a man of such style, wit and discrimination, Oscar Wilde was capable of writing the most terrible tosh.
>
> Charles Spencer *Daily Telegraph*

> He [Philip Prowse] has allowed the cast to be scarcely more wooden and padded than the stuff they are sitting on.
>
> Robert Hewison *Sunday Times*

> She [Francesca Annis] rises above the implausibilities of the plot to convey genuine passion and pain
>
> John Gross *Sunday Telegraph*

1997 Gate Theatre, Dublin.

Director	Alan Stanford
LORD WINDERMERE	Michael James Ford
LORD DARLINGTON	Robert O'Mahoney
LORD AUGUSTUS LORTON	Tom Hickey
MR DUMBY	Philip O'Sullivan
CECIL GRAHAM	Pat Kinevane
MR HOPPER	Mark O'Halloran
PARKER	Terence Orr
SIR JAMES ROYSTON	Russell Smith
LADY WINDERMERE	Hilary Reynolds
THE DUCHESS OF BERWICK	Susan FitzGerald
LADY AGATHA CARLISLE	Emily Nagle
LADY STUTFIELD	Sharon Devlin
LADY JEDBURGH	Lyn Fullerton
MRS COWPER-COWPER	Emma Moohan
LADY PLYMDALE	Claudia Carroll

MRS ERLYNNE	Olwen Fouere
MISS GRAHAM/ROSALIE	Angela Crowe

The production was updated to 1947.

> Alan Stanford's new production at the Gate takes what, to this reviewer, is a daringly original line in apparently trying to separate the two threads by giving the occupants of society an air of slightly over-the-top caricature while the protagonists of the melodrama are invested with an almost over-the-top air of wilful innocence. So marked are the differences of characterisation between the two groups that it is almost possible to detect the slide of certain characters from wickedness to innocence, or vice versa, by changes in their acting style.
>
> David Nowlan *Irish Times*

> Hilary Reynolds's Lady Windermere and Olwen Fouere's Mrs Erlynne bring to their roles a controlled vulnerability and physicality, infusing their characters' inner lives with a depth and complexity which belie the ease of their performances.
>
> Jocelyn Clarke *Sunday Tribune*

1997 Royal Exchange, Manchester.

Director	Braham Murray
Designer	Simon Higlett

LORD WINDERMERE	Richard Hansell
LORD DARLINGTON	Simon Robson
LORD AUGUSTUS	James Saxon
MR DUMBY	Ian Pepperell
CECIL GRAHAM	Nick Caldecott
MR HOPPER	Damian Warren
PARKER	Gerry Hinks
LADY WINDERMERE	Rebecca Johnson
THE DUCHESS OF BERWICK	Rosalind Knight
LADY AGATHA	Sarah Kirkman
LADY PLYMDALE	Claire Porter
LADY STUTFIELD	Clare Bloomer
LADY JEDBURGH	Marie Collett

MRS COWPER-COWPER	Sarah Quinn
MRS ERLYNNE	Gabrielle Drake
ROSALIE	Sarah Quinn

The production transferred to the Theatre Royal, Haymarket, London, with the following changes of cast:

LORD AUGUSTUS	Malcolm Rennie
MR DUMBY	Gerard Logan
CECIL GRAHAM	Jonathan Weir
MR HOPPER	Joseph Morton

Simon Robson played Lord Darlington for the true friend Wilde had always wanted him to be. But why had the designer given him Moorish apartments, which immediately hinted at all sorts of perversions? And what were all those bachelor dandies doing, lolling about on the cushions on the floor? (Since this was the Naughty Nineties, they were swapping epigrams.)

Lord Windermere was cast much younger than usual. Mrs Erlynne (elegant Gabrielle Drake), hiding her true feelings, and putting manners before morals, punctuated his priggish and rude lecture with tart irony.

Rebecca Johnson's Lady Windermere was touchingly virtuous and gullible. The Duchess of Berwick is not that witty, but Rosalind Knight, a stylish trouble-maker dressed in red velvet, acted her as if she were, and delivered her lines with a hard, cutting edge.

The production was better in the round in Manchester than it was behind a proscenium arch in London. The ball scene was far too static. Malcolm Rennie's Lord Augustus was very cheap caricature and grossly inferior to James Saxon, who had been excellent butt for Nick Caldecott's camp Graham and Ian Pepperell's camp Dumby. Designer Simon Higlett's sloping floor gave Wilde a completely new slant.

> Rosalind Knight provides the most delicious feast of comic acting now available in London as an elderly Duchess whose fountain of malice never runs dry.
>
> Nicholas de Jongh *Evening Standard*

1997 Chichester Festival Theatre, Sussex.

Director	Richard Cottrell
LORD WINDERMERE	Tim Wallers
LORD DARLINGTON	David Rintoul
LORD AUGUSTUS	John McCallum
MR DUMBY	John Turnbull
CECIL GRAHAM	James Wallace
MR HOPPER	Daniel O'Grady
PARKER	Stanley Page
LADY WINDERMERE	Siri O'Neal
THE DUCHESS OF BERWICK	Googie Withers
LADY AGATHA	Laura Bazeley
LADY PLYMDALE	Belinda Ross
LADY STUTFIELD	Mary Chater
LADY JEDBURGH	Mollie Savile
MRS COWPER-COWPER	Amanda Waldy
MRS ERLYNNE	Stephanie Beacham
ROSALIE	Sasha Waddell
MISS GRAHAM	Julia Rounthwaite
SIR JAMES ROYSTON	Peter Yapp
GUY BERKELEY	Paul Kelly
LORD PAISLEY	Simon Coxon
LADY PAISLEY	Sasha Waddell
FOOTMAN	Simon Coxon

The set was absurdly opulent. The acting was shallow and histrionic. Tim Wallers and Siri O'Neal, cast as the Windermeres, did a lot of shouting. Googie Withers was insecure as the Duchess of Berwick. John McCallum was dull as Lord Augustus. There is more to Mrs Erlynne than cleavage; though you would never have guessed this from Stephanie Beacham's hard-boiled performance which emphasised all the worst melodrama, failed to deliver the wit, and missed the pathos completely.

> She [Googie Withers] sails through the production like the Queen Mother celebrating her 206th birthday, all bosom, feathers, and parasol, wrapping scandal up in a blanket like a Victorian agony aunt. If only she could have stifled the needless excesses of this baroque melodrama.
>
> James Christopher *The Times*

1998 Shaw Festival, Niagara-on-the-Lake, Canada.

Director	Christopher Newton
LORD WINDERMERE	Ben Carlson
LORD DARLINGTON	Gordon Rand
LORD AUGUSTUS	Barry MacGregor
MR DUMBY	Neil Barclay
CECIL GRAHAM	Mike Shara
MR HOPPER	Ian Leung
MR RUFFORD	Patrick R Brown
MR ARTHUR BOWDEN	Brian Elliott
LORD PAISLEY	Neil Foster
SIR JAMES ROYSTON	Randy Ganne
PARKER	Richard Farrell
LADY WINDERMERE	Colombe Demers
DUCHESS OF BERWICK	Patricia Hamilton
LADY AGATHA	Shauna Black
LADY PLYMDALE	Karen Wood
LADY STUTFIELD	Robin Hutton
LADY JEDBURGH	Mary Haney
MRS COWPER-COWPER	Patty Jamieson
MRS ERLYNNE	Fiona Reid
ROSALIE	Stephanie McNamara
MRS ARTHUR BOWDEN	Stephanie McNamara
MRS PAISLEY	Gabrielle Jones

North American audiences do not know *Lady Windermere's Fan* and presume, because it is by Wilde, that it is going to be as funny as *The Importance of Being Earnest*. They roared with laughter when Mrs Erlynne sacrificed her honour to save her daughter from disgrace. Christopher Newton's production was extremely handsome and the ball scene, with couples waltzing on the revolving stage, had the sort of glamour you might expect to find in a Broadway musical.

Normally actresses are cast as Mrs Erlynne because they look like 'an edition de luxe of a wicked French novel meant specially for the English market.' These actresses can usually be relied on to do the tart wit but are not so good with those scenes which call for a mother's feelings. Fiona Reid, who, strangely, acted Mrs Erlynne for a silly woman, did the mother part best.

Ben Carlson was a bit young to be calling Lady Windermere 'child'. The best acting was by Mike Shara and Neil Barclay who handled Wilde's epigrams with polished ease.

Salomé (1892)

A Tragedy in One Act

'To my friend Lord Alfred Bruce Douglas the translator of my play'

Characters:

HEROD ANTIPAS, Tetrarch of Judaea
JOKANAAN, The Prophet
THE YOUNG SYRIAN, Captain of the Guard
TIGELLINUS, A Young Roman
A CAPPADOCIAN
FIRST SOLDIER
SECOND SOLDIER
THE PAGE OF HERODIAS
JEWS, NAZARENES, ETC.
A SLAVE
NAAMAN, The Executioner
HERODIAS, Wife of the Tetrarch
SALOMÉ, Daughter of Herodias
THE SLAVES OF SALOMÉ
FIRST GREEK

The scene of the play:
A great terrace in the Palace of Herod, set above the banqueting hall.

The Plot

Herod lusts after Salomé. Salomé lusts after Jokanaan. The Young Syrian lusts after Salomé. The young Page lusts after the Young

Syrian, who commits suicide when his love for Salomé is not reciprocated. Salomé wants to touch Jokanaan's body and kiss his lips, but he rejects her. Herod offers Salomé anything she wants if she will dance for him. She asks for Jokanaan's head. He offers her instead half his kingdom, the largest emerald in the world, fifty peacocks, all his jewellery, the mantle of the high priest, and the veil of the sanctuary. She still wants Jokanaan's head. When she gets the head, Herod is so appalled by the slobbering exhibition she makes of herself, that he orders his soldiers to kill her. She is crushed beneath their shields.

The Characters

SALOMÉ has no name in the Bible. She is merely the daughter of Herodias. The Dance of the Seven Veils is Wilde's invention. She claims she was a virgin until she met Jokanaan. Likened to a dove and a silver flower, she is neither wanton nor a harlot, but a simple girl who wanted everything on a plate.

JOKANAAN (John the Baptist) is a chaste young man. 'Back, daughter of Sodom! Touch me not.' His body is white as snow and as thin as an ivory statue. 'It is above all his eyes that are terrible. They are like black holes burned by torches in a Tyrian tapestry.'

HEROD, not Salomé, is the leading role. The Tetrarch is sensual, vain, superstitious, sexually frustrated, incestuous, cruel, mad, and ridiculous. According to his wife, his father was a camel driver and a robber. He doesn't mind Christ cleansing lepers, healing the blind and changing water into wine, but draws the line at his bringing back the dead. Herod has a magnificent aria when he pleads with Salomé to ask for anything but the head of Jokanaan and offers her half his kingdom, the largest emerald in the world, fifty peacocks, jewels, topazes, opals, onyxes, moonstones, and the veil of the temple.

HERODIAS is Herod's wife. 'I do not believe in miracles,' she says. 'I have seen too many.'

THE YOUNG SYRIAN is in love with Salomé: 'She is like a dove that has strayed,' he sighs. 'She is like a narcissus trembling in the wind.' When he observes Salomé kissing Jokanaan on the mouth he kills himself. The Page of Herodias, his young boy friend, is heartbroken.

THE MOON, pale, cold, chaste, naked, changes colour (from white to red to black) and is the premonition of doom and disaster. The Moon – 'You must not look at the moon!' – is likened to a woman rising from a tomb, to a little princess who wears a veil, a woman who is dead, a mad woman, a piece of money, a little silver flower, a dead woman who is seeking to cover herself with a shroud, and a dead woman who is seeking everywhere for lovers. An exasperated Herodias says the moon is the moon and that is all. Wilde said the Moon was the leading character.

Salomé was written in French in the autumn of 1890. The text, based on the Gospels of Matthew and Mark, owed also something to *The Song of Songs*, and a great deal to Wilde's interest in such writers and painters as Flaubert (*Hérodias*, 1876), Gustave Moreau (*Salomé Dansant*, exhibited 1876), Massenet (*Hérodiade*, 1881), Huysmans (*À Rebours*, 1884), Mallarmé (*Hérodiade*, 1891), Maurice Maeterlinck (*La Princesse Maleine*, 1889) and the Symbolist movement.

Wilde was obsessed with Salomé. 'Do you think she would be better naked?' he asked Gomez Carillo, a Guatemalan diplomat. 'Yes, totally naked, but draped with heavy necklaces made of jewels of every colour, warm with the fervour of her amber flesh? . . . Her lust must needs be infinite, and her perversity without limits. Her pearls must expire on her flesh.'

Wilde read the play to Sarah Bernhardt, who declared: 'Mais c'est héraldique; on dirait une fresque . . . Le mot doit tomber comme une perle sur un disque de cristal; pas de mouvements rapides, des gestes stylisés.' She said she would perform it in London.

Wilde made it clear, in a letter to *The Times*, that though he was delighted that 'the greatest tragic actress of any stage now living' should wish to produce and appear in his play, it had not been written for her. 'I have never written a play for any actor or actress, nor shall I ever do so. Such work is for the artisan in literature, not for the artist.'

Bernhardt was in the middle of rehearsals in 1892 when the Lord Chamberlain, Edward F Smyth Pigott (described by Bernard Shaw as 'a walking compendium of vulgar insular prejudice') refused the play a licence on the ground that biblical characters were not allowed on the English stage.

Wilde thought it ridiculous that the Lord Chamberlain could forbid plays like Massenet's *Hérodiade*, Gounod's *La Reine de Saba* and Rubinstein's *Judas Maccabaeus* and yet permit Victorien Sardou and Emile de Najac's explicit comedy about adultery, *Divorçons*. In an interview with *Le Gaulois*, he said he would renounce his British citizenship and become a Frenchman.

William Archer, drama critic of the *World* and advocate for the abolition of censorship, wrote a letter to the *Pall Mall Gazette* which appeared in the issue of 1 July 1892:

> Ever since Mr Oscar Wilde told me a fortnight ago, that his *Salomé* had been accepted by Madame Sarah Bernhardt, I have been looking forward, with a certain malign glee, to the inevitable suppression of the play by the Great Irresponsible. Quaint as have been the exploits of that gentleman and his predecessors in the past, the record of Censorship presents nothing quainter than the present conjuncture. A serious work of art, accepted, studied, and rehearsed by the greatest actress of our time, is peremptorily suppressed, at the very moment when the personality of its author is being held up to ridicule, night after night, on the public stage, with the full sanction and approval of statutory Infallibility. But it is surely unworthy of Mr Wilde's lineage to turn tail and run away from a petty tyranny which lives upon the disunion and apathy of English dramatic authors.

The play Archer was referring to was *The Poet and the Puppets* by Charles Brookfield and J M Glover, a travesty of *Lady Windermere's Fan*, which was playing at the Comedy Theatre in 1892.

In a letter to his brother, Will, Wilde complained that not a single actor had protested ('not even Irving, who is always prating about the Art of the Actor') and proclaimed that all the actors and drama critics, with the exception of Archer, were Philistines.

The play was published in French in Paris in February 1893 and received the following reviews:

> It is an arrangement in blood and ferocity, morbid, bizarre, repulsive, and very offensive in its adaptation of scriptural phraseology to situations the reverse of sacred. It is not ill-suited to some of Mme Bernhardt's dramatic genius, and it is vigorously written in some parts.
>
> *The Times*

Maeterlinck paints in washes of water-colour. Mr Wilde attains to depth and brilliancy in oils. *Salomé* has all the qualities of a great historical picture, pedantry and conventionality excepted.

William Archer *White and Black*

Salomé, published in English by John Lane in February 1894, was translated by Lord Alfred Douglas, and was dedicated to him. Douglas was not pleased when it dawned on him 'that the difference between the dedication of *Salomé* to me by the author and the appearance of my name on the title-page is the difference between a tribute of admiration from an artist and a receipt from a tradesman.'

I suppose the play is unhealthy, morbid, unwholesome, and un-English, *ça va sans dire*. It is certainly un-English, because it is written in French, and therefore unwholesome to the average Englishman, who can't digest French. It is probably morbid and unhealthy, for there is no representation of quiet domestic life, nobody slaps anybody else on the back all through the play, and there is not a single reference to roast beef from one end of the dialogue to the other, and though it is true there is a reference to Christianity, there is no muscular Christianity. Anyone, therefore, who suffers from that most appalling and widespread of diseases which takes the form of a morbid desire for health had better avoid and flee from *Salomé*, or they will get a shock that will take months of daily papers and Charles Kingsley's novels to counteract. But the less violently and aggressively healthy, those who are healthy to live and do not live to be healthy, will find in Mr Oscar Wilde's tragedy the beauty of a perfect work of art, a joy for ever, ambrosia to feed their souls with honey of sweet-bitter thoughts.

Lord Alfred Douglas *The Spirit Lamp*

Wilde didn't care for either Douglas's translation or Aubrey Beardsley's illustrations. He objected to the artwork because much of it – *The Woman in the Moon*, *A Platonic Lament*, *Eyes of Herod*, *Enter Herodias* – included grotesque and obscene caricatures of himself.

'They are cruel and evil,' he said, 'and so like dear Aubrey, who has a face like a silver hatchet, with grass-green hair . . . They are all too Japanese, while my play is Byzantine. My Herod is like the Herod of Gustave Moreau – wrapped in jewels and sorrows. My

Salomé is mystic, the sister of Salammbô, a Sainte Thérèse who worships the moon; dear Aubrey's designs are like naughty scribbles a precocious schoolboy makes on the margins of his copybook.'

Bernhardt promised to produce the play at her own theatre but she didn't keep her promise and the world premiere took place under another management.

1896 11 February Premiere: Théâtre de l'Œuvre, Paris.

Director	Aurélien Lugné-Poë
HEROD	Aurélien Lugné-Poë
JOKANAAN	Max Barbier
YOUNG SYRIAN	M Lerey
HERODIAS	Gina Barbieri
SALOMÉ	Lina Munte

Despite the fact that *Salomé* was to be performed in a private theatre, the possibilities of a ban still remained. Lugné-Poë, therefore, did not make an announcement that he was going to stage Oscar Wilde's play until the very last moment.

An actress was cast as the Page so that, hopefully, nobody would be able to complain that the Page's affection for the Young Syrian was homosexual.

Rehearsals did not go smoothly. Jokanaan's property head (which had been borrowed from a waxworks museum) was smashed. A dress caught fire and it looked, for a moment, as if the fire-brigade (rather than the censor) would close the theatre.

The actual theatre programme was designed by Toulouse-Lautrec and included his portrait of Wilde which has the Thames and Big Ben in the background.

The reviews were mixed. There were those who thought the applause on the first night had been for the playwright rather than for the play.

1901 Breslau. German premiere in a translation by Dr Kisper.

1902 Kleines Theater, Berlin.

Translator	Hedwig Lachmann
Director	Max Reinhardt
	Friedrich Kayssler
Designers	Lovis Corinth
	Max Kruse
Music	Max Marschalk
	Friedrich Bermann
HEROD	Emanuel Reicher
JOKANAAN	Friedrich Kayssler
HERODIAS	Luise Dumont
SALOMÉ	Gertrud Eysoldt

The play was acted in a double bill with *Bunbury (The Importance of Being Earnest)*. The performances were private. Richard Strauss, the composer, was one of the people who came to see it. Such was the success of the production, it was revived the following year for the general public with the following cast:

1903 Neues Theater, Berlin.

HEROD	Emanuel Reicher/Ludwig Wullner
JOKANAAN	Max Eisfeldt
HERODIAS	Luise Dumont/Hedwig Wangel/ Tilla Durieux
SALOMÉ	Gertrud Eysoldt/Tilla Durieux

The play was a major turning point in Max Reinhardt's career. The production, spectacular in setting, costume and lighting, ran for 200 performances.

1903 Munich. Lili Marberg acted Salomé with great success. It was Robert Ross, Oscar's friend, who said that *Salomé* made Oscar Wilde a household name wherever English was not spoken. English and American critics have never much cared for the play, generally dismissing it as 'paste jewellery', 'embroidered Oriental junk' and kitsch.

1905 English premiere: Bijou Theatre, Bayswater, London.

Director	Florence Farr
HEROD	Robert Farquharson
JOKANAAN	Vincent Nello
HERODIAS	Louise Salom
SALOMÉ	Millicent Murby

There were two private performances by the New Stage Club which were attended by a fashionable audience who received the play, said *The Times*, 'with applause, but with no special rapture.'

> The average sight-seer might term it extraordinary, if he did not understand it, and ridiculous, if he did. The Philistine would dismiss it as rot. For ourselves we are inclined to agree in no small measure with the Philistine. It was a singular combination of puerility and putrescence. Its purple passages struck one, at all events as they were delivered last night, as turgid and extravagant . . . *Salomé* is clearly a play to be read in the study – not to be seen on the boards.
>
> *Daily Telegraph*

> Yesterday's performance left much to be desired. It was taken in much too slow time, a monotonous chant was sometimes heard, and the stage was on occasions so dark that the action was obscure. Whatever merits the play can claim are literary rather than dramatic, and though strong situations seem more than once near at hand they are carefully shunned. *Salomé* is only in one act, but its language is prolix.
>
> *The Times*

> The actress at the Bijou was just a young lady – a clever young lady, a conscientious and promising young lady, whose career I shall watch with interest, but who never for one moment last Wednesday began to become *Salomé* or began to cease to be a young lady . . . Mr Farquharson's performance was especially laudable in that he never let his minute expression of Herod's self in all its hideousness interfere with his musical delivery of the elaborate cadences. He performed two tasks in perfect fusion. Passages that might have been merely beautiful he made

> dramatically hideous, without loss of their beauty. Passages that might have been merely hideous he made beautiful, without loss of their appropriateness. Of course he played all the other people off the stage, figuratively. Literally, they remained there, I regret to say.
>
> Max Beerbohm *Saturday Review*

1905 American premiere: Berkeley Lyceum, New York.

The play was acted by the Progressive Stage Society, an avant-garde group of volunteer actors.

> Oscar Wilde was a person of slender talent and of no lasting importance, and, considering the baleful associations that hang about his name, it would be 'progressing' in the right direction to allow his works and all memory of him to pass at once into oblivion that surely awaits him.
>
> William Winter *New York Daily Tribune*

1905 Premiere of Richard Strauss's opera at Royal Opera House, Dresden.

Libretto	Hedwig Lachmann
Director	Wilhelm Wirk
Conductor	Ernest von Schuch
HEROD	Carl Burrian
JOKANAAN	Carl Perron
SALOMÉ	Marie Wittich

> The recurring phrases of *Salomé* that bind it together like a piece of music with recurring motifs, are, and were to me, the artistic equivalent of the refrains of the old ballads.
>
> Oscar Wilde *De Profundis*

Richard Strauss's Salomé (unlike Wilde's Salomé) was no virgin. Marie Wittich, a Wagnerian soprano, appalled by what she was expected to do on stage, threatened to go on strike. 'I won't do it,' she said. 'I'm a respectable married woman.' A dancer, Bianca Froehlich, danced in her stead.

Strauss insisted on two things: one, that the dance should be serious, decent, aristocratic and stylish; and, two, that the Page should be played by a girl.

On the first night there were thirty-eight curtain-calls. The critics described the opera as immoral and cacophonous. Many of them thought it was degrading for composer and audience alike. Some thought it was the ideal entertainment for homosexuals, lesbians, masochists and sadists.

Arnold Bax in his autobiography, *Farewell My Youth* (Longman, 1943), said that Carl Burrian 'created a quite horrifying Herod, slobbering with lust, and apparently almost decomposing before our disgusted but fascinated eyes.'

Within the next two years Strauss's *Salomé* would be performed in fifty other opera houses.

1906 Astor, New York.

HEROD	William McVay
HERODIAS	Huida Englund
SALOMÉ	Mercedes Leigh

The play was dismissed as 'bloodily degenerate' by the *Sun* and 'decadent stuff, unworthy of notice' by the *Tribune*.

> The dance was not a dance, but a removal of veils – the seven veils of the text – and some posturing. Her [Mercedes Leigh's] voice was often too weak. In the earlier scenes she was not the Princess but too much the common flirt. She improved, however, as the act proceeded.
>
> *New York Times*

1906 Richard Strauss conducted the Austrian premiere of his opera in Graz, where it was seen by Giacomo Puccini, Gustav Mahler, and Adolf Hitler. He also conducted the Italian premiere in Turin. Arturo Toscanini conducted the opera at La Scala in Milan. The Kaiser allowed *Salomé* to be produced in Berlin but only on the condition that the Star of Bethlehem appeared on the backcloth during the closing scene.

1906 King's Hall, Covent Garden, London.

Director	C S Ricketts
Costumes	C S Ricketts
HEROD	Robert Farquharson
JOKAANAN	Lewis Casson
YOUNG SYRIAN	Orlando Barnett
HERODIAS	Florence Farr
SALOMÉ	Miss Darragh

The play was performed by the Literary Theatre Club in a double bill with *A Florentine Tragedy*. Charles Ricketts invited Constance Collier and Mrs Patrick Campbell to play Salomé. Both of them turned down the role. The press boycotted the performance. *The Times* returned their tickets. No illustrated paper would publicise the photographs.

The first-night audience included George Bernard Shaw, W B Yeats, Thomas Hardy, George Moore, Max Beerbohm, Arthur Symons, Eleanora Duse and Roger Fry. Fry said that he had never seen anything so beautiful on the stage.

Ricketts and Wilde had had endless discussions about the décor and what Salomé should wear. Ricketts thought she should be in black 'like the night'. Wilde wanted her in green 'like a curious poisonous lizard'. Ricketts wanted the moonlight to fall upon the ground, the source not being seen. Wilde wanted 'some strange dim pattern in the sky'.

> The most notable feature of the production of *Salomé* was the costumes designed by Mr C S Ricketts – a marvellous harmony of blue and green and silver. Here praise must end. The stage was left ridiculously bare, and never for a moment produced the illusion of the terrace outside Herod's banqueting hall. Not even the cistern out of which the Prophet rises was discoverable – *Hamlet* without the Prince of Denmark. And the actors! Without being too exigent, I cannot but suggest that before attempting such a play they ought to have been sent by special train to Berlin. Even then Miss Darragh would have been an impossible Salomé. She lacked nearly everything required by this complex character. The Dance of the Seven Veils was executed with all the propriety of a British governess. Mr Robert Farquharson, whose Herod delighted us

last year, has now elaborated it to the verge of caricature. He emphasises far too much the neuropathic element, and revels in the repulsive symptoms of incipient softening of the brain.

Max Meyerfeld

In the role of Salomé Miss Darragh seemed to be overweighted with the difficulties of the character which would tax the resources of the finest actress; but the earnestness infused into her delivery of the lines made the representation remarkably striking and impressive. Mr Robert Farquharson lined in deep colours the imbecility of Herod, and quite succeeded in creating an impression of loathing for the unscrupulous monarch. Mr Lewis Casson was a dignified John the Baptist, and embellished the character with many elocutionary graces which were invaluable in the part.

Era

1906 Dance: *The Vision of Salomé*

Vienna. Maud Allan danced to music by Marcel Rémy. Allan and Rémy had been to see the Max Reinhardt production in Berlin. Frederick Ponsonby in his autobiography, *Recollection of Three Reigns* (Eyre & Spottiswoode, 1951), said that 'Her dance of Salomé with the head of John the Baptist was really most dramatic, and although I can't say that she wore many clothes, there was nothing in the least indecent about her performance.'

1907 Metropolitan Opera, New York.
American premiere of Richard Strauss's opera.

Conductor	Alfred Hertz
Director	Anton Schertel
HEROD	Carl Burrian
JOKANAAN	Anton Van Rooy
HERODIAS	Marion Weed
SALOMÉ	Olive Fremstad

Strauss's opera opened on 22 January and closed the same day. The dancing and especially the kissing of the severed head caused deep offence. Some members of the audience left the theatre in the most ostentatious manner.

One person wrote to the *New York Times* to say he 'had never heard, read or imagined such detailed and explicit expressions of the most horrible, disgusting, revolting and unmentionable features of degeneracy.'

H E Krembiel writing in the *New York Herald-Tribune*, found it 'abhorrent, bestial and loathsome'. It was obvious to him that 'Decent people did not want to have the house polluted with the stench with which Oscar Wilde's play had filled the nostrils of humanity.'

J Pierrepont Morgan's daughter persuaded her father to use his influence to have the opera taken off. There were no further performances at the Met until 1934.

1907 Dance: *La Tragédie de Salomé*

Paris. Lois Fuller (who had already been seen as Salomé in four tableaux at the Comédie-Parisienne in 1895) danced to music by Florent Schmitt. Her costume of 4,500 peacock feathers was based on Aubrey Beardsley's drawing. The dance was based on a poem by Robert d'Humières.

1907 Irving Place Theatre, New York.

HEROD	Friedrich Holthaus
JOKANAAN	Carl Machold
HERODIAS	Marie Immisch
SALOMÉ	Hedwig von Osterman

The play was performed in German. The staging was elaborate and the theatre was crowded.

1908 Dance: *The Vision of Salomé*

Maud Allan danced at the Palace Theatre, London. 'There is,' said *The Times*, no extravagance and sensationalism about Miss Allan's dancing.'

Phyllis Dare sang a song at Allan's expense in *The Dairymaids*, a farcical musical play by A M Thompson and Robert Courtneidge. Dare was attended by four little girls dressed as Salomé, each with her own decapitated head.

1908 American film.
Alternative title: *The Dance of the Seven Veils*.

Director	J Stuart Blackton
CAST	Maurice Costello Ralph Ince Florence Lawrence

1908 Vera Komissarzhevkaya's Theatre, St Petersburg.

Director	Nikolai Evreinov
Designer	Nikolai Kalmakov
HEROD	A Arkad'ev
JOKAANAN	A Zakushnyak
SALOMÉ	N Volkhova

The Russian production, explicitly erotic, was banned by the Holy Synod just as it was about to open.

1908 St Petersburg.
A ballet by Mikhail Fokine.

Music	Alexander Glazunov
Décor	Leon Bakst
SALOMÉ	Ida Rubinstein

Since the censor and the Church did not allow either Wilde's text or the severed head, all Ida Rubinstein could do was dance.

1909 St Petersburg. Nikolai Evreinov's production was banned for a second time.

1909 Berlin Deutches Theater, New York.

HEROD	Ludwig Wuellner
JOKANAAN	Ferdinand Stell
HERODIAS	Juliette Barthelmy
SALOMÉ	Hedwig Reicher

Miss Reicher has the sumptuous physical charm, beauty of face and grace of figure, and she plays with excellent understanding . . . On the stage Dr Wuellner looks nearly 7 feet in height and in the swarthy makeup he presents a truly sinister appearance.

New York Times

1910 British film.

1910 Paris premiere of Antoine Mariotte's opera at the Gaîté.

1910 French film.

A magnificent adaptation of the great Biblical tragedy of love, hatred, and passion. A fine Pathé-color drama superbly staged and enacted by a company of Italian artists. Grand settings and elaborate costumes characterize the play.

Bioscope

1910 Royal Opera House, London.
British premiere of Richard Strauss's opera.

Director	Louis Verande
Conductor	Thomas Beecham

HEROD	Ernst Kraus
PROPHET	Clarence Whitehill
HERODIAS	Ottilie Metzger
NARRABOTH	Maurice D'Oisly
PAGE	Edna Thornton
SALOMÉ	Aino Ackte

A large crowd had gathered on the day the booking opened and the production was sold out in eighty minutes. The management said 'they had never been so hustled, metaphorically speaking.'

Thomas Beecham (conducting an orchestra of 112 instruments) described *Salomé* as 'the most daring and original of modern opera musically, artistically and dramatically.'

The critics described *Salomé* as 'a brilliant fungus sprung from a decaying genius' and 'decadent melodrama gorgeously embroidered with splendid hyperbole'.

The censor had decreed that Jokanaan could only be called The Prophet and that the decapitated head should not be seen. So Salomé sang to an empty tray with a bit of blood on it. The censor had also insisted on cuts in the text in order to make her passion a little more spiritual and a little less carnal. Beecham ignored the cuts, presuming the censor did not speak German and therefore would not notice.

Aino Ackte had been selected by Strauss himself to sing Salomé. Her performance, a *tour de force*, made the rest of the cast seem amateurish; but vocally she was uneven.

Beecham devoted himself almost entirely to the orchestra, giving the singers little help.

> Thus much may be said that, as presented at Covent Garden, it is a stupid travesty of the real thing.
>
> *Globe*

> She [Aino Ackte] looked like an Aubrey Beardsley drawing but she spoiled her effects by monotony.
>
> *Pall Mall Gazette*

1911 Court Theatre, London.

Director	Harcourt Williams
Costumes	C S Ricketts
HEROD	Herbert Grimwood
JOKANAAN	Arthur Wontner
YOUNG SYRIAN	Harcourt Williams
HERODIAS	Edyth Olive
SALOMÉ	Adeline Bourne
PAGE	Eric Maturin

> The performance of *Salomé* at the Court attracted a large audience, mostly women, who came, no doubt, not only to procure themselves an emotion but in the belief that they were assisting at an intellectual entertainment instead of a mere sham . . . For the thinking playgoer and the unthinking such a play as *Salomé* can have no attraction, for it has no great interest either as literature or drama . . . When all is said and done I think we may take it that we have now seen the first and last of *Salomé*.
>
> Modred *Referee*

> The remarkable grip of the play on the European stage, irrespective of the opera, is probably due to the excessive modernity and the tense dramatic opportunity it affords for exhibiting the phenomena of neurosis in different phases . . . Miss Adeline Bourne did not succeed in giving any idea of Wilde's Salomé. Her high-pitched voice often produced discomfort only in passages where it should have been most moving. Her gestures were without significance; her death was equally undignified.
>
> *The Times*

> It is pretentious – morbid – epileptic . . . it was a sorry spectacle, fit only for sexless women and 'pussy cat' men.
>
> Magog *Penny Illustrated Paper*

1911 Mimodrama at Hippodrome Theatre, London.

Author	M Xanrof
Music	Puget
HEROD	M Pascuale
JOKANAAN	M Boldrini
HERODIAS	Madame Deleck
SALOMÉ	Sahary Djeli

The *Illustrated London News* reported that the barely nineteen-year-old Sahary Djeli, 'the rage of women and men throughout France and the continent, had been electrifying crowded audiences at the Hippodrome with her wonderful dancing.'

1911 Dance: *La Tragédie de Salomé*

Paris. Lois Fuller danced to music by Florent Schmitt and choreography by Boris Romanov.

1912 Dance: *The Dance of the Seven Veils*

Rome. Mata Hari danced at a private party given by Prince di San Faustino.

1912 National Theatre, Prague. Olga Grovskaya dressed in white to emphasise Salomé's virginity.

1912 Théâtre du Châtelet, Paris.

Director	Vsevolod Meyerhold
Designer	Leon Bakst
Music	Aleksandr Glazunov
Choreography	Mikhail Fokine
SALOMÉ	Ida Rubinstein
HEROD	Edouard de Max

Ida Rubinstein acted in the play for the first time.

1913 Comedy Theatre, New York.

Mimi Agulin, acting in a condensed version in Italian, was said to have out Saloméd all other Salomés.

> There were many Italians in the audience who understood and appreciated the performance. There were many more Americans who did not begin to sit up and take notice until Salomé discarded her outer clothing and danced the Dance of the Seven Veils. From then on there was no one in the theatre who did not understand the remainder of the entertainment.
>
> *New York Times*

1913 Italian film.

Director	Dr Garriazzo
HERODIAS	Signorina Costamegno
SALOMÉ	Signorina De Labroy

While the whole thing is most artistically done there is nothing in the reels to create sufficient excitement to call out the police – or anybody else. It is a most excellent example of 'celluloid' drama – nothing more. Any effort to create the impression that it is 'indecent' or 'suggestive' would be foolish to press.

Jolo *Variety*

The story is unfolded with lucidity and great dramatic force; the leading parts are in the hands of artists of undoubted ability; the management of vast crowds is effective in the extreme; and the mounting and dressing are on the most sumptuous scale . . . The elaborate production shows evidence of minute attention to every detail of costume and accessory, and its result is a gorgeous picture of oriental splendour. Signorina Costamegno gives a dramatic performance as Herodias and Signorina de Labroy is graceful and seductive as Salomé.

Bioscope

1913 *La Tragédie de Salomé*
A ballet by Boris Ramonov.
Presented by Les Ballets Russes.

Premiere: Théâtre des Champs-Elysées, Paris.

Poem	Robert d'Humières
Music	Florent Schmitt
Designer	Sergei Yurevitch Soudeikine
SALOMÉ	Tamara Karsavina

A note in the programme stated: The scene takes place after the execution of the Baptist. Salomé's dance is at first frantic and insane; then more proud and sorrowful, more remote and ecstatic.

> It is the expression and avowal of her sensual torment and of her atonement through the misery, the very misery of her unassuageable desire.

The ballet, a solo, was specially choreographed for Karsavina. She wore long, false eyelashes, her breasts were almost bare, and a rose was stencilled on her leg. She was attended by eight Negroes and four executioners. The designs (in purple, black and silver) were influenced by Aubrey Beardsley.

Les Ballets Russes brought the production to the Theatre Royal, Drury Lane, London.

> The thing is preposterously absurd, childish, without any redeeming feature, save the exhibition of Mme Karsavina's extraordinarily graceful movement.
>
> *Pall Mall Gazette*

> She came down the steps trailing a gorgeously decorated train behind her. After a few moments' pause she tears off her wraps and appears in a wonderful costume by M. Sergei Soudeikine (who also designed the scenery), and from that moment she gradually works herself up into a frenzy while the music grows more and more animated, and eventually the curtain descends as she is left panting up against the stand staring up at the head above her. Mme Karsavina's dancing was an extraordinary *tour de force*. There was not a touch of exaggeration and not an ugly movement and the way in which longings and regrets were expressed by purely choreographic means are quite extraordinary.
>
> *The Times*

1916 Russian film directed by Nikandk Turkin.

1917 Maly Theatre, Moscow.

Translator	Konstantin Balmont
Director	Ivan Platon
HEROD	M Lenin
HERODIAS	N Smirnova
SALOMÉ	Olga Grovskaya

1917 Kamernyi Theatre, Moscow.

Translator	Konstantin Balmont
Director	Aleksandr Tairov
Designer	Aleksandra Ekster
Music	Jules Gyutel
HEROD	Ivan Arkadin
JOKANAAN	Nikolai Tseretelli
SALOMÉ	Alisa Koonen

A famous production with Cubist-inspired sets and costumes.

> Now the princess increases the tempo of the dance, pulls a green veil from about her breast, and sinks suddenly to the floor. Slowly, sinuously, she rises again and her whole body loses itself in the dance. Again and again she faces the well, rushing at it with a fury and a swiftness that lash the beads of her skirt against its sides, and then turning away from it violently. She tears the fourth veil from her breast and the rhythm becomes quieter and more regular. A slow, free dance of ecstatic joy carries Salomé from one side of the terrace to the other, first towards Herod and then towards the well. The dance becomes wilder and faster . . .
>
> Oliver M Sayler *The Russian Theatre* (London, 1923)

1918 Comedy Theatre, New York.

HEROD	Louis Calvert
JOKANAAN	Walter Hampden
HERODIAS	Helen Westley
SALOMÉ	Marie Yorska

> Mme Yorska exhibited an unfortunate lack of the rudimentary, most indispensable qualifications – the physical. That was not her fault, of course; but there you are. She did not look the part to begin with. She read her lines with the traditional sing-song delivery of the French school, which exaggerated the artificiality without intensifying the verbal richness of Alfred Douglas's really poetic translation.
>
> *New York Post*

The play is still, of course, a presentiment in poetic guise of extreme moral degeneracy, and most people will prefer to give it a wide berth . . . the figure of Herod especially, thanks to the ripe and vigorously human art of Louis Calvert, stood forth as one of the most memorable creations of modern drama.

New York Times

1918 American film.

Director	J Gordon Edwards
HEROD	G Raymond Nye
JOKANAAN	Albert Roscoe
HERODIAS	Genevieve Blinn
SALOMÉ	Theda Bara

Miss Bara is in her element as the arch vampire who finds little or no difficulty in luring every male to destruction that strikes her fancy . . . The scarcity of her attire, to aid to the allurement, was artistically handled making it most fascinating and devoid of vulgarity.

Jolo *Variety*

Even Oscar Wilde's conception of the Princess does not achieve the complete heartlessness and abandoned devilry of the heroine of this film. Theda Bara succeeds, however, in making the character convincing and her performance is a thoroughly effective piece of work, despite her inclination for rather prolonged poses. She receives adequate support from G Raymond Nye, who makes a virile and dignified Herod; Herbert Hayes as the impassioned Selanus whose suicide suggests the death of the Young Syrian in Wilde's drama; and Albert Roscoe as the prophet, who should surely have been bearded.

Bioscope

1918 Court Theatre, London.

Director	Alix Grein
HEROD	George Relph
JOKANAAN	Ernest Milton
YOUNG SYRIAN	Rayson Cousens
HERODIAS	Alix Grein
SALOMÉ	Maud Allan

The production was originally going to open at the Kensington Theatre, but the manager cancelled the performance when the Lord Chamberlain refused to give the play a licence. The performance at the Court Theatre was private and open only to members of the Independent Theatre.

Alix Grein, speaking from the stage, said that Wilde's work was not impure. The *Stage* disagreed, finding it 'a very impure work, impure in theme, impure in atmosphere and charged with sickly voluptuousness.'

Noel Pemberton Billing, MP, attacked Maud Allan's performance, which led to a case of libel, which escalated into a full-blown trial. Pemberton Billing believed that one of the reasons the British were not winning the war was because of the wholesale corruption of the nation. He said the Germans had compiled a dossier of 47,000 people who had been corrupted.

> This kind of stuff has no relation to art. It is animalism, or worse; for animals have their decencies. As a study in decadent expression and also from the personal point of view as a human document, *Salomé* is interesting in the library, but it is not fitted for stage representation . . . *Salomé* is little more than a mass of luscious verbiage with the adjective doing most of the work . . . In the dance Miss Maud Allan was naturally in her element, for she is mistress of expressive and graceful movements. In her acting she seemed to feel more than she could express, and her elocution was very faulty . . . Mr George Relph gave much realistic intensity to the repulsively neurotic Herod . . . Mr Ernest Milton was a picturesque Jokanaan, if rather wanting in the ecstasy of the prophet.
>
> *Stage*

> Miss Maud Allan as Salomé gave an artistic and delicate performance, although occasionally her delivery became a little monotonous. Graceful and interesting as was her 'Dance of the Seven Veils' it did not represent her art at its highest point. Mr George Relph gave a really magnificent impersonation of Herod; and good work was done by Mr Ernest Milton as Jokanaan, Mr Rayson Cousens as the young Syrian, and Miss Alix Grein as Herodias.
>
> *Era*

1919 Charles Ricketts's designs, destined for a production by the Shehiku Company in Tokyo, were impounded by US customs.

1919 Dance: *La Tragédie de Salomé*

Opera House, Paris. Ida Rubinstein danced to choreography by Nicola Guerra and music by Florent Schmitt.

1920 American film: *A Modern Salomé*

Director	Leonce Perret
Screenplay	Leonce Perret
VIRGINIA HASTINGS	Hope Hampton
ROBERT MONTI	Sidney L Mason
JAMES VANDAM	Percy Standing
WALTER GREENE	Arthur Donaldson
HARRY TORRENCE	Wyndham Standing
HELEN TORRENCE	Agnes Ayres

Virginia Hastings sacrificed the life of an innocent man to save her reputation. Later she dreamt she was Salomé and this led her to confess the truth.

1921 Moscow. Premiere of Alexander Gorsky's ballet, to music by Richard Strauss.

1922 Klaw Theatre, New York.
Produced by Players' Forum.

HEROD	Fred Eric
JOKANAAN	Noel Leslie
HERODIAS	Alma Kruger
SALOMÉ	Thelma Harvey

Thelma Harvey, a South Seas dancer, who had been arrested by the police and charged with violence of movement and paucity of clothes, was cast as Salomé. The result was, according to the *Commercial* critic 'disgustingly stupid'.

> It is obviously the desire of this producing company to invite police interference and notoriety for the purpose of making money through the summer. There is neither art, beauty nor intelligence in the production to justify Wilde's *Salomé.*
>
> *Commercial*

1922 Leningrad. Premiere of Leonid Leontiev's ballet, to music by Alexander Glazunov.

1923 Frazee Theatre, New York.
Produced by Ethiopian Art Theatre of Chicago.

Director	Raymond O'Neil
HEROD	Sydney Kirkpatrick
JOKANAAN	Solomon Bruce
YOUNG SYRIAN	Arthur Ray
HERODIAS	Laura Bowman
SALOMÉ	Evelyn Preer

1923 American film.

Director	Charles Bryant
Screenplay	Peter M Winters
Designer	Natasha Rambova
Photography	Charles Van Enger

HEROD	Mitchell Lewis
JOKANAAN	Nigel de Brulier
YOUNG SYRIAN	Earl Schenck
HERODIAS	Rose Dione
SALOMÉ	Nazimova
PAGE	Arthur Jasmine
EXECUTIONER	Frederick Peters
TIGELLINUS	Louis Dumar

It was said that Nazimova, the Russian-born stage and film actress, employed only homosexual actors as a homage to Wilde. She also wrote the script under the pseudonym of Peter M Winters. Her Salomé, a slip of a girl in a slip, was a pouting 1920s Forty-Second-Street vamp, who looked all set to audition for the chorus of a Broadway musical. The Dance of the Seven Veils was in the manner of Lois Fuller enveloped in tulle. Jokanaan, his body white as snow, looked quite demented. Herod was a grotesque, rouged baby. The executioner was played by a giant. The scantily clad, half-naked cast wore extraordinary headdresses and waved palms. The highly stylised black and white and gold sets were based on Aubrey Beardsley's illustrations.

> Other than the facial contortions indulged in by the Madame there is little to the picture, likewise little to her costume, which, however, was all that the law required and a bit more, so the box office won't get any great draw because of any lack of dress on the part of the star . . . *Salomé* as a picture is going to please a few who are Nazimova devotees, a few that like higher art in all its form perversions, and then its box office value will end.
>
> Fred *Variety*

> Try as she will she cannot be seductive . . . She tosses her head impudently, grimaces repeatedly, and rolls her eyes with a vitreous stare. The effect is comic.
>
> *New Republic*

> You have your warning. This is bizarre stuff.
>
> *Photoplay*

1923 American film.

Director	Malcolm Strauss
HEROD	Vincent Coleman
HERODIAS	Christine Winthrop
SALOMÉ	Diana Allen

1924 Cherry Lane Theatre, New York.

HEROD	Albert W Patrick
HERODIAS	Ardelle Mitchell Dabney
SALOMÉ	Hemsley Winfield

The play was acted by an all-black cast.

> What the performance would have been like without the ludicrous performance of Hemsley is hard to conjecture.
>
> *Evening Graphic*

1928 Gate Theatre, Dublin.

Director	Hilton Edwards
HEROD	Hilton Edwards
JOKANAAN	Micheál Mac Liammóir
SALOMÉ	Coralie Carmichael

Years later, addressing the Drama League, Micheál Mac Liammóir said: 'Looking back on the way we were forced to do it, and the cast was the best we could collect, I wonder whether it wouldn't have been better not to have attempted it at all.'

1929 Festival Theatre, Cambridge.

Director	Terence Gray
Music	Constant Lambert
Movement	Hedley Briggs
Choreographer	Ninette de Valois

HEROD	George Coulouris
YOUNG SYRIAN	Hedley Briggs
JOKANAAN	Noel Iliff
HERODIAS	Doria Paston
SALOMÉ	Vivienne Bennett

A note in the programme stated: 'The duty of the modern theatre artist in producing *Salomé* is to present it in its full artificiality as an abstract work of art, which is its essential character and the source of its real value and permanence as a work of theatre.'

1931 The Cambridge Festival production was revived.

HEROD	Robert Morley
JOKANAAN	Noel Iliff
YOUNG SYRIAN	Hedley Briggs
HERODIAS	Alison Pickard
SALOMÉ	Beatrix Lehmann

Beatrix Lehmann was an inhuman and terrifying Salomé. Robert Morley played Herod for comedy. Jokanaan's head was represented by a mask.

1931 Oxford University. The Vice-Chancellor refused the Oxford Repertory Company permission to perform *Salomé.*

1931 Gate Theatre Studio, London.

Director	Peter Godfrey
Choreographer	Ninette de Valois

HEROD	Robert Speaight
JOKANAAN	John Clements
YOUNG SYRIAN	Esmond Knight
HERODIAS	Flora Robson
SALOMÉ	Margaret Rawlings

It is surprising that it does not collapse under a superfluity of metaphor, and indeed it does threaten to collapse at the outset. Mr John Clements's Prophet has not the voice or presence enough to strike the stage with terror, and Miss Rawlings's early approach to him is robbed of its effect . . . The performance seemed to us too suppressed, but within the limits of the producer's deliberate design Mr Speaight gave an impressive performance, and Miss Margaret Rawlings attained to a chill, feline evil very closely in the tradition of the Beardsley drawings.

The Times

1931 Savoy Theatre, London.

Director	Nancy Price
Choreographer	Ninette de Valois
HEROD	Robert Farquharson
JOKANAAN	Lawrence Anderson
YOUNG SYRIAN	Robert Donat
HERODIAS	Nancy Price
SALOMÉ	Joan Maude

The play was performed in a triple bill with Strindberg's *The Stronger* and Wilde's *The Selfish Giant*, the latter set to music by Liza Lehmann. The production transferred to the Duke of York's with the same cast with the exception of Austin Trevor who played Jokanaan.

I think Salomé has been generally misjudged. She was not altogether bad. She was an experienced girl, but liable, through being a daughter of that perverted family, to evil impulses of the blood. There is nothing more dreadful than the sight of a girl who is naturally good, in the grip of an evil passion which she cannot control. That was the character I tried to play. It would have been easy to make Salomé a common vamp – but how crude, and how untrue!

Joan Maude *Evening Standard*

The part of Salomé has been held to be unactable. Wilde stipulated for it 'an actress of troubling beauty and of flute-like voice'. Beauty Joan Maude certainly has – not I am glad to say, of that unearthly Beardsleyesque quality – and her voice, save on occasions, is agreeable. But much more than that is required to express the unholy seething passion that is the essence of the character. For all her sighings for the red mouth of Jokanaan and her grovellings before the gruesome trophy she remained, I am afraid, not the creature of evil perversity, but obviously a nice English girl in Eastern undress.

A E Wilson *Star*

There is nothing voluptuous, sadistic, or passionate in her interpretation of the part. She appears just a nice little High School girl slightly offended because John the Baptist refused to partner her in a tennis tournament.

Illustrated London News

1932 Premiere of Gluck-Sandor's ballet to music by Richard Strauss, with Felicia Sorl as Salomé and Charles Laskey as Jokanaan.

1933 Warsaw. Premiere of Abramovitsch's ballet.

1934 Los Angeles. Premiere of Lester Horton's ballet.

1945 American film: *Salomé Where She Danced*

Director	Charles Lamont
CAST	Yvonne de Carlo Rod Cameron Albert Dekker

The story was updated to the Franco-Prussian War and starred Yvonne de Carlo as a Viennese dancer, who, suspected of being a spy, fled to Arizona.

1946 Cambridge Theatre, London.
Presented by Monte Carlo Ballet.

Choreographer	Serge Lifar
Music	Richard Strauss
SALOMÉ	Olga Adabache
CAST	Lilian Leander Leo Lauer Gerard Mulys

> In *Salomé* he [Serge Lifar] fails to interpret the beauty of Oscar Wilde's poem or Richard Strauss's music. What we saw was angular acrobatics which came dangerously near to farce when the veils were discarded. Surely Salomé did not dance on her toes like a Cossack; nor did she use French circus and cabaret tricks.
>
> *Dancing Times*

1947 Rudolph Steiner Hall, London.

Director	Peter Zadeck
HEROD	Michael Yannis
JOKANAAN	Neville Bewley
HERODIAS	Renee Goddard
SALOMÉ	Bernice Rubens

The Centaur Company presented the play in a double bill with T S Eliot's *Sweeney Agonistes*.

> Requiring as it does the actor's every artifice to save the author from sounding stilted and ridiculous, Wilde's play is at present beyond them.
>
> *The Times*

1949 Richard Strauss's opera at Royal Opera House, London.

Conductor	Karl Rankl
Director	Peter Brook
Designer	Salvador Dali
HEROD	Franz Lechleitner
JOKANAAN	Kenneth Schon
YOUNG SYRIAN	Edgar Evans
HERODIAS	Constance Shacklock
SALOMÉ	Ljuba Welitsch
SECOND SOLDIER	Geraint Evans

> Why should we be afraid of fantasy and imagination, even in an opera house? When the curtain rises, strange vulture-like wings beat slowly under the moon; a giant peacock's tail, opening with

the opening of the dance, suggests the decadent luxury of Herod's kingdom. A handful of such touches over the ninety-six minutes of the opera are designed to lift the audience into the strange Wilde–Strauss world and to point the essential stages of the tragedy. I feel I can safely say that wherever *Salomé* departs from the traditional production, the aim is a musical one. This *Salomé* is designed much more for singers than the traditional production.

Peter Brook

Peter Brook was director of productions at Covent Garden. Salvador Dali provided a background of gigantic peacock feathers, yards and yards of scarlet nylon net, huge spiked shields. Herodias could barely move inside her head-dress and collar. The designs caused an uproar.

Of the production generally it is difficult to speak in the restrained language appropriate to a Sunday paper.

Ernest Newman *Sunday Times*

In sheer vocalism she [Ljuba Welitsch] dwarfed everyone else. *Salomé* is nothing if not a story of horror and lust. To dress it in *Alice in Wonderland* costume is quite out of artistic keeping.

Peter Wildeblood *Daily Mail*

She sings magnificently – almost too much so, for she cannot resist making so many climaxes that they begin to kill each other long before the end.

Eric Blom *Observer*

Peter Brook responded to the critics in a letter to the *Sunday Times*:

An opera producer must work entirely from what he finds in the score. He will be surrounded by good people who will tell him where the door and window have stood for generations, where in fact they *must* stand for evermore. He will be told how it was all done in the past and how it is done in Milan today. He must, of course, listen. But then he must do exactly what the score seems to dictate to him and what he believes to be right.

1950 American film: *Sunset Boulevard*

Director	Billy Wilder
CAST	Gloria Swanson William Holden Eric von Stroheim

Famous silent film star Norma Desmond (Gloria Swanson) engages a young writer (William Holden) to work on a script which will relaunch her screen career. The role she chooses for her comeback is Salomé. The soundtrack quoted from Richard Strauss's opera.

1951 Ballet: *The Dance of Salomé*
Presented by the National Ballet of Canada.

Choreographer	Celia Franca
Music	James Hartley
HEROD	Jury Gottshalk
HERODIAS	Natalie Bulko
SALOMÉ	Celia Franca

The production was originally created for television and then adapted for the stage.

> Celia Franca as Salomé combined the sinuous allure of the seductress with an appeal to the pity of her audience.
>
> *Dance and Dancers*

1952 New Torch Theatre, London.

Director	Ronald Lane
HEROD	Richmond Nairne
JOKANAAN	Kenneth Macleod
YOUNG SYRIAN	Peter Smallwood
HERODIAS	Elizabeth Kentish
SALOMÉ	Prudence Hyman

> Oscar Wilde's *Salomé* seems to have lost, if it ever possessed, the power to horrify, enthral or even hold the attention, its

repetitions, pretentious imagery, and exaggerated theatricality are all the more obvious when Herod is as absurd a figure as Mr Richmond Nairne makes him.

The Times

1953 American film.

Director	William Dieterle
HEROD	Charles Laughton
JOKANAAN	Alan Badel
HERODIAS	Judith Anderson
SALOMÉ	Rita Hayworth
CLAUDIUS	Stewart Granger
PILATE	Basil Sydney

Harry Kleiner's screenplay was an adaptation of Dieterle's *The Good Tidings*. Salomé, virginal and Christian, removed only six veils which was the maximum allowed by the law and the Breen office. The story was given a completely new twist. Salomé danced to *save* John the Baptist's life. She also had a boyfriend, Claudius, and together, at the end of the film, they listened to the Sermon on the Mount.

1954 Richard Strauss's opera on American television.

Director	Kirk Browning
Conductor	Peter Herman Adler
Designer	William Molyneux
HEROD	Andrew McKinley
JOKANAAN	Norman Atkins
HERODIAS	Lorna Sidney
SALOMÉ	Elaine Malbin
PAGE	Carol Jones

Norman Atkins and Carol Jones sang only. Their roles were acted by John Cassavetes and Sal Mineo.

> Miss Malbin gave a high-keyed interpretation. There were times during this taxing session when she was so high-pitched vocally and dramatically that the performance seemed shrill.
>
> Jose *Variety*

1954 Ballet: *Daughter of Herodias*
St Alphonsus Theatre, Chicago. Premiere of Ruth Page's ballet, to music by Richard Strauss.

1954 Q Theatre, Kew, Surrey.
Transferred St Martin's Theatre, London.

Director	Frederick Farley
HEROD	Frank Thring
JOKANAAN	John Springett/John Boyd-Brent
YOUNG SYRIAN	Michael Browning/Julian Sherrier
HERODIAS	Vivienne Bennett
SALOMÉ	Agnes Bernelle
PAGE	Peter Kerr
Cast incl.	John Schlesinger

The production played in a double bill with Jean-Paul Sartre's *The Respectable Prostitute* and was variously described as sickly, vulgar, repulsive, boring, cloying and soporific.

Frank Thring's Herod was as bloated, as voluptuous, and as lascivious, as an Aubrey Beardsley drawing. Thring was at his best when he was failing to make Salomé change her mind 'You're not listening!' he cried. Some critics thought the Australian actor's ferocious performance was 'the lustiest exhibition of old-time ham'.

> A thin line separates Wilde's notorious study in decadence from the ludicrous. This revival contrives somehow to stay on the right side of the line but it is often a near thing.
>
> *The Times*

> Combines the morbid horrors of Grand Guignol with a suggestion of the Folies Bergère in its celebrated Dance of the Seven Veils and with an almost indigestible richness of phrase.
>
> A E Wilson *Star*

> Done in cold blood without music and not very well at that, it must now give even the least sensitive acute discomfort not because of the necrophilia but because of the transparent shabbiness of this gilt and fustian.
>
> Philip Hope Wallace *Manchester Guardian*

1955 American television.

Adaptation	Ellen Violett
Music	Leonard Bernstein
Director	John Stix
HEROD	Leo Genn
JOHN	Martin Landau
CAPTAIN	Mario Alcalde
HERODIAS	Patricia Neal
SALOMÉ	Eartha Kitt

Many viewers complained that the production was shown on a Sunday.

> Miss Kitt, in the title role, probably had the hardest task of all, working out a satisfactory characterisation for Salomé. The outcome left much to be desired. Salomé was in turn portrayed as dreamer, flirt, first wishy-washy, then determined and finally an unrequited lover (although chopping a man's head off for unrequited love is going some). Her portrayal, though competently delivered, lacked consistency and strength.
>
> *Variety*

1956 Davenport Theatre, New York.

Director	Joseph Guzzetti
HEROD	James Coco
JOKANAAN	Dan Hogan
SALOMÉ	Jane Norvell

Salomé played in a double bill with *A Florentine Tragedy* under the title of *An Evening with Oscar Wilde.*

James Coco as a petulant Herod and Jane Norvell as a rather mature Salomé do their best to create vital theatre.

Variety

1964 Stockholm. Premiere of Birgit Cullenberg's ballet, to music by H Rosenberg.

1967 Der Grüne Kakadu Theatre, New York.

Director	J S Vogel
CAST	Bob Beardsley Peter Bumstead Randy Jay Ada McAllister M A Whiteside

1968 Polish television.
Presented by the Wroclaw Pantomime Ensemble.

Director	Andrzej Brzozowski
CAST	Danuta Kisiel Mette Sem Abdresen

1968 Amiens. Premiere of Joseph Lazzini's ballet, to music by Francis Miroglio.

1970 Richard Strauss's opera at the Royal Opera House, London.

Conductor	Georg Solti
Director	August Everdong
Designer	Andrzej Majewski
HEROD	Ragnar Ulfung
JOKANAAN	Peter Glossop
YOUNG SYRIAN	Ermanno Mauro
HERODIAS	Josephine Vesay
SALOMÉ	Grace Bumbury

The moon was represented by a richly embossed metal gong hanging in the sky. The enormous bejewelled rocks, either side of a crumbling staircase, looked liked fossilised reptiles. The cistern was covered by a glass roof which, when raised by huge iron hawsers, looked like a huge spider's web. Ragnar Ulfung's Herod was a young, Bacchus-like tyrant with a soft centre.

> Grace Bumbury sang the title role with unfailing beauty of tone, only revealing in occasional top notes that the part is outside her normal range. She looked the part of the spoiled child to perfection, and her dance combined art and seduction more skilfully than any I have ever seen.
>
> Martin Cropper *The Times*

1970 East Berlin.
A ballet by Jorge Lefèbre.

JOKANAAN	David Holmes
SALOMÉ	Anne Marie

Jorge Lefèbre, in an interview, said his ballet was 'a very sexy pas de deux, expressing Salomé's dream of having this man, of her love of him, and of her hate.'

1970 Glasgow. Premiere of Peter Darrell's ballet for Scottish Theatre Ballet, at Theatre Royal.

1970 French television.

Director	Pierre Koralnik
Choreographer	Maurice Béjart
HEROD	Michel Auclair
JOKANAAN	Jean-Paul Zehnacker
YOUNG SYRIAN	Christian Delangre
HERODIAS	Madeleine Solange
SALOMÉ	Ludmilla Tcherina

One of the settings for Pierre Koralnik's adaptation was Antoni Gaudí's Church of the Holy Family in Barcelona.

> But as the director and adapter Pierre Koralnik laid on the atmosphere thicker and thicker, it became quite visibly grotesque with Herod peering out from what looked like a giant shoe horn and Salomé's dance turning out to be a masturbatory writhe around an ice-rink, neither destructive nor sensuous and extremely ugly.
>
> Philip Purser *Sunday Telegraph*

1971 West German film.

Director	Werner Schroeter
CAST	Mascha Elm
	Rabben
	Ellen Umlauf
	Magdalena Montezuma
	Thomas von Keyserling
	Rene Schenenberger
	Joachim Paede

1971 Antwerp. Premiere of André Leclair's ballet, to music by William Walton, for Ballet of Flanders.

1972 Jean Cocteau Theatre, New York.

Director	Eve Adamson
HEROD	Seamus O'Brien
JOKANAAN	Charles Richetelle
YOUNG SYRIAN	Sydney Shaw
HERODIAS	Jere Jacob
SALOMÉ	Druscilla Harris

The production was prefaced with Mallarmé's poem, *Hérodiade*.

> The temperature in the theatre rises appreciably during the veil dance . . . Mr O'Brien shows the king's human side, his humour, his compassion, his lust, his fear of what Christ just might represent.
>
> Hugh Heckman *Our Town*

1972 Italian film.

Director	Carmelo Bene
HEROD	Carmelo Bene
JOKANAAN	Giovanni Davoli
HERODIAS	Lydia Mancinelli
SALOMÉ	Donyale Luna
Cast incl.	Veruschka

Bene is on the screen (in the part of Herod) practically the whole time. His favourite form of delivery is to slobber the words across dripping lips, not always intelligibly, to repeat them, to have a second voice speak them simultaneously, and to writhe pitifully the while, in close-up before the camera, which lovingly caresses his tonsils, larynx, tongue, and every drop of saliva that those organs produce . . . If you can find Wilde in this orgy, he remains remarkably unscathed, which speaks more for Wilde's strength than for Bene's deference.

Gideon Bachmann *Film Quarterly*

The failure of the film lies in Bene's inability to find a visual correlative for the carefully constructed milieu whereby Wilde justified, in his play, an atmosphere of distortion and delirium.

Jack Babuscio *Gay News*

1972 Helsinki. Premiere of Van Vlaaderer's ballet.

1973 Ballet: *Face of Violence*
Subtitle: *Salomé*

Presented by Cincinnati Ballet.

Choreographer	James Truitte
Music	Lester Horton
HEROD	David Blackburn
JOKANAAN	Michael Bradshaw
HERODIAS	Steffi McFarlane
SALOMÉ	Karen Kuetz

> The most potent imagery is when she dances with the gory bloodstained cloth that covered John the Baptist's head. Clutched between her teeth, pressed against her body, the material assumes its own sinister character. And in the end, Herod uses it to strangle her.
>
> Nancy Mason *Dance Magazine*

1973 Paris. An all-male production.

CAST	Gilbert Beugniot
	Philippe Miglioli
	Pierre Nayaert
	Daniel Abjean
	Sylvestre Laboue
	Louis Tilly

1973 Toronto. Canadian premiere of Wilde's play at New Theatre.

1974 Horizons Theatre Company, New York.

Director	Mark Jessurum-Lobo
HEROD	Robert Hazelton
JOKANAAN	Daniel Snow
HERODIAS	Judith Mayes
SALOMÉ	Marie Amsell

Howard Thompson in the *New York Times* praised Robert Hazelton's 'moving, biting portrayal' which vividly conveyed Herod's lust and guilt.

1974 Ballet on French television.

Choreographer	Maurice Béjart
Music	Jean Prodomides
SALOMÉ	Ludmilla Tcherina

> Sad to say she was covered from neck to ankle in translucent blue tights, which in moments of stress revealed anatomical details . . . The dance itself was sensual, erotic, self-indulgent and partly self-satisfying, and it is not surprising that Herod considered the price too high.
>
> Michael Bayston *Dancing Times*

1975 Fortune Theatre, New York.

Director	Lindsay Kemp
HEROD	David Meyer
JOKANAAN	David Haughton
YOUNG SYRIAN	Tony Maples
HERODIAS	The Incredible Orlando
SALOMÉ	Lindsay Kemp

> Where the production fails most of all, however, aside from too much improvisation, is with Oscar Wilde's text, which when spoken by these mimes, sounds ludicrous if not campy, producing a strangely comic effect when the poetry should soar.
>
> David Sears *Villager*

> Perhaps most trying of all (for the audience) is that there is a complete absence of humour. This *Salomé* is as serious as a stone.
>
> Mel Gussow *New York Times*

1975 *Now She Dances*
Written and directed by Doric Wilson.

Premiere: Tosos Theatre Company, New York.

Now She Dances was a gay guide to *Salomé*. The trial of Jokanaan was equated with the trial of Wilde. The chorus was represented by Victorian servants: a closet-queen butler, a Cockney maid, and an American page boy. Sally Eaton played Salomé.

1975 Richard Strauss's opera at the London Coliseum.

Translation	Tom Hammond
Conductor	Mark Elder
Director	Joachim Herz
Designer	Rudolph Heinrich
HEROD	Emile Belcourt
JOKANAAN	Neil Howlett
YOUNG SYRIAN	Ramon Remedios
HERODIAS	Elizabeth Connell
SALOMÉ	Josephine Barstow

> We want to avoid the notion that Salomé is a perverted, decadent girl. She's brought up in this old-fashioned court but it's not infected her. Out of this contradiction rises the special charm of Salomé. She is very childish and innocent which Josephine Barstow is ideally built for.
>
> Rudolph Heinrich talking to Tom Sutcliffe in the *Guardian*

Strauss's erotic score is even more vulgar than Wilde, rolling in its own narcissism and hysteria. Josephine Barstow produced a thrilling sound. Neil Howlett's voice, ringing from the bowels of a deep prison, was highly dramatic. The surprise, as always, was that for all the sensationalism (and onanism) there was such purity of feeling. Joachim Herz's production needed a choreographer and a dancer.

> Her performance [Josephine Barstow's] is altogether extraordinary. She acts with complete conviction and sings with much exquisite refinement of detail and considerable reserves of power.
>
> Desmond Shaw-Taylor *The Times*

1977 Spanish film, directed by Teo Hernandez. *Ecran* thought that if Wilde had been alive and he had been a film director this was the sort of film he would have made.

1977 Spanish television.

Director	Sergio Schaaf
HEROD	Enrique Casamitjana
JOHN	Enric Majo
HERODIAS	Conchita Bardem
SALOMÉ	Nuria Espert

Terence Moix's adaptation of the Oscar Wilde play is a disappointment. The over-familiar yarn is handled in a static manner, with an over-emphasis on flowery phraseology and a paucity of anything like excitement . . . John the Baptist dangles throughout most of the seg from ropes in the palace, looking like an out-of-work anarchist.

Variety

1977 African Centre Stage, London.

Director	Mark Heath
HEROD	Ivan Fraser
JOKANAAN	Mark Heath
HERODIAS	Gigi Gurpinav
SALOMÉ	Ellen Thomas

An all-black production in which Mark Heath was heard but not seen.

1977 The Round House, London.

Director	Lindsay Kemp
HEROD	Vladek Sheybal
JOKANAAN	David Haughton
HERODIAS	The Incredible Orlando
SALOMÉ	Lindsay Kemp
CAST	Neil Caplan
	Michael Matou

Following its New York premiere in 1975, Lindsay Kemp revived and coniderably revised his production in Sydney before it came to London.

The show, a homo-erotic spectacle, was one for the boys, an all-male mixture of triteness and grotesque theatrics, reeking of morbidity and decaying perversion. Beautiful, sordid, and a bit of a drag, it had all the familiar Kemp trademarks: deafening drum beat, incense, naked flames, naked buttocks, a flying angel, a live snake, ritual sacrifice, and plenty of make-up and sequins. Ironically, the show was at its best *before* Salomé came on.

Once the company started speaking snippets of Wilde in English and French, the whole thing became embarrassingly amateur. The text was heavily cut. It would have been better to have had no Wilde at all.

Kemp was a decidedly middle-aged, small and dumpy Salomé, a Folies Bergère has-been. He gave himself a characteristic slow, very slow, star entrance and, taking his cue from Wilde's line, 'Her little white hands are fluttering like doves that fly to their dovecots,' his hands fluttered. The Dance of the One Veil was a cabaret turn. He was finally crushed to death between mirrored shields.

Vladek Sheybal's weedy Herod played a supporting role not only to Salomé but to the Incredible Orlando cast as a blind, bald, bare-bosomed, black-lipped, macabre and obscene Herodias.

The finale, with the murder of the beautiful, milk-white Jokanaan enveloped in Salomé's cloak, followed by a slow-motion curtain-call, had the right decadent magic.

Salomé was variously described as 'luscious hodge podge,' 'voluptuous mishmash,' and 'gelding the lily'. It ran in tandem with Kemp's sado-masochistic *Flowers*, a patina for Jean Genet.

> There seems a genuine idea here – *Salomé* as a dream of a paranoid homosexual – but it is trapped in a kind of ornate banality.
>
> Alexander Bland *Observer*

> And though Vladek Sheybal is a fine actor, he under-Herods Herod to such an extent that his supposedly intemperate lust for his step-daughter suggests nothing more than that he has got a pebble in his shoe.
>
> Michael Billington *Guardian*

1978 Cirkus Theater, Copenhagen.
A ballet by Flemming Flindt.

Music	Peter Maxwell Davies
Conductor	Janos Furst
HEROD	Flemming Flindt
JOKANAAN	Johnny Eliasen
HERODIAS	Lizzie Rode
SALOMÉ	Vivi Flindt

Salomé's love for Jokanaan was such that she helped him escape from prison. When they were captured she danced naked to save his life. It was Herodias who asked for his head.

The nudity caused an enormous controversy in Denmark and Flemming Flindt was accused of pornography and commercialisation. It was estimated that nearly a million people watched the ballet when it was danced uncut on television.

1978 Spanish film (16 mm, 14 minutes).

Director	Pedro Almodovar
CAST	Isabel Mestres
	Fernando Hilbeck
	Augustin Almodovar

1981 Philippine film.

Director	Laurice Guillen
SALOMÉ	Gina Alajar
CAST	Johnny Delgado
	Dennis Roldan

Salomé murdered her lover. In the manner of *Rashomon*, the film offered three different versions of the same story.

1984 *Salomé oder Auf dem Dach der Welt*
English title: *Salomé or On the Roof of the World*
A play by Fritz Scheidiwy.

Premiere: Studio Wolfbach, Zurich.

Directors	Fritz Scheidiwy Gerhard Fielder
SALOMÉ/DORIAN	Sven-Eric Bechtolf
JOKANAAN/LORD HENRY	Christopher Bantzer
HEROD/BASIL HALLWOOD	Jurgen Cziesla
HERODIAS/SYBIL VANE	Anne-Marie Kuster

Fritz Scheidiwy's play was based on *Salomé* and *The Picture of Dorian Gray* with texts by Flaubert, Baudelaire, Kafka, Borges and others. *Variety* said the result was 'bewildering, often weird, sometimes confusing and, most of the time, quite fascinating.'

1985 City Centre Theatre, New York.
Presented by Ballet of the 20th Century.

Choreography	Maurice Béjart
Music	Riccardo Drigo
SALOMÉ	Patrick Dupond

Patrick Dupond, in an interview in New York, said: 'Seduction is pushed until destruction. It is inspired by Kabuki and Oscar Wilde. I have to act as much as I dance. I'm not a boy or a girl but in between. It's very strange and very tricky.'

> Despite Mr Dupond's unflagging energy, the solo was only intermittently interesting for its gimmicks were not always related to well-developed ideas about human character.
>
> Jack Anderson *New York Times*

1985 French/Italian film.

Director	Claude D'Anna
Screenplay	Claude D'Anna
HEROD	Tomas Milian
JOKANAAN	Fabrizio Bentivoglio
HERODIAS	Pamela Salem
SALOMÉ	Jo Champa
NERVA	Tim Woodward

The production was a science-fiction fantasy and much nearer to *Star Wars* and Strauss than it was to Wilde. 'I am always closer to music than to words,' said Claude D'Anna. 'The opera provided me with an erotic universe of flames, blood, violence.'

Jokanaan was a modern terrorist. Herod descended to the dungeon in a 1930s hotel lift. The soldiers wore Red Army greatcoats. Salomé was a revolutionary. Jokanaan's head was presented to her wrapped in a copy of the *Wall Street Journal.* The dialogue was risible. Victoria Mather in the *Daily Telegraph* dismissed the film as 'pernicious rubbish'.

> The script is based on a play by Oscar Wilde, who might however be at a loss to recognize the convoluted political argument as leaden as *Hansard.*
>
> David Robinson *The Times*

> The inevitable seduction scene occurs in such listless fashion that Salomé's climactic dance of the seven veils looks like an arty aerobic exercise. There's a fair amount of nudity in the pic spiced by simulated sex with a decided whiff of kinkiness. Despite this, *Salomé*'s erotic quotient is slightly to the left of *Song of Bernadette.*
>
> Sege *Variety*

> Oscar Wilde might well have said that you'd need a heart of stone beating beneath your dirty raincoat not to laugh at *Salomé.*
>
> Philip French *Observer*

1986 Canadian television film of Strauss's opera.

Director	Jean-Yves Landry
HEROD	William Ingle
JOKANAAN	Peter Wimberger
HEREDIAS	Janice Myerson
SALOMÉ	Laila Anderson

The opera is pretty racy stuff, with lust, seduction and decapitation. Just the thing to spice up a Sunday afternoon.

Devo *Variety.*

1987 British film: *Salomé's Last Dance*

Director	Ken Russell
Screenplay	Ken Russell
HEROD/ALFRED TAYLOR	Stratford John
JOKANAAN/BOSIE	Douglas Hodge
OSCAR WILDE	Nikolas Grace
HERODIAS/LADY ALICE	Glenda Jackson
SALOMÉ/ROSE	Imogen Millais-Scott

Elgar, Prokofiev, Debussy, Bartok, Delius, Strauss, Isadora Duncan, Mahler, Liszt, Tchaikovsky, Delius, Valentino, etc., etc., Ken Russell had done them all. The only surprise was that he hadn't got round to Oscar Wilde sooner.

His conceit was that on 5 November 1892 Oscar watched a private performance of *Salomé* at a Victorian male brothel run by Alfred Taylor.

Salomé was played by a skivvy. Taylor himself played a very rude and very rouged Herod. Lord Alfred Douglas played Jokanaan. Lady Alice (whoever she might be) played Herodias. The rest of the cast were drawn from clients and courtesans. The soldiers were played by rough trade, the Hassidic Jews by dwarves, and the Nazarenes by raving queens. Russell himself appeared as a photographer. 'If your acting is as grossly indecent as your photographic studies,' said Wilde, 'we are in for an outrageous evening.' He wished him luck: '*Merde!*'

Merde, indeed. It would probably be best to draw a veil over the opening tableau which showed Jokanaan in a cage being whipped by topless women in leather who then rammed a red-hot poker up his backside.

Salomé ate a banana and blew smoke in Herod's face. Herodias got into a trunk with two soldiers, and every time Herod mentioned the wind, Tigellinus farted.

The whole cast watched the final scene. There was a great deal of fidgeting. 'What are you looking for?' asked Herodias. 'A handbag,' replied the young chap behind her. 'A handbag?' she ejaculated in the Edith Evans manner. When Herod said he would give Salomé the veil of the sanctuary, they all exclaimed, 'I say!' in unison.

At the end of her dance, Salomé revealed all, and all included a penis. Finally, she sat astride Jokanaan's decapitated head and masturbated. 'Utterly monstrous . . . it's a vile crime,' said Herod, who was, probably, speaking of Russell's production.

Wilde, who sat on a sofa drinking champagne, didn't bother to watch the whole performance (wise man) and disappeared behind a curtain to have it off with a young actor who was playing the Young Syrian and was covered in gold body paint. He came back in time for the beheading and expressed his delight at having found he had written another comedy.

'Bravo!' he cried. 'What, no curtain-calls? It wasn't as bad as all that.' (Yes, it was.) Next time they did the play, he thought Bosie should play Salomé and he should play the prophet.

The police then arrived (three years too early) to cart Wilde off to prison. Alfred Taylor was also arrested for keeping a disorderly house (and for putting on a dreadful production of *Salomé*?).

Vivian Russell's modern translation of the French original robbed the play of its poetry. The whole film was a rotten send-up from start to finish. The production, shot very quickly and on the cheap (very cheap), was badly staged, badly photographed (endless close-ups), and badly acted. 'I make no excuse for my performance,' said Glenda Jackson in character as Lady Alice.

> It is the kind of film that gives decadence a bad name.
>
> Charles Osborne *Daily Telegraph*

> The execution is execrable, quite the worst film Ken Russell has made in 25 years.
>
> Philip French *Observer*

1987 Shaw Festival, Niagara-on-the-Lake, Canada.

Director	Sky Gilbert
HEROD	Barry MacGregor
JOKANAAN	Dwight Koss
YOUNG SYRIAN	Patric Masurkevitch
HERODIAS	Robin Craig
SALOMÉ	Camille Mitchell

Director Sky Gilbert, in a programme note, wrote: 'We have set the play in parallel reality where sexual idols exist on TV (a reality much like our reality) and dressed Herod in his court in a fashion with which we can all identify. We have modernised some of the language to make the play's message more real to us today.'

The updating meant that Herod was in uniform and Jokanaan in boots and jeans. Salomé stripped to Billie Holiday's 'Not Much To Look At.' Television sets were set up round the stage. She didn't kiss the prophet's decapitated head but his face on the screen.

> *Salomé* has been updated by director Sky Gilbert with results that are tedious and predictable. There may be a more charitable view but I can't find it. The production looks like a cross between a cheap sci-fi movie and *I Claudius.*
>
> Terry Doran *Buffalo News*

> Gilbert's production often has the forced earnestness of a university show and doesn't really catch fire until Barry MacGregor's entrance as a buffoonish King Herod.
>
> Stewart Brown *Hamilton Spectator*

1988 The Gate Theatre, Dublin.
Transferred to Edinburgh Festival in 1989. Transferred to Spoleto Festival, Charlston, South Carolina, in 1990.

Director	Steven Berkoff
HEROD	Alan Stanford
JOKANAAN	Joe Savino
YOUNG SYRIAN	David Heap
HERODIAS	Barbara Brennan
SALOMÉ	Olwen Fouere

Steven Berkoff, writing in the programme, said: 'I like the play because he gave his actors 'arias', not unlike Shakespeare, and the actor can spread his wings and be allowed to fly. He gave the most lyrical and incandescent images to his characters and was not concerned with being 'real,' as was most Victorian theatre at the time. The play is not about real people, it is about our wildest dreams and desires. It is desire itself, unadulterated pure desire and, as such, is the fuel of theatre. The real theatre, as Wilde found, was boring and vacant and spent most of its time being a mirror to an ugly face. But even the ugly love to stare at themselves. Wilde gives us a beautiful image. Decadent, ornate, but still closer to the stuff we think about after we have closed our eyes than what we see with them open.'

Stanford shows you the half-fearful, half-fearsome potentate, a pudgily unstable creature starting out of superstitious broodings to pursue some barbaric whim. Whenever his gaze fixes on his step-daughter, his features slacken into sick voluptuousness of a drawing by Beardsley.

Peter Kemp *Independent*

Alan Stanford makes a splendidly repellent Herod – fleshy, self-indulgent, craven and corrupt – and his list of the priceless treasures he will give Salomé is relished like a man gorging himself on an impossibly rich banquet.

Charles Spencer *Daily Telegraph*

1989 Royal National Theatre, London.
Transferred to Phoenix Theatre in 1990.

Director	Steven Berkoff
HEROD	Steven Berkoff
JOKANAAN	Rory Edwards
YOUNG SYRIAN	Jason Carter
HERODIAS	Carmen Du Sautoy
SALOMÉ	Katharine Schlesinger

Personally, I like my comedy to be intensely modern and I like my tragedy to walk in purple and be remote.

Oscar Wilde

Steven Berkoff's memorably decadent production was excessively mannered, vocally and physically. Everything was stylised. Every movement was in slow motion. Every line was clearly enunciated to the very last languorous syllable. Wilde was given the full hypnotic narcotic treatment to a tinkling Satie-esque accompaniment on a grand piano.

The production was a Symbolist's wet dream, a triumph of style over matter, as arch and as ornate and as grotesque as the text. The soldiers were turned into a chorus of 1920s Bright Young Things. All the props were mimed.

Berkoff as Herod (a dangerous, lascivious, dead common, shoulder-heaving, bullet-headed, natty-waistcoated Berkoff yobo) gave an extraordinary display of vocal gymnastics. He offered Salomé up to half his kingdom if she would daaaaance for him.

Katharine Schlesinger mimed the dance of the seven veils and without having taken anything off persuaded a hushed audience that she was standing there totally naked. As she 'stripped' the audience actually leaned forward to see her 'nakedness' the better.

Rory Edwards's Jokanaan, his denunciation ringing out, was the lone Biblical figure on stage.

> This is *Salomé* as performed by lobotomised somnambulists, or perhaps by the inmates of an asylum of upper-class shell-shocked officers and their wives who have survived the First World War.
>
> Charles Osborne *Daily Telegraph*

> Because everyone moves as if they were totally submerged in water and talks as if every word were weighted with lead, Wilde's dialogue takes on the fascination and irrationality of a dream.
>
> Milton Shulman *Evening Standard*

> For all its virtuosity and visual excellence, *Salomé* seems hollow at heart and no amount of brilliance can disguise the inadequacies of the play itself.
>
> Kate Kellaway *Observer*

1992 British film, directed by Lucy Enfield, premiered at the Edinburgh Film Festival.

1992 Ballet: *Ich Werde Deinen Mund Küssen*
Premiere: Nationaltheaters, Mannheim.

Choreographer	Philippe Talard
Music	Arnold Schönberg
JOKANAAN	Olaf Schmidt
SALOMÉ	Rosangela Calheiros

1992 Circle in the Square, New York.

Director	Robert Allan Ackerman
HEROD	Al Pacino
JOKANAAN	Arnold Vosloo
YOUNG SYRIAN	Esai Morales
HERODIAS	Suzanne Bertish
SALOMÉ	Sheryl Lee

Mr Pacino lives dangerously . . . He could easily fall flat on his face as a red-lipped, zonked out, near falsetto Herod. He could easily spill over into high camp, easily lose it. What saves him – or makes him – is his good humour! Al Pacino as the epitome of decadence and tyranny sees the funny side! Herod is laughable.

John Heilpern *New York Observer*

He does not edge into this role; he dives headlong . . . But there are far too many unintentional laughs, some of them provided by the ingenuous delivery of pretentious dialogue, others by the skimpy costumes.

Mel Gussow *New York Times*

Pacino's Herod is an effete, prissily languid, rabbity little fellow – a camp Roman out of a De Mille spectacle . . . Sheryl Lee's Salomé is pure high-school amateurishness.

Michael Feingold *Village Voice*

The result is often campy, usually overwrought and sometimes plain goofy.

Greg Evans *Variety*

1992 Richard Strauss's opera at the Royal Opera House, London.

Conductor	Edward Downes
Director	Peter Hall
Designer	John Bury
HEROD	Kenneth Riegel
JOKANAAN	Michael Devlin
YOUNG SYRIAN	Robin Leggate
HERODIAS	Gillian Knight
SALOMÉ	Maria Ewing

Strauss is much more vulgar than Wilde's jewelled and perfumed prose. There is so much drama going on in the music that you don't need the singers. Certainly the sexual turmoil is so energetically scored after Jokanaan has returned to his cell as to make any visual statement by Salomé superfluous.

'Daughter of Sodom! I will NOT have her looking at me!' sang Michael Devlin, literally at the end of his tether, standing there emaciated, long-haired, ivory-white, buttock naked. It was no surprise that Herodias's hair had turned blue (just as Wilde had wanted). She had to sit on the terrace listening to the prophet screaming abuse at her all day long.

Kenneth Riegel's Herod (vain, sensual, ridiculous) remained unperturbed: 'He never says anything rude about me.' It seemed odd that, during his step-daughter's final *tête à tête* with Jokanaan, he should face the proscenium arch. Given the Tetrarch's kinky taste, you would think he would, surely, snatch the occasional look. Maria Ewing's Salomé revealed all at the end of the Dance of the Seven Veils.

Salomé was very loud, masturbatory kitsch, awash in its multiple orgasms. Edward Downes drowned the singers, Ewing and Devlin's voices often too light to soar above the orchestra. John Bury provided a pretty Art Nouveau backcloth.

1994 Citizens' Theatre, Glasgow.

Director	Jon Pope
HEROD	James Duke
YOKANAAN	John Ireland
NARRABOTH	Beatrice Comins
ISSACHAR	Brendan Hopper
HERODIAS	Anna Savva
SALOMÉ	Julie Saunders

This production offers us a rundown slum with bare rafters, piles of rubble, a dirty sink and the kind of elderly radio receiver which featured in Second World War movies . . . Most of the lines are deleted, with some deliberately pedestrian ones inserted . . . The pity of this reduced version is primarily that it does not make evident sense . . . The second reason for regret is that it obscures the acting, especially that of Julie Saunders in the title role. This wispy creature with electrifying sensuality and captivating presence is already outstanding and it would have been fascinating to see her in the part originally written.

Joseph Farrell *Scotsman*

1998 Riverside Studios.

Director	Mick Gordon
HEROD	Greg Hicks
JOKANAAN	Tristan Sturrock
YOUNG SYRIAN	Tom Smith
HERODIAS	Veronica Quilligan
SALOMÉ	Emily Woof

Mick Gordon's minimal production stripped Wilde bare and played out the action within a taped area. There was no poetry, no beauty, no gaudy ornateness, no severed head, no voluptuousness, no Grand Guignol, no nudity. Jokanaan was discovered up a ladder speaking into a microphone. Salomé, wearing white jeans, reclined on a large wooden circle, as if she were a dish on a plate. Herod wore an eye patch and a long black cloak, bared his chest and feet, and lurched about, sloshing his turquoise drink all over the place.

The production falls short of words; it feels like a rehearsal.

Kate Kellaway *Observer*

It's a contest between the histrionics of stage acting and the withdrawn intensity of screen acting. Woof's muteness wins hands down.

Robert Butler *Independent on Sunday*

A Woman of No Importance (1893)

A New and Original Play of Modern Life

'To Gladys Countess de Grey'

Characters in the Play:
LORD ILLINGWORTH
SIR JOHN PONTEFRACT
LORD ALFRED RUFFORD
MR KELVIL, MP
THE VENERABLE ARCHDEACON DAUBENY, DD
GERALD ARBUTHNOT
FARQUHAR, Butler
FRANCIS, Footman
LADY HUNSTANTON
LADY CAROLINE PONTEFRACT
LADY STUTFIELD
MRS ALLONBY
MISS HESTER WORSLEY
ALICE, Maid
MRS ARBUTHNOT

The scenes of the play:
Act I Lawn in front of the terrace of Hunstanton Chase.
Act II Drawing-room at Honstanton Chase after dinner.
Act III The Picture Gallery at Hunstanton Chase.
Act IV Sitting-room at Mrs Arbothnot's house at Wrockley.

Time: The present. The action takes place within twenty-four hours.

The Plot

ACT I Lady Hunstanton is entertaining her guests at her country house. Gerald Arbuthnot informs his hostess that Lord Illingworth has just offered to make him his secretary. Lady Hunstanton writes a letter inviting Arbuthnot's mother to come to dinner and meet Lord Illingworth. Mrs Allonby, who detests Hester Worsley's puritanism and candour, challenges Lord Illingworth to kiss her. As they exit he spies a letter and recognises the handwriting.

ACT II After dinner, the ladies are alone. Mrs Allonby's 'clever talk' shocks Hester, who lectures the company on morality. Mrs Arbuthnot arrives just in time to hear a ringing condemnation of herself. She is horrified to find that Lord Illingworth is the man who seduced her twenty years ago, who fathered their child, and then abandoned them both. She pleads with him not to take Gerald away from her but she cannot bring herself to tell her son the real reason for her objection to Illingworth.

ACT III Illingworth attempts to seduce Gerald. Mrs Arbuthnot attempts to stop Gerald going abroad. He cannot understand why she should object to his bettering himself. If he were Illingworth's secretary, he feels, he would be in a financial position to propose to Hester. She tells him obliquely the story of her life but he is too stupid to realise she is talking about herself and naively says that no nice girl would have run off with a man in the first place. Illingworth attempts to kiss Hester (off-stage). Gerald attempts to throttle Illingworth. 'Stop, Gerald, stop!' cries Mrs Arbuthnot. 'He is your own father.'

ACT IV Gerald declares he will not go to India with Illingworth but will stay with his mother. He insists it is her duty to herself (and to all other women) to marry his father. She refuses. Hester agrees with Mrs Arbuthnot and says she is happy to marry Gerald and for her to come and live with them. Illingworth asks Mrs Arbuthnot to share their son with him, and offers to marry her. She refuses.

The Characters

LORD ILLINGWORTH, a man of flinty intellect, is both hero and villain. The hero is an elegant, flippant, vain dandy, and effortlessly witty. ('The peerage is the best thing in fiction the English have done.') The villain is a bisexual, who having seduced the mother, now wants to seduce her son. Illingworth, who has read *The Picture of Dorian Gray* and quotes Lord Henry Wotton endlessly, is, in fact, Wotton in another guise and his true character (vicious, blasé, coarse) is revealed in the last act: 'You gave yourself to me like a flower, to do anything I liked with. You were the prettiest plaything, the most fascinating of small romances.'

Wilde wanted him acted with great distinction. 'He is like no one who existed before . . . He is certainly not natural. He is a figure of art. Indeed, if you can bear the truth he is myself.' He certainly sounds like Wilde in full flow:

> To get into the best society, nowadays one has either to feed people, amuse people or shock people.
>
> A man who can dominate a London dinner-table can dominate the world. The future belongs to the dandy. It is the exquisites who are going to rule.

The role of Lord Illingworth was created by Herbert Beerbohm Tree, of whom Oscar Wilde said, 'Ah, every day, dear Herbert becomes *de plus en plus Oscarisé*; it is a wonderful case of Nature imitating art.'

MRS ALLONBY ran away twice before she married and then married a tedious virgin called Ernest. (If he is called Ernest, does this mean he's gay?) She says women have a much better time than men have. 'There are far more things forbidden us than are forbidden them.' Elegant, incorrigible, waspishly witty, she and Lord Illingworth are the direct descendents of Millamant and Mirabell in William Congreve's *The Way of the World*. Their witty exchanges and Mrs Allonby's definition of 'the ideal man' are in the Restoration comedy tradition:

> The ideal Man! Oh, the Ideal Man should talk to us as if we were goddesses, and treat us as if we were children. He should refuse all our serious requests, and gratify every one of our whims. He should encourage us to have caprices, and forbid us to have missions. He should always say much more than he means, and always mean much more than he says. He should never run down other pretty women. That would show he had no taste, or make one suspect that he had too much. No; he should be nice about

them all, but say that somehow they don't attract him. If we ask him a question about anything, he should give us an answer all about ourselves. He should invariably praise us for whatever qualities he knows we haven't got. But he should be pitiless, quite pitiless, in reproaching us for the virtues that we have never dreamed of possessing. He should never believe that we know the use of useful things. That would be unforgivable. But he should shower on us everything we don't want. He should persistently compromise us in public, and treat us with absolute respect when we are alone. And yet he should always be ready to have a perfectly terrible scene, whenever we want one, and to become miserable, absolutely miserable, at a moment's notice, and to overwhelm us with reproaches in less that twenty minutes, and to be positively violent at the end of half an hour, and to leave us for ever at a quarter to eight, when we have to go and dress for dinner. And when, after that, one has seen him for really the last time, and he has refused to take back the little things he has given one, and promised never to communicate with one again, or to write one any foolish letters, he should be perfectly broken-hearted, and telegraph to one all day long, and send little notes every half hour by a private hansom, and dine quite alone at the club so that every one should know how unhappy he was. And after a whole dreadful week, during which one has gone about everywhere with one's husband, just to show how absolutely lonely one was, he may be given a third last parting, in the evening, and then, if his conduct has been quite irreproachable, and one has behaved really badly to him, he should be allowed to admit that he has been entirely in the wrong, and when he has admitted that, it becomes one's duty to forgive, and one can do it all over again from the beginning, with variations.

Mrs Allonby's 'clever talk' shocks Lady Hunstanton. Hester Worsley loathes her. As the play progresses, she and Lord Illingworth are seen to be much closer in character to the Marquise de Merteuil and Vicomte de Valmont in Laclos's *Les Liaisons Dangereuses*.

MRS ARBUTHNOT, the woman of no importance, lives a life of a recluse with her illegitimate son. Dressed and veiled all in black, she looks like a ghost from the past. 'She is a woman who drags a chain like a guilty thing. She is a woman who wears a mask like a thing that is a leper. The fire cannot purify her. The waters cannot quench her anguish.' The Biblical rhetoric can be embarrassing, especially when she is pleading with Illingworth: 'Leave me the little vineyard of my life; leave me the walled-in garden and the well of water; the ewe-lamb God sent me, in pity or wrath, oh! leave me that. George, don't take Gerald from me.'

GERALD ARBUTHNOT, nineteen years old, Lord Illingworth's illegitimate son, is employed as a junior, underpaid, clerk in a provincial bank in a third-rate provincial town. He is, on his own admission, an awful duffer, naive, unworldly and fearfully idle. He wants to get into society and would give anything to be like Illingworth. He cannot believe anything infamous of him until he attempts to kiss the girl he loves. Gerald, an awful prig, is a mother's boy, and likely to remain so. Wilde insisted the actor most be charming and young.

HESTER WORSLEY, a pretty eighteen-year-old American heiress, harangues the entire company in a high-handed manner:

> You rich people in England, you don't know how you are living. How could you know? You shut out from your society the gentle and the good. You laugh at the simple and the pure. Living, as you all do, on others and by them, you sneer at self-sacrifice, and if you throw bread to the poor, it is merely to keep them quiet for a season. With all your pomp and wealth and art you don't know how to live – you don't even know that. You love the beauty you can see and touch and handle, the beauty that you can destroy, and do destroy, but of the unseen beauty of life, of the unseen beauty of a higher life you know nothing. You have lost life's secret. Oh, your English society seems to me shallow, selfish, foolish. It has blinded its eyes, and stopped its ears. It lies like a leper in purple. It sits like a dead thing smeared with gold. It is all wrong, all wrong.

Hester is vehement in her beliefs that a woman who has sinned should be punished and not allowed into good society. She also agrees that 'the sins of the parents should be visited on the children.' Like Lady Windermere (who has similar fast-and-hard rules) she has to learn to modify her opinions, otherwise the sins would be visited on the man she wants to marry.

LADY HUNSTANTON, the empty-headed, absent-minded hostess, intellectually out of her depth, chatters away inconsequentially: 'I was in hope he would have married Lady Kelso. But I believe he said her family was too large. Or was it her feet? I forget which.'

LADY CAROLINE, a hard, bitter woman, has been married four times. 'Twenty years of marriage had made her look something like a public building.' She spends the whole evening looking for her husband, convinced he is making love to some woman.

ARCHDEACON DAUBENY'S sole topic of conversation is his wife.

MRS DAUBENY, the hypochondriacal wife of the Archdeacon, is one of the great unseen characters of English literature. She suffers from headaches, deafness, poor eyesight, arthritis and Alzheimer's Disease. She never eats solids and lives entirely on jellies. But she is never morbid and remains resolutely cheerful, taking an active interest in her own health. 'She is a perfect martyr, happiest when she is alone,' says the Archdeacon, who clearly can't wait to get out of the house.

LADY STUTFIELD, who hasn't a brain in her silly, effusive head, finds everything either 'quite, quite' or 'very, very' or 'so, so'. Will she end up in bed with Sir John Pontefract? More than likely, if they can escape Lady Caroline's vigilance. Wilde said she was very serious and romantic and that she must be played as if she was playing the heroine of a romance.

LORD ALFRED RUFFORD (a portrait of Lord Alfred Douglas?) makes a brief appearance. The role is so small – no more than a handful of lines – that it is usually cut. Alfred smokes gold-tipped cigarettes. 'They are awfully expensive,' he says. 'I can only afford them when I'm in debt. One must have an occupation nowadays. If I hadn't my debts I shouldn't have anything to think about.'

> Plots are tedious. Anyone can invent them. Life is full of them. Indeed one has to elbow one's way through them as they crowd across one's path. I took the plot of this play from the *Family Herald*, which took it – wisely, I feel – from my novel *The Picture of Dorian Gray*. People love a wicked aristocrat who seduces a virtuous maid, and they love a virtuous maiden for being seduced by a wicked aristocrat. I have given them what they like so that they may learn to love what I like to give them.
>
> Oscar Wilde, quoted by Beerbohm Tree in Hesketh Pearson's *Beerbohm Tree: His Life and Laughter* (Methuen, 1956)

Asked if he had produced the play with the assistance of Wilde, Tree replied that he had produced it with the interference of Wilde.

> I am not nervous on the night I am producing a new play. I am exquisitely indifferent. My nervousness ends at the last dress rehearsal. I know then what effect my play, as presented upon the stage, has produced upon me. My interest in the play ends there, and I feel curiously envious of the public – they have such wonderfully fresh emotions in store for them.
>
> Oscar Wilde

1893 19 April Premiere: Theatre Royal, Haymarket, London.

Licensee and manager	Herbert Beerbohm Tree
LORD ILLINGWORTH	Mr Tree
SIR JOHN PONTEFRACT	Holman Clark
ALFRED RUFFORD	Mr Lawford
MR KELVIL	Mr Allan
ARCHDEACON DAUBENY	Mr Kemble
GERALD ARBUTHNOT	Mr Fred Terry
FARQUHAR	Mr Hay
FRANCIS	Mr Montagu
LADY HUNSTANTON	Miss Rose Leclercq
CAROLINE PONTEFRACT	Miss Le Thière
LADY STUTFIELD	Miss Horlock
MRS ALLONBY	Mrs Tree
HESTER WORSLEY	Julia Neilson
ALICE	Miss Kelly
MRS ARBUTHNOT	Mrs Bernard Beere

On the first night, there were cries of 'Author! Author!' A large gentleman rose in one of the boxes. 'Ladies and gentlemen, I regret to inform you that Mr Oscar Wilde is not in the house.' The large gentleman spoke with authority. He was Oscar Wilde.

There was a big rush for tickets. Wilde said they were having to turn royalty away. The Prince of Wales attended the second night. When Wilde suggested that he was going to have to cut the play, the Prince begged him not to cut a single line.

The *Stage* said its success could be attributed to the fact that society liked to see itself reflected even if the glass was distorted and the vision seen was imperfect. The play ran for a total of 113 performances.

> As a play *A Woman of No Importance* is nought; it merely consists of a few scenes borrowed from French drama, dropped into an impossible social milieu; on the other hand, as an entertainment it is a success. Mr Oscar Wilde has diligently collected jokes, done them up so cleverly that some sound almost new, and the result is an amusing chitter-chatter of impossible aristocrats.
>
> *Sketch*

> In this play all the personages make on us the impression of a set of wonderfully clever people, who say wonderfully clever things, couched in such a grace of language that their very distinction becomes tedious, because there is no soul, no real sentiment behind their talk. They are all *poseurs*, and in all their actions and words we do not feel the spontaneity of natural motives; but we see the author who holds the wires in his hand, pulls them at his will, and makes them speak, as he would speak, as a ventriloquist who works his dolls. To listen to the bright conversation of a man like Mr Oscar Wilde is always pleasant for a time, but when a whole play is padded out with such conversation, and when the action and the characters seem to float rudderlessly about in an ocean of words, then weariness must step in, and one cannot pronounce the play a good drama.
>
> *Saturday Review*

> In intellectual calibre, artistic competence – ay, and in dramatic instinct to boot – Mr Wilde has no rival among his fellow-workers for the stage.
>
> William Archer *World*

> The play is fresh in idea and execution and is written with a literary polish too rare on the English stage . . . Cleverly written as it is, the play would gain by compression alike in its flippant and its serious passages . . . Mrs Beere, an eminently good woman, sober in costume, demure in manner, with Titian red hair, irreproachable in morals, was strongly pathetic and dignified.
>
> *The Times*

> I really do not think that Mr Beerbohm Tree has ever shown such mastery of subtle effect, acquired by apparently the simplest means, than as the cool, blasé, man-of-the-world, husband and father in this particular play. Mr Tree has the wonderful art of completely transforming himself . . . Notice his air of distinction, how he holds himself, how he wears his clothes, how he becomes another man, not because he is dressed up differently, but for the time being he is in another man's skin. There is the art of it. Polish and breeding and subliminated insolence are in every pore of this man's skin. And withal the wretch has a vein of tenderness through it all. Society has given him the veneer, but scratch it off and you will find a remnant of a heart. The man must have something lovable about him or that particular woman would never have loved him. I wish we could see more of Mr Tree in these characters. He is one of the first of our English comedians, observant, pungent, analytic.
>
> Clement Scott *Era*

> No words could praise too highly the boundless humour of Miss Leclercq as a worldly old woman without whom the play would be well-nigh intolerable, or the airy flippancy and ingenious audacities of the society butterfly of Mrs Tree. These were examples of high comedy perfect of their kind.
>
> *Theatre*

The play went on tour with Lewis Waller in the role of Lord Illingworth. Wilde saw a production at the Theatre Royal, Jersey, in September 1893 and thought it was good on the whole. Gerald, he said, was excellent but Hester lacked decision and strength.

1893 American premiere: Fifth Avenue Theatre, New York.

LORD ILLINGWORTH	Maurice Barrymore/Charles Coghlan
SIR JOHN PONTEFRACT	Grant Stewart
ALFRED RUFFORD	Edgar Norton
MR KELVIL	Robert Fischer
ARCHDEACON DAUBENY	Thomas Whiffen
GERALD ARBUTHNOT	Robert Taber/Aubrey Boucicault
FARQUHAR	Edwin James
FRANCIS	Damon Lyon
LADY HUNSTANTON	Ada Dyas

CAROLINE PONTEFRACT	Mrs Bowers
LADY STUTFIELD	Constance Levien
MRS ALLONBY	Mrs Dion Boucicault
HESTER WORSLEY	Effie Shannon
ALICE	Alice G Cleather
MRS ARBUTHNOT	Rose Coghlan

The chief characteristic of Mr Wilde as a writer is that he thinks of nothing except himself. For that reason his works are invariably subjective, and in drama that condition is not advantageous. No such society exists anywhere on earth as the society depicted by Mr Wilde . . . There is no play. The proportion of talk to action is about ten to one, and, worse gabble was never known outside of a dime novel . . . Amid Mr Wilde's laborious folly – wherein impertinence passes for wit and tinsel for brilliancy – there was comingled a weak strain of ethical observation . . . The London audience must be hard up for entertainment . . . There is not a good part in the piece – that of Mrs Arbuthnot being particularly dull.

New York Tribune

Mr Wilde writes smart dialogue easily and there is too much of it. His plot is very slight . . . Mr Wilde's wit, however, often seems like the refuse of Sheridan's workshop filtered through mire. His piquancy is sometimes only dirt. Nevertheless, there are strong dramatic passages that reveal a feeling for theatrical effect . . . Mr Barrymore, who in the present lamentable stage of his career did not even know the words of his part, whose acting was coarse, ill-mannered, formless and without variety . . . Miss Coghlan acted her part with admirable discretion and tact. Her impersonation was beyond reproach technically and seemed to have all the emotional force and pathos the part is capable of producing. Her sweet, powerful voice was used with excellent skill, and there were moments when she raised the mind of the spectators quite beyond Oscar Wilde.

New York Times

Miss Coghlan, as the heroine, was forceful, but not at all emotional, and did not arouse the sympathy of the audience . . . The play is an intellectual success. There are few good things in it, but no end of good things are said.

New York Herald

1903 Empire Theatre, Balham, London.

LORD ILLINGWORTH	Charles Hartley
SIR JOHN PONTEFRACT	Gerald Smythe
ALFRED RUFFORD	Eric Perceval
MR KELVIL	James Benwell
ARCHDEACON DAUBENY	Dudman Bromwich
GERALD ARBUTHNOT	Arthur Godsale
FARQUHAR	Leonard Lorrain
FRANCIS	F Cowley Wright
LADY HUNSTANTON	Di Forbes
CAROLINE PONTEFRACT	Muriel Herbert
LADY STUTFIELD	R. Mayne Young
MRS ALLONBY	Ethel Gordon Paul
HESTER WORSLEY	Ethel Beale
ALICE	Ruth Fox
MRS ARBUTHNOT	Lydia Busch

1907 His Majesty's Theatre, London.

Director	Mr Tree
LORD ILLINGWORTH	Mr Tree
SIR JOHN PONTEFRACT	J Fisher White
ALFRED RUFFORD	Langhorne Burton
MR KELVIL	Charles Allan
ARCHDEACON DAUBENY	Edmund Maurice
GERALD ARBUTHNOT	Charles Quartermaine
FARQUHAR	Clive Currie
FRANCIS	F Cowley Wright
LADY HUNSTANTON	Mrs Charles Calvert
CAROLINE PONTEFRACT	Kate Bishop
LADY STUTFIELD	Kate Cutler
MR ALLONBY	Ellis Jeffreys
HESTER WORSLEY	Viola Tree
ALICE	Hilda Moore
MRS ARBUTHNOT	Marion Terry

The repartee dragged on the first night due to the actors' imperfect recollection of their lines.

Nowadays people don't talk in plays as Oscar Wilde made them talk – for one reason because there is no playwright among us capable of inventing that brilliant talk, and for another, because playgoers would not be disposed to listen to it with enthusiasm. The truth is a little of it goes a long way and in *A Woman of No Importance* there is far too much of it.

The Times

Mr Tree's style has ripened and matured since *A Woman of No Importance* was produced, and the air of leisured ease and cynical calmness with which he played Lord Illingworth in 1893 is even more perfectly polished and perfected.

Era

Marion Terry never strikes a deep enough note of distress in the earlier acts nor displays enough contempt in the closing scene.

Illustrated London News

1912 American silent film.

1915 Kingsway Theatre, London.

Director	Madge McIntosh
LORD ILLINGWORTH	Lawrence Hanray
SIR JOHN PONTEFRACT	William Armstrong
ALFRED RUFFORD	Frederick Cooper
MR KELVIL	Harvey Adams
ARCHDEACON DAUBENY	William Dexter
GERALD ARBUTHNOT	Percy Marmont
FARQUHAR	Arthur C Rose
LADY HUNSTANTON	Edith Barnwell
CAROLINE PONTEFRACT	Nina Henderson
LADY STUTFIELD	Kathleen Johnston
MRS ALLONBY	Estelle Winwood
HESTER WORSLEY	Edith Smith
ALICE	Gwynifrede Sardon
MRS ARBUTHNOT	Madge McIntosh

Lawrence Hanray played Lord Illingworth very cleverly with excellent polish and suavity but was rather too youthful in appearance for the part. Lady Hunstanton was delightfully played by Edith Barnwell and Miss Estelle Winwood was very alluring and flippant as Lady Allonby and rattled through her lines in an easy, graceful way, but we should like to have seen the part played with more distinction.

Era

1916 Fulton Theatre, New York.

Director	Ira Hards
LORD ILLINGWORTH	Holbrook Blinn
SIR JOHN PONTEFRACT	Max Montesole
ALFRED RUFFORD	Lionel Pape
MR KELVIL	Ivan T Simpson
ARCHDEACON DAUBENY	Richard Temple
GERALD ARBUTHNOT	George Le Guere
FARQUHAR	Ralph Kemmett
FRANCIS	George Thorne
LADY HUNSTANTON	Fanny Addison Pitt
CAROLINE PONTEFRACT	Marguerite St John
LADY STUTFIELD	Alice Lindahl
MRS ALLONBY	Annie Hughes
HESTER WORSLEY	Ottola Nesmith
ALICE	Carolyn Darling
MRS ARBUTHNOT	Margaret Anglin

Whatever the reason for its non-production, it cannot be claimed it has aged. Wilde, like Shaw, wrote not for the moment but the century. The very artificiality and the undramatic qualities of Wilde's plays prevent their aging; their outstanding feature is the substance – not the form . . . Mr Blinn, acting always with his intelligent restraint, was a suave and polished Illingworth, although there was nothing of the gentleman about him. As a gentleman he was precise and elegant; his caddish moments sat on him with less ease.

New York Daily Tribune

It is when the epigrams cease and the action begins that this Wilde comedy shows its age. When the play is bright it is frivolous, and when it is serious it is dull . . . It is Miss Anglin's misfortune, therefore, that she's cast as the solemn Mrs Arbuthnot, who does not have a single witty line. Her great dramatic talent is wasted on a wholly artificial part.

New York Sun

It takes acting of a very high order to quicken the moribund portions of Wilde's drama, and it is only the fine, glowing work of Miss Anglin which keeps the fourth act from crumbling at the touch. That is why she is such a tower of strength in the present revival. With the real fire, skilfully, discreetly, and reservedly used, she imparts something of the old tingle to the 'big scene'.

New York Times

Mr Le Guere is not to be blamed if his heroic threats against his father become somewhat laughable when one compares the slender boy with the adamantine parent.

Christian Science Monitor

1921 British film.

Director	Denison Clift
Screenplay	Arthur Q Walton
LORD ILLINGWORTH	Milton Rosmer
GERALD ARBUTHNOT	Ward McAllister
FARQUHAR	Henry Vibart
LADY HUNSTANTON	Daisy Campbell
HESTER WORSLEY	Lillian Walker
MRS ARBUTHNOT	Fay Compton
ELSIE FARQUHAR	Gwen Carton
SIR THOMAS	M Gray Murray
LADY CECILIA	Hetta Bartlett
LADY RUFFORD	Julie Hartley-Milburn
NURSE	Joey Sanderson

It is a notable British film . . . Fay Compton is a screen acquisition; with an extremely difficult part she makes a powerful appeal to the sympathy without a trace of overacting; in close-ups her facial expressions are excellent. Restraint is one of the great virtues of Milton Rosmer's work; he is much more happily cast than in some recent films and gives a subtle and convincing study of a typical Wilde creation.

Kinematograph Weekly

1926 Elephant Theatre, London.

Director	N Carter Slaughter
LORD IILLINGWORTH	N Carter Slaughter
SIR JOHN PONTEFRACT	Wm J Miller
ALFRED RUFFORD	Lionel Scott
MR KELVIL	Harry Tresham
ARCHDEACON DAUBENY	Frank Corfield
GERALD ARBUTHNOT	Geoffrey Carlisle
FARQUHAR	Floyd Gwynne
FRANCIS	Gilbert de Yonson
LADY HUNSTANTON	Gladys Spencer
CAROLINE PONTEFRACT	Ivy Shepherd
LADY STUTFIELD	Greta Wood
MRS ALLONBY	Enid Lindsay
HESTER WORSLEY	Dodo Watts
ALICE	Sadie Martin
MRS ARBUTHNOT	Grace Sweeting

1936 German film: *Eine Frau ohne Bedeutung*

Director	Hans Steinhoff
Screenplay	Thea Von Harbou
	Bernd Hoffmann
SYLVIA	Kathe Dorsch
LORD ILLINGWORTH	Gustav Grundgens
GERALD	Albert Lieven
HESTER	Marianne Hoppe

Much of the brilliant dialogue which distinguishes this satire on English society has been lost. An incongruous note results from the physical modernisation of the setting while the motivation remains rather outmoded.

New York Times

1937 French film: *Une Femme sans Importance*

Director	Jean Choux
Screenplay	Charles Spaak
LORD ILLINGWORTH	Pierre Blanchar
ESTHER	Lisette Lanvin
GERALD	Gilbert Gil
LADY PATRICIA	Catherine Fonteney
THE PASTOR	Charles Granval
ILLINGWORTH'S FATHER	Jean Perier
CAROLINE	Laure Diana
SYLVIA	Line Noro
HESTER	Lisette Lanvin
LADY HUNSTANTON	Marguerite Templey
LORD HUNSTANTON	Jean Tissier

Pierre Blanchar is the only actor who is truly in the style of Wilde's plays: sharp, well-bred, ardent at the beginning, then icy and bitter, with a superiority which was really perfect, he dominated the film.

La Cinématographie Française

1945 Spanish film: *Una Mujer sin Importancia*

Director	Luis Bayon Herrera
Adaptor	Arturo S Mom
LORD ILLINGWORTH	Santiago Gomez Cou
GERALD	Hugo Pimentel
MRS ARBUTHNOT	Mecha Ortiz
CAST	Lidla Denis
	Golde Flami
	Bianca Vidal
	Sara Barrie
	Yolanda Alexandrini
	Carlos Enriquez

Wilde's plot was transferred to Cordoba. Mrs Arbuthnot ran a curio shop and her son was a bank clerk.

Miss Ortiz gives a restrained interpretation of the role of Mrs Arbuthnot. Santiago Gomez Cou is stilted as Lord Illingworth and Hugo Pimentel as Gerald is uneven.

Nid *Variety*

1953 Savoy Theatre, London.

Director	Michael Benthall
Settings and costumes	Loudon Sainthill
LORD ILLINGWORTH	Clive Brook
SIR JOHN PONTEFRACT	William Mervyn
ALFRED RUFFORD	Charles Perry
MR KELVIL	Philip Burton
ARCHDEACON DAUBENY	Aubrey Mather
GERALD ARBUTHNOT	Peter Barkworth
FARQUHAR	Stringer Davis
FRANCIS	Peter Bayliss
LADY HUNSTANTON	Athene Seyler
CAROLINE PONTEFRACT	Jean Cadell
LADY STUTFIELD	Joan Benham
MRS ALLONBY	Isabel Jeans
HESTER WORSLEY	Frances Hyland
ALICE	Daphne Newton
MRS ARBUTHNOT	Nora Swinburne

It was John Gielgud who suggested that the fourth act should be rewritten to make the play more revivable. Paul Dehn (the adaptor – initially uncredited until the critics complained) combined Acts II and III and stripped away the melodrama and heavy moralising. 'Child of my shame be no longer child of shame' was cut. The play did not end on Mrs Arbuthnot's famous last line. Instead, Illingworth, having made his exit, returned for some more comedy and another exit.

Dehn also provided his own pastiche epigrams. 'Nothing should be rewritten but the classics' was one of his wittier efforts. Part of the evening's entertainment was guessing which were his lines and which were Wilde's.

1953 was Queen Elizabeth's coronation year and the play was lavishly produced with an all-star cast. Clive Brook, ill at ease on the first night, mistimed most of his lines and offered no critical interpretation of Lord Illingworth's character. The chief joy was Isabel Jeans, a high-comedy actress of elegance and wit, who handled both the malice and the definition of 'an ideal husband' superbly.

Athene Seyler, genial, loveable, kind (the very qualities Wilde wanted) was delightful as the rambling, forgetful Lady Hunstanton. Jean Cadell, as Caroline Pontefract, punctured Hester Worsley's lengthy lecture on morality perfectly: 'Might I, dear Miss Worsley, as you are standing up, ask you to ring the bell?' Frances Hyland was a charming Puritan and Joan Benham was very funny as Lady Stutfield who finds everything either 'very, very' or 'quite, quite'.

Nora Swinburne as 'sweet, simple, good Mrs Arbuthnot' had lost most of her lines. She was excellent with the pathos; but, not surprisingly, defeated by 'Stop, Gerald, stop! He is your own father.'

Loudon Sainthill's costumes were so sumptuous that at times it seemed as if the cast was taking part in a mannequin parade.

> This is not so much a revival as a disinterment. Clever embalmers have been at work on this inferior Wilde and they have embalmed it almost out of recognition.
>
> *Sketch*

> It is all like a saunter through a wax museum.
>
> John Barber *Daily Express*

> I couldn't think of a single actor who could carry off the poised display of arrogance, ill-judged charm and caddishness. Mr Brook was perfect.
>
> T C Worsley *New Statesman and Nation*

1960 British television.

Adaptor	Paul Dehn
Director	Joan Kemp-Welch
LORD ILLINGWORTH	Griffith Jones
SIR JOHN PONTEFRACT	Nicholas Hannen
ALFRED RUFFORD	Tony Bateman

MR KELVIL	Michael Logan
ARCHDEACON DAUBENY	Charles Lloyd Pack
GERALD ARBUTHNOT	Clifford Elkin
FARQUHAR	Stringer Davis
FRANCIS	Michael Ely
LADY HUNSTANTON	Athene Seyler
CAROLINE PONTEFRACT	Marian Spencer
LADY STUTFIELD	Marcia Ashton
MRS ALLONBY	Helen Cherry
HESTER WORSLEY	Eira Heath
ALICE	Coral Fairweather
MRS ARBUTHNOT	Gwen Watford

'I love the play and its gaiety and style,' said Athene Seyler, who repeated the performance she had given in the 1953 stage revival. 'There's too much emphasis on second-rate people and squalor these days.' Her remark (quoted in *TV Times*) ignored the fact that the characters in *A Woman of No Importance* are second-rate people and that their behaviour is squalid.

It seemed somewhat perverse to cut Wilde and then leave in Dehn's pastiche epigrams, which were served on a plate in a very mechanical and very monotonous manner. The play came across as a lot of empty and very self-indulgent chatter.

The melodrama was poorly handled. Griffith Jones's Lord Illingworth lacked charm. Charles Lloyd Pack (as the Archdeacon) was so busy being odiously oily that the joke at the expense of his hypochondriacal wife went completely by the board.

The best performances were by Seyler (though she waved her fan too much) and Marcia Ashton who played Lady Stutfield as Joan Greenwood might have played her.

The women's lavish hats were absurdly big for the small screen.

> Athene Seyler's Lady Hunstanton was perfection; she had the croaking quality of the amiable, worldly old toad which suits this type down to the last fold of its jewelled dewlap.
>
> Maurice Richardson *Observer*

1967 Vaudeville Theatre, London.

Adaptor	Paul Dehn
Director	James Gillhouley
LORD ILLINGWORTH	Tony Britton
SIR JOHN PONTEFRACT	George Desmond
ALFRED RUFFORD	Dixon Adams
MR KELVIL	Robert Dean
ARCHDEACON DAUBENY	James Hayter
GERALD ARBUTHNOT	Michael Pennington
FOOTMAN	Allan Lee
LADY HUNSTANTON	Agnes Lauchlan
CAROLINE PONTEFRACT	Billie Hill
LADY STUTFIELD	Diane Hart
MRS ALLONBY	Pauline Jameson
HESTER WORSLEY	Portland Mason
ALICE	Terry Crotty
MRS ARBUTHNOT	Phyllis Calvert

The *Illustrated London News* thought the play was even more tedious than it had been fourteen years previously. 'A hollow and flatulent evening,' said the *Sunday Times*. The headline in the *Daily Mail* was 'Wilde turkey served up cold.'

But then there was not much sense in reviving the play with an all-star cast of no stars. James Gillhouley's sluggish production lacked style. The epigrams could not bear the weight, pause and smirks Pauline Jameson and Tony Britton gave them. Phyllis Calvert made nothing of Mrs Arbuthnot's big scene when she pleads with Lord Illingworth not to take her son away. Gerald (rather than the actor) played to a lot of unwanted laughter. The inexperienced Portland Mason was totally out of her depth as Hester. Agnes Lauchlan was an amusingly dotty and gushing Lady Hunstanton. The best performance was by James Hayter as the Archdeacon and he stole most of the notices.

> James Hayter walked away with the evening as the Archdeacon. (How revealing it was that the biggest laughs went to pieces of character-playing as opposed to purely verbal witticism.) . . . An evening, I fear, of no importance.
>
> Hugh Leonard *Plays and Players*

1978 Chichester Festival Theatre, Sussex.

Director	Patrick Garland
LORD ILLINGWORTH	Keith Baxter
SIR JOHN PONTEFRACT	George Howe
ALFRED RUFFORD	Martin Chamberlain
MR KELVIL	Martin Milman
ARCHDEACON DAUBENY	John Warner
GERALD ARBUTHNOT	Tim Woodward
FARQUHAR	Robert Perceval
FRANCIS	Simon Shepherd
LADY HUNSTANTON	Ambrosine Phillpotts
CAROLINE PONTEFRACT	Margaretta Scott
LADY STUTFIELD	Rosie Kerslake
MRS ALLONBY	Barbara Murray
HESTER WORSLEY	Gayle Hunnicutt
ALICE	Judith Davis
MRS ARBUTHNOT	Siân Phillips

The first act was boring. The supposedly clever talk, the facile paradoxes and the glib epigrams quickly palled, even more so since they were poorly delivered. The play didn't come alive until the young American's outburst against English society. In any normal production Illingworth and Mrs Allonby are the best parts; but at Chichester they were not well enough acted and the emphasis shifted to Mrs Arbuthnot.

Siân Phillips, in a role few modern actresses have wanted to play, was extraordinarily successful. She looked tragic; the depth of her feeling was never in any doubt. The melodrama was totally subdued, even on the notorious 'Stop, Gerald, stop! He is your own father!' – a line worthy of *East Lynne* and guyed by Noël Coward in *Hay Fever*. Phillips carried the play through its trickier passages and played the last scene as if it were by Ibsen.

Patrick Garland's lavish and elegant production placed such an unexpected emphasis on the melodrama that Lord Illingworth's witty lines in the middle of the most serious scenes became a ludicrous intrusion. Keith Baxter was miscast, looking far too young to be playing the cynical corrupter of youth. Since the play was being performed at Chichester (home to theatre's lost middle-class audience) there was, of course, no hint of homosexuality.

George Howe enriched the small part of Sir John Pontefract and Ambrosine Phillpotts gradually talked herself into Lady Hunstanton, but Barbara Murray merely boomed away as Mrs Allonby.

> The worst thing about the play is the very thing that Wilde's reputation rests on: the famous epigrams. The brutal truth is that they are mostly *terrible*: lumpish, stupid, meaningless and rancid with midnight oil.
>
> Bernard Levin *Sunday Times*

> Keith Baxter lends distinction to this monstrous bore, flipping each verbal pellet with a whimsical grace.
>
> John Barber *Daily Telegraph*

> Why revive such an orgy of mawkish sentiment and melodramatic revelation?
>
> *Country Life*

1984 Gate Theatre, Dublin.

Director	Patrick Mason
LORD ILLINGWORTH	Alan Stanford
SIR JOHN PONTEFRACT	Aiden Grennell
MR KELVIL	Robert Carrickford
ARCHDEACON DAUBENY	Christopher Casson
GERALD ARBUTHNOT	Lorcan Cranitch
FARQUHAR	Tony Coleman
FRANCIS	Neil Linden-Johnson
HENRY	Philip Hardy
LADY HUNSTANTON	Daphne Carroll
CAROLINE PONTEFRACT	Pamela Mant
LADY STUTFIELD	Anita Reeves
MRS ALLONBY	Barbara Brennan
HESTER WORSLEY	Niamh Cusack
MRS ARBUTHNOT	Kate Flynn

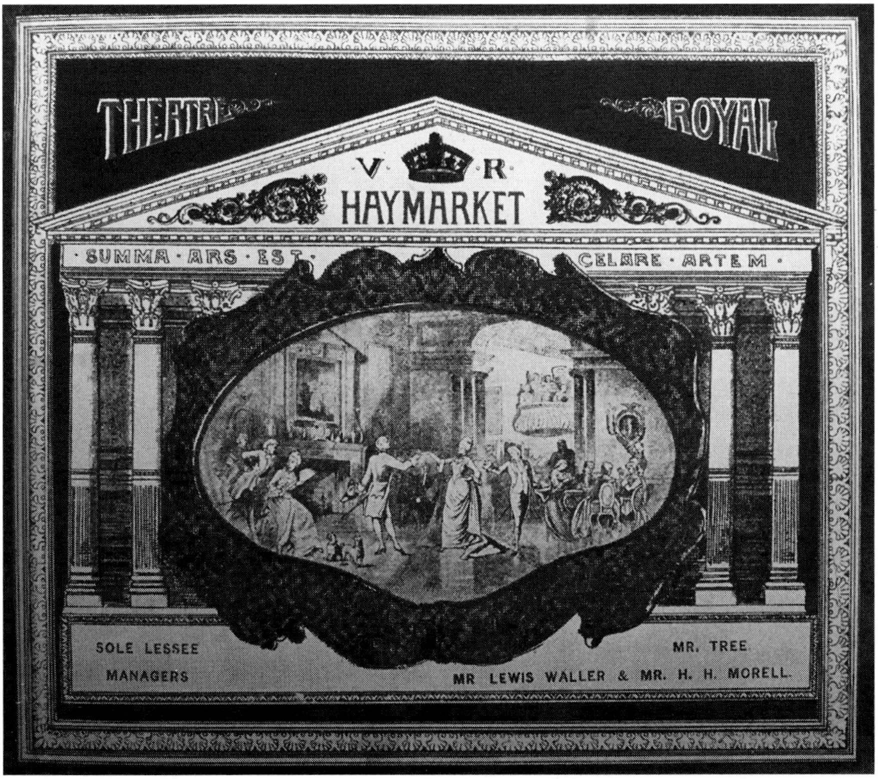

The programme cover and the exterior of Theatre Royal, Haymarket, where *A Woman of No Importance* and *An Ideal Husband* were performed.

Speak, sir! Why is my wife here? Answer me! By God!
I'll search your rooms, and if my wife's here, I'll –

Ben Webster as Cecil Graham, George Alexander as Lord Windermere and Nutcombe Gold as Lord Darlington in Act III of *Lady Windermere's Fan,* 1892.

Marion Terry as Mrs Erlynne in *Lady Windermere's Fan,* 1892.

Illustration in *Illustrated London News.*

Stop, Gerald, stop! He is your own father! Fred Terry as Gerald Arbuthnot, Mrs Bernard Beere as Mrs Arbuthnot and Beerbohm Tree as Lord Illingworth in Act III of *A Woman of No Importance,* 1893.

Jack, you're at the muffins again! I wish you wouldn't. There are only two left.

Allen Aynesworth as Algernon Moncrieff and George Alexander as John Worthing in Act II of *The Importance of Being Earnest,* 1895.

Florence West as Mrs Cheveley in *An Ideal Husband,* 1895.

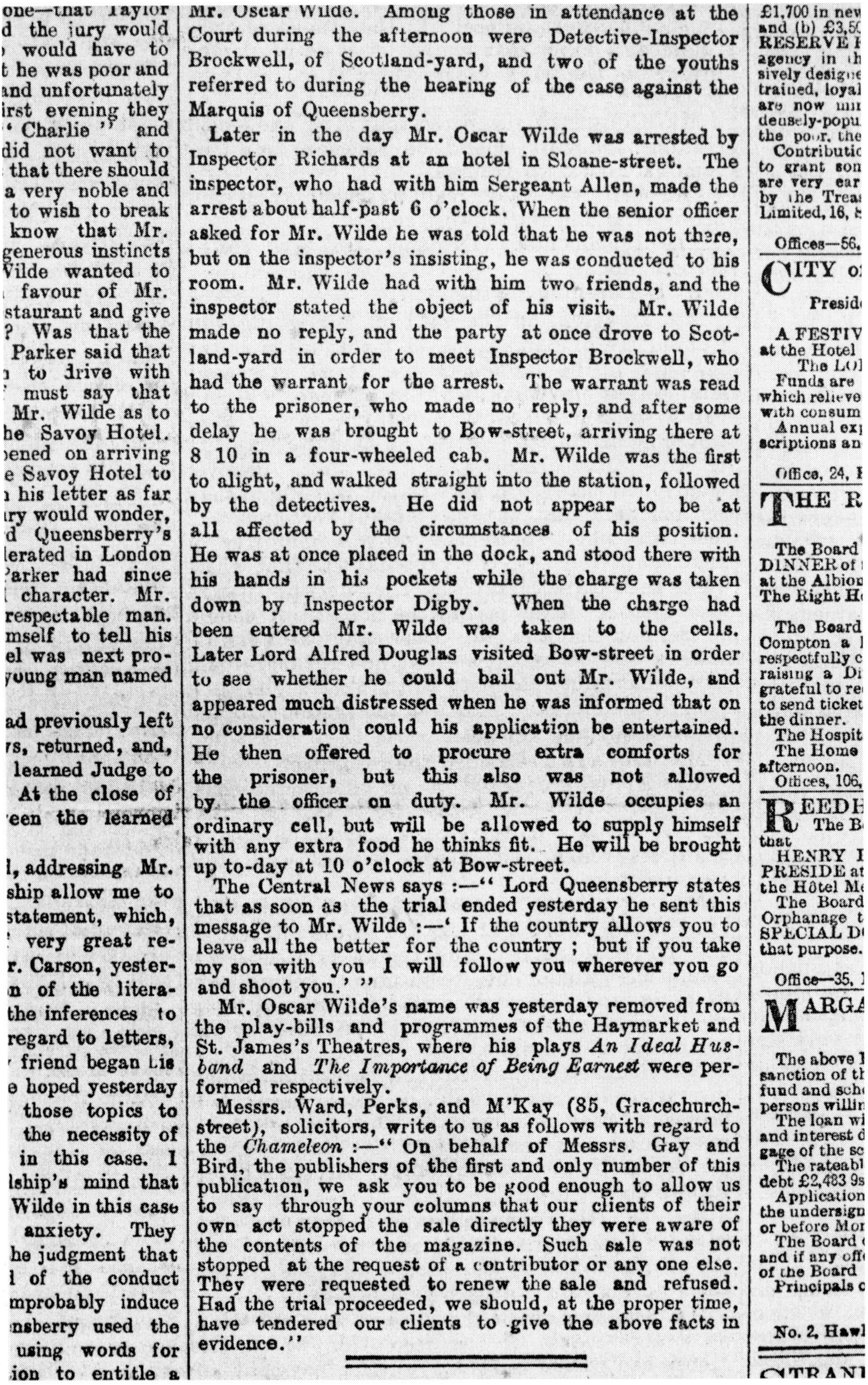

Mr. Oscar Wilde. Among those in attendance at the Court during the afternoon were Detective-Inspector Brockwell, of Scotland-yard, and two of the youths referred to during the hearing of the case against the Marquis of Queensberry.

Later in the day Mr. Oscar Wilde was arrested by Inspector Richards at an hotel in Sloane-street. The inspector, who had with him Sergeant Allen, made the arrest about half-past 6 o'clock. When the senior officer asked for Mr. Wilde he was told that he was not there, but on the inspector's insisting, he was conducted to his room. Mr. Wilde had with him two friends, and the inspector stated the object of his visit. Mr. Wilde made no reply, and the party at once drove to Scotland-yard in order to meet Inspector Brockwell, who had the warrant for the arrest. The warrant was read to the prisoner, who made no reply, and after some delay he was brought to Bow-street, arriving there at 8 10 in a four-wheeled cab. Mr. Wilde was the first to alight, and walked straight into the station, followed by the detectives. He did not appear to be at all affected by the circumstances of his position. He was at once placed in the dock, and stood there with his hands in his pockets while the charge was taken down by Inspector Digby. When the charge had been entered Mr. Wilde was taken to the cells. Later Lord Alfred Douglas visited Bow-street in order to see whether he could bail out Mr. Wilde, and appeared much distressed when he was informed that on no consideration could his application be entertained. He then offered to procure extra comforts for the prisoner, but this also was not allowed by the officer on duty. Mr. Wilde occupies an ordinary cell, but will be allowed to supply himself with any extra food he thinks fit. He will be brought up to-day at 10 o'clock at Bow-street.

The Central News says :—" Lord Queensberry states that as soon as the trial ended yesterday he sent this message to Mr. Wilde :—' If the country allows you to leave all the better for the country ; but if you take my son with you I will follow you wherever you go and shoot you.' "

Mr. Oscar Wilde's name was yesterday removed from the play-bills and programmes of the Haymarket and St. James's Theatres, where his plays *An Ideal Husband* and *The Importance of Being Earnest* were performed respectively.

Messrs. Ward, Perks, and M'Kay (85, Gracechurch-street), solicitors, write to us as follows with regard to the *Chameleon* :—" On behalf of Messrs. Gay and Bird, the publishers of the first and only number of this publication, we ask you to be good enough to allow us to say through your columns that our clients of their own act stopped the sale directly they were aware of the contents of the magazine. Such sale was not stopped at the request of a contributor or any one else. They were requested to renew the sale and refused. Had the trial proceeded, we should, at the proper time, have tendered our clients to give the above facts in evidence."

The Times reports on Oscar Wilde's arrest in the issue of 6 April, 1895.

1984 Citizens' Theatre, Glasgow.

Director and designer	Philip Prowse
LORD ILLINGWORTH	Robert David MacDonald
SIR JOHN PONTEFRACT	Robin Sneller
MR KELVIL	Laurance Rudic
ARCHDEACON DAUBENY	Derwent Watson
GERALD ARBUTHNOT	Paul Rhys
FRANCIS	Colin Wells
LADY HUNSTANTON	Ida Schuster
CAROLINE PONTEFRACT	Fidelis Morgan
LADY STUTFIELD	Anne Lambton
MRS ALLONBY	Roberta Taylor
HESTER WORSLEY	Yolanda Vasquez
MRS ARBUTHNOT	Jill Spurrier

The Citizens' exaggerated and unsympathetic acting style adds to the moral confusion by making Jill Spurrier's Mrs Arbuthnot – a pinch-lipped and sentimentally self-flagellating figure straight out of Victorian melodrama – seem almost as absurd as the house-party poseurs.

Joyce McMillan *Guardian*

Jill Spurrier wears her shame with arrogance . . . Robert David MacDonald plays Lord Illingworth as a disconcertingly charmless *vicieux* who believes everything he says even when it is untrue . . . in Paul Rhys – the Citizens' produce their ace: a young actor of rare spontaneity, innocence and warmth, who for most of the evening brimming with ruthlessness and wit persuades us to forget that young Gerald will, alas, turn into a perfect prig.

Michael Ratcliffe *Observer*

1988 Cambridge Theatre Company tour.

Director	Bill Pryde
LORD ILLINGWORTH	Malcolm Sinclair
SIR JOHN PONTEFRACT	David Stoll
MR KELVIL	Alec Linstead

ARCHDEACON DAUBENY	Hubert Rees
GERALD ARBUTHNOT	Gerard Logan
FRANCIS	Ben Miles
LADY HUNSTANTON	Andree Evans
CAROLINE PONTEFRACT	Georgine Anderson
LADY STUTFIELD	Isabelle Amyes
MRS ALLONBY	Bernice Stegers
HESTER WORSLEY	Catherine Roman
ALICE	Joanna Hartley
MRS ARBUTHNOT	Susan Brown

The cast rise confidently to the occasion with the wit and do remarkably well with the anger.

Jeremy Kingston *The Times*

1991 Barbican Theatre, London (Royal Shakespeare Company).

Director and designer	Philip Prowse
LORD ILLINGWORTH	John Carlisle
SIR JOHN PONTEFRACT	Leonard Kavanagh
LORD ALFRED RUFFORD	Marston Bloom
MR KELVIL	David Killick
ARCHDEACON DAUBENY	John Bott
GERALD ARBUTHNOT	Andrew Havill
FARQUHAR	Bill McGuirk
FRANCIS	Simon Day
LADY HUNSTANTON	Barbara Leigh-Hunt
CAROLINE PONTEFRACT	Cherry Norris
LADY STUTFIELD	Mary Chater
MRS ALLONBY	Nichola McAuliffe
HESTER WORSLEY	Julie Saunders
ALICE	Jayne Boniface
MRS ARBUTHNOT	Carol Royle
FOOTMAN	Stuart Hutchison

The Royal Shakespeare Company was so broke that they were going to have to shut their Barbican doors. In the circumstances, it seemed a bit odd that this enormously successful revival played for only twenty-five performances.

The biggest laugh was reserved for the scene where Gerald Arbuthnot attempted to throttle Lord Illingworth. 'Stop, Gerald, stop! He is your own father.' The second big laugh was when Gerald informed his mother that he was going to write a letter telling Illingworth that he must marry her.

The revival was sumptuous. ('Moderation is a fatal thing, Lady Hunstanton. Nothing succeeds like excess.') Philip Prowse emphasised the glittering artificiality with garden urns, a pond, banks of flowers, ivy-clad walls, gilt, velvet, roses, and a landscape by Claude. He sprang a number of surprises. The first was casting a black actress to play Hester Worsley. (Presumably, she was the illegitimate daughter of a white millionaire?) The cross-casting gave a new edge to Hester's strong belief that the sins of the father should be visited on the children, but it didn't seem very likely that the conservative Mrs Arbuthnot would have approved of her son marrying a black girl.

The second surprise was the introduction of a beautiful, silent young man who remained on the periphery and whom everybody ignored. His feet were bare. He wore flannels, an open neck, and an old school tie for a belt. Who was he? The programme identified him as Lord Alfred Rufford. He looked like Lord Alfred Douglas. Had Lady Hunstanton invited Oscar? Would Lord Illingworth pick Rufford up before Oscar did? Or would Oscar steal Gerald from Illingworth?

The third major surprise was that there was not a whiff of homosexuality about the production. Illingworth wanted Gerald for his private secretary and nothing else. John Carlisle played him for an aged dandy, ice-cold, supercilious, self-absorbed, a decadent villain without any redeeming charm, openly contemptuous of Mrs Arbuthnot. 'What a typical woman you are,' he said. Carlisle, languid in his cynicism and savage in his cruelty, was utterly obnoxious. Nichola McAuliffe's Mrs Allonby was equally charmless and ruthless.

Contrary to all expectation it was the melodramatic last act, heavy in Old Testament morality, which worked best. Carol Royle was gently tragic. There was a stillness about her performance. The intensity of her loathing for Illingworth was never in any doubt.

Barbara Leigh-Hunt was a delightfully vacuous Lady Hunstanton. Cherry Morris was a formidable Lady Caroline Pontefract and Mary Chater's silly Lady Stutfield was a common flirt.

The ladies wore their opulent clothes with style. Even the curtain-call was taken to the manner born.

> This is an impeccable production of an under-rated play and should do both Wilde and the RSC a lot of good.
>
> John Peter *Sunday Times*

> The melodramatic episodes are just a risible embarrassment.
>
> Paul Taylor *Independent*

> As soon as it's over, you realise that it's the stilted period piece that you always thought it was; but it is oddly moving while it lasts.
>
> John Gross *Sunday Telegraph*

1992 Theatre Royal, Haymarket, London.
Philip Prowse's production was revived with the following changes in the cast:

LORD ALFRED RUFFORD	Simon Day
MR KELVIL	Patrick Hannaway
ARCHDEACON DAUBENY	John Gill
FRANCIS	James Tucker
MRS ALLONBY	Jennifer Hilary
HESTER WORSLEY	Jaye Griffiths
ALICE	Nada Sharp
FOOTMAN	George Giles

> In its psychological command, Wilde never wrote a more substantial play. Prowse gives us the substance and with his own designs, the glittering surface.
>
> Jeremy Kingston *The Times*

> Many of Wilde's epigrams and deliciously catty social observations are served up with self-conscious emphasis, a travesty of the soufflé-light confection of guile and spontaneity he reputedly brought to the dinner table.
>
> Antonia Denford *City Limits*

1996 Abbey Theatre, Dublin.

Director	Ben Barnes
LORD ILLINGWORTH	Ian McElhinney
SIR JOHN PONTEFRACT	Barry McGovern
ALFRED RUFFORD	Philip Judge
MR KELVIL, MP	Malcolm Douglas
ARCHDEACON DAUBENY	Peadar Lamb
GERALD ARBUTHNOT	Andrew Scott
FRANCIS	Paschal Friel
FARQUHAR	Gavin O'Connor
LADY HUNSTANTON	Joan O'Hara
CAROLINE PONTEFRACT	Barbara Brennan
LADY STUTFIELD	Claudia Carroll
MRS ALLONBY	Donna Dent
HESTER WORSLEY	Andrea Irvine
ALICE	Maeve McGrath
MOLLY	Catherine Punch
MRS ARBUTHNOT	Catherine Byrne

The play isn't worth a bother, but the cast strive manfully and womanfully to do something with it.

Eamonn Sweeney *In Dublin*

It remains a poor play and Ben Barnes's new production of it, faithful to both the text and the theatrical constructs of its period, does little to invest it with dramatic life.

David Nowlan *Irish Times*

1997 Haymarket Theatre, Leicester.

Director	Paul Kerryson
LORD ILLINGWORTH	Richard Willis
SIR JOHN PONTEFRACT	John Atterbury
ALFRED RUFFORD	Vernon Thompson
MR KELVIL, MP	Claude Close
ARCHDEACON DAUBENY	Philip Anthony
GERALD ARBUTHNOT	Edmund Moriarty

SERVANT	Vernon Thompson
LADY HUNSTANTON	Janet Brown
CAROLINE PONTEFRACT	Margaret Robertson
LADY STUTFIELD	Celia White
MRS ALLONBY	Tracy Sweetinburgh
HESTER WORSLEY	Fo Cullen
ALICE	Celia White
MRS ARBUTHNOT	Shirley Stelfox

Paul Kerryson's production, handsomely costumed by Paul Farnsworth, was deliberately artificial. The cast, all in white, having made a mannered entrance, like mannequins on a catwalk, lined up, faced front, and ponged the wit, maxims, paradoxes and epigrams straight at the audience. Kerryson was always more interested in how Wilde looked and sounded rather than in what he had to say and felt.

The set had two statues. One was a caricature of Queen Victoria looking down her nose. This was removed the moment the play began. The other was of Oscar Wilde lounging on top of one of four huge portals, and there he remained throughout the action. Just in case the audience should miss the connection between the statue and Illingworth, Richard Willis adopted exactly the same position when he was attempting to seduce Gerald.

Willis emphasised Illingworth's vanity. He was a bit on the young side; or, at any rate, too young to be playing opposite Shirley Stelfox's Mrs Arbuthnot, who carried twenty years of sorrow (and Wilde's embarrassing rhetoric) as if she were in some Greek tragedy.

Gerald emerged a major character, Edmund Moriarty stressed what an awful duffer he is. A brilliant future is never on the cards. If he had become Illingworth's secretary, he would presumably have become his lover, to be discarded when somebody less naive, less gauche and less unworldly came along. Gerald is so pompous. The audience gasped when he told his mother that it was her duty to marry Illingworth.

Mrs Allonby, who lets her clever tongue run away with her (and not only her tongue) may be vulgar but she is never quite as vulgar as Tracy Sweetinburgh made her out to be. Hester Worsley harangued the idle rich, as if she were on a soap-box in Hyde Park. Lord Alfred Rufford (a role which is usually cut) was so common he might have been a rent boy.

It was to the credit of the actors that lines like, 'Stop, Gerald, stop! He is your own father!' and 'Child of my shame be still the child of my shame,' did not raise a titter. But then the audience did not laugh very much at the wit, either.

An Ideal Husband (1895)

To Frank Harris: A Slight Tribute to his Power and Distinction as an Artist, his Chivalry and Nobility as a Friend

Characters:

THE EARL OF CAVERSHAM, K G
LORD GORING, his son
SIR ROBERT CHILTERN, Bart., Under-Secretary for Foreign Affairs
VICOMTE DE NANJAC, Attaché at the French Embassy in London
MR MONTFORD
MASON, Butler to Sir Robert Chiltern
PHIPPS, Lord Goring's servant
JAMES, Footman
HAROLD, Footman
LADY CHILTERN
LADY MARKBY
THE COUNTESS OF BASILDON
MRS MARCHMONT
MISS MABEL CHILTERN, Sir Robert's sister
MRS CHEVELEY

The scenes of the play:

Act I Octagon Room in Sir Robert Chiltern's house in Grosvenor Square.
Act II Morning-room in Sir Robert Chiltern's house.
Act III Library of Lord Goring's house in Curzon Street.
Act IV As in Act I.

Time: The present *Place:* London
The action of the play is completed within twenty-four hours.

The Plot

ACT I Sir Robert Chiltern, Under-Secretary for Foreign Affairs, and his wife are holding a reception. Lady Markby brings a friend, Mrs Cheveley, who asks for his support in the House of Commons for the Argentine Canal Scheme. He refuses, saying it is a swindle. She tells him that she knows that he laid the foundation of his fortune by selling a cabinet secret and that she has a letter of his to prove it and if he doesn't do as she says, she will sell the letter to the press. Lady Chiltern (unaware of her husband's shady past) is amazed when he tells her that he has changed his mind and is going to support the Argentine Canal. She insists he write Mrs Cheveley a letter, retracting his offer.

ACT II Chiltern seeks advice from his best friend, Lord Goring, who urges him to tell his wife the truth. Mrs Cheveley calls to find if she had dropped a brooch the previous night. (She had, and it had been picked up by Goring who had recognised it and deliberately not handed it in.) Lady Chiltern tells Mrs Cheveley that, had she known who she was (a despised school contemporary who had been expelled for theft), she would not have admitted her to her house. Mrs Cheveley tells her the truth about her husband's wealth and Lady Chiltern, horrified, turns on her husband.

ACT III Lord Goring receives a letter from Lady Chiltern saying she is coming to see him urgently. His father arrives and he tells his manservant that a lady is arriving and to show her into the next room. Mrs Cheveley arrives and Phipps, thinking she is the person Goring is expecting, shows her into the next room. Chiltern arrives. Both men are amazed to find Mrs Cheveley in the next room. Chiltern, believing that Goring knew she was there, leaves, angrily. Mrs Cheveley, who had once been Goring's mistress, and knowing of his deep friendship with Chiltern, attempts to blackmail Goring, saying she will give him Chiltern's incriminating letter if he marries her. Goring produces the brooch and puts it on her wrist, accusing her of having stolen it from his cousin. Mrs Cheveley (who didn't know the brooch could also be used as a bracelet) cannot remove it. Goring threatens to call the police. Mrs Cheveley hands over the letter, but manages to steal Lady Chiltern's letter.

ACT IV Goring tells Lady Chiltern that Mrs Cheveley has stolen her letter and counsels her to tell her husband the truth, namely that the woman Goring thought was concealed in his rooms was her and not Mrs Cheveley; but Lady Chiltern says she can't do that. Just as she is about to try and intercept the letter, Chiltern comes in with it, presuming (since there is no name on the letter – a fact not noticed by Mrs Cheveley!) she had addressed it to him. Chiltern (who, bravely, had roundly denounced the Argentine Scheme in the House of Commons when he still thought Mrs Cheveley had his letter) is offered a post in the cabinet. His wife persuades him he should refuse. Goring persuades them to change their minds and asks for Chiltern's sister's hand in marriage. Chiltern, convinced that Goring is having an affair with Mrs Cheveley, refuses. Lady Chiltern confesses all.

The Characters

LORD GORING is on perfectly good terms with the world. Thirty-four years old, idle, rich, languorous and vain, he is the flawless dandy. But though excessively trivial on the surface, underneath he is totally reliable, a good, solid friend to Lord and Lady Chiltern. His scenes, with Mrs Cheveley (his ex-mistress), Mabel Chiltern (his future fiancée), and his father, are in the best tradition of the English comedy of manners, which owes so much to the Irish playwrights. Goring is Wilde's witty self:

> In modern life nothing produces such an effect as a good platitude.
>
> A man who cannot talk morality twice a week to a large, popular, immoral audience is quite over as a serious politician.
>
> To love oneself is the beginning of a lifelong romance.

MRS CHEVELEY, twice married, clever, handsome, dangerous, is a scarlet woman *par excellence*, a scheming Victorian stage villainess, as adept with epigrams as she is with blackmail. 'Morality,' she says, 'is simply the attitude we adopt towards people whom we personally dislike.' She adores scandal and wears it like a new bonnet. Politics, she claims, are her only pleasure.

ROBERT CHILTERN, Under-Secretary for Foreign Affairs at forty, and with a brilliant career ahead of him, is fatally compromised and liable to be hounded out of political life. Chiltern is Wilde. 'Do you think what I did eighteen years ago should be brought up against me now?' he asks. 'Do you think it fair that a man's whole career should be ruined for a fault done in one's boyhood almost?' Chiltern, a weak and shallow man, argues that public life and private life are two different things and that no one should he judged by his past. His wife disagrees: 'One's past is what one is. It is the only way one should be judged.'

LADY CHILTERN is a woman of the highest principles. Cold, stern and without mercy, she expects her husband (whom she has idolised for his ideals, principles, purity, nobility and honesty) to be beyond reproach and when she finds he is not, she turns on him. 'Don't come near me! Don't touch me!' One critic, unusually percipient (four months ahead of Wilde's trial) complained, 'To parody Ibsen, "Woman don't do that"; they stick to a man they love to the last instant. They would bribe warders to visit him in Holloway gaol. They would kiss him in the dock before he went down to penal servitude.'

MABEL CHILTERN, Sir Robert's sister, is a pert, strong-minded, self-possessed young lady, who is determined to marry Lord Goring; and indeed she is the ideal match (and the ideal 'beard'?) for him. Wilde says Mabel is the perfect example of the English type of prettiness, the apple-blossom type and that she looks like a Tanagra statuette.

THE EARL OF CAVERSHAM, an old gentleman of seventy, is the father of Lord Goring, whom he is always criticising and whom he obviously adores.

LADY MARKBY is a pleasant, kindly, popular woman who (says Mrs Cheveley) 'talks more and says less than anybody I ever met.'

> Nothing is so dangerous as being too modern. One is apt to grow old-fashioned quite suddenly.

BARON ARNHEIM, a character who is never seen, is vividly described by Chiltern as 'a man of most subtle and refined intellect, a man of culture, charm, and distinction . . . One of the most intellectual men I have ever met . . . with a strange smile on his pale, curved lips.' Arnheim corrupted Chiltern when he was twenty-two in much the same way that Illingworth attempted to corrupt Gerald Arbuthnot in *A Woman of No Importance.* The scene Chiltern describes is clearly a seduction scene.

1895 3 January Premiere: Theatre Royal, Haymarket, London. Transferred: Criterion Theatre on 13 April.

Lessee	Herbert Beerbohm Tree
Manager	Lewis Waller
THE EARL OF CAVERSHAM	Alfred Bishop
LORD GORING	Charles H Hawtrey
SIR ROBERT CHILTERN	Lewis Waller
VICOMTE DE NANJAC	Cosmo Stuart
MR MONTFORD	Henry Stanford
MASON	H Deane
PHIPPS	C H Brookfield
JAMES	Charles Meyrick
HAROLD	Mr Goodhart
LADY CHILTERN	Julia Neilson
LADY MARKBY	Fanny Brough
COUNTESS OF BASILDON	Vane Featherston
MRS MARCHMONT	Helen Forsyth
MABEL CHILTERN	Maude Millett
MRS CHEVELEY	Florence West

Anyone happening to look in at the Haymarket Theatre on the fall of the curtain last night would have come to the conclusion that Mr Oscar Wilde had written a brilliant play, and no doubt many of those who cheered so lustily were quite of that opinion. But viewed dispassionately, *An Ideal Husband* was a thing of shreds and patches, a stringing together of a number of inconsequent incidents whose only dramatic value was that they have been in use for years past, and are therefore to be borne with as we bear with the ancient jokes of an eldery, highly respectable and, above all, wealthy member of one's family. There is nothing which gives Mr Wilde the right to class himself as a playwright either of promise or experience.

Morning Advertiser

We doubt not that the play will be successful, it is so smart and so characteristic of its author, who has the rare art of embroidering vulgarity with a passing show of wit. If the mere story be found tedious, artificial, and of the calibre of the 'penny in the slot' order of dramatic literature, it will pass because of its frank insincerity. There is scarcely a sincere line or character in the play; but neither Mr Oscar Wilde nor his dramatic exercises are to be taken very seriously. It will amuse the thoughtless and that is better than disgusting the earnest.

Daily Telegraph

And now, behold! the artist has turned mechanic, and a cheap, second-rate workman at that. Much of the dialogue is forced and strained, and the exposition of character is shallower than ever. We owe too much to Mr Wilde to be angry with him; we can only mourn in sorrow, not in anger, over his degeneration.

Era

One could believe easily that it was written by a disciple of Mr Wilde, who had been studying, insufficiently, the school of Scribe, as well as the joke-manufacturing process of the famous pseudo-epigrammatist. It may seem strange that Mr Wilde should be old-fashioned, since the author is supposed to be ultra-modern; yet no one could well deny that the sense of weariness it sometimes causes is due partly to the fact that it is antiquated in method, and that the method is not well handled. There is hardly a character in the piece in whom one detects any signs of life.

Monocle *Sketch*

The fact remains that Mr Wilde's work is not only poor and sterile, but essentially vulgar.

A B Walkley *Speaker*

As far as I can ascertain, I am the only person in London who cannot sit down and write an Oscar Wilde play at will. The fact that his plays, though apparently lucrative, remain unique under these circumstances, says much for the self-denial of our scribes. In a certain sense Mr Wilde is to me our only thorough playwright. He plays with everything: with wit, with philosophy, with drama, with actors and audience, with the whole theatre. Such a feast scandalises the Englishman, who can no more play with wit and philosophy than he can with a football or a cricket bat.

George Bernard Shaw *Saturday Review*

Following the first night, Robert Ross interviewed Oscar Wilde for the *St James's Gazette*:

> 'But are you satisfied with the interpreters of the "Ideal Husband"?'
>
> 'I am charmed with all of them. Perhaps they are a little too fascinating. The stage is the refuge of the too fascinating.'
>
> 'Have you heard it said that all the characters in your play talk as you do?'
>
> 'Rumours of that kind have reached me from time to time,' said Mr Wilde, lighting a cigarette, 'and I fancy that some such criticism has been made. The fact is that it is only in the last few years that the dramatic critic has had the opportunity of seeing plays written by any one who has a mastery of style. In the case of a dramatist also an artist it is impossible not to feel that the work of art, to be a work of art, must be dominated by the artist. Every play of Shakespeare is dominated by Shakespeare. Ibsen and Dumas dominate their works. My works are dominated by myself.'
>
> 'Have you ever been influenced by any of your predecessors?'
>
> 'It is enough for me to state definitely, and I hope once for all, that not a single dramatist in this century has ever in the smallest degree influenced me. Only two have interested me.'
>
> 'And they are?'
>
> 'Victor Hugo and Maeterlinck.'

1895 American premiere: Lyceum Theatre, New York.

EARL OF CAVERSHAM	W J LeMoyne
LORD GORING	Herbert Kelcey
SIR ROBERT CHILTERN	Stephen Grattan
VICOMTE DE NANJAC	David Elmer
MR MONTFORD	Frank Short
MASON	Charles A Goettler
PHIPPS	Ernest Tarleton
LADY CHILTERN	Isabel Irving
LADY MARKBY	Mrs Charles Walcot
COUNTESS OF BASILDON	Bessie Tyree
MRS MARCHMONT	Mrs Thomas Whiffen

MABEL CHILTERN	Katherine Florence
MRS CHEVELEY	Rhoda Cameron

This drama is no less flimsy and ephemeral than its predecessors. There is, however, an audience for stories of amatory and semi-political intrigues and for 'smart' or more or less ill-bred talk and to that audience. 'An Ideal Husband' may prove temporarily acceptable. Mr Wilde's plays always blow over, and this smoke-wreath will vanish with the rest. There is no solidity to Mr Oscar Wilde.

New York Daily Tribune

It is a fragile thing of course, for Oscar loves fragility as he loves violets and the sound of his own voice, but it is full of that fluent talk that is a very clever imitation of wit, and has made Mr Wilde the little Congreve of the present hour . . . Mr Grattan and Miss Irving act the trying characters of the husband and wife with much zeal, both being seemingly conscious that they are very young, and anxious to overcome as far as possible that pleasant deficiency.

New York Times

'A lot of d— nobodies talking about nothing.' This is a wonderfully sincere self-criticism on the part of Mr Wilde, and an admirable summary of the whole first act . . . Miss Irving is a most sprightly and engaging comedienne but not at all an emotional actress and Lady Chiltern is emotional to the point of hysteria. Miss Cameron, as a lady who loves to speculate in canals, was superb in speech and bearing.

New York Herald

1905 Munich. German premiere at Residenz Theater.

1914 St James's Theatre, London.

Licensee and Manager	George Alexander
EARL OF CAVERSHAM	Alfred Bishop
LORD GORING	George Alexander
SIR ROBERT CHILTERN	Arthur Wontner
VICOMTE DE NANJAC	J S Russell
MR MONTFORD	George Bishop

MASON	A Glascodine
PHIPPS	E Vivian Reynolds
JAMES	Guy Dawson
HAROLD	W Coats Bush
LADY CHILTERN	Phyllis Neilson-Terry
LADY MARKBY	Henrietta Watson
COUNTESS OF BASILDON	Elizabeth Chesney
MRS MARCHMONT	Muriel Barnby
MABEL CHILTERN	Amy Brandon-Thomas
MRS CHEVELEY	Hilda Moore

Robert Ross, Wilde's literary executor, attempted to bring the play up to date. There were references to eugenics instead of higher education, to motor cars instead of carriages, to golf instead of the Scottish novel, and to the Sahara Irrigation Scheme instead of the Argentine Canal.

> How can the players of today put life into his saw-dust padded types? They do their best. Sir George Alexander works hard to pit feeling as well as humour into the speeches of the *raisonneur* . . . But really the play as a whole is *vieux jeu.*
>
> *Illustrated London News*

> Sir George Alexander plays as only Sir George Alexander can the flippant *raisonneur* and wears a moustache, the mild ferocity of which would do credit to a German subaltern! . . . Mr Arthur Wontner, on the other hand, is a splendidly sincere and incisive Sir Robert Chiltern, and his present performance is one of the best things he has done.
>
> *Stage*

> The Lady Chiltern of Miss Phyllis Neilson-Terry looks as beautiful as a statue and seems almost as cold until the flood-tide of her emotion is let loose. Then she exhibits extraordinary power and pathos, with a tenderness that is wonderfully natural and touching.
>
> *The Times*

> I have never seen Miss Hilda Moore to better advantage than as Mrs Cheveley, the unscrupulous, deep, designing villainess of the play. The part suits her admirably.
>
> *World*

1918 Comedy Theatre, New York.

EARL OF CAVERSHAM	Cyril Harcourt
LORD GORING	Julian L'Estrange
SIR ROBERT CHILTERN	Norman Trevor
VICOMTE DE NANJAC	George Hayes
MR MONTFORD	S V Phillips
MASON	Alfred Helton
PHIPPS	Henry Crocker
LADY CHILTERN	Beatrice Beckley
LADY MARKBY	Alice Augarde Butler
COUNTESS OF BASILDON	Merle Maddern
MRS MARCHMONT	Elizabeth Deimel
MABEL CHILTERN	Gretchen Yates
MRS CHEVELEY	Constance Collier

No English dramatist is as narrowly limited in his abilities as Wilde is; but few have qualities that are as distinct and unapproachable. No one who cares for intelligent and genuine gaiety can afford to miss *An Ideal Husband.*

New York Times

Goring is the real part in the play, the real dominant, interesting character. Sir Robert is an ass, and a pompous, sentimental ass into the bargain. Mr L'Estrange does as well as his weight will permit but the part is beyond his register . . . Gretchen Yates looks twenty-eight, to be euphemistic, and she speaks the sparkling froth as though she were ashamed of it and of the author . . . Mrs Cheveley is supposed to look 'rather like an orchid'. The only flower Constance Collier suggested to my mind was a particularly flourishing chrysanthemum.

Louis Herwin *Globe*

Miss Collier played the practical Mrs Cheveley with great suavity and delicate force. She clothed the crudity of some of her situations with an air of worldliness and self-possession that made them seem positively convincing.

New York Daily Tribune

1923 Toronto. Canadian premiere at Regent Theatre.

1935 German film: *Ein Idealer Gatte*

Director	Herbert Selpin
Screenplay	Thea von Harbou

EARL OF CAVERSHAM	Paul Henckels
LORD GORING	Georg Alexander
SIR ROBERT CHILTERN	Karl Ludwig Diehl
VICOMTE DE NANJAC	Werner Scharf
MASON	Heinz Förster-Ludwig
PARKER	Karl Dannemann
LADY CHILTERN	Brigitte Helm
LADY MARKBY	Toni Tetzlaff
MABEL CHILTERN	Annie Markart
MRS CHEVELEY	Sibylle Schmitz
MR VICKERS	Hermann Fink
MISS HARRIET	Babette Jensen

Miss Schmitz – despite hard work – is badly miscast. Generally enrolled as a heavy, she's asked to do a sophisticated job here, and the results are somewhat mangled. At least they might have taken away her gay '90s feathers and some of the grease paint.

Edga *Variety*

1943 Westminster Theatre, London.

Director	Jack Minster
Scenery and costumes	Rex Whistler

EARL OF CAVERSHAM	Esme Percy
LORD GORING	Roland Culver
SIR ROBERT CHILTERN	Manning Whiley
VICOMTE DE NANJAC	Ian Lubbock
MR MONTFORD	Charles Deane
MASON	John Vere
PHIPPS	Townsend Whitling
JAMES	John Baker
HAROLD	Ian Morris

LADY CHILTERN	Rosemary Scott
LADY MARKBY	Irene Vanbrugh
COUNTESS OF BASILDON	Nan Hopkins
MRS MARCHMONT	Rosamund Greenwood
MABEL CHILTERN	Peggy Bryan
MRS CHEVELEY	Martita Hunt

Wilde's indolent way with the story and with the characterisation of this comedy has the odd effect of rousing the suspicion that he was laughing not only at public morality, but at his audience . . . Miss Martita Hunt speaks her immoral paradoxes as though she were inventing them . . . Dame Irene Vanbrugh has a few minutes of comic perfection . . . Esme Percy burlesques a 'heavy' father with much delicacy and humour.

The Times

Miss Martita Hunt, drawn as a third-rate adventuress, looked like a Sargent and displayed inimitable breeding.

James Agate *Sunday Times*

1947 Theatre Royal, Bristol.

Director	Hugh Hunt
EARL OF CAVERSHAM	Paul Rogers
LORD GORING	Robert Eddison
SIR ROBERT CHILTERN	William Devlin
VICOMTE DE NANJAC	Rolf Lefebvre
MR MONTFORD	Joseph James
MASON	Edward Stanley
PHIPPS	Jack Moss
LADY CHILTERN	Elizabeth Sellars
LADY MARKBY	Dorothy Lane
COUNTESS OF BASILDON	Anne Salisbury
MRS MARCHMONT	Joan Cairncross
MABEL CHILTERN	Jane Wenham
MRS CHEVELEY	Catherine Lacey

1947 British film.

Producer and director	Alexander Korda
Screenplay	Lajos Biro
EARL OF CAVERSHAM	C Aubrey Smith
LORD GORING	Michael Wilding
SIR ROBERT CHILTERN	Hugh Williams
VICOMTE DE NANJAC	Michael Anthony
MR MONTFORD	Peter Hobbes
MASON	John Clifford
PHIPPS	Fred Groves
MR TRAFFORD	Michael Ward
LADY CHILTERN	Diana Wynyard
LADY MARKBY	Constance Collier
COUNTESS OF BASILDON	Harriette Johns
MRS MARCHMONT	Christine Nordon
MABEL CHILTERN	Glynis Johns
MRS CHEVELEY	Paulette Goddard
DUKE OF NONSUCH	Michael Medwin

The Naughty Nineties crows upon the screen
Victoria reigns – but FASHION is the Queen.

The above legend and the tinkling playing of 'After the Ball' behind the credit titles did not augur well for Alexander Korda's approach.

Hugh Williams and Diana Wynyard, as the Chilterns, were the perfect dull couple. Williams was very stiff and wooden (perhaps deliberately so) and the film showed no awareness of the comic irony that anybody should think Chiltern ideal Prime Minister material. Wynyard was a solemn prig, as beautiful and as cold as a classical statue. She looked exactly the sort of person who would always get the Good Conduct medal at school.

Michael Wilding played Lord Goring with a pleasant, light touch. He was very much the conceited young puppy, though never quite aristocratic enough; in truth, despite having been coached by Martita Hunt (*grande dame* of *grandes dames*) he was a bit common. He was fine with the wit ('Vulgarity is simply the conduct of other people'), fine with the vanity ('To love oneself is the beginning of a lifelong romance'), fine in his relations with his father, his manservant, and the girl he loves; but he was not so good when he had to be serious. He was a poor listener and offered Hugh Williams no support in Chiltern's long confession scene, visibly not paying attention. Korda had wanted Rex Harrison for the role.

Paulette Goddard (who was in the cast for the US box office) was ravishingly gowned by Cecil Beaton in emerald green, flaming pink, and waspish yellow and black; she brought a brash, metallic, American vulgarity to Mrs Cheveley's mischief-making.

Glynis Johns, a husky charmer, was absolutely enchanting as Mabel Chiltern. Her tears-in-the-eyes confession of her love for Lord Goring was most touching: 'If you knew anything, which you don't, you would know that I adore you. Everyone in London knows it except you. It is a public scandal the way I adore you. I have been going about for the last six months telling the whole of society that I adore you. I wonder you consent to have anything to say to me. I have no character left at all. At least, I feel so happy that I am quite sure I have no character left at all.' It was difficult to imagine it being better done.

C Aubrey Smith, an actor of the old school, who had appeared in the second revival of *Lady Windermere's Fan* in 1904, was cast as Lord Caversham. He was his usual immensely distinguished, crusty, bushy-eyebrowed self, a fine Whig type who might well have been painted by Lawrence.

Constance Collier, who had played Mrs Cheveley in New York in 1918, was cast as Lady Markby, but her part had all but disappeared. Left without any lines, she jutted her jaw and rattled her teeth.

An Ideal Husband always looked like a photographed play. The actors invariably entered and exited the frame as if they were in a theatre and had been standing about in the wings waiting to come on. Vincent Korda provided over-furnished sets rather than rooms. The rooms were framed with heavy curtains giving them a proscenium-arch effect. The opulence (tapestries, chandeliers, balustrades) was overpowering. The luxury was clearly there for the British public as a much-needed antidote to post-war austerity.

A considerable portion of the dialogue was sacrificed in favour of looking at a panorama of Hyde Park Corner (reconstructed at Shepperton Studios) and observing the phaetons, broughams, horse-riders, Household Cavalry, etc., parading by. It was mere spectacle, a waste of time. A more relevant scene, but repeated too often, was the picture of the crush on the Chilterns' crowded staircase. The actors were waxworks wearing costumes. They and their costumes were there to dress the set. The garish Technicolor was unflattering to their complexions.

Seldom have such polished manners been wedded to such good technique in an English studio.

Matthew Norgate *Tribune*

Poor Paulette Goddard vainly trying to be a sophisticated and ageing siren is wrong even down to her corsets.

Annabel Farjeon *Time and Tide*

I must confess I find the whole thing magnificently indigestible. It's worth seeing all the same.

Daily Graphic

1959 Sofia. A production by the Bulgarian National Theatre.

1965 Strand Theatre, London.

Director	James Roose-Evans
EARL OF CAVERSHAM	Roger Livesey/Raymond Huntley
LORD GORING	Richard Todd
SIR ROBERT CHILTERN	Michael Denison/Michael Goodliffe
VICOMTE DE NANJAC	Richard Dennis
MR MONTFORD	Keith Bowles
PHIPPS	Cyril Wheeler
LADY CHILTERN	Dulcie Gray/Rachel Gurney
LADY MARKBY	Ursula Jeans
COUNTESS OF BASILDON	Anne Cameron
MRS MARCHMONT	Gillian Raine
MABEL CHILTERN	Perlita Neilson
MRS CHEVELEY	Margaret Lockwood

The cast, very much a second eleven, was drawn from the British film stars of the 1940s and 1950s. The production was uninspired and the epigrams didn't sparkle. Margaret Lockwood (a famous *Wicked Lady*) knew how to mix epigrams and blackmail as Mrs Cheveley, but Richard Todd, returning to the stage after a seventeen-year absence, was too old to be playing Lord Goring and had neither the charm nor the wit. The best performance was by Perlita Neilson as a sweet and pert Mabel.

> Her [Margaret Lockwood] elegant timing of the delivery of a stinging insult, her mocking triumphant laughter, her precise sense of period and character make the performance the best thing in an otherwise limp revival.
>
> *Punch*

> Michael Denison and Dulcie Gray, as the blackmailed statesman and his highly principled wife, play with an anonymous restraint which suggests embarrassment.
>
> *The Times*

1969 British television.

Director	Rudolph Cartier
EARL OF CAVERSHAM	Charles Carson
LORD GORING	Jeremy Brett
SIR ROBERT CHILTERN	Keith Michell
VICOMTE DE NANJAC	Michel Faure
MASON	Raymond Graham
PHIPPS	Erik Chitty
LADY CHILTERN	Dinah Sheridan
LADY MARKBY	Zena Dare
COUNTESS OF BASILDON	Madge Miller
MRS MARCHMONT	Penelope Lee
MABEL CHILTERN	Susan Hampshire
MRS CHEVELEY	Margaret Leighton

'To love oneself,' said Lord Goring, 'is the beginning of a life-long romance.' Jeremy Brett and Erik Chitty (as Phipps) established a flippant note in a pre-credit sequence drawn from Act III. But once the play began Rudolph Cartier concentrated on the seriousness.

Keith Michell (as Robert Chiltern) sported a caddish moustache and looked more than capable of compromise, and sooner rather than later. The high spot of his performance was when he turned on his wife and blamed her for his crisis: 'Why can't women love us, faults and all? Why do you place us on monstrous pedestals?' he roared.

The ending was changed, or rather the play stopped on Chiltern's decision to do the honourable thing and resign, thus negating Wilde's satire on political life and society.

Margaret Leighton did not disguise what a horrid woman the blackmailing and no-longer-young Mrs Cheveley was. Zena Dare, playing Lady Markby, was easily the most aristocratic-looking person in the cast.

> Miss Leighton shone, was witty, glamorous, poised and, in defeat, quite human.
>
> A P Ryan *The Times*

1973 West German television: *Ein Idealer Gatte*

1976 Yvonne Arnaud Theatre, Guildford, and UK tour.

Directed	Val May
EARL OF CAVERSHAM	Wilfrid Hyde White
LORD GORING	Simon Williams
SIR ROBERT CHILTERN	Edward Hardwicke
VICOMTE DE NANJAC	Graham Callan
MR MONTFORD	Simon Clarke
MASON	Barry Wilmore
PHIPPS	Robert Tunstall
JAMES	John Benjamin
LADY CHILTERN	Rachel Gurney
LADY MARKBY	Margaretta Scott
COUNTESS OF BASILDON	Bernice Stegers
MRS MARCHMONT	Julie Neubert
MABEL CHILTERN	Judy Geeson
MRS CHEVELEY	Sylvia Syms
LADY BARFORD	Deborah Snook
DUCHESS OF MARYBOROUGH	Ethel Drew
MAID	Ethel Drew

1978 Churchill Theatre, Bromley, and UK tour.

Director	Patrick Lau
THE EARL OF CAVERSHAM	Geoffrey Toone
LORD GORING	Edward de Souza
SIR ROBERT CHILTERN	Lewis Jones

VICOMTE DE NANJAC	Gareth Armstrong
MR MONTFORD	Michael Napier Brown
MASON	Douglas Milvain
PHIPPS	Paddy Ward
JAMES	Martin Gower
HAROLD	David Woodcock
LADY CHILTERN	Renee Asherson
LADY MARKBY	June Jago
COUNTESS OF BASILDON	Margo Johns
MRS MARCHMONT	Jane Collins
MABEL CHILTERN	Jacquie-Ann Carr
MRS CHEVELEY	Sylvia Syms

1979 Horseshoe Theatre Company (UK tour).

Director	David Gilmore
THE EARL OF CAVERSHAM	Raymond Francis
LORD GORING	John Fraser
SIR ROBERT CHILTERN	Richard Coleman
VICOMTE DE NANJAC	Mark Dowse
MR MONTFORD	Marc Ashley
MASON	Michael Sharvell-Martin
PHIPPS	Jonathan Cecil
LADY CHILTERN	Bridget de Courcy
LADY MARKBY	Betty Marsden
COUNTESS OF BASILDON	Mary Mitchell
MRS MARCHMONT	Sheila Felvin
MABEL CHILTERN	Karen Dotrice
MRS CHEVELEY	Hildegard Neil
MAID	Jane Myerson
A GUEST	Nicholas Bell

The production alternated with *Lady Windermere's Fan*. Lord Goring was played with considerable charm by John Fraser and his scenes with Mabel, with his father, and with his servant were all delightful. It was interesting to note that whereas Lord Goring's epigrams served to make him more likeable, Mrs Cheveley's epigrams only increased her essential nastiness. Hildegard Neil caught the glib tone exactly.

Betty Marsden played Lady Markby in an impossibly stagey manner and the result was a tiresome and very faded copy of Edith Evans's Lady Bracknell. Much more authentically Wilde was Karen Dotrice, whose self-possessed Mabel Chiltern was clearly a first draft for Cecily Cardew in *The Importance of Being Earnest.*

1981 Russian film: *Idealny Muzh*

Director	Viktor Georiyev
Screenplay	Viktor Kadochnikov

EARL OF CAVERSHAM	Pavel Kadochnikov
LORD GORING	Eduard Martsevich
SIR ROBERT CHILTERN	Yuri Yakovlev
LADY CHILTERN	Anna Tvelenyova
LADY MARKBY	E Khanayeva
MABEL CHILTERN	Elena Korenyeva
MRS CHEVELEY	Ludmila Gurchenko

Miss Mabel is an ineffably Russian ingénue, though none the worse for that; but the actors playing Sir Robert and Lord Goring are credible English gentlemen, despite the latter's wheaten locks.

John Pym *Monthly Film Bulletin*

1986 Citizens' Theatre, Glasgow.

Director and designer	Philip Prowse

THE EARL OF CAVERSHAM	Robert David MacDonald
LORD GORING	Harry Gibson
SIR ROBERT CHILTERN	Mark Lewis
VICOMTE DE NANJAC	Laurence Rudie
LADY CHILTERN	Anne Lambton
LADY MARKBY	Jill Spurrier
MABEL CHILTERN	Claire Hirsh
MRS CHEVELEY	Roberta Taylor

Philip Prowse's set had a hot-house opulence, with golden spangled draperies, black marble urns, and ormolu bowls filled with artificial fruit. The production opened with Mrs Marchmont and Lady Basildon dead drunk.

When Mrs Cheveley was struggling to get the bracelet off her arm, she said 'Fuck!', which surprised everybody (though Wilde's stage direction does say 'a curse breaks from her'). So that Goring would not attempt to stop her departure and make a scene in front of his manservant, she ripped open her bodice to suggest that there had been a bit of hurly-burly on the chaise longue.

Lady Chiltern was played for a stupid woman. Chiltern was played for what he was: an unattractive politician, a vulgar *arriviste*. At the end of the play he asked her if she loved him or merely pitied him. Prowse left the question unanswered, cutting the kiss and the last lines.

Tommy Trafford, who keeps proposing to Mabel Chiltern off-stage and never appears, made an appearance.

> The point, that Wilde's society is predatory and violent rather than effete, is mercilessly made. People approach each other purposefully and brutally. Conversation is used as a two-edged sword. Lord Goring (Harry Gibson) is a thoughtful, unsmiling dandy who uses wit as a melancholy diversion while he considers the next move (or his next evasion).
>
> *Observer*

> Philip Prowse provides a bilious portrait of a coarse and raffish English upper-crust . . . As a director he brings out the spiritual squalor behind the chiselled phrases.
>
> Michael Billington *Guardian*

1987 Chichester Festival Theatre, Sussex.

Director	Tony Britton
EARL OF CAVERSHAM	William Fox
LORD GORING	Clive Francis
SIR ROBERT CHILTERN	David Gwillim
VICOMTE DE NANJAC	Collin Johnson
MR MONTFORD	Alexander Hanson
MASON	John Peters
PHIPPS	Peter Fontaine

FOOTMAN	Malcolm Browning
LADY CHILTERN	Lucy Fleming
LADY MARKBY	June Whitfield
COUNTESS OF BASILDON	Rebecca Roper-Caldbeck
MRS MARCHMONT	Lynn Clayton
MABEL CHILTERN	Amanda Waring
MRS CHEVELEY	Joanna Lumley
DUCHESS OF MARYBOROUGH	Valerie Minifie
LADY JANE BARFORD	Caroline Lintott

Joanna Lumley's Mrs Cheveley is acted off the stage by her sensational dresses.

Nicholas de Jongh *Guardian*

Never have the epigrams throbbed so mirthlessly as when Mr Francis reels them off.

Martin Hoyle *Financial Times*

1989 Gate Theatre, Dublin.

Director	Ben Barnes
EARL OF CAVERSHAM	Aiden Grennell
LORD GORING	Stephen Brennan
SIR ROBERT CHILTERN	Alan Stanford
VICOMTE DE NANJAC	Derek Chapman
MASON	Christopher Fitz-Simon
PHIPPS	Mal Whyte
MR MONTFORD	Peter Hanly
LADY CHILTERN	Susan Fitzgerald
LADY MARKBY	Doreen Hepburn
COUNTESS OF BASILDON	Marion O'Dwyer
MRS MARCHMONT	Fiona Douglas-Stewart
MABEL CHILTERN	Orla Charlton
MRS CHEVELEY	Barbara Brennan
DUCHESS OF MARYBOROUGH	Laura Fagan

1989 Westminster Theatre, London.

Director	Patrick Sandford
EARL OF CAVERSHAM	Richard Murdoch
LORD GORING	Jeremy Sinden
SIR ROBERT CHILTERN	Jeremy Child
VICOMTE DE NANJAC	Sean Aita
MASON	Deborah Blake
PHIPPS	Roy Boutcher
LADY CHILTERN	Liz Bagley
LADY MARKBY	Moira Redmond
COUNTESS OF BASILDON	Rachel Preece
MRS MARCHMONT	Shauna Baird
MABEL CHILTERN	Emma Watson
MRS CHEVELEY	Delia Lindsay

The production cut Lord Goring's speech about a man's life being worth more than a woman's.

> This is an elegant and sinister show as relevant to modern politics as it is to Wilde's downfall.
>
> Dan Jones *Sunday Telegraph*

> . . . curiously lifeless . . . the characters seem little more than witty waxworks.
>
> Annalena McAfee *Evening Standard*

1992 Globe Theatre, London.

Director	Peter Hall
EARL OF CAVERSHAM	Michael Denison
VISCOUNT GORING	Martin Shaw
SIR ROBERT CHILTERN	David Yelland
VICOMTE DE NANJAC	Dominic Hawksley
MR MONTFORD	Peter Gordon
MASON	Robin Browne
PHIPPS	Peter Gordon
JAMES	Roderick Nicolson

LADY CHILTERN	Hannah Gordon
LADY MARKBY	Dulcie Gray
COUNTESS OF BASILDON	Deborah Makepeace
MRS MARCHMONT	Kate Isitt
MABEL CHILTERN	Victoria Hasted
MRS CHEVELEY	Anna Carteret
MR BARFORD	Roderick Nicolson
LADY JANE BARFORD	Teresa Forsyth

All Wilde's characters are extravagantly emotional and are quite naturally eccentric. But they do not show their feelings or release their emotions; that would be un-English. They utter witticisms instead. The more emotional they become, the more extravagant the wit. It is a type of English stiff upper lip; and it informs all Wilde's theatre. Beneath the wit there is always an intense emotional reality. The actor must investigate it, know it, and create it every night. Then he must mask it completely with the wit.

Peter Hall *Guardian*

'Scandal,' says Mrs Cheveley, 'used to lend charm or at least interest to a man. Now they crush him.' Oscar Wilde's play about corruption in high places was as topical as ever, opening as it did in the middle of the Matrix Churchill 'arms for sale for Iraq' scandal. Politicians have always had to be economical with the truth.

'Truth,' says Chiltern, 'is a very complex thing, and politics is a very complex business. There are wheels within wheels . . . Sooner or later in political life one has to compromise. Everyone does.'

A Victorian gold sovereign hung in front of the stage. Elgar played. Peter Hall's triumph was the actors' confident handling of the melodrama. David Yelland was first-rate as Chiltern. Hannah Gordon, cold, stern and quite pitiless in her perfection, was a worthy rival for Anna Carteret's handsome, scheming adventuress. Hall's major innovation was to play the mistaken identities of Act III as if Chiltern and Lord Goring were in a scene from a farce by Georges Feydeau.

There was a great deal of Oscar in Martin Shaw, whose sad-eyed, languorous, epicene, gay Goring, was clearly modelled on photographs of Wilde. It was a bit difficult to imagine him marrying such a plain and bespectacled Mabel Chiltern unless, of course, she was to be a cover for his extra-mural activity. But gay though he was, the production did not take the next step and suggest that there was or had ever been anything between him and Chiltern. Shaw's outstanding performance was not only witty in what he said but also witty in his silent and ironic comments directed to the audience, which he signalled by a weary and resigned raising of the eyebrow. The flippancy was a mask. He used his epigrams to disguise his innate decency, his essential charity and compassion, his moral seriousness. The acting in some of the other roles was a bit reppy.

> There is not one cabinet minister's wife that should not rush along to see this play. It would be better yet if their husbands would accompany them but are they men enough to take it? Oscar Wilde's 1895 treatment of political corruption and cover-up – as exposed and handled at home – return to the London stage at so ripe a moment that the audience gasps at the nerve it touches. Not that *An Ideal Husband* is scathing. On the contrary it is so morally pellucid and so witty, generous and humane that it might well reduce our political masters to embarrassed tears.
>
> Alistair Macaulay *Financial Times*

1995 Théâtre Antoine, Paris, *Un Mari Idéal.*

Adaptor	Pierre Laville
Director	Adrian Brine
EARL OF CAVERSHAM	Jacques Debary
LORD GORING	Didier Sandre
SIR ROBERT CHILTERN	Frédéric Van den Driessche
LADY CHILTERN	Dominique Sanda
LADY MARKBY	Edith Perret
MABEL CHILTERN	Florence Darel
MRS CHEVELEY	Anny Duperey

The Théâtre Antoine, in financial difficulties and in danger of closing, could not afford either the full sets or the full cast. The characters were cut. The text was cut and reordered. The play ran for fifteen months and saved the theatre. Didier Sandre's subtle yet luminous performance as Lord Goring was particularly admired for its depth.

> The play is strong and beautiful . . . Didier Sandre is as admirable in the comedy as he is in the serious moments.
>
> Michel Cournot *Le Monde*

1995 Shaw Festival, Niagara-on-the-Lake, Canada.

Director	Duncan McIntosh
EARL OF CAVERSHAM	Michael Ball
LORD GORING	Allan Gray
SIR ROBERT CHILTERN	Norman Browning
VICOMTE DE NANJAC	Neil Barclay
MR MONTFORD	Richard Binsley
MASON	Gordon Rand
PHIPPS	Jack Medley
JAMES	Matt Handy
HAROLD	Bruce Davies
LADY CHILTERN	Helen Taylor
LADY MARKBY	Nora McLellan
COUNTESS OF BASILDON	Jillian Cook
MRS MARCHMONT	Alison Woolridge
MABEL CHILTERN	Ann Baggley
MRS CHEVELEY	Jan Alexandra Smith

Duncan McIntosh's sterile, old-fashioned, mechanical, busy production was badly acted. Nora McLellan as the chattering Lady Markby played to the gallery and was unspeakably vulgar. The exchanges between Goring and his father were also acted for cheap laughs. What was interesting was the audience's reaction. They not only laughed at the wit, epigrams and paradoxes, they roared with delight all the way through the seriousness in the last act, presuming that since Oscar Wilde had written the play, it must all be funny.

> By employing pretentious music by the likes of Gorecki, Rachmaninoff and Janecek and enlisting a lighting design so lacking that it reduces some scenes to sludge, the production makes a futile effort to achieve a weighty solemnity. Meanwhile McIntosh is encouraging some performers to indulge in such shrieking, histrionic, bosom-heaving and brow-smiting excesses that the end result is embarrassing parody.
>
> Jamie Portman *London Free Press*

1996 Shaw Festival, Niagara-on-the-Lake, Canada.

Revival of Duncan McIntosh's production with the following changes in the cast:

VICOMTE DE NANJAC	Simon Bradbury
MR MONTFORD	Sandy Webster
MASON	Mike Shara
JAMES	Malcolm Scott
HAROLD	Brian Marler
LADY MARKBY	Jennifer Phipps
MABEL CHILTERN	Isolde O'Neill

1996 Peter Hall's production transferred to the Ethel Barrymore Theatre, New York, with the London cast with one major change: Pennie Downie played Lady Chiltern. Six months later the play was recast:

EARL OF CAVERSHAM	Michael Allinson
LORD GORING	Nicky Henson
SIR ROBERT CHILTERN	James Warwick
LADY CHILTERN	Madeleine Potter
LADY MARKBY	Kim Hunter
MABEL CHILTERN	Cheryl Gaysunas
MRS CHEVELEY	Stephanie Beacham

> [Nicky] Henson gives Goring a languid grace and effete decency that seems even more of a Wilde self-portrait than [Martin] Shaw's portrayal. He only needs a green carnation . . . Perhaps Stephanie Beacham as the wicked Mrs Cheveley overdoes the hissing melodrama a little bit – Hall's determinedly urbane version of Wilde is a shade more subtle than that.
>
> Clive Barnes *New York Post*

1996 Meanwhile, the play continued in London with different casts in a number of theatres: the Theatre Royal, Haymarket, the Old Vic, the Globe Theatre, the Albery Theatre and the Lyric Theatre:

EARL OF CAVERSHAM	John McCallum/Richard Todd
LORD GORING	Nicky Henson/Simon Ward/ Christopher Cazenove

SIR ROBERT CHILTERN	David Rintoul/Robert East/ Simon Ward
LADY CHILTERN	Kim Thomson/Deborah Grant/ Madeleine Potter
LADY MARKBY	Googie Withers/Barbara Murray
MABEL CHILTERN	Susannah Hitching/Rebecca Thorn
MRS CHEVELEY	Diane Fletcher/Carol Drinkwater/ Kate O'Mara/Susannah York

Robert East, meeting the melodrama head-on, did not attempt to disguise the fact that Chiltern, ambitious for luxury and power, was despicable. The idea that he represented 'what is best in English public life' and was potential Prime Minister material was a good cynical joke.

Simon Ward played the witty, conceited and likeable Lord Goring as if Goring were Wilde. However, the flowing locks, the portly padding, the waddling gait, the rouged lips (!) and the self-satisfied puppy smile made him look like a *Punch* caricature rather than the genuine article; and, at fifty-five, Ward was too old to be cast as a man twenty-one years his junior.

1997 Peter Hall's production toured Australia with the following cast:

EARL OF CAVERSHAM	John McCallum
LORD GORING	Nicky Henson
SIR ROBERT CHILTERN	John Waters
LADY CHILTERN	Josephine Byrnes
LADY MARKBY	Googie Withers
MABEL CHILTERN	Penny Cook
MRS CHEVELEY	Stephanie Beacham

> When it comes to high comedy with a light touch these veterans [John McCallum and Googie Withers] are a hard act to beat . . . [Nicky] Henson is a farceur who can prance light-footedly and play the licensed clown when required.
>
> Veronica Kelly *Australian*

1999 British film.

Director	Oliver Parker
Adaptation	Oliver Parker

EARL OF CAVERSHAM	John Wood
LORD GORING	Rupert Everett
SIR ROBERT CHILTERN	Jeremy Northam
MASON	Neville Phillips
PHIPPS	Peter Vaughan
LADY CHILTERN	Cate Blanchett
LADY MARKBY	Lindsay Duncan
COUNTESS OF BASILDON	Marsha Fitzalan
MABEL CHILTERN	Minnie Driver
MRS CHEVELEY	Julianne Moore
TOMMY TRAFFORD	Ben Pullen
SIR EDWARD	Simon Russell Beale
MISS DANVERS	Anna Patrick
MISS PRISM	Janet Henfrey
ALGY	Andy Harrison
RED-HAIRED ACTRESS	Nancy Carroll
BURLINGTON	Stephen May
LADY BASILDON	Delia Lindsay

In 1999 there were two screen versions of *An Ideal Husband*, one set in its correct period, the other updated. The great strength of Oliver Parker's Victorian production was that the opening sequences never felt like a photographed play. The introduction of the characters in handsome locations, the sharp editing, and the rearranging of the text, were all executed most skilfully.

The major surprise of the screenplay was that it dispensed altogether with the stolen bracelet, the key prop in the play, the linchpin. In Wilde's Act III Mrs Cheveley promises she will hand over Chiltern's letter to Goring on the day Goring marries her. Parker went one step further and introduced a wager: if Chiltern condemned the Argentine Canal scheme in the House of Commons she would give up the idea of marrying him. On the other hand, should Chiltern support the scheme, Goring would have to marry her. This led to a scene in the House of Commons where it looked as if Chiltern was going to support the scheme. Goring (to protect his own interests) immediately started coughing very loudly, prompting Chiltern to do an immediate volte-face and roundly condemn the canal, launching into a speech in which he was 'standing at the end of the century, stepping into the next century,' lambasting 'commerce without conscience', and generally underlining the parallels with the millennium in the most obvious manner.

Act IV was completely rewritten. Chiltern did not presume the letter his wife wrote to Lord Goring was for him. Goring, Lady Chiltern and Mabel found themselves forced to lie and behave as if they were in a French farce, which they acted to a romantic musical accompaniment on the soundtrack. The rewriting did not improve on Wilde; it merely cheapened him. Lady Chiltern's confession that she had lied was also played for comedy. The triviality did neither the role nor Cate Blanchett any favours. The one innovation which did work was her sudden realisation that Mrs Cheveley's blackmailing of her husband was revenge: 'It occurs to me the whole issue is just about you and me.'

A scene which was in keeping with Wilde was the one when Goring (a man unable to commit himself to marriage) found it difficult to get down on his knees and actually propose to Miss Mabel. The words, 'Marry me', stuck in his throat.

The most interesting interpolation was to have all the characters attend the first night of *The Importance of Being Earnest*, though they did seem to be spending more time looking at each other through their opera-glasses than watching the play. Wilde took a curtain call and delivered the speech which he had delivered in real life on the first night of *Lady Windermere's Fan*. It was his appearance which prompted Lady Chiltern to turn to her husband and ask, 'Is there any secret dishonour or disgrace? Tell me at once.' It was the only time in the whole film that even a hint of the homosexual subtext surfaced. An earlier opportunity in a Turkish bath was not taken. Goring and Chiltern sat back to back but only so that the camera could get them in the same frame. Their towels remained firmly in place. Presumably, they were not in the notorious Turkish Bath in Jermyn Street, so notorious that it was finally closed down by the police.

Jeremy Northam's Chiltern was visibly a man of weak character, who had no regrets for his past actions; his only regret was being found out. When he told Goring that Arnheim had given him £110,000 and Goring commented that he was 'worth more' the criticism was totally lost on him. Chiltern presumed Goring was talking finance rather than morality.

Just in case anybody might have suspected that Goring, a resolute bachelor, was homosexual, the film opened with him in bed with a prostitute. The character was much darker than usual; Rupert Everett, elegantly in period, might have been playing Lord Henry Wotton. Goring came across as slightly sinister and unpleasant, short on charm, quick with the acerbity. When Mrs Cheveley failed to seduce him, he immediately seduced her with kisses and champagne. Julianne Moore, eyes twinkling, always bemused, underplayed Wilde's villainess to present a quieter, subtler, and, in keeping with the rewritten script, a more sentimental reading of Mrs Cheveley's character.

1999 British film: *Oscar Wilde's An Ideal Husband*

Director	Bill Cartlidge
Adaptation	Bill Cartlidge
LORD CAVERSHAM	Robert Hardy
ARTHUR GORING	Jonathan Firth
ROBERT CHILTERN	James Wilby
VICOMTE DE NANJAC	Roger May
PHIPPS	Tyler Butterworth
TOMMY TRAFFORD	Mark Gillis
GERTRUDE CHILTERN	Trevyn McDowell
LADY MARKBY	Prunella Scales
OLIVIA BASILDON	Tara Palmer-Tomkinson
MARGARET MARCHMONT	Tamara Beckwith
MABEL CHILTERN	Karen Hayley
LAURA CHEVELEY	Sadie Frost

Bill Cartlidge's modern version did not have the production values of Oliver Parker's film and looked as if it might have been a film made for television. The action was moved out of London, brought down market, and shot mainly on location in the Shires. The major surprise was that, despite being set in the 1990s, the screenplay was completely faithful to Wilde. Chiltern was now a county councillor, who had sold a council secret rather than a government secret. The shares had been in a local canal rather than the Argentine Canal; otherwise, there was no tampering with the text.

At first it didn't seem as if the updating was going to work. Wilde's dialogue didn't sound right in modern dress, but once the film had got past the opening party in the town hall and Chiltern and Goring were playing golf, Wilde worked perfectly. There was nothing dated about such remarks as, 'In England, a man who can't talk morality twice a week to a large popular immoral audience is quite over as a serious politician.'

There was a delightful moment, too, when Chiltern was arguing that it wasn't fair to be judged by the follies of one's youth. 'Life is never fair,' said Goring, sinking the put and winning the game. Part of the fun (as it is with productions which update Shakespeare's plays) was seeing how Cartlidge reinterpreted scenes and lines. Chiltern sent Mrs Cheveley a fax. Goring met Lady Chiltern at the hairdressers. 'Why are you looking so strangely at me?' she asked him. The line was given a new spin because she had just emerged from under the dryer to reveal her hair in an extraordinary range of curlers.

When Mrs Cheveley stole Lady Chiltern's letter, Goring chased after her in his car. His Ferrari broke down and he had to sleep the night in it. In the morning he was woken by his father driving past on a motorbike and Mabel riding by on a horse. She gave him a lift home. The whole sequence might have been out of a 1930s American screwball comedy. Jonathan Firth, not nearly as studied and artificial as Rupert Everett, and much more charming, acted with a light comedy touch.

'Nowadays,' says Mrs Cheveley, 'with our modern mania for morality, everyone has to pass for paragons of purity and incorruptibility.' James Wilby's Chiltern, weak and flabby, looked exactly the sort of politician who would ask questions for cash. Cartlidge, as Parker had done, ignored the homosexual subtext. Chiltern and Goring, admittedly, did strip naked in the sauna but once they were in the pool they kept a very wide berth of each other.

Prunella Scales, playing that frightful snob, Lady Markby, a very conservative Conservative, was ideal for Wilde and the Shires. She had more lines than Lindsay Duncan (who played Markby in the Parker film) and was therefore able to make more impact. 'I am a little too old now to set a good example myself,' she confided, 'but I always admire people who do.' Attending a jumble sale, the room was suddenly invaded by the local youth. 'The fact is that our society is terribly overpopulated,' she whispered. 'Really someone should arrange a proper scheme of assistance for emigration.'

The major weakness of the film was the casting of Sadie Frost as Mrs Cheveley. Taking her cue from Goring's observation that she wears far too much rouge and not quite enough clothes, Frost wore her cleavage low and her skirts high. 'Morality,' she snapped at Lady Chiltern, 'is simply the attitude we adopt towards people we personally dislike.' She was so dreadfully common that it was difficult to imagine Goring ever having fancied her. There was certainly nothing 'brilliant' about this shoddy blackmailer.

The Importance of Being Earnest (1895)

A Trivial Comedy for Serious People

'To Robert Baldwin Ross in appreciation and affection'

Characters:
JOHN WORTHING, JP, of the Manor House, Woolton, Hertfordshire
ALGERNON MONCRIEFF, his friend
REV. CANON CHASUBLE, DD Rector of Woolton
MERRIMAN, Butler to Mr Worthing
LANE, Mr Moncrieff's Manservant
LADY BRACKNELL
GWENDOLEN FAIRFAX, her daughter
CECILY CARDEW, John Worthing's Ward
MISS PRISM, her Governess

Time: The present.

Scenes:

Act I Algernon Moncrieff's rooms in Piccadilly.
Act II Garden at the Manor House, Woolton.
Act III Morning-room at the Manor House, Woolton.

The Plot

ACT I John Worthing has invented a fictitious brother, Ernest, who allows him to escape to London. His best friend, Algernon

Moncrieff, has invented a permanent invalid, Mr Bunbury, who allows him to escape any duties he may find irksome. Algernon discovers that Worthing has a pretty young ward in the country called Cecily Cardew. Worthing wants to marry Algernon's cousin, Gwendolen Fairfax. He proposes to her and she reveals that she has had a lifelong passion to marry somebody of the name of Ernest. When Lady Bracknell, her mother, learns that he does not know who his parents are and that he was found in a handbag in Victoria Station, she advises him to find at least one parent before she can consider allowing her daughter to marry him.

ACT II Algernon turns up at Worthing's country estate, unannounced, pretending to be Ernest, and falls in love with Cecily Cardew, who confesses she has been in love with him ever since she learned her guardian had a wicked brother called Ernest. She, too, has always wanted to marry someone of that name. Worthing arrives, dressed in deepest mourning, to announce that Ernest is dead, only to find that Ernest is staying in his house. Gwendolen arrives and is entertained to tea by Cecily. The girls are not amused to find that, having each become engaged to Ernest Worthing, neither fiancé is in fact called Ernest.

ACT III Lady Bracknell arrives. She agrees to Algernon's marriage to Cecily the moment she discovers Cecily is coming into a fortune, but refuses to countenance Worthing marrying Gwendolen until she learns from a former employee, Miss Prism, now Cecily's governess, that the baby Prism mislaid at Victoria Station twenty-seven years ago is none other than Worthing, the long-lost son of Lady Bracknell's sister.

The Characters

LADY BRACKNELL is a monster without being a myth, a Wagnerian gorgon, implacable in her snobbery and unashamedly mercenary. The role is part Queen Victoria, part Wilde, part transvestite. Lady Bracknell makes pronouncements:

> I do not approve of anything that tampers with natural ignorance. Ignorance is like a delicate exotic fruit; touch it and the bloom is gone. The whole theory of modern education is radically unsound. Fortunately in England, at any rate, education produces no effect whatsoever. If it did, it would prove a serious danger to the upper classes and probably lead to acts of violence in Grosvenor Square.

To lose one parent, Mr Worthing, may be regarded as a misfortune; to lose both looks like carelessness.

To be born, or at any rate bred, in a handbag, whether it had handles or not, seems to me to display a contempt for the ordinary decencies of family life that reminds one of the worst excesses of the French Revolution. And I presume you know what that unfortunate movement led to? As for the particular locality in which the handbag was found, a cloakroom at a railway station might serve to conceal a social indiscretion – has probably, indeed, been used for that purpose before now – but it could hardly be regarded as an assured basis for a recognised position in good society.

ALGERNON MONCRIEFF is a conceited, over-dressed, over-educated and ostentatiously eligible young man. 'He has nothing but he looks everything.' He has invented an invaluable permanent invalid called Bunbury in order that he may be able to go down to the country whenever he chooses.

JOHN (JACK) WORTHING, also a secret Bunburyist, pretends to have a younger, louche, brother, Ernest, who is always getting into the most dreadful scrapes and debts. Worthing doesn't actually know who he is by birth. He was found in a handbag in the cloakroom of Victoria Station, the Brighton line. ('The line is immaterial.')

Moncrieff and Worthing fall in love with two girls who have a fixation about being married to men called Ernest.

JACK: I'll bet you anything you like that half an hour after they have met, they will be calling each other sister.

ALGERNON: Women only do that when they have called each other a lot of other things first.

GWENDOLEN FAIRFAX, a fashionable and sophisticated young lady, has been brought up by Lady Bracknell to be extremely short-sighted. She is always smart and never wrong. 'I never change,' she says, 'except in my affections.'

JACK: You don't think there is any chance of Gwendolen becoming like her mother in about a hundred and fifty years, do you, Algy?

ALGERNON: All women become like their mothers. That is their tragedy. No man does. That's his.

CECILY CARDEW, Jack's extremely pretty ward, is just eighteen but always admits to twenty when she goes to parties. She falls in love with her guardian's wicked brother, writes all his love letters and becomes engaged, and all this before they have even met. In the battle with Gwendolen, over tea, she wins game, set, and match. 'It seems to me, Miss Fairfax, that I am trespassing on your valuable time. No doubt you have many other calls of a similar character to make in the neighbourhood.'

MISS PRISM is Cecily Cardew's governess and the authoress of a three-volume novel of 'revolting sentimentality'. In a moment of mental abstraction she deposited the manuscript in a perambulator and deposited the baby in her charge in a handbag which she left in the cloakroom of Victoria Station. She is delighted to have the handbag so unexpectedly restored to her. 'It has been a great inconvenience being without it all these years.'

CANON CHASUBLE, the local vicar, has one sermon on the meaning of the manna in the wilderness, which he can adapt for harvest celebrations, christenings, confirmations, on days of humiliation, and festal days.

In July 1894 Oscar Wilde, seriously pressed for money, wrote a letter to the actor George Alexander, licensee and general manager of the St James's Theatre, asking for £150 in return for first refusal of his new play. The plot, he admitted, was slight. The real charm, he said, lay in the dialogue. Wilde retreated to Worthing ('Worthing is a place in Sussex. It is a seaside resort') to escape his London creditors and the emotional and financial demands of Lord Alfred Douglas.

The play (initially set in the eighteenth century and called *Lady Lancing*) was finished in October and Wilde sent a copy to Alexander with an accompanying letter saying that he did not think Alexander was suitable for his comedy (since he was a romantic actor) and that what the play really needed was actors like Charles Wyndham and Charles Hawtrey.

Wyndham was then sent the script. In the meantime Alexander had an unexpected failure with Henry James's *Guy Donville*, and, in sudden need of a play to fill his theatre, asked for the script to be returned to him.

At Alexander's request Wilde cut the play from four acts to three, to allow for Langdon E Mitchell's curtain-raiser, *In the Season*, to be performed. Among the cuts were Moulton the gardener, and a passage which referred to Robert Hichens's *The Green Carnation*, a novel recently published, which satirised Wilde and his circle. A more serious loss was an amusing scene in which a solicitor, Gribsby, arrived to arrest Algernon for his debts.

Robert Ross interviewed Wilde for the 18 January 1895 issue of the *St James's Gazette*:

> 'Do you think that the critics will understand your new play, which Mr George Alexander has secured?'
>
> 'I hope not.'
>
> 'I dare not ask, I suppose, if it will please the public?'
>
> 'When a play that is a work of art is produced on the stage what is being tested is not the play, but the stage; when a play that is *not* a work of art is produced on the stage what is being tested is not the play, but the public.'
>
> 'What sort of play are we to expect?'
>
> 'It is exquisitely trivial, a delicate bubble of fancy, and it has its philosophy.'
>
> 'Its philosophy!'
>
> 'That we should treat all the trivial things of life very seriously, and all the serious things of life with sincere and studied triviality.'

Ada Leverson described Wilde's appearance on the first night for the *New Criterion*:

> That evening he was dressed with elaborate dandyism and a sort of florid sobriety. His coat had a black velvet collar. He held white gloves in his small pointed hands. On one finger he wore a large scarab ring. A green carnation – echo of the ring – bloomed savagely in his buttonhole, and a large bunch of seals on a black moire ribbon watch chain hung from his white waistcoat. This costume, which on another man might have appeared perilously like fancy dress and on his imitators was nothing less, seemed perfectly to suit him; he seemed at ease and to have a great look of the first gentleman in Europe.

The Importance of Being Earnest was a big success. 'In my fifty-three years of acting,' said Allan Aynesworth, who played Algernon Moncrieff, 'I never remember a greater triumph. The audience rose in their seats and cheered and cheered again.'

At the final curtain Wilde and Alexander were called for. Wilde refused to take a bow. The audience, expecting one of his witty first-night speeches, was disappointed.

'You see,' he explained later, 'I took one only last month at the Haymarket and one feels so much like a German band.'

The truth is that Wilde spent most of his time backstage trying to avoid the Marquis of Queensberry. Wilde had been tipped off that the Marquis was planning a demonstration at the theatre. Queensberry did indeed arrive, with a prize-fighter, but policemen from Scotland Yard barred his entrance. Failing to gain admittance, he left a grotesque bouquet of vegetables at the stage door. After he had gone, Wilde was still afraid that he might have placed hecklers in the gallery to make a disturbance.

1895 14 February St James's Theatre, London.

Licensee and manager	George Alexander
JOHN WORTHING	George Alexander
ALGERNON MONCRIEFF	Allan Aynesworth
REV. CANON CHASUBLE	H H Vincent
MERRIMAN	Frank Dyall
LANE	F Kinsley Peile
LADY BRACKNELL	Rose Leclercq
GWENDOLEN FAIRFAX	Irene Vanbrugh
CECILY CARDEW	Evelyn Millard/Violet Lyster
MISS PRISM	Mrs George Canninge

The popular success of *The Importance of Being Earnest* was never for a moment in doubt. To use a current vulgarism, the piece 'caught on' immediately.

Morning Post

The Importance of Being Earnest sends wave after wave of laughter curling and foaming round the theatre; but as a text for criticism, it is barren and delusive. It is like a mirage-oasis in the desert, grateful and comforting to the weary eye – but when you come close up to it, behold! it is intangible, it eludes your grasp. What can a poor critic do with a play which raises no principle, whether of art or morals, creates its own canons and conventions, and is nothing but an absolutely wilful expression of an irrepressibly witty personality? . . . Its theme, in other hands, would have made capital farce; but 'farce' is far too gross and commonplace a word to apply to such an iridescent filament of fantasy.

William Archer *World*

I cannot say that I greatly cared for *The Importance of Being Earnest*. It amused me, of course; but unless comedy touches me as well as amuses me, it leaves me with a sense of having wasted my evening. I go to the theatre to be moved to laughter, not to be tickled or bustled into it; and that is why, though I laugh as much as anybody at a farcical comedy, I am out of spirits before the end of the second act, and out of temper before the end of the third, my miserable mechanical laughter intensifying these symptoms at every outburst . . . On the whole I decline to accept *The Importance of Being Earnest* as a day less than ten years old; and I am altogether unable to perceive any uncommon excellence in its presentation.

George Bernard Shaw *Saturday Review*

Whether in farce or drama, plot continues to be Mr Oscar Wilde's most vulnerable point. The story of this latest production is, indeed, almost too preposterous to go without music.

The Times

The mantle of Mr Gilbert has fallen on the shoulders of Mr Oscar Wilde, who wears it in jauntiest fashion . . . It is easy to find fault with Wilde's latest piece. It is, indeed, difficult to do anything else.

Athenaeum

It has not a relish of reason or sparkle of sanity; it is absurd, preposterous, extravagant, idiotic, saucy, brilliantly clever, and unedifyingly diverting . . . To say that a play of this airy and unsubstantial kind requires a particularly brisk order of acting is

> merely to state the obvious. But there is scarcely any one in this cast who will not benefit by a full realisation of this truth.
>
> *Daily Telegraph*

> George Alexander played Worthing just as a part of this sort should be played, i.e., with entire seriousness and no indication of purposed irony. He never once ceased to realise that the effect of the author's conception in a piece of this kind is marred immediately that the artists appear to see the fun.
>
> *Era*

> Mr Alexander's grave, almost solemn, style in the part of the hero gave the utmost point to the burlesque and it was agreeably contrasted with Mr Allan Aynesworth's airs of gay insouciance as Moncrieff. Miss Vanbrugh also adopted the mock-heroic manner. Miss Evelyn Millard, on the other hand, admirable actress as she is in emotional characters, seemed ill-assorted with her companion, her earnest manner being unsuited to the utterance of cynical aphorisms.
>
> *Daily News*

One of the major surprises of reading the original reviews is that Rose Leclercq's Lady Bracknell is barely mentioned. It could be that she was not at her best on the first night, since she was suffering from cold. Irene Vanbrugh in her autobiography, *To Tell My Story* (Hutchinson, 1948), praised her highly:

> A great personal success was made by that famous old actress Rose Leclercq – the natural *grande dame* of the stage with all the true polish and innate dignity of the unmistakable 'lady'. Her walk, her voice, her carriage, her every detail was marvellous. The handkerchief she used, the long bottle of eau-de-Cologne, the way she sat – such details marked her as the lady of rank and blue blood that she portrayed; she was never stagey or exaggerated.

On 5 April 1895 Wilde was arrested on a charge of gross indecency. On 6 April, his name was removed from the programme and all advertising. The box office collapsed immediately. The play closed on 8 May, having run 83 performances. In July Wilde was declared bankrupt and Alexander was able to snap up the rights to the play at a very advantageous price to him.

1895 American premiere: Empire Theatre, New York.

JOHN WORTHING	Henry Miller
ALGERNON MONCRIEFF	William Faversham
REV. CANON CHASUBLE	W H Crompton
MERRIMAN	W J Whitman
LANE	E Y Backus
LADY BRACKNELL	Ida Vernon
GWENDOLEN FAIRFAX	Viola Allen
CECILY CARDEW	Agnes Miller
MISS PRISM	May Robson

The chief characteristic of the play is its highly-elaborate dialogue, a travesty in the manner of Congreve. Almost every line is avowedly and laboriously witty. About one-half of the dialogue last night proved diverting. Of the other half much fell flat, while some was actually tiresome . . . Such a play, to be thoroughly enjoyed, needs the finest possible performances; at the Empire, unhappily, it misses that. The acting of Mr Frohman's company last night was moderately efficient. No single actor was quite at home in his or her role. All worked diligently.

New York Times

It was a fairly appreciative audience but not a very large one. The present unpopularity of Mr Wilde's personality has evidently stigmatised his play and many of the first nighters who in their totality would have crowded the house but for the recent revelations were conspicuously absent . . . It is an extravaganza, full of topsy-turvy humor . . . Once or twice the witticisms were boomerangs that hit back ominously at the author as when Miss Gwendolen Fairfax sententiously remarks that 'modern culture is not the sort of thing that one cares to talk about in public.' . . . William Faversham as Algernon Moncrieff carried himself with an uneasy attempt at ease that was slightly irritating. The other players were good, but not excellent.

New York Herald

1901 Coronet Theatre, London.

JOHN WORTHING	George Alexander
ALGERNON MONCRIEFF	W Graham Browne
REV. CANON CHASUBLE	E Lyall Swete
MERRIMAN	R E Goddard
LANE	H Dansey
LADY BRACKNELL	M Talbot
GWENDOLEN FAIRFAX	Mabel Dubois
CECILY CARDEW	Lillian Braithwaite
MISS PRISM	Mrs Thomas Laverton

Wilde's name did not appear on the programme. The play was described as being by the author of *Lady Windermere's Fan*.

1902 St James's Theatre, London.

JOHN WORTHING	George Alexander
ALGERNON MONCRIEFF	W Graham Browne
REV. CANON CHASUBLE	E Lyall Swete
MERRIMAN	R E Goddard
LANE	H Dansey
LADY BRACKNELL	M Talbot
GWENDOLEN FAIRFAX	Margaret Halstan
CECILY CARDEW	Lillian Braithwaite
MISS PRISM	Mrs Thomas Laverton

What differentiates this farce from any other, and makes it funnier than any other, is the humourous contrast between its style and matter. To preserve its style fully, the dialogue must be spoken with grave unction. The sound and sense of the words must be taken seriously, treated beautifully. If mimes rattle through the play and anyhow, they manage to obscure much of its style, and much, therefore, of its fun. They lower it towards the plane of ordinary farce.

Max Beerbohm *Saturday Review*

Miss Lillian Braithwaite is wonderfully well-suited to the role of Cecily Cardew and her sweet simplicity and personal charm, combined with a serenity which would be difficult to surpass.

Era

Exhilarating champagne farce . . . delightful imbroglio of just sufficiently inconsequent fooling is just what late diners of today require at the theatre.

Illustrated London News

1902 Empire Theatre, New York.

JOHN WORTHING	Charles Richman
ALGERNON MONCRIEFF	William Courtenay
REV. CANON CHASUBLE	W H Crompton
MERRIMAN	Frank Brownlee
LANE	George Osbourne, Jr
LADY BRACKNELL	Ethel Hornick
GWENDOLEN FAIRFAX	Margaret Anglin
CECILY CARDEW	Margaret Dale
MISS PRISM	Mrs Thomas Whiffen

The play happens to be inextricably associated with the saddest and most revolting scandal in the history of the English drama, perhaps of all drama. Every man of intelligence, no doubt, wishes to disassociate the man Oscar Wilde from the playwright.

New York Times

In construction *The Importance of Being Earnest* is as crude as the comediettas written for an occasion, seen on drawing room stages; the people come on and go off without any reason, but as they are openly puppets the author perhaps was wise in making no attempt to hide the wires which make them dance. The trifle is excellently acted. Miss Anglin, as a solemn society maid, who takes down her lover's proposal verbatim in her diary, is deliciously funny.

Theatre

1902 Berlin. German premiere, *Bunbury*, at Kleines Theater, directed by Driedrich Kayssler. *Bunbury* played in a double bill with *Salomé*.

1904 *Bunbury* played at the Stadttheater Altona, Hamburg. First major German production of the play.

1909 St James's Theatre, London.

JOHN WORTHING	George Alexander
ALGERNON MONCRIEFF	Allan Aynesworth
REV. CANON CHASUBLE	E Vivian Reynolds
MERRIMAN	Erik Stirling
LANE	T Weguelin
LADY BRACKNELL	Helen Rous
GWENDOLEN FAIRFAX	Stella Patrick Campbell
CECILY CARDEW	Rosalie Toller
MISS PRISM	Alice Beet

Mr Alexander's second revival of the piece is very welcome and especially as he himself figures as the pseudo-Ernest and rattles off his speeches with all his old sly and smirking humour.

Illustrated London News

Every epigram, every paradox was received with just as uproarious outbursts of laughter as when they first fell on the listener . . . Mr Aynesworth's unabashed coolness and suave diplomacy are conceived in the best spirit of drollery . . .

Era

Taken as a whole the acting is 'nothing to write home about' but the piece is so good that laughter is continuous nevertheless. Some of the wit has got a trifle tarnished. The fashion of inverted aphorism has passed away. But the humour is as irresistible as ever. It is certainly the best farce of our time.

H Hamilton Fyfe *World*

1910 Lyceum Theatre, New York.

JOHN WORTHING	Hamilton Revelle
ALGERNON MONCRIEFF	A E Matthews
REV. CANON CHASUBLE	Albert Tavernier
MERRIMAN	Frederick Raymond
LANE	Robert Reese
LADY BRACKNELL	Ethel Winthrop
GWENDOLEN FAIRFAX	Jane Oaker
CECILY CARDEW	May Blayney
MISS PRISM	Florence Edney

> One can imagine almost any assemblage of healthy-minded English people seeing the fun of it in spite of the fact that it discloses something of the weakness of a traditional, and sometimes sacredly regarded aristocracy . . . Miss Winthrop missed making point after point. Her playing illustrated in a way the general shortcomings in a performance where brittle speeches were not infrequently lingered on over too long or given again with so little authority that they failed of their effect.
>
> *New York Times*

> Matthews was an immovable countenance. Vocally, his expression left nothing to be wished for, but even Algy Moncrieff must have had a pliable muscle or two in his face . . . Cecily somewhat taxed your imagination when she said she was eighteen.
>
> *New York Daily Tribune*

1911 St James's Theatre, London.

JOHN WORTHING	Hamilton Revelle
ALGERNON MONCRIEFF	A E Matthews
REV. CANON CHASUBLE	Vivian Reynolds
MERRIMAN	G Trevor Roller
LANE	Arthur Royston
LADY BRACKNELL	Mrs G Kemmis
GWENDOLEN FAIRFAX	Dorothy Green
CECILY CARDEW	Gladys Cooper
MISS PRISM	Alice Beet

Gladys Cooper (whose beauty caused the audience to gasp) was admired for her self-possession, delightful sense of humour, and dainty archness. Initially she had not liked the play, not finding it very funny.

'To be perfectly honest,' she wrote in her autobiography, *Gladys Cooper* (Hutchinson, 1935), 'I had never heard of the play, did not know if "Ernest" was spelled with or without an "a" and knew next to nothing of Oscar Wilde. Seeing my ignorance he [A E Matthews] used to take me to one side, tell me what a great chance had come my way, and coach me in the part. He was a brick, and I shall always be grateful to him for his help.'

Dorothy Green caught the artificial manner to a nicety and spoke with distinction, and acted with tact and humour throughout . . . Mr Matthews made his points with a most convincing air of nonchalance and Mr Revelle contrived to be really humourous in his mock seriousness.

The Times

1911 Paris. *De l'Importance du Sérieux.*

1913 St James's Theatre, London.

JOHN WORTHING	Gerald Ames
ALGERNON MONCRIEFF	A E Matthews
REV. CANON CHASUBLE	E Vivian Reynolds
MERRIMAN	Austin Fehrman
LANE	Alfred Harris
LADY BRACKNELL	Helen Rous
GWENDOLEN FAIRFAX	Dorothy Fane
CECILY CARDEW	Rosalie Toller
MISS PRISM	Alice Beet

There are few modern plays that have the same power of making the audience shake with laughter.

The Times

1918 Theater zur Kaufleuter, Zurich.

James Joyce (as business manager) and Claud Sykes (as artistic director and actor) formed a new stage company, the English Players, to put on plays in English. Their first production was *The Importance of Being Earnest* with a semi-professional cast.

Joyce and Henry Carr (an amateur actor who played Algernon) had a huge argument over the reimbursement of the cost of a pair of trousers Carr had bought specially for the production. They finally went to law to settle their differences.

The incident was later used by Tom Stoppard in his play, *Travesties.*

1923 Theatre Royal, Haymarket, London.

Director	Allan Aynesworth
JOHN WORTHING	Leslie Faber
ALGERNON MONCRIEFF	John Deverell
REV. CANON CHASUBLE	H O Nicholson
MERRIMAN	Walton Palmer
LANE	Douglas Jefferies
LADY BRACKNELL	Margaret Scudamore
GWENDOLEN FAIRFAX	Doris Kendal
CECILY CARDEW	Nancy Atkin
MISS PRISM	Louise Hampton
MAID	Betty Sturgess

The play was updated to the 1920s.

> Time has taken the curl out of many of the epigrams, and they cannot be brought up to date merely by the ladies of the cast wearing the latest from Curzon Street . . . Miss Louise Hampton, the Miss Prism, should have been the Lady Bracknell – whom Margaret Scudamore played entirely for aggressiveness instead of humour . . . It can do his reputation [Leslie Faber's] no harm to point out that for light fantastic comedy he has no talent whatsoever.
>
> *Observer*

> Mr John Deverell's Algernon was the hit of the evening. His engaging fatuity was at ease and at home in a part which is nothing if not engagingly fatuous.
>
> *The Times*

1926 Repertory Theatre, Birmingham.

Director	H K Ayliff
JOHN WORTHING	Perceval Clark
ALGERNON MONCRIEFF	Edward Chapman
REV. CANON CHASUBLE	Frank Moore
MERRIMAN	Charles Leighton

LANE	Ralph Richardson
LADY BRACKNELL	Ormonde Wynne
GWENDOLEN FAIRFAX	Dorothy Black
CECILY CARDEW	Muriel Hewitt
MISS PRISM	Dorothy Hall
FOOTMAN	Stringer Davis

1926 Abbey Theatre, Dublin.

Director	Lennox Robinson
JOHN WORTHING	F J McCormick
ALGERNON MONCRIEFF	Arthur Shields
REV. CANON CHASUBLE	Barry Fitzgerald
MERRIMAN	P J Carolan
LANE	Michael J Dolan
LADY BRACKNELL	Maureen Delany
GWENDOLEN FAIRFAX	Eileen Crowe
CECILY CARDEW	Shelagh Richards
MISS PRISM	May Craig

In a programme note, Lennox Robinson wrote:

> The time seems to have come when *The Importance of Being Earnest* needs to be definitely dated . . . Played in shingled hair and plus fours, it will seem a little absurd and démodé but played in costumes that to our eyes will be curious and in scenery that is extravagant it will take its proper place among the stage masterpieces of the world. Doubtless there will come a time when producers and public will weary of seeing the play in the costume of the '90s and some producer will conceive the brilliant idea of presenting it in 'modern dress'. But that time has not yet come.

> The costumes last night, no doubt, gave rise to many a smile but what effect they had on the understanding of the dialogue is a matter of opinion. The impression one got last night was that the players did not feel quite at home.
>
> *Irish Times*

> In the early stages the company appeared to be more conscious of their clothes than of the parts the author intended them to

play. Fortunately this awkwardness diminished as the action developed and though throughout the epigrams were exploded much as a boy touches off a squib, the fun is so infectious that what began almost as a funeral march ends in a glorious gallop.

Irish Independent

1926 Comedy Theatre, New York.

Director	Dudley Digges
JOHN WORTHING	Vernon Steele
ALGERNON MONCRIEFF	Reginald Owen
REV. CANON CHASUBLE	Dudley Digges
MERRIMAN	Gerald Hamer
LANE	Wallace Roberts
LADY BRACKNELL	Lucille Watson
GWENDOLEN FAIRFAX	Haroldine Humphreys
CECILY CARDEW	Patricia Collinge
MISS PRISM	Catherine Proctor

To our amazement, however, the old piece seemed as fresh as an orchid and quite the most iridescent bit of nonsense that is fluttering these evenings in the Broadway breeze. Compared to the infant wisecracking indulged in by the modern wags and jokers, the remarks of this aged harlequin are the life of the party . . . Miss Lucille Watson, as the wise and frosty Lady Bracknell, was humourously imperial in the best manner in such things.

New York Daily Tribune

If the pace were quicker and the acting of the various characters were blended more sympathetically these sparkling lines would doubtless seem fresher than they do.

J Brooks Atkinson *New York Times*

For the most part it was acted tooth and nail, if I may say so. They went at it ruthlessly. They jumped through it; they tore at it; they rumpled and crumpled it; they lurched on it; they certainly had little respect for it. It sounded like comic opera minus the music.

Alan Dale *American*

1927 Musical: *Oh, Ernest*

Premiere: Royale Theatre, New York.

Book and lyrics	Francis De Will
Music	Robin Hood Bowers
Director	William J Wilson

ALGY	Henry McNaughton
WORTHING	Hal Forde
LADY BRACKNELL	Flavia Arcaro
GWENDOLEN	Marjorie Gateson
CECILY	Dorothy Dilley
MISS PRISM	Sonia Winfield
CHAUSUBLE	Jethro Warner

The musical was described as 'the lowest ebb of the theatrical season' and dismissed as: 'noisy butchery', 'just another dance show', 'sodden, tasteless and utterly dreary', 'a wasted evening in the theatre'. 'The effect was like drinking dead champagne.'

1930 Lyric Theatre, Hammersmith, London.

Director	Nigel Playfair

JOHN WORTHING	John Gielgud/Nicholas Hannen
ALGERNON MONCRIEFF	Anthony Ireland
REV. CANON CHASUBLE	Charles Staite
MERRIMAN	Scott Russell
LANE	Richard Caldicot
LADY BRACKNELL	Mabel Terry-Lewis
GWENDOLEN FAIRFAX	Iris Baker
CECILY CARDEW	Heather Angel
MISS PRISM	Jean Cadell/Athene Seyler

Nigel Playfair's production was mounted entirely in black and white and looked as if it had been designed by Aubrey Beardsley. *The Times* thought that the artificial décor (pleasing though it was to the eye) was more often at war with the play than in accord with it.

John Worthing is played with immensities of perception, industry and resolution by Mr John Gielgud, who is totally unfitted for the part, not because he is a tragic actor, but because he is a serious one.

James Agate *Sunday Times*

And how should Wilde be played? There is one simple answer, that he should be played as Miss Mabel Terry-Lewis plays Lady Bracknell. Her dry, incisive, unforced wit; her proud carriage; the exquisite precision of her emphasis; above all her great personal dignity that preserves a great lady in one who might have been a butt – these things make of her acting a standard by which other acting in this piece must be judged . . . Mr Gielgud and Miss Terry-Lewis together are brilliant. They have what the others collectively lack – the rhythm of the play, for it is very like a piece of formal music; and they have the supreme grace of always allowing Wilde to speak for himself in his own voice and not in the voice of a modern imitator.

The Times

According to John Gielgud, Mabel Terry-Lewis had no idea the lines were funny and wondered what the audience was laughing at.

1932 German film: *Liebe, Scherz und Ernst*
A musical by B E Luthge and Curt J Braun.

Director	Franz Wenzler
CAST	Charlotte Ander
	Georg Alexander
	Harald Paulsen
	Adele Sandrook
	Ilse Korseck
	Gertrud Wolle
	Julius Falkenstein
	Erich Kestin
	Hilde Hildebraud
	Kurt Lilien

1932 French film: *Touchons du Bois*
Also known as Soyons Sérieux.

Director	Maurice Champreux
Screenplay	Louis Verier
	Ninon Steinhoff
CAST	Armand Bernard
	Suzet Mais
	Jeanne Cheiril
	Lily Zevaco
	Suzy Pierson
	Marcelle Barry
	Jules Moy
	Roland Armontel

Wilde was turned into farce and was barely recognisable.

1933 Gate Theatre, Dublin.

Director	Hilton Edwards
JOHN WORTHING	Cyril Cusack
ALGERNON MONCRIEFF	Micheál Mac Liammóir
REV. CANON CHASUBLE	Edward Lexy
LADY BRACKNELL	Kirkwood Hackett
GWENDOLEN FAIRFAX	Ria Mooney
CECILY CARDEW	Betty Chancellor
MISS PRISM	Coralie Carmichael

1934 Old Vic Theatre, London.

Director	Tyrone Guthrie
JOHN WORTHING	Roger Livesey
ALGERNON MONCRIEFF	George Curzon
REV. CANON CHASUBLE	Charles Laughton
MERRIMAN	James Mason
LANE	Morland Graham
LADY BRACKNELL	Athene Seyler
GWENDOLEN FAIRFAX	Flora Robson

CECILY CARDEW	Ursula Jeans
MISS PRISM	Elsa Lanchester

Charles Laughton was originally cast to play John Worthing, but Tyrone Guthrie thought him too unpleasant for the role and persuaded him to play Chasuble instead.

In his book *A Life in the Theatre* (Hamish Hamilton, 1960), Tyrone Guthrie wrote: '*The Importance* was not a wise choice. Nobody was really well suited. My direction was galumphing and uninteresting. This revival must be unique in that Canon Chasuble (Charles Laughton in a devastating, brilliant and outrageous lampoon) appeared to be the leading part.'

> Mr Charles Laughton's Chasuble is thick with the oil of gentlemanly hypocrisy.
>
> *The Times*

> Mr Charles Laughton's unctuous Vicar was both perfectly audible and preeminently unfrockable.
>
> Harold Hobson *Observer*

> As Lady Bracknell Miss Seyler, who normally looks like some magnanimous mouse, swelled to Wagnerian size and gave a performance of such bite and gusto that every line was in danger of being lost through being drowned in the laughter greeting the one before.
>
> James Agate *Sunday Times*

1938 First British television performance.

Director	Royston Morley
JOHN WORTHING	Alan Wheatley
ALGERNON MONCRIEFF	John Wyse
REV. CANON CHASUBLE	Reginald Brooke
MERRIMAN	Stuart Latham
LANE	Mario Francelli
LADY BRACKNELL	Barbara Everest
GWENDOLEN FAIRFAX	Vivienne Bennett
CECILY CARDEW	Winifred Willard
MISS PRISM	Thea Holme

1939 Vanderbilt Theatre, New York.

Director	Estelle Winwood
JOHN WORTHING	Clifton Webb
ALGERNON MONCRIEFF	Derek Williams
REV. CANON CHASUBLE	Ainsworth Arnold
MERRIMAN	A G Andrews
LANE	Guy Spaull
LADY BRACKNELL	Estelle Winwood
GWENDOLEN FAIRFAX	Helen Trenholme
CECILY CARDEW	Florence McGee
MISS PRISM	Hope Williams

Earnest may be a lark for the players but it is distinctly too dated to get past first base.

Ibee *Variety*

A perfect joy for forty minutes and a pleasant bore for sixty.

Burns Mantle *New York Daily News*

On the whole, however, *The Importance of Being Earnest* seems to have reached its dotage.

Richard Watts, Jr *Tribune*

You cannot help admiring the brilliance of some of the results. Yet you soon get heartily sick of the trick. You find yourself resenting the emptiness of the writing. You begin to feel as if you had lived on a diet of truffles for a month. Especially when the play is done with as little style or relish as it is at Vanderbilt.

John Mason Brown *New York Post*

1939 Globe Theatre, London.

Director	John Gielgud
JOHN WORTHING	John Gielgud
ALGERNON MONCRIEFF	Ronald Ward
REV. CANON CHASUBLE	David Horne
MERRIMAN	Felix Irwin

LANE	Leon Quartermaine
LADY BRACKNELL	Edith Evans
GWENDOLEN FAIRFAX	Joyce Carey
CECILY CARDEW	Angela Baddeley
MISS PRISM	Margaret Rutherford
FOOTMAN	John Justin

For many people, even for those who never saw it, this production (with its magnificent cast) has remained the definitive one. Gielgud, in a radio interview with John Miller for the BBC in 1978, which was published under its radio title, *An Actor and His Time* (Sidgwick & Jackson, 1979), said: *The Importance of Being Earnest* has to be played very strictly; it is like chamber music. You must not indulge yourself, or caricature. You must play it with your tongue in your cheek, like a solemn charade.'

Bryan Forbes in his autobiography of Edith Evans, *Ned's Girl (*Elm Tree Books, 1977), quoted Evans on Lady Bracknell: 'I know those kind of women. They ring the bell and ask you to put a lump of coal on. They were caricatures, these people – absolutely assured, arrogant, and that's the way they spoke . . . They spoke meticulously, they were all very good looking and they didn't have any nerves.'

> If the past theatrical decade has to be represented by a single production, this is the one many good judges would choose.
>
> *The Times*

> Mr John Gielgud's John Worthing is full of rare comedy; he passes from mourning to muffins with measured dignity that is never over-done and he adds subtlety and freshness to the value of familiar lines.
>
> Ivor Brown *Observer*

> John Gielgud's light, clear, civilised performance unfalteringly holds the balance of the comedy true. It is a masterpiece of artificial acting.
>
> A V Cookman *Bystander*

> Mr John Gielgud, as John Worthing, is nothing short of brilliant. He has, so to speak, disappeared into the period, so right is he and so unforced is his comedy.
>
> W A Darlinton *Daily Telegraph*

> Of Miss Rutherford I must be content to say that she could not miss perfection if she aimed wide of it.
>
> *Sunday Times*

The production was given eight special matinee performances in January and February and then revived in August with the following changes of cast:

ALGERNON MONCRIEFF	Jack Hawkins
REV. CANON CHASUBLE	George Howe
MERRIMAN	Kingstone Trollope
LANE	Parde Woodman
GWENDOLEN FAIRFAX	Gwen Ffrangcon-Davies
CECILY CARDEW	Peggy Ashcroft/ Celia Johnson (on tour)
FOOTMAN	Douglas Malcolm

> . . . though Mr Hawkins has the air of a Margate tripper, rather than a man about town, he gave an immensely amusing performance . . . The depth of horror she [Edith Evans] gets into her voice when she learns that John was found at Victoria Station (the Brighton line) was so funny it made one regret that nowadays few actresses dare to play tricks with their voices.
>
> *Illustrated London News*

> Descending like some great fowl from splendid and uncharted skies, she [Edith Evans] can see no roost without ruling it and hear no crow without o'ercrowing it. For her to say 'a handbag' is to bring all the heavens of Mayfair crashing in one thunderbolt.
>
> Ivor Brown *Observer*

> Peggy Ashcroft's Cecily is dead right, artifice providing an entrancing impression of simplicity.
>
> Richard Clowes *Sunday Times*

Jack Hawkins in his autobiobraphy *Anything for a Quiet Life* (Elm Tree Books, 1973); thought that, 'Maybe part of the play's astonishing success stemmed from the fact that somehow that brittle period piece reflected the unbelieving, almost frivolous view we all took of the war, and even when it was obvious that this was real war, and no longer phoney, it still had a magic all its own.'

1942 Phoenix Theatre, London.

Director	John Gielgud
JOHN WORTHING	John Gielgud
ALGERNON MONCRIEFF	Cyril Ritchard
REV. CANON CHASUBLE	J H Roberts
MERRIMAN	Charles Maunsell
LANE	Deering Wells
LADY BRACKNELL	Edith Evans
GWENDOLEN FAIRFAX	Gwen Ffrangcon-Davies
CECILY CARDEW	Peggy Ashcroft
MISS PRISM	Jean Cadell

Miss Edith Evans as Lady Bracknell is the Koh-i-noor of this bediamoned and *fin-de-siècle* fairy-tale.

Ivor Brown *Observer*

1946 British television.

Director	George More O'Ferrall
JOHN WORTHING	Robert Eddison
ALGERNON MONCRIEFF	Mackenzie Ward
REV. CANON CHASUBLE	David Horne
MERRIMAN	Stringer Davis
LANE	Alban Blakelock
LADY BRACKNELL	Margaret Rutherford
GWENDOLEN FAIRFAX	Margaret Vines
CECILY CARDEW	Dorothy Hyson/Deryn Kerbey
MISS PRISM	Betty Potter

1947 New York and tour.

Director	John Gielgud
JOHN WORTHING	John Gielgud
ALGERNON MONCRIEFF	Robert Flemyng
REV CANON CHASUBLE	John Kidd
MERRIMAN	Stringer Davis
LANE	Richard Wordsworth

LADY BRACKNELL	Margaret Rutherford
GWENDOLEN FAIRFAX	Pamela Brown
CECILY CARDEW	Jane Baxter
MISS PRISM	Jean Cadell
FOOTMAN	Donald Bain

John Gielgud, in *An Actor and His Time*, said:

> It has to be played with the most enormous solemnity. But inside you must play the whole play as if you were doing a practical joke – with immense seriousness, knowing yourself that you are being killingly funny. And yet if you were to betray with the slightest flicker of an eyelash that you know you're funny, you are not funny either.

> Mr Gielgud plays with an ascetic arrogance that is enormously witty quite apart from the dialogue.
>
> Brooks Atkinson *New York Times*

> Margaret Rutherford is a magnificent snobbish Lady Bracknell. She resembles a grande dame of the bulldog breed and conducts herself with the same tenacity.
>
> William Hawkins *New York World Telegraph*

> Good as individual performances are, it is the teamwork of the cast that contributes chiefly to a memorable production and an evening of theatrical delight.
>
> Richard Watts, Jr *New York Post*

> It is distinctly for the minority . . . Is this superannuated comedy worth all this skilled effort?
>
> *Brooklyn Eagle*

1947 American television.

Director	Stanley Quinn
JOHN WORTHING	John Stephen
ALGERNON MONCRIEFF	Eliott Held
REV. CANON CHASUBLE	Guy Spaull
LADY BRACKNELL	Anna Russell

GWENDOLEN FAIRFAX	Romola Robb
CECILY CARDEW	Margaret Phillips
MISS PRISM	Silvia Davis

1950 American television.

Director	Williams Corrigan
JOHN WORTHING	John Buckmaster
ALGERNON MONCRIEFF	Hurd Hatfield
REV. CANON CHASUBLE	Dayton Lummis
MERRIMAN	Huntington Watts
LANE	Byron Russell
LADY BRACKNELL	Bertha Belmore
GWENDOLEN FAIRFAX	Brooke Bryon
CECILY CARDEW	Margaret Phillips
MISS PRISM	Hazel Jones

Hurd Hatfield and John Buckmaster played the foppish British gentlemen in search of the name Ernest and each gave a sock readings of the role.

Variety

1952 American television.

Eddie Dowling and the Dublin Players appeared in a scene from the play on the Ed Sullivan Show, *Toast of the Town*.

The social spoofing received a letter-perfect enactment by a trio of thesps . . . these Dubliners are better than Okay by a wide margin.

Variety

1952 British film.

Director	Anthony Asquith
JOHN WORTHING	Michael Redgrave
ALGERNON MONCRIEFF	Michael Denison
REV. CANON CHASUBLE	Miles Malleson

MERRIMAN	Aubrey Mather
LANE	Walter Hudd
SETON	Richard Wattis
LADY BRACKNELL	Edith Evans
GWENDOLEN FAIRFAX	Joan Greenwood
CECILY CARDEW	Dorothy Tutin
MISS PRISM	Margaret Rutherford

Anthony Asquith made no concessions to cinema. The production remained a filmed play, opening and closing in a theatre with the curtain rising and falling. The actors were deliberately stagey. 'Brilliant,' said C A Lejeune in the *Observer*. 'Total failure,' said Richard Winnington in the *News Chronicle*.

The film paid homage to both Wilde and Edith Evans, preserving her Lady Bracknell for posterity. 'I didn't try to modify her performance in any way,' said Asquith, 'because it seemed to me quite splendid.' Evans, awesome, monumental, was much less of a caricature than her numerous imitators have imagined.

Asquith asked her to change 'perambulator' to 'baby carriage' for American audiences. She refused. On being told that if she went straight on to the second mark the camera wouldn't be on her any more, she replied, 'Well, I don't know what it is about me, but I always feel the camera should come to me instead of me going to the camera.'

Michael Denison was a conceited and debonair Algernon, tossing off the epigrams in a bumptious manner. Michael Redgrave, a bland, tired, moustached dandy, acted in a quieter, more subtle, more serious key, but was far too old to be playing Worthing.

Joan Greenwood's exquisite, short-sighted Gwendolen ('I intend to develop in many directions') produced all sorts of vibrations. When she told Cecily that she was known for the gentleness of her disposition and the extraordinary sweetness of her nature, the claws were practically visible. There were moments when Greenwood sounded like Evans. In an earlier age, in a different country, this Gwendolen would have gone straight to the guillotine.

Margaret Rutherford was an ample-bosomed and motherly Prism. Miles Malleson's Chasuble was the perfect foil.

John Gielgud once described the role of Cecily as being one which should be played by someone who is first cousin to Alice-in-Wonderland. Asquith thought Dorothy Tutin (who was pretty, charming and sharp) fitted that description perfectly.

> *The Importance of Being Earnest*, without possessing the specific cinematic virtues, sets a standard in style, elegance, and sheer acting genius which will not easily be surpassed.
>
> *The Times*

> Dame Edith demonstrates her utter contempt for those who would have their screen acting different from the theatre and makes the other actors, with their more refined camera technique, appear a little thin-blooded when they are forced to share the screen with her.
>
> Karel Reisz *Sight and Sound*

> There is a Dresden china elegance, daintiness and precision about the work of Joan Greenwood – who delivers witticisms in a way that says 'Have I been clever!' instead of 'How clever I am.'
>
> *Sydney Morning Herald*

> They work so hard at it that now and then there is an awareness of the strain and effort necessary to keep the whole unstable structure of mistaken identities and Victorian notions from collapsing.
>
> Hollis Alpert *Saturday Review*

Michael Redgrave in his autobiography, *In My Mind's Eye* (Weidenfeld & Nicolson, 1983) wrote:

> I was very disappointed. The tempo, which it is true, must not be hurried, was ponderous, and sometimes the players, as Shaw noted of the original production, were too much in awe of Wilde to give their lines the air of conversation. I missed the audience terribly. Wilde's epigrams demand their tribute of laughter and, without it, both the actor and the story seemed very vulnerable.

1954 *Il est important d'être aimé.*

Théâtre Comédie des Champys-Élysées.

Adaptors	Jean Anouilh Claude Vincent
Director	Claude Sainval

JOHN WORTHING	Yves Robert
ALGERNON MONCRIEFF	Claude Sainval
REV. CANON CHASUBLE	Maurice Meric
MERRIMAN	Marcel Delaittre/Jean Vallienne
LANE	Henri Gaultier/Yves Gladine
LADY BRACKNELL	Françoise Rosay
GWENDOLEN FAIRFAX	Laurence Bataille
CECILY CARDEW	Jacqueline Ellis
MISS PRISM	Thérèse Dorny

1954 Le Théâtre en Rond, Paris.

Adaptor	Charles Cambilard
Director	André Villiers

1955 Munich. Premiere of *Bunbury*, an opera by P Burkhardt.

1956 Playhouse, Oxford.

Director	James Grout
JOHN WORTHING	Toby Robertson
ALGERNON MONCRIEFF	James Grout
REV. CANON CHASUBLE	Ken Wynne
MERRIMAN	David King
LANE	Brian Rawlinson
LADY BRACKNELL	Ena Burrill
GWENDOLEN FAIRFAX	Hazel Penwarden
CECILY CARDEW	Jacqueline Ellis
MISS PRISM	Barbara Atkinson

1957 Hermione Gingold played Lady Bracknell on American television.

1957 Television musical: *Who's Earnest?*

Director	David Alexander
JOHN WORTHING	David Atkinson
ALGERNON MONCRIEFF	Edward Mulhare
REV. CANON CHASUBLE	Martyn Green
MERRIMAN	Gordon Peters
LANE	Rex O'Malley
LADY BRACKNELL	Edith King
GWENDOLEN FAIRFAX	Louise Troy
CECILY CARDEW	Dorothy Collins
MISS PRISM	Nydia Westman

1957 Musical: *Found in a Handbag*

Premiere: Theatre Royal, Margate.

Music and lyrics	Allon Bacon
Director	Douglas Rye
JOHN WORTHING	Michael Spice
ALGERNON MONCRIEFF	John Ruck Keene
REV. CANON CHASUBLE	Peter Hill
MERRIMAN	Douglas Rye
LANE	Philip John
LADY BRACKNELL	Carol Raymount
GWENDOLEN FAIRFAX	June Wyndham Davies
CECILY CARDEW	Patricia Mortimer
MISS PRISM	Geraldine Newman

The scene with Gribsby (which George Alexander had cut during the first production) was played for the first time on any stage. The production was revived the following year at the Paris Theatre, Brighton, with Barry Sinclair playing John Worthing.

1957 Anna Russell played Lady Bracknell at Bucks County Playhouse, Pennsylvania.

1957 Dublin Festival.

Director	Michael MacOwan
JOHN WORTHING	Robert Eddison
ALGERNON MONCRIEFF	Derek Blomfield
LADY BRACKNELL	Margaret Rutherford

Many theatregoers will remember most clearly the magnificent Lady Bracknell of Margaret Rutherford, a man-o-war in full sail; this is a comedy performance of great tradition.

Irish Times

1958 Musical: *Half in Earnest*

Premiere: Belgrade Theatre, Coventry.

Music and lyrics	Vivian Ellis
Director	Bryan Bailey
JOHN WORTHING	Brian Reece
ALGERNON MONCRIEFF	Bryan Johnson
REV. CANON CHASUBLE	Henry Manning
MERRIMAN	Patrick Noble
LANE	Jon Livermore
LADY BRACKNELL	Marie Lohr
GWENDOLEN FAIRFAX	Pamela Jordan
CECILY CARDEW	Stephanie Voss
MISS PRISM	Phillada Sewell
FOOTMAN	Patrick O'Connell

As early as 1950 C B Cochran, the London theatre producer, had intended to present *Half in Earnest* with Marie Lohr, Michael Redgrave and Brian Reece in the West End. The production never materialised.

The Belgrade Theatre was the first regional theatre to be built after World War Two.

> This adaptation suggests no good reason why this particular classic should ever be set to music.
>
> *The Times*

> Mr Ellis might have fused the old and new more successfully if the words and music had smacked of the late 'nineties instead of the early 'thirties.
>
> *Punch*

1958 British television.

Director	Ronald Marriott
JOHN WORTHING	Michael Denison
ALGERNON MONCRIEFF	Tony Britton
REV. CANON CHASUBLE	Richard Goolden
LANE	Robert Webber
LADY BRACKNELL	Martita Hunt
GWENDOLEN FAIRFAX	Dulcie Gray
CECILY CARDEW	Maureen Swanson
MISS PRISM	Madeleine Christie

Michael Denison and Dulcie Gray, in their joint autobiography, *Double Act*, described how they all waited for Martita Hunt's delivery of 'A handbag!' and how deeply disappointed they were when she whispered it. 'They can't say I'm trying to copy Edith [Evans] now, can they?' she said.

> It is hard to think of any play less apt for television . . . The cast made an indecisive compromise between whole-hearted stylisation and realist moderation. On the whole the ladies came off worst. The idea of a 'real' Lady Bracknell is preposterous; and as Miss Martita Hunt presented the part it dwindled from one of imperturbably grotesque grandeur to a portrait of a shifty purse-proud obstinacy.
>
> *The Times*

1959 Old Vic Theatre, London.

Director	Michael Benthall
JOHN WORTHING	John Justin
ALGERNON MONCRIEFF	Alec McCowen
REV. CANON CHASUBLE	Miles Malleson
MERRIMAN	William McAllister
LANE	Norman Scace
LADY BRACKNELL	Fay Compton
GWENDOLEN FAIRFAX	Barbara Jefford
CECILY CARDEW	Judi Dench
MISS PRISM	Rosalind Atkinson
FOOTMAN	Dyson Lovell

The first London revival in seventeen years invited unfavourable comparisons with John Gielgud's production. Fay Compton forgot her lines and was prompted from the audience. Alec McCowen was camp. Miles Malleson was not as good as he had been in the film. But Judi Dench, a pert pink rose, vibrated to the sound of the name 'Ernest' and Rosalind Atkinson was a formidable governess. The main surprise (and disappointment) was that Maggie Smith, a member of the company, had not been cast as Gwendolen.

> Fay Compton's genteel, subdued, uncertain reading of the role is but a tinkling ice-cube compared with Dame Edith's unforgettable, formidable, unsinkable iceberg.
>
> Milton Shulman *Evening Standard*

1960 Musical: *Ernest in Love*

Premiere: Gramercy Arts Theatre, New York.

Book and lyrics	Anne Croswell
Music	Lee Pockriss
Director	Harold Stone
JOHN WORTHING	John Irving
ALGERNON MONCRIEFF	Louis Edmonds
REV. CANON CHASUBLE	George Hall
LANE	Alan Shayne

LADY BRACKNELL	Sara Seegar
GWENDOLEN FAIRFAX	Lelia Martin
CECILY CARDEW	Gerrianne Raphael
MISS PRISM	Lucy Landau

Ernest in Love was a pocket-sized musical, praised for its deft music, clever lyrics and its respect for the original. Lady Bracknell sang 'A Handbag Is Not A Proper Mother'. The chorus included a greengrocer, a bootmaker, a piano teacher, a tobacconist, a dancing master, and two maids.

1963 Madison Avenue Playhouse, New York.

Director	Douglas Seale
JOHN WORTHING	Michael Allison
ALGERNON MONCRIEFF	Louis Edmonds/John Neville
REV. CANON CHASUBLE	Melville Cooper
MERRIMAN	Carey Nairnes
LANE	Claude Horton
LADY BRACKNELL	Ann Shoemaker/Rene Gadd
GWENDOLEN FAIRFAX	Maureen Hurley
CECILY CARDEW	Carrie Nye/Jean Henderson
MISS PRISM	Jean Cameron

Often it turns out to be more barbed than its age and servitude give it any right to be.

Howard Taubman *New York Times*

It lacks that quality of easy expertise which would lift it from upper-middle mediocrity into theatrical peerage.

Michael Smith *Village Voice*

This is the cup of tea for a particular palette and it might have a tedious taste for someone impatient with its style.

Martin Gottfried *Woman's Wear Daily*

1963 Musical: *Wilde About Marriage*

Premiere: San Francisco.

Book, music and lyrics by Don De Mistral.

1964 Musical: *Mein Freund Bunbury*

Premiere: Metropol Theater, Berlin.

Music	Gerd Natschinski
Libretto	Helmut Bez
	Jurgen Degenhardt
Conductor	Tiberiu Popovici

1964 British television.

Director	Bill Bain
JOHN WORTHING	Ian Carmichael
ALGERNON MONCRIEFF	Patrick Macnee
REV. CANON CHASUBLE	Wilfrid Brambell
MERRIMAN	Charles Lloyd Pack
LANE	William Redmond
LADY BRACKNELL	Pamela Brown
GWENDOLEN FAIRFAX	Fenella Fielding
CECILY CARDEW	Susannah York
MISS PRISM	Irene Handl

Cathleen Nesbitt was to have played Lady Bracknell, but she was taken ill just as rehearsals were about to begin. Pamela Brown stepped in. It has often been said that Gwendolen will eventually become like her mother; what Brown was able to do was to remind audiences that Lady Bracknell had once been like Gwendolen. She was the youngest and prettiest Lady Bracknell. Taking the lines at a spanking pace, Brown got right away from Edith Evans's famous portrayal and opened up the role to a whole host of younger actresses.

Fenella Fielding, never afraid to be stagey, gave the tea scene a crisp edge. Though Ian Carmichael did not have the same feeling for the period, he was very funny in his quarrels with Algy, which were played like a lovers' quarrel. For a moment it seemed as if it were Oscar and Bosie having one of their many rows.

Patrick Macnee and Susannah York were not at their ease. Irene Handl was miscast and Wilfrid Brambell was just bad.

> Pamela Brown's Lady Bracknell was, perhaps, not quite the heavily gunned battleship she should have been – rather more of the cruiserweight, shall we say.
>
> Lynn Lockwood *Daily Telegraph*

> The performance was generally lightweight . . . Ian Carmichael was polished but in a different idiom; his John Worthing was charming, but blurred round the edges. Patrick Macnee's Algernon in searching for relaxed ease, merely seemed lackadaisical.
>
> *Variety*

1966 Flora Robson played Lady Bracknell in Newcastle at the theatre named after her, the Flora Robson Playhouse, and didn't enjoy the experience one bit. Two years later in London she would score a big success as Miss Prism.

1967 A musical version by Miroslav Ponc and Jiri Kosina was performed in Czechoslovakia.

1968 British television.

Director	George More O'Ferrall
JOHN WORTHING	Keith Barrow
ALGERNON MONCRIEFF	Barry Justice
LANE	Michael Finlayson
LADY BRACKNELL	Margaretta Scott
GWENDOLEN FAIRFAX	Angela Thorne

The programme was introduced by John Gielgud. Only Act I was performed.

1968 Musical: *Found in a Handbag*

Revival: Devonshire Park Theatre, Eastbourne.

Music and lyrics	Allon Bacon
Director	Richard Burnett
JOHN WORTHING	David Hall-Green
ALGERNON MONCRIEFF	Jonathan Prince
REV. CANON CHASUBLE	Colin Cresswell
MERRIMAN	Peter Power
LANE	Brue Bennett
LADY BRACKNELL	Adele Strong
GWENDOLEN FAIRFAX	Jean Lloyd
CECILY CARDEW	Diane Raynor
MISS PRISM	Patricia Ivey
CABBIE	Peter Power

Liberally laced with nineteen tantalising catchy lyrics, cleverly contrived lyrics that amusingly maintain the continuity of the plot, Allon Bacon's *The Importance of Being Earnest* has all the possibilities of becoming one of the top musicals of the decade.

Stage

1968 Theatre Royal, Haymarket, London.

Director	Robert Chetwyn
JOHN WORTHING	Daniel Massey
ALGERNON MONCRIEFF	John Standing
REV. CANON CHASUBLE	Robert Eddison
MERRIMAN	Lee Fox
LANE	Geoffrey Edwards
LADY BRACKNELL	Isabel Jeans
GWENDOLEN FAIRFAX	Helen Weir
CECILY CARDEW	Pauline Collins
MISS PRISM	Flora Robson
FOOTMAN	Paul Greaves

Isabel Jeans's Lady Bracknell was an elegant, mercenary old lady, who talked a lot of nonsense with hilarious deadpan seriousness.

Snobbish, hard, quite ruthless, she allowed nothing to stand in her way. What was said in parenthesis was often just as funny as the choicest epigram and paradox. When she said, 'To be born, or at any rate bred, in a handbag, whether it had handles or not, seems to me to display a contempt for the ordinary decencies of family life and reminds one of the worst excesses of the French Revolution,' it was the 'whether it had handles or not' which was so delicious.

John Standing's Algy, an ostentatiously elegant young man, had plenty of style, whether he was smugly coining epigrams or gobbling muffins. Pauline Collins was a pert Cecily.

Flora Robson's Miss Prism was a delightful mixture of anguish and coquettishness. Robert Eddison's Chasuble was a very gentle and very nervous celibate. Robson and Eddison made much of their coyness and embarrassment in each other's company.

Kenneth Barrow in his biography of Flora Robson, *Flora* (Heinemann, 1981), quoted her as saying that she knew her 'only chance of success was to play her seriously, tragically even'.

> With brilliant inspiration, they [Flora Robson and Robert Eddison] play as an elderly Héloïse and Abelard. Gleaming at each other like pale-eyed impassioned sheep, they languish and swoon in panting, tragic infatuation. Beside their lust, the leads indeed seem trivial.
>
> Ronald Bryden *Observer*

> Mr Standing strikes a nice balance between smugness and solemnity, giving moral force to his most frivolous assertion.
>
> Henry Popkins *The Times*

1968 Roundabout, New York.

Director	Gene Feist
JOHN WORTHING	Joe Ambraski
ALGERNON MONCRIEFF	John Mitchell
REV. CANON CHASUBLE	David Baker
MERRIMAN	Barry Goldberg
LANE	Robert Barger
LADY BRACKNELL	Irene Bejarno
GWENDOLEN FAIRFAX	Madeleine Le Roux
CECILY CARDEW	Jane E House
MISS PRISM	Elizabeth Owens

1973 Abbey Theatre, Dublin.

Director	Alan Barlow
JOHN WORTHING	John Kavanagh
ALGERNON MONCRIEFF	Desmond Cave
REV. CANON CHASUBLE	Ronnie Walsh
MERRIMAN	Bill Foley
LANE	Clive Geraghty
MOULTON	Harry Brogan
LADY BRACKNELL	Joan O'Hara
GWENDOLEN FAIRFAX	Deirdre Donnelly
CECILY CARDEW	Bernadette McKenna
MISS PRISM	May Cluskey

Mr Barlow produces it as an hilarious lark, sometimes almost a send-up of the Wilde convention into the attic realms of *Charley's Aunt* and it suffers nothing at his hands.

Seamus Kelly *Irish Times*

It gives what is undoubtedly the most painfully tasteless production I have ever seen of Mr Wilde's play on any stage anywhere and I have seen some grim efforts . . . Through hamming, camping, guying and caricaturing, through comic opera servants, acrobats, and bits of music-hall business, it offers us a production which starts at a low level and goes steadily downhill.

Desmond Rushe *Irish Independent*

1973 Musical: *Nobody's Earnest*

Premiere: Williamstown Theatre, Massachusetts.

Adaptor	Arnold Sundgaard
Music	Alec Wilder
Lyrics	Ethan Eyer
Director	Nikos Psacharopoulos
JOHN WORTHING	Clifford David
ALGERNON MONCRIEFF	John Cunningham
REV. CANON CHASUBLE	Emery Battis

MERRIMAN	Glen Mure
LANE	Kent Stephens
LADY BRACKNELL	Elizabeth Parrish
GWENDOLEN FAIRFAX	Marian Mercer
CECILY CARDEW	April Shawhan
MISS PRISM	June Gable

Everyone has been too respectful of the original text, with the result that too often a song seems simply an interpolation.

Edwin Wilson *Wall Street Journal*

He [Clifford David] conveys about as much wit as a graffito in an off-limits bar . . . Elizabeth Parrish plays Lady Bracknell as a French cocotte formerly active in Montmartre's music halls.

John Simon *New York*

1974 British television.

Director	James MacTaggart
JOHN WORTHING	Michael Jayston
ALGERNON MONCRIEFF	Julian Holloway
REV. CANON CHASUBLE	Richard Pearson
MERRIMAN	Arthur Hewlett
LANE	Douglas Milvain
LADY BRACKNELL	Coral Browne
GWENDOLEN FAIRFAX	Gemma Jones
CECILY CARDEW	Celia Bannerman
MISS PRISM	Lally Bowers

The production was prosaic and generally unfunny. Coral Browne, who had a reputation off-stage for being very ladylike and very vulgar at the same time, should have been perfect casting for Lady Bracknell, yet in the event she was disappointing.

Coral Browne's Lady Bracknell was less monstrous than the author suggested, rather too attractive, scaled down rather than played up.

Shaun Usher *Daily Mail*

She [Celia Bannerman] was poised without archness, modest without coyness, charming without cuteness.

Clive James *Observer*

1974 Shaw Theatre, London.

Director	Peter James
JOHN WORTHING	Richard Kay
ALGERNON MONCRIEFF	Terry Taplin
REV. CANON CHASUBLE	Edward Jewesbury
MERRIMAN	Gordon Richardson
LANE	Kenneth Benda
LADY BRACKNELL	Betty Marsden
GWENDOLEN FAIRFAX	Polly Adams
CECILY CARDEW	Louise Purnell
MISS PRISM	Rosamund Greenwood

1974 Italy. Premiere of *L'Importanza d'Essere Franco*, a musical by Mario Castelnuovo-Tedesco.

1974 Arts Theatre, New York.

Director	Robert Sterling
JOHN WORTHING	Terrence O'Hara
ALGERNON MONCRIEFF	Thomas MacGeevy
REV. CANON CHASUBLE	John Dorrin
LADY BRACKNELL	Jean Campbell
GWENDOLEN FAIRFAX	Lee Terri
CECILY CARDEW	Berryl Man
MISS PRISM	Muriel Mason

Berryl Man – beset with dreadful problems in the second act when her dress nearly fell down – caught that unnerving habit of upperclass English girls of punctuating each sentence with nervous giggles, half a plea for mercy, half an invitation to put your hand up her skirt.

Alexander Coburn *Village Voice*

1974 Musical by Hot Peaches.

Premiere: Nighthouse Theatre, New York.

Lyrics	Marie D'Antoni
Director	Paulita Sedgwick
JOHN WORTHING	Sister Tui
ALGERNON MONCRIEFF	Ian McKay
LADY BRACKNELL	Michael Akian
GWENDOLEN FAIRFAX	Byron Thomas
CECILY CARDEW	Chris Kapp

The musical (described by one critic as 'elegant trash') was a drag show with 'thirties torch songs and jazz numbers.

> What we get instead are drag queenlets in drag. Young blades in need of sharpening, and scenes that cry to heaven for vengeance. What we don't get is a savour of the delectable Wildean wit. The cast is made to call so much attention to its own burlesqueries that it runs roughshod over the dialogue, wishing it would somehow go away. The result is a shallow surface façade that runs no deeper than the tiny silver sequin planted as a dimple on an Algerian chin.
>
> Edward Moran *Show Business*

1974 *Travesties*
A play by Tom Stoppard.

Premiere: Aldwych Theatre (Royal Shakespeare Company).

Tom Stoppard has described *Travesties* as a bit of singing and dancing mixed up with political debate. The comedy looked at the past through the faulty memory of Henry Carr, formerly a casual employee of the British Consulate General in Zurich.

In his dotage Carr confuses the minor role he had played in a major political event (the Russian Revolution) with a major role (Algernon Moncrieff) he had played in an amateur production of *The Importance of Being Earnest*. John Wood had tremendous vitality as both the young and the old Carr.

To enjoy Stoppard's play it was not necessary to know anything about either Lenin, James Joyce or Tristan Tzara (founder member of Dada); but it was absolutely essential to know Oscar Wilde's play because Stoppard relied for his wit on direct quotation and pastiche. Cecily and Gwendolen sang their tea scene. Ideally, as they do regularly in America, the two plays should be revived in tandem.

The Royal Shakespeare Company revived *Travesties* in 1993 at the Barbican. Antony Sher (Carr) and David Whitehead (very stylish as Tzara) gave an amusing imitation of the way some actors carry on when they act in Wilde's comedy.

1975 Greenwich Theatre.

Director	Jonathan Miller
JOHN WORTHING	David Horovitch
ALGERNON MONCRIEFF	Robert Swann
REV. CANON CHASUBLE	Benjamin Whitrow
MERRIMAN	Alan Brown
LANE	Alan Hay
LADY BRACKNELL	Irene Handl
GWENDOLEN FAIRFAX	Angela Down
CECILY CARDEW	Charlotte Cornwell
MISS PRISM	Joan Sanderson

'German sounds a thoroughly respectable language and indeed, I believe it is so,' says Lady Bracknell. Irene Handl, famous for her Cockney roles, played Lady Bracknell as a German Jewess. Dumpy, frumpish, and cosy, she was no gorgon. The interpretation blunted the lines.

'What Handl does to Lady Bracknell,' said one critic, 'is nothing to what the real Lady Bracknell would have done to Miss Handl.'

The truth is that she had adopted the German accent to disguise her fluffing of lines. After the first night she dropped the accent, much to the disappointment of theatregoers who had gone specially to Greenwich to hear it. Joan Sanderson was such a stern and forbidding Miss Prism that many people thought the two actresses should have swapped roles.

Jonathan Miller had originally wanted to stage an all-male production at the National Theatre, with either Leo McKern or Peter Bull as Lady Bracknell, but the idea had been vetoed by Harold Pinter who was on the NT's Board.

> She [Irene Handl] sounds mysteriously Central European, disarming opposition not through patrician obstinacy but by impenetrable gemütlich silliness.
>
> Robert Cushman *Observer*

> Joan Sanderson delivers Prism's lunatic irrelevancies as though they were Socratic truths.
>
> Jeremy Kingston *Plays and Players*

1975 Stratford Festival, Canada.

Director	Robin Phillips
JOHN WORTHING	Nicholas Pennell
ALGERNON MONCRIEFF	Richard Monette
REV. CANON CHASUBLE	Tom Kneebone
MERRIMAN	John Innes
LANE	Rod Beattie
LADY BRACKNELL	William Hutt
GWENDOLEN FAIRFAX	Pat Galloway
CECILY CARDEW	Marti Maradan
MISS PRISM	Meg Hogarth

William Hutt, well over six foot, fox-furred, gloved, parasoled, played Lady Bracknell as a reincarnation of Queen Mary, wife of King George V. Stately, haughty, imperious, and intimidating, he kept his natural male voice and played the part straight.

Lady Bracknell was dumbfounded when John Worthing told her that he had been born in a handbag. Hutt looked at his tiny handbag, he looked at Mr Worthing, he looked at the handbag, he looked at Mr Worthing, a double, triple, quadruple, quintuple take, and then, when Worthing made a slight move towards him, he clasped the handbag to his bosom as if he feared Worthing might do some unspeakable outrage to it.

1976 Stratford Festival revived Robin Phillips's production.

JOHN WORTHING	Nicholas Pennell
ALGERNON MONCRIEFF	Barry McGregor
REV. CANON CHASUBLE	Eric Donkin

MERRIMAN	John Innes
LANE	Richard Curnock
LADY BRACKNELL	William Hutt
GWENDOLEN FAIRFAX	Pat Galloway
CECILY CARDEW	Marti Maradan
MISS PRISM	Amelia Hall

1976 West German television: *Keine Hochzeit ohne Ernst.*

1977 Citizens' Theatre, Glasgow.

Director	Giles Havergall
Designer	Philip Prowse
JOHN WORTHING	James Gibb
ALGERNON MONCRIEFF	Mark Lewis
REV. CANON CHASUBLE	Barry Philips
MERRIMAN	Ciaran Hinds
LANE	Brough Cooper
LADY BRACKNELL	Jonathan Hyde
GWENDOLEN FAIRFAX	Jill Spurrier
CECILY CARDEW	Julia Blalock
MISS PRISM	Gerard Murphy
MR GRIBSBY	David Hayman
MOULTON	Douglas Heard

The Glasgow Citizens' used the four-act version, which included Gribsby's arrival to accompany Algernon to Holloway Prison, Chasuble's proposal to Miss Prism, and Moulton, the gardener.

> It is a fully fledged, controlled and brilliantly funny piece of feminine characterisation. Mr Hyde has a superb voice, a commanding stage presence and great style. Here he sounds like Edith Evans (except at the obvious moments!) and looks like Martita Hunt. With black bustle, parasol and galleon hat, he sweeps imperiously and (nice touch) slightly myopically through the play.
>
> Michael Coveney *Financial Times*

1977 The Round House Theatre, London, and tour.

Director	Tenniel Evans
JOHN WORTHING	John Harding
ALGERNON MONCRIEFF	Martin Connor
REV. CANON CHASUBLE	Edward Petherbridge
MERRIMAN	Tenniel Evans
LANE	Tenniel Evans
LADY BRACKNELL	Ann Firbank
GWENDOLEN FAIRFAX	Rosie Kerslake
CECILY CARDEW	Ann Hasson
MISS PRISM	Brenda Peters

Tenniel Evans's production for the Actors Company was dominated by Edward Petherbridge's skeletal, nasal, lip-licking, wild-haired Chasuble, who was much given to involuntary phallic gestures. 'A masterpiece of fumbling indecision,' said Allen Saddler in *Plays and Players*.

> He has the semblance of a drainpipe and the demeanour of a mad bumblebee and whenever he is on the stage the play comes alive.
>
> *Sunday Times*

1977 Circle in the Square, New York.

Director	Stephen Porter
JOHN WORTHING	James Valentine
ALGERNON MONCRIEFF	John Glover
REV. CANON CHASUBLE	G Wood
MERRIMAN	Thomas Ruisinger
LANE	Munson Hicks
LADY BRACKNELL	Elizabeth Wilson
GWENDOLEN FAIRFAX	Patricia Conolly
CECILY CARDEW	Kathleen Widdoes
MISS PRISM	Mary Louise Wilson

> This is a farce walking the tightrope of absurdity. But it is also farce at its most urbane – as insolently monocled in manner as it is killingly high-toned in language.
>
> T E Kalem *Time*

> Perhaps Wilde had a nostalgia for heterosexual respectability that was deeper than he knew.
>
> Julia Novick *Village Voice*

1977 Young Vic Theatre, London.

Director	Denise Coffey
JOHN WORTHING	David Henry
ALGERNON MONCRIEFF	Simon Chandler
REV. CANON CHASUBLE	Job Stewart
MERRIMAN	Hugh Hastings
LANE	Ian Taylor
LADY BRACKNELL	Teddy Green
GWENDOLEN FAIRFAX	Amanda Boxer
CECILY CARDEW	Natasha Pyne
MISS PRISM	Rosalind Boxall

Simon Chandler was a waspish Algy. David Henry was a teddy-bear Ernest. Amanda Boxer's Gwendolen was an apprentice gorgon. The trouble with casting Teddy Green as Lady Bracknell was that the play became a crude romp, and much nearer to *Charley's Aunt* (Algy's Aunt?) than *The Importance of Being Earnest*.

> He tends neither in the direction of Danny La Rue nor Barry Humphries and remains somewhere in a gender limbo and about as terrifying as an elderly pigeon.
>
> Nicholas de Jongh *Guardian*

1979 Chichester Festival Theatre, Sussex.

Director	Peter Dews
JOHN WORTHING	Ian Ogilvy
ALGERNON MONCRIEFF	Michael Cochrane

REV. CANON CHASUBLE	John Clements
MERRIMAN	John Gill
LANE	David Glover
LADY BRACKNELL	Googie Withers
GWENDOLEN FAIRFAX	Hayley Mills
CECILY CARDEW	Mel Martin
MISS PRISM	Patsy Byrne

Michael Cochrane wore a green carnation. Ian Ogilvy wore a pin-striped suit. The actors, loud in voice and dress, lacked wit and bite. The company as a whole had a poor sense of period and their diction was not good.

> Ian Ogilvy plays Jack Worthing caddishly enough with one of those awful perpetual half-smiles that informs everyone that he knows he is a handsome man-about-town.
>
> Keith Nurse *Daily Telegraph*

> She [Googie Withers] plays Aunt Augusta instead as a *fin de siècle* Mrs Thatcher and sustains her formidable authority that way. No fireworks on 'A handbag!' – but instead a crashing chord for the death of Bunbury when she had to utter 'Exploded!
>
> Anthony Curtis *Plays and Players*

> John Clements is an unusually, rather pleasantly timorous Canon Chasuble; and Miss Byrne's Prism is a bulldog lady not at all suitable for a romantic conclusion.
>
> B A Young *Financial Times*

1980 Old Vic Theatre, London.

Director	Frank Hauser
JOHN WORTHING	Richard Easton
ALGERNON MONCRIEFF	David Downer
REV. CANON CHASUBLE	James Bree
MERRIMAN	Terence Soall
LANE	Desmond Jordan
GRIBSBY	Kenneth Waller
MOULTON	Desmond Jordan

LADY BRACKNELL	Margaretta Scott
GWENDOLEN FAIRFAX	Polly Adams
CECILY CARDEW	Isabelle Amyes
MISS PRISM	Joyce Grant

The production was advertised as the four-act version, but it was in fact a mixture of the four-act and three-act versions.

The advantages of the four-act version are a stronger story line and a greater development of Algernon's character. The weakness is that the actual dialogue is not so tight and the situation is over-stretched.

Moulton, the gardener, has so little to do that he might as well not be there, but Gribsby, the solicitor, has such a good scene that it is a pity that it is not played more often. The scene in question is the one where Algy, disguised as Ernest, finds himself arrested for Jack's debts, a classic case of mistaken identity and poetic justice. The solicitor's remarks, with hindsight, are painfully prophetic.

GRIBSBY: I am sorry to disturb this pleasant family meeting but time presses. We have to be at Holloway not later than four o'clock; otherwise it is difficult to obtain admission. The rules are very strict.

ALGERNON: Well, really I am not going to be imprisoned in the suburbs for having dined out in the West End.

Richard Easton, well into his forties, had a hangdog, seedy, look, and his mouth was constantly agape. His performance would have been better suited to the Ralph Lynn parts in the farces of Ben Travers. David Downer's moment came when Algy dictated his love for Cecily very, very slowly so that she could take it down in her diary. The best performance was by Polly Adams, a passionate and idealistic Gwendolen, who exercised the firmest of hands.

Margaretta Scott as Lady Bracknell had one memorable moment when she learned that Ernest had been found in a handbag. She closed her book with its list of eligible young men and returned it to her purse which shut with a dismissive click which reverberated throughout the theatre as loud as the last trumpet.

1980 Musical: *Ernest in Love*

Premiere: Theatre-off-Park, New York.

Book and lyrics	Anne Croswell
Music	Lee Pockriss
Director	Jay Stephens
CAST	Dan Ahearn
	Susan Bigelow
	Virginia Dowling
	Kathleen Greenon
	Alex Korff
	Jack Kyrieleison
	Doreen Richardson
	Barbara Surosky
	Geri Winbarg
	Ray Xifo

1981 Palace Theatre, Watford.

Director	Michael Attenborough
JOHN WORTHING	Gary Bond
ALGERNON MONCRIEFF	Jeremy Clyde
REV. CANON CHASUBLE	Henry Moxon
MERRIMAN	Sydney Arnold
LANE	Alan Hay
LADY BRACKNELL	Wendy Hiller
GWENDOLEN FAIRFAX	Gabrielle Drake
CECILY CARDEW	Ann Thornton
MISS PRISM	Rosamund Greenwood

The production was televised.

> The production looked exceptionally bright and appropriate for the petulantly romantic tone of the satire as *Earnest* proved to a new era why Wilde comedy is considered a masterpiece.
>
> B K *Variety*

1982 American television: *Who Am I This Time?*
A short story by Kurt Vonnegut, Jr.

Adaptor	Neal Morton Miller
Director	Jonathan Demme

By day Harry Nash (Christopher Walken) was a cripplingly shy, tongue-tied, bespectacled shop assistant. But at night, when he was appearing with the local amateur theatre, his whole personality was transformed. He became the parts he played: Stanley Kowalski, Cyrano, Abraham Lincoln. His girlfriend (Susan Sarandon) decided that the best way for him to overcome his shyness would be for him to play stage roles off-stage as well. He courted her in the guise of Mark Antony, Professor Henry Higgins and Henry V. He proposed to her in the character of John Worthing.

1982 Mercer Street Theatre, New York.

Director	Evan Thompson
JOHN WORTHING	Owen Thompson
ALGERNON MONCRIEFF	David H Hamilton
REV. CANON CHASUBLE	Evan Thompson
LANE	John McGrane
LADY BRACKNELL	Quentin Crisp
GWENDOLEN FAIRFAX	Anne Burr
CECILY CARDEW	Cecile Callan
MISS PRISM	Joan Shepard

The results are disastrous, except in the case of Quentin Crisp, who, as Lady Bracknell, ignores acting, characterisation, gender, and sometimes even Wilde's exact wording and still gives a successful performance, because he has his own style, which is compatible with Oscar's, while his cohorts, styleless creatures all, are being fiendishly Wildean all over the stage to no effect whatsoever.

Michael Feingold *Village Voice*

1982 National Theatre, London.

Director	Peter Hall
JOHN WORTHING	Martin Jarvis
ALGERNON MONCRIEFF	Nigel Havers
REV. CANON CHASUBLE	Paul Rogers
MERRIMAN	John Gill
LANE	Brian Kent
LADY BRACKNELL	Judi Dench
GWENDOLEN FAIRFAX	Zoë Wanamaker
CECILY CARDEW	Elizabeth Garvie
MISS PRISM	Anna Massey

The unspeakably vulgar programme-cover drawing of a baby in a handbag did not augur well. Nor did there seem much sense in casting Judi Dench as Lady Bracknell if Zoë Wanamaker were to be cast as her daughter. There was not much sense in casting Judi Dench in the first place. Immaculately preserved, she was no gorgon. She flirted openly with Algy, her hand on his knee.

Her distaste, as she listened to Jack's account of how he had been abandoned in a handbag, was very funny. She tore up her notes. Dench's timing and delivery of Wilde's lines, as when she commented on Bunbury's death ('He seems to have had a great confidence in the opinion of his physicians') was perfect. But in no way was she ever Lady Bracknell.

Martin Jarvis, far too old, was the most earnest of Ernests; he was so grave he might have been the undertaker. His best moment was his outrage when he found Algy masquerading as his brother. The comedy was in his silent outrage. No less funny was the way he promised Lady Bracknell the handbag rather than the parents by the end of the month.

Nigel Havers, who should have been a natural for Algernon, was inadequate. Paul Rogers found a new way to play Chasuble: bad-tempered.

> Whereas Edith Evans was like some powerful mare, Miss Dench is like some mettlesome pony.
>
> Francis King *Sunday Telegraph*

> She [Judi Dench] has an icy authority and elegance. She is formidably funny, with finger-tip control of nuclear comic energy, needing only to remove her spectacles when she comes to the notorious hurdle of the handbag line. Here is the definitive Lady Bracknell in her own kind, to match Dame Edith in power, if not in extravagance, and perhaps to surpass it in humanity. With a touch *less* humanity she will be just about perfect.
>
> Richard Findlater *Plays and Players*

> This is probably the best *acted* Lady Bracknell there has ever been. (Edith Evans was a Happening.) And somehow, through sheer technical prowess, this uncompromising portrayal floods the auditorium with more warmth than has been generated by any actress since Miss Dench played O'Casey's Juno
>
> Robert Cushman *Observer*

1983 *The Importance of Being Wilde*
by James Hogue.

Premiere: Nameless Theatre, New York.

Director	James Hogue
FRANKFORD SURREY	Walter Dunlap
JACK WORTHING	Mitchell Sugarman
ALGERNON MONCRIEFF	Thomas Abrams
ALICE LITTLE	Siri Wanamaker
MR LITTLE	J Lee Flynn
MR BUNNBURY	Kevin Scott
LADY CONSTANCE	Christine Gillespie

The Importance of Being Wilde was a sequel to *The Importance of Being Earnest*. Frankford Surrey, the leading character, was a friend of Algernon Moncrieff.

> Hogue has quoted from Lord Byron, Shakespeare, Gilbert and Sullivan, and shamelessly plagiarised Wilde for characters and situations. Several encounters he sets up merely to try his hand at aphorisms. But his flop.
>
> Sy Syna *New York Tribune*

1984 Musical: *The Importance*

Premiere: Ambassadors Theatre, London.

Music and lyrics	John Hugh Dean
Director	Tony Craven
LAKE	Peter Loury
MR ATKINS	Barry Stean
JOHN WORTHING	Patrick Ryecart
ALGERNON MONCRIEFF	David Firth
DR CHASUBLE	Robert Dorning
MERRIMAN	Nicholas Amer
LANE	Llewellyn Rees
LADY BRACKNELL	Judy Campbell
GWENDOLEN FAIRFAX	Ruth Mayo
CECILY CARDEW	Karen Lancaster
MISS PRISM	Sheila Bernette
MR BROWNE	Joseph Young

John Hugh Dean's adaptation and Tony Craven's production managed to exceed everybody's worst expectations with cloying Victorian ballads, undistinguished tunes, and tatty prettiness.

> It is coarse, incompetent, joyless, simpering and, not to mince words, dreadful.
>
> Kenneth Hurran *Mail on Sunday*

1984 Wilde Theatre, Bracknell, Berkshire.

Director	John Ginham
JOHN WORTHING	Mark Tandy
ALGERNON MONCRIEFF	Alex Jennings
REV. CANON CHASUBLE	David Rose
MERRIMAN	Nigel Harrison
LANE	Adam Kurakin
LADY BRACKNELL	Dilys Laye
GWENDOLEN FAIRFAX	Nicola King
CECILY CARDEW	Deborah Poplett
MISS PRISM	Margot Cunningham

The play was chosen to inaugurate a new theatre.

> Its chief glory is the Lady Bracknell of Dilys Laye . . . making the barbed or imperious comments all the more telling for being delivered in the small, clear voice of someone who must have once, not so long ago, been a charming girl . . . Alex Jennings' youthful, mischievous, pampered Algernon can only have been the fag of Mark Tandy's balding, elongated, sad-faced Jack when both of them were at Eton.
>
> *Sunday Telegraph*

1985 Samuel Beckett Theatre, New York.

Director	Philip Campanella
JOHN WORTHING	Samuel Maupin
ALGERNON MONCRIEFF	Anthony Fusco
REV. CANON CHASUBLE	William Denis
MERRIMAN	Robert North
LANE	A D Cover
LADY BRACKNELL	Dina Merrill/Peg Small
GWENDOLEN FAIRFAX	Cynthia Dozier
CECILY CARDEW	Cherry Jones
MISS PRISM	Carmella Ross

1985 Playhouse, Oxford.

Director	Richard Williams
JOHN WORTHING	David Mallinson
ALGERNON MONCRIEFF	Chris Hunter
REV. CANON CHASUBLE	John Rolfe
MERRIMAN	David Goodland
LANE	Godfrey Jackman
LADY BRACKNELL	Andrée Melly
GWENDOLEN FAIRFAX	Christine Kavanagh
CECILY CARDEW	Natalie Ogle
MISS PRISM	Elizabeth Kelly

The production played in tandem with Tom Stoppard's *Travesties*.

Mr Hunter who announces his love for Cecily by rolling on the floor and kicking his legs in the air gives us a magnetic display of emotional frenzy; but it owes slightly more to Jerry Lewis than the insouciant elegance of Wilde's Algernon

Michael Billington *Guardian*

1985 Jean Cocteau Repertory Theatre, New York.

Director	Gils Hogya
JOHN WORTHING	Patrick Boyington
ALGERNON MONCRIEFF	John Emmert
LADY BRACKNELL	Craig Cook
GWENDOLEN FAIRFAX	Margaret Dulaney
CECILY CARDEW	Stephanie Lett

Craig Cook's Lady Bracknell is a big, over-inflated figure, a towering indomitable cartoon pasted on the scene. Before her are arranged the combatants, as before a sphinx.

Michael Grumley *New York Native*

1986 Musical: *Borne in a Handbag*

Revival: Key Theatre, Peterborough.

Music and lyrics	Sean O'Mahony
Director	Derek Killeen

Author John Hugh Dean, who had been banned from the London production of his musical *The Importance* and feeling that justice had not been done to his musical adaptation, revived it with a new title, under his own name, Sean O'Mahony, and at his own expense.

1987 Royalty Theatre, London.

Director	Donald Sinden
JOHN WORTHING	Clive Francis
ALGERNON MONCRIEFF	Denis Lawson
REV. CANON CHASUBLE	Harold Innocent

MERRIMAN	Patrick Ludlow
LANE	Ken Wynne
LADY BRACKNELL	Wendy Hiller
GWENDOLEN FAIRFAX	Gabrielle Drake
CECILY CARDEW	Natalie Ogle
MISS PRISM	Phyllida Law

The actors and the director killed off Wilde in much the same way that Algy had killed off Bunbury. The play was so dead, it was like watching a very brightly lit museum piece.

The audience applauded Lady Bracknell rather than Wendy Hiller, who was no gorgon and looked old enough to be everybody's grandmother. Clive Francis, no longer twenty-seven (Jack's real age), admitted to being thirty-five but looked as if he were well into his forties.

The most serious error of Donald Sinden's production was to deny Worthing his centre-stage entrance when he arrives in deepest mourning for the death of his brother. Francis came on from stage right and was half-way across the stage before most of the audience realised he was there, thus robbing him of one of the biggest laughs of the play.

The most likeable performance was Denis Lawson's slightly camp and slightly common Algernon. Ken Wynne was allowed to turn Lane into an extended comic music-hall turn before the play proper started.

> Lady Bracknell is one of society's vultures, swooping on her prey with the creature's autocratic instinct for survival. Yet as played by Wendy Hiller, she resembles more a beady-eyed budgerigar pecking crossly at its millet.
>
> Jack Tinker *Daily Mail*

> She copes with memories of Dame Edith's way with the 'handbag' line by the simple expedient of turning that famous upward inflection into a downward one.
>
> Charles Osborne *Daily Telegraph*

> The lightest of meringues should be served crispy, warm and fresh (just as it once was); here it's more of a school dumpling.
>
> Robert Gore Langton *Plays and Players*

1987 Whitehall Theatre, London.

Adaptor/director	Lou Stein
JOHN WORTHING	Simon Dutton
ALGERNON MONCRIEFF	Robin Kermode
REV. CANON CHASUBLE	Fred Evans
MERRIMAN	Chubby Oates
LANE	Chubby Oates
LADY BRACKNELL	Dame Hilda Bracket
GWENDOLEN FAIRFAX	Tara Ward
CECILY CARDEW	Kate O'Sullivan
MISS PRISM	Dr Evadne Hinge

Lou Stein's Pirandellian conceit was that two middle-aged women were acting *The Importance of Being Earnest* in their own front parlour.

Lady Bracknell and Miss Prism were played by two drag artists. They also played Gwendolen Fairfax and Cecily Cardew when the two actresses, who were to have played them, were delayed at Victoria Station by a missing handbag.

Wilde's comedy was acted for chintzy suburban camp and sexual innuendo. The result was an amateur send-up of an amateur performance with a cheap imitation of Edith Evans.

The critics described this bizarre and ribald travesty as 'a memorably appalling evening' (*Evening Standard*), 'a subversion of a great comedy: an evening of lumpen satire' (*Guardian*), and 'utterly loathsome' (*Jewish Chronicle*).

> There can't be a worse conceived production anywhere in London.
>
> Christopher Edward *Spectator*

> The question is: who needs it?
>
> Clive Hirschhorn *Sunday Express*

1987 *La Graveco de la Fideligio*

Premiere: Bloomsbury Theatre, London.

The play was performed in Esperanto.

1987 Gate Theatre, Dublin.

Director	Patrick Mason
Designer	Robert Ballagh
JOHN WORTHING	Bosco Hogan
ALGERNON MONCRIEFF	Lorcan Cranitch
REV. CANON CHASUBLE	Alan Stanford
MERRIMAN	Christopher Casson
LANE	David Heap
LADY BRACKNELL	Kate Flynn
GWENDOLEN FAIRFAX	Ingrid Craigie
CECILY CARDEW	Lise-Ann McLaughlin
MISS PRISM	Maire Hastings
GRIBSBY	J J Murphy
FOOTMAN	Rod Chichignoud

Robert Ballagh's portrait of Oscar Wilde was unveiled in the foyer of the Gate Theatre on the opening night of this production.

1988 British television.

Director	Stuart Burge
JOHN WORTHING	Paul McGann
ALGERNON MONCRIEFF	Rupert Frazer
REV. CANON CHASUBLE	Alec McCowen
MERRIMAN	John Quarmby
LANE	John Woodnutt
LADY BRACKNELL	Joan Plowright
GWENDOLEN FAIRFAX	Amanda Redman
CECILY CARDEW	Natalie Ogle
MISS PRISM	Gemma Jones
GRIBSBY	Peter Copely

Joan Plowright played the imperious mother with a gulping disbelief which reduced the greatest lines to a contorted hiccough. But at least she and Paul McGann's genuinely pre-Raphaelite Jack had a glimmer of consistent style.

William Holmes *The Times*

Instead of camped-up Wilde, a uniformly strong cast gave us Wilde the trenchant social observer who ebulliently caught the chauvinism and Philistinism of the British upper-class.

Patricia Morison *Daily Telegraph*

It was as if the cast were so busy rooting their characters in some form of reality that there was no energy left over to deliver the lines with the relish they so obviously demand.

Malcolm Hay *Plays and Players*

1989 *Without Apologies*
A play by Thom Thomas.

Premiere: Hudson Guild Theatre, New York.

Director	Edgar Lansbury
ALGY BEAUMONT	Kurt Knudson
GWENDOLEN	Pauline Flanagan
ERNIE BEAUMONT	Peter Pagan
CECILY	Carrie Nye
BRENDA	Laura Brutsman
WILLIE JUKES	Edmund Lewis

Thom Thomas set his play in 1933, 1937 and 1940. Algernon was married to Gwendolen. They lived in shabby gentility in the borough of Camden Town, London. They were strictly lower-middle class. Algy had grown stout and was a writer of obituary notices. Gwendolen raised chickens. Jack had married Cecily. They were bankrupt. Lady Bracknell did not appear.

It would have been no loss if *Without Apologies* had been left in a handbag in a cloakroom at Victoria Station.

Mel Gussow *New York Times*

This mirthless farce by Thom Thomas . . . is a cuckoo's egg laid in Oscar Wilde's nest.

New York

1989 Bloomsbury Theatre, London.
Transferred: Jeanette Cochrane Theatre, London.

Director	Yvonne Brewster
JOHN WORTHING	Gary McDonald
ALGERNON MONCRIEFF	Ben Thomas
REV. CANON CHASUBLE	Oscar James
MERRIMAN	Andrew Goth
LANE	Christopher Tajah
LADY BRACKNELL	Mona Hammond
GWENDOLEN FAIRFAX	Juanita Waterman
CECILY CARDEW	Jeohna Williams
MISS PRISM	Leonie Forbes

The Talawa Theatre Company presented an all-black production, which was broad, funny, and totally conventional, though, inevitably, some lines – 'I hope your hair curls naturally' and 'I am glad to say I have never seen a spade' – took on a completely new meaning.

Director Yvonne Brewster, writing in the programme, made this statement:

> We set out to be as truthful to the text as it was humanly possible to be, bearing in mind that an all-black production of *The Importance of Being Earnest* was probably very far from Wilde's wildest imagination. We found great support in his attitude to English society; his commentary was all the clearer because he was Irish. We felt it was important to set the play in England in 1895, but not to disguise or trivialise the fact that we were black.

> Ben Thomas's elegant Algernon Moncrieff, a smooth aesthete done out in crisp moustache and cream suit, manages the authentic Wildean noise and cultivates the right languor and artifice.
>
> Nicholas de Jongh *Guardian*

1989 Jean Cocteau Repertory Theatre, New York.

Director	Robert Perillo
JOHN WORTHING	Christopher Oden
ALGERNON MONCRIEFF	Robert Ierardi
REV. CANON CHASUBLE	Zenon Zelenich
MERRIMAN	Harris Berlinsky
LANE	Harris Berlinsky
LADY BRACKNELL	Joseph Menino
GWENDOLEN FAIRFAX	Carol Dearman
CECILY CARDEW	Lyn Wright
MISS PRISM	Angela Vitall

The Cocteau staging amounts to little more than a campy burlesque of manners.

Wilborn Hampton *New York Times*

Too often Menino is impassive rather than imperious – more a Buddha than a dragon lady.

David Barbour *Backstage*

1990 *Lady Bracknell's Confinement*
A monologue by Paul Doust.

Premiere: Pleasance Theatre, Edinburgh Festival.
Transferred: Battersea Arts Centre, London.

Director	Christopher G Stanford
LADY BRACKNELL	Paul Clayton

The fifty-five minute monologue, described as a sequel to *The Importance of Being Earnest*, was a drag act. Lady Bracknell turned out to be a man. Gwendolen Fairfax was her sister's daughter, which meant that John Worthing couldn't marry her because she was his sister.

1990 Pearl Theatre Company, New York.

Director	Anthony Cornish
JOHN WORTHING	Stuart Lerch
ALGERNON MONCRIEFF	Michael John McGuinness
REV. CANON CHASUBLE	Frank Geraci
MERRIMAN	Bruce Harpster
LANE	Bruce Harpster
LADY BRACKNELL	Margaret Hilton
GWENDOLEN FAIRFAX	Donnagh Welby
CECILY CARDEW	Laura Rathgeb
MISS PRISM	Joanna Camp

Margaret Hilton is a credible Lady Bracknell although she occasionally more resembles a stern nanny than a Mayfair matron.

Wilborn Hampton *New York Times*

1991 Touring production, UK.

Director	Val May
JOHN WORTHING	Neil Daglish
ALGERNON MONCRIEFF	Benedict Taylor
REV. CANON CHASUBLE	Michael Denison
MERRIMAN	Greg Wagland
LANE	Michael Denison
LADY BRACKNELL	Penelope Keith
GWENDOLEN FAIRFAX	Jessica Turner
CECILY CARDEW	Sally Cookson
MISS PRISM	Dulcie Gray
MAID	Sarah Chard

Neil Daglish at one performance inadvertently skipped a line in answer to Lady Bracknell's question as to where he had been found and replied that he had been found in a cloakroom at Victoria Station and made no mention of the handbag at all. Mortified, he rushed to Penelope Keith's dressing-room in the interval to apologise. The actress, charmingly, said it was such a relief not to have to say 'A handbag!' But *The Importance of Being Earnest* without the handbag (whether it has handles or not) is like *Hamlet* without the Prince of Denmark. Did the public besiege the box office and ask for their money back?

1991 Sydney, Australia.

JOHN WORTHING	Jonathan Biggins
ALGERNON MONCRIEFF	Andrew Tighe
REV. CANON CHASUBLE	Bob Hornery
MERRIMAN	Gordon Chater
LANE	Gordon Chater
LADY BRACKNELL	Ruth Cracknell
GWENDOLEN FAIRFAX	Jane Menelaus
CECILY CARDEW	Rachel Szalay
MISS PRISM	Monica Maugham

1992 American film.

Director	Kurt Baker
JOHN WORTHING	Daryl Roach
ALGERNON MONCRIEFF	Wren T Brown
REV. CANON CHASUBLE	Brock Peters
MERRIMAN	Barbara Issacs
LANE	Obba Babatunde
BUTLER	Sylvester Hayes
LADY BRACKNELL	Ann Weldon
GWENDOLEN FAIRFAX	Chris Calloway
CECILY CARDEW	Lanei Chapman
MISS PRISM	C C H Pounder

The film isn't bad enough to be campy or good enough to fully exploit the surprise of the premise: an all-black update of Wilde.

Gary Dauphin *Village Voice*

The ensemble vocal style might be described as a caricature of generic hoity-toitiness, with the la-di-da cadences accompanied by stiff, affected body language.

Stephen Holden *New York Times*

1993 Aldwych Theatre, London.

Director	Nicholas Hytner
JOHN WORTHING	Alex Jennings
ALGERNON MONCRIEFF	Richard E Grant
REV. CANON CHASUBLE	Richard Pearson
MERRIMAN	Hugh Munro
LANE	Michael Stroud
LADY BRACKNELL	Maggie Smith
GWENDOLEN FAIRFAX	Susannah Harker
CECILY CARDEW	Claire Skinner
MISS PRISM	Margaret Tyzack

Maggie Smith, a high-comedy actress incomparable in Congreve, Farquhar and Coward, is capable of getting three laughs on the trot where other actresses would be hard-pressed to find one. She got her first laugh before she had uttered a word, merely by the way she looked John Worthing up and down. Dressed all in grey, she was like some highly-strung bird. There was disapproval in every glance and every fidget. She wielded her umbrella like a weapon, urging her fellow actors to speak faster.

'Style,' says Lady Bracknell, 'depends on the way the chin is worn. They are worn very high at present.' Smith wore her chin exceedingly high. She brought a welcome *arriviste* vulgarity to the role. Who was Lady Bracknell before she married Lord Bracknell? She had no fortune of any kind ('But I never dreamed for a moment of allowing that to stand in my way.') Was she on the stage, perhaps, and, like one of the Gaiety Girls of the Edwardian age, had she married into the aristocracy?

Smith's timing, as always, was a joy throughout. She solved the problem of the handbag by ignoring the handbag completely and getting her big laugh on 'The line is immaterial.' (Jonathan Hyde had done the same thing in the Glasgow Citizens' revival in 1977.) Her drive and energy were invaluable in the last act; only the thought of one hundred and thirty thousand pounds in the funds stopped her in her tracks.

Alex Jennings, an actor of elegance, was admirable in the scene where Worthing arrives in deepest mourning for an imaginary brother who is that moment being impersonated by his best friend. Richard E Grant's Algernon (an ostentatious dandy in crushed velvet and a fancy waistcoat) had considerable charm. The two men greeted each other with a kiss, which may have raised false hopes in some quarters that the director Nicholas Hytner was about to explore a gay subtext and that the true meaning of being 'Ernest' and 'Bunburying' would be revealed to a West End audience.

Gwendolen and Cecily (pronounced Cicely) were undercast. So was Miss Prism. Richard Pearson found nothing in Chasuble.

Bob Crowley's sets gave the comedy a new angle, a surreal skewwhiff sweep, providing outsize portraits, outsize sofas, outsize peacock topiaries and outsize windows (from which, no doubt, five counties could be seen). The portrait of Algy looked as if it had been painted by Sargent.

> This, surely, is a role she [Maggie Smith] was born to play, and she lays into it with a relish and a precision that leaves the spectator helpless with admiration and laughter.
>
> Charles Spencer *Daily Telegraph*

> She [Maggie Smith] gives a splendid, hard-boiled performance, punctuated with exquisite sour looks and grimaces very much in her own style, but perfectly consistent with what Wilde wrote.
>
> John Gross *Sunday Telegraph*

> Maggie Smith simply offers us a battery of comic effects. The result is to unbalance an otherwise excellent evening. Wilde was not writing a star vehicle for Lady Bracknell. In stealing the show, Dame Maggie's hyperactive performance subtly undermines it.
>
> Michael Billington *Guardian*

1993 Royal Exchange, Manchester.

Director	James Maxwell
JOHN WORTHING	Neil Dudgeon
ALGERNON MONCRIEFF	Samuel West
REV. CANON CHASUBLE	John Branwell
MERRIMAN	James Masters
LANE	James Masters
LADY BRACKNELL	Avril Elgar

GWENDOLEN FAIRFAX	Zara Turner
CECILY CARDEW	Melanie Ramsay
MISS PRISM	Marcia Warren

The play was updated to the early twentieth century. The accents were down-market, the clothes ill-fitting, and the actors drank tea from mugs.

> Played with as much style as a suburban Tupperware party.
>
> Robin Thornber *Guardian*

> Lady Bracknell should be a dreadnought in heavy seas, but here seems more like a cutter in light winds.
>
> Andrew St George *Financial Times*

1993 Stratford Festival, Ontario, Canada.

Director	David William
JOHN WORTHING	Colm Feore
ALGERNON MONCRIEFF	Lorne Kennedy
REV. CANON CHASUBLE	Richard Curnock
MERRIMAN	William Needles
LANE	Brian Tree
LADY BRACKNELL	Pat Galloway
GWENDOLEN FAIRFAX	Lucy Peacock
CECILY CARDEW	Marion Day
MISS PRISM	Barbara Bryne
FOOTMEN	Marc Ruel
	Frank Zotter

Audiences entering the theatre were greeted by a front-drop curtain with Wilde's signature followed by C33, which made some people wonder if Algy was also going to be arrested for Bunburying.

The play, with the possible exception of Lorne Kennedy as Algy, was miscast, yet Wilde's wit and absurdity still played to continuous laughter. Lucy Peacock, as Gwendolen, enunciated her lines so clearly that it seemed as if she had been having lessons with Professor Henry Higgins. Every syllable was heard, and practically every letter.

1994 Thorndike Theatre, Leatherhead.

Director	Michael Denison
JOHN WORTHING	Mark Greenstreet
ALGERNON MONCRIEFF	Robert Beck
REV. CANON CHASUBLE	Michael Denison
MERRIMAN	Peter Fontaine
LANE	Peter Fontaine
LADY BRACKNELL	Dulcie Gray
GWENDOLEN FAIRFAX	Catherine Rabett
CECILY CARDEW	Eleanor Tremain
MISS PRISM	Carmen Silvera

1995 Repertory Theatre, Birmingham.
Transferred: Old Vic Theatre, London.

Director	Terry Hands
JOHN WORTHING	Roger Allam
ALGERNON MONCRIEFF	Philip Franks
REV. CANON CHASUBLE	Patrick Godfrey
MERRIMAN	Martin Wimbush
LANE	Martin Wimbush
LADY BRACKNELL	Barbara Leigh-Hunt
GWENDOLEN FAIRFAX	Abigail Cruttenden
CECILY CARDEW	Jacqueline Defferary
MISS PRISM	Rosalind Knight

Barbara Leigh-Hunt (as Lady Bracknell her eyes constantly pierced the auditorium) found an original way to say 'A handbag!' by the simple expedient of not saying it at all. She merely mouthed it.

Philip Franks tried to make up for the fact that he was far too old to be playing Algy by donning a wig, dressing up in a velvet suit (such as Wilde wore on his American tour) and bouncing about the stage in an ostentatious manner when he was not lying down on the floor (not the best position for audibility). He did not seem to be playing Algernon Moncrieff so much as Reginald Bunthorne in Gilbert and Sullivan's *Patience*.

Roger Allam was also too old to be playing John Worthing but had the right pained expression. There were times when, in his delivery, stance and manner, he recalled Rex Harrison, an actor who never played in Wilde and should have. Rosalind Knight's Miss Prism was the most severe of governesses.

1995 Touring production, UK.

Director	Nicholas Wright
JOHN WORTHING	Geoffrey Church
ALGERNON MONCRIEFF	Charles Edwards
REV. CANON CHASUBLE	John Nettelton
MERRIMAN	Simon Markey
LANE	Simon Markey
LADY BRACKNELL	Bette Bourne
GWENDOLEN FAIRFAX	Jennifer Scott-Malden
CECILY CARDEW	Jessica Lloyd
MISS PRISM	Deirdre Doone

Algernon Moncrieff's room in the Albany had a prominent hookah. There were no chairs, only cushions on the floor. Lady Bracknell had to sit on a tea-chest.

A programme note reminded theatregoers that it was almost obligatory these days to view the play in terms of coded homosexuality, which no doubt explained why Charles Edwards's very camp Algy looked as if he had been Bunburying all his life. Edwards would have been perfect for an all-male production.

What was so unexpected about drag artist Bette Bourne's performance was that, though he acted Lady Bracknell with all the out-front aplomb of a drag artist, he never let the mask drop. He never tipped the audience the wink and remained in character throughout, even in the curtain-call. He was a waxwork gorgon of Wagnerian proportions, far less camp than Maggie Smith and far more formidable than Edith Evans. His delivery of such lines as 'Mr Worthing, is Miss Cardew at all connected with any of the large railway stations in London?' and 'The general was essentially a man of peace except in his domestic life' were exemplary.

1996 Théâtre National de Chaillot, Paris. *L'Importance d'Etre Constant.*

Director	Jérôme Savary
Translator	Jean-Michel Départs

JOHN WORTHING	Samuel Labarthe
ALGERNON MONCRIEFF	Rupert Everett
REV. CANON CHASUBLE	Yves Jacques
MERRIMAN	François Borysse
LANE	Yves Jacques
LADY BRACKNELL	Danièle Lebrun
GWENDOLEN FAIRFAX	Claire Keim
CECILY CARDEW	Clotilde Pourau
MISS PRISM	Nanou Garcia
MR GRIBSBY	Jacques Herlin
MOULTON	François Borgsse

Perdre un parent peut être considéré comme un malheur . . . mais perdre les deux, cela ressemble à de l'étourderie.

[Jérôme Savary] has chosen good actors but he makes them hold back rather than letting them off the leash. He has made them act character-types rather than let them enjoy the subtle quirkiness that is the play's essence. You have to wait until the second act and the 'muffin' scene before you get really involved. Here Oscar Wilde's inimitable virtuosity veers towards nonsensical burlesque. It is at this point that one has a really good time: Rupert Everett and Samuel Labarthe's talents do not go unwasted. But it is only a brief moment.

Salino Brigitte *Le Monde*

1996 The play was performed at Theatre Lampeti, Athens, directed by Marios Plorites.

1996 *L'Importanza di Essere Onesto* was performed in Verona.

1996 Irish Repertory Theatre, New York.

Director/designer	Tony Walton

JOHN WORTHING	Daniel Gerroll
ALGERNON MONCRIEFF	Eric Stoltz
REV. CANON CHASUBLE	John Fielder
MERRIMAN	Thomas Carson
LANE	Thomas Carson
LADY BRACKNELL	Nancy Marchand
GWENDOLEN FAIRFAX	Melissa Errico
CECILY CARDEW	Schuyler Grant
MISS PRISM	Sloane Shelton

1997 Abbey Theatre, Dublin.

Director	Patrick Mason
JOHN WORTHING	Frank McCusker
ALGERNON MONCRIEFF	Darragh Kelly
REV. CANON CHASUBLE	Harry Towb
MERRIMAN	Niall O'Brien
LANE	Des Cave
LADY BRACKNELL	Rosaleen Lineham
GWENDOLEN FAIRFAX	Alison McKenna
CECILY CARDEW	Dawn Bradfield
MISS PRISM	Doreen Keogh

One further way to express distaste for his comedies might be to mount a production of *Earnest* in which corseted tension appears in place of intricate spirals of frivolity, in which comedy and seriousness work antagonistically, and in which the show almost shudders to a halt every time Lady Bracknell speaks. The Abbey's latest production of *The Importance of Being Earnest*, directed by Patrick Mason, is guilty of all three transgressions to some extent, but none more seriously than the last.

Luke Clancy *The Times*

The faint Irish tones lurking under the actors' voices reveal one of the greatest English comedies as being a brilliant parody of English upperclass life by an Irish observer of genius . . . Mason's production has an airy frivolity and a hard-edged drive. The characters eye one another in that apparent English puzzlement that disguises the most complete understanding.

John Peter *Sunday Times*

Although the Irish actors do the play with faux-posh English accents, they manage not to turn it into a Victorian-camp version of Noël Coward. The show also boasts an attractive Lady Bracknell who – for once – doesn't look or sound like something from the black lagoon.

Robert Gore-Langton *Daily Express*

1997 *The Kaos Importance of Being Earnest* (UK tour)

Director	Xavier Leret
JOHN WORTHING	Ralf Higgins
ALGERNON MONCRIEFF	Jack Corcoran
REV. CANON CHASUBLE	Oliver Parham
LANE	Oliver Parham
LADY BRACKNELL	Sharon Schaffer
GWENDOLEN FAIRFAX	Jordan Whyte
CECILY CARDEW	Jill Norman
MISS PRISM	Judith Aitken

Kaos Theatre has its own house style, a very physical, acrobatic style. Algernon wore leopard-printed trousers and screwed up his face and body. He looked as if he had been Bunburying all over the place. John Worthing, no less contorted, had ginger hair and wore PVC trousers. Bracknell screamed her head off and on 'A handbag!' was lifted up by the rest of the cast to become almost airborne. Cecily Cardew had her hair in curlers and looked as if she might play rugby. In the famous tea scene she and Gwendolen had a wrestling match in which no holds were barred and bottoms were severely smacked.

Wilde's verbal humour played an entirely subordinate role to the posturing actors and the slapstick. The text was tampered with only once when Worthing was asked what his politics were and replied, 'I'm New Labour!' The next line was Wilde's: 'They count as Tories,' said Lady Bracknell.

1998 Renaissance Theater, Berlin. All-male production.

Director	Hans Holman
JOHN WORTHING	Christoph Jacobi
ALGERNON MONCRIEFF	Christian Schmidt
REV. CANON CHASUBLE	Ralf Wolter
MERRIMAN	Wolfgang Grindemann
LANE	Horst Schultheis
LADY BRACKNELL	Peter Matic
GWENDOLEN FAIRFAX	Boris Aljinovic
CECILY CARDEW	Matthias Bundschuh
MISS PRISM	Gerhard Friedrich

1998 Alabama Shakespeare Festival, Montgomery, USA.

Director	Barry Boys
JOHN WORTHING	Ray Chambers
ALGERNON MONCRIEFF	Sam Gregory
REV. CANON CHASUBLE	Paul Hebron
MERRIMAN	Greg Thornton
LANE	Greg Thornton
LADY BRACKNELL	Jill Tanner
GWENDOLEN FAIRFAX	Monica Bell
CECILY CARDEW	Elizabeth Long
MISS PRISM	Sonja Lanzener

Lady Bracknell's observation that 'Fortunately in England, at any rate, education produces no effect whatsoever' was received with a roar of laughter and a round of applause. So, too, was Gwendolen's comment that 'In matters of great importance, style, not sincerity is the vital thing.' The style of the performance was often nearer to Gilbert than Wilde but then so, occasionally, is Wilde. Gwendolen booming away was far more of a gorgon than her mother, who displayed an unexpected sense of humour.

It was a pity that the director, having decided to include one of the scenes that George Alexander had cut in 1895, did not retain the dialogue as well. Jack, handing out the Army Lists to the company at the end of the play, by mistake gives a copy of *Bradshaw* to Canon

Chasuble, the *Price Lists of the Civil Stores* to Miss Prism and *The Green Carnation* (Robert Hichens's satiric novel on Wilde and his homosexual circle) to Lady Bracknell!

On a point of design, while Jack might well have Aubrey Beardsley's prints of *Salomé* in his London apartment (under lock and key) he would most certainly not have them on the walls of the morning-room of his country residence.

1998 Red Room Theatre, Fringe Festival, New York.

Director	Hugh Hysell
JOHN WORTHING	Jack Figlioli
GWENDOLEN FAIRFAX	Adam Beckworth

The action was updated to the present and set in the Hamptons.

> This contemporary reworking plays like a dream . . . Many of Wilde's lines actually now ring truer being performed by an all-male cast. Wilde's writing has a strong gay sensibility.
>
> Chip Deffaa *New York Post*

1998 Edinburgh Festival Fringe and Etcetera Theatre, London.

Director	Berwyn Kinsey
JOHN WORTHING	Tom Brown
ALGERNON MONCRIEFF	Ryan Kiggell
LADY BRACKNELL	Hana Thalova
GWENDOLEN FAIRFAX	Annalie Wilson
CECILY CARDEW	Sophie Lovett
MISS PRISM	Marketa Vickova
MR GRIBSBY	Richard Mathews

The truth is rarely pure and never simple. Since most theatregoers these days know that Algernon Moncrieff and John Worthing were 'confirmed and secret Bunburyists', it may not have come as a total surprise to learn that they were also lovers. A great deal of kissing went on in this very earnest (i.e., gay) production which began with Worthing having a bath on stage after a shag off-stage with

Moncrieff and ended in tears when Algy discovered he had been committing incest.

The text, adapted from the fourth-act version and including invented lines, ripped Wilde apart. There was no Jack in mourning, no tea scene, no Chasuble, and Lane and Merriman were heard but not seen. Berwyn Kinsey attempted to cut the laughter and play the lines totally seriously. It didn't work because the idea hadn't been thought through and because the acting (with the exception of Ryan Kiggell who had some idea of the style) was so bad. Lady Bracknell was embarrassing.

1998 *Handbag*
or *The Importance of Being Someone*
by Mark Ravenhill.

Premiere: Renaissance Theater, Berlin.
Transferred to Lyric Studio, Hammersmith, London, followed by UK tour.

Director	Nick Philippou
TOM/CARDEW	Tim Crouch
LORRAINE/PRISM	Faith Flint
PHIL	Paul Rattray
SUZANNE/CONSTANCE	Julie Riley
MAURETTA/AUGUSTA	Celia Robertson
DAVID/MONCRIEFF	Andrew Scarborough

Thanks to Edith Evans's upward inflection, 'A HANDBAAAG!' is the most quoted exclamation in British theatre and most audiences would have guessed immediately that Mark Ravenhill's play must have something to do with *The Importance of Being Earnest*. The play was, in fact, a marriage of Wilde and *Shopping and F***ing* with acknowledgements to Caryl Churchill's *Cloud Nine* and Edward Bond's *Saved*.

Ravenhill set the action in two alternating and overlapping eras, Victorian and modern. In 1867 (twenty-eight years before *The Importance of Being Earnest* begins) Lady Bracknell was unmarried and arrived in England from Ireland to bag herself a husband. Miss Prism, who was more interested in her three-volume novel than the baby in her charge, did not accidentally put the baby in the handbag.

It was a deliberate action so that Thomas Cardew could have the boy. The pun is intended. Mr Cardew (Wilde's 'old gentleman of a very charitable and kindly disposition with a first-class ticket to Worthing') ran an orphanage, and, in Ravenhill's play, had just been run out of town for fondling the foundlings. In the modern era a lesbian couple, who wanted a child, asked a gay couple to provide the sperm, which one of them did in a teacup.

Child-rearing is difficult. Wilde said, 'Children begin by loving their parents; after a time they judge them; rarely, if ever, do they forgive them.' Ravenhill asked who then was best qualified to bring up a child if not the mother and father? Lesbians? Gays? Bisexuals? Victorian nannies? Modern child-minders? Heroin addicts? Paedophiles? The sperm-donor? The language was as explicit as the music was loud.

1998 Theatre Royal, Windsor, and UK Tour

Director	Val May
JOHN WORTHING	Robin Lermitte
ALGERNON MONCRIEFF	Matthew Finney
REV. CANON CHASUBLE	Geoffrey Davies
MERRIMAN	Mark Burgess
LANE	Geoffrey Davies
LADY BRACKNELL	Liza Goddard
GWENDOLEN FAIRFAX	Tracey Childs
CECILY CARDEW	Sophie Millett
MISS PRISM	Dora Bryan

Upholstered like a Victorian sofa and bristling with contempt, Liza Goddard's fierce Bracknell advances on Ernest as if she were going to dismember him for daring to propose to her daughter, Gwendolen. While some Bracknells are measured by their warbles, Goddard should be measured for her steel . . . Dora Bryan's ripe old governess, Miss Prism, drops a wonderful lilt of lechery in her voice when she declares to the venerable Reverend Chasuble that ripeness can be trusted.

James Christopher *The Times*

A Florentine Tragedy (1894)

The Plot

SIMONE, an old Jewish merchant, comes home to find his wife entertaining Guido, the son of one of Florence's most noble families. Simone pretends that he thinks Guido is there to buy his rich fabrics. Guido asks Simone if he is willing to sell his wife. The two men engage in banter which ends with Simone engineering a duel, which he wins.

A Florentine Tragedy, written in blank verse, is a pastiche Renaissance drama set in the sixteenth century. Wilde began writing it in 1894 but never finished it, though he attempted to do so in prison and later in France when he was desperate for money. After his death, Robert Ross commissioned the poet T Sturge Moore to write an opening scene. Maria does not appear in the play Wilde wrote.

1906 10 June Premiere: King's Hall, London.

Director	Charles Ricketts
Designer	Charles Ricketts
GUIDO	Reginald Owen
SIMONE	George Ingleton
BIANCA	Gwendolen Bishop

The Literary Theatre Club presented the play as a curtain-raiser to *Salomé* for members and guests, for two performances.

> Obviously, the part of Simone is a fine part for an actor. I should like to have seen it played by Sir Henry Irving. I know of no one

else who could have given fully the sardonic essence of it. Mr George Ingleton, however, who played it the other night, is a very capable actor and his performance seemed really distinguished in the glare of incapacity shed by the young lady and gentleman who played the other two parts.

Max Beerbohm *Saturday Review*

1907 New English Players performed the play in London.

1908 Mrs Patrick Campbell played Bianca in Edinburgh.

1909 Tivoli Theatre, Manchester.

GUIDO	Bartlett Garth
SIMONE	Philip Sanders
BIANCA	Violet Vorley
MARIA	Madge Raqer

1911 The play was performed in Swansea.

1912 The play was performed by the Liverpool Repertory Theatre, directed by Basil Dean.

1913 American film.

1914 Repertory Theatre, Birmingham.

Director	Frank D Clewlow
GUIDO	Felix Aylmer
SIMONE	Barry V. Jackson
BIANCA	Cecily Byrne
MARIA	Hylda Spall

1917 Opera: *Eine Florentinische Tragodie*

Premiere: Opera House, Stuttgart.

Music	Alexander Zemlinsky
Libretto	Max Meyerfeld
Conductor	Max Von Schillings

Arnold Schoenberg described the opera as a 'magnificent work'.

1921 Kingsway, London.

Matinee performance by the 1920 Players.

Director	Cyril Hardingham
GUIDO	Cyril Hardingham
SIMONE	John Merry
BIANCA	Marjorie Gabain
MARIA	Edith Ryland

1926 New York. American premiere staged by the American Cooptimists, directed by Carlo de Angello.

1927 Arts Theatre, London.

Director	A E Filmer
GUIDO	Walter Hudd
SIMONE	Ion Swinley
BIANCA	Dorothy Black
MARIA	Joan Pereira

> It takes Mr Ion Swinley, for instance, fully five minutes to strangle Mr Walter Hudd for the simple reason that he is engaged in an envenomed picturesque tirade against the deceitfulness of mankind during the time.
>
> *The Times*

1927 Grove Street Theatre, New York.

Presented by American Grand Guignol Inc.

Director	Georges Renavent
GUIDO	Georges Renavent
SIMONE	Clarence Derwent
BIANCA	Mary Blair
MARIA	Helen Malmud

An audience, very willing to yield itself, found much to applaud in Wilde's drama. It was charmingly set and costumed, and capably performed by Miss Blair, Mr Renavent and Mr Derwent.

New York Times

1956 Davenport Theatre, New York.

Director	Joseph Guzzetti
GUIDO	Lou Spiegel
SIMONE	George Bartenieff
BIANCA	Shirley Wilber
MARIA	Ellen Holly

A Florentine Tragedy played in a double bill with *Salomé* under the title of *An Evening with Oscar Wilde*.

It is conceivable they could do much better with something less tricky. Only the most skilful professionals, accustomed to the stylised acting tradition, could give verve to these slender poetical exercises.

A G *New York Times*

1964 British television.

Adaptor	Robert Shaw
Director	Herbert Wise
GUIDO	Robert Shaw
SIMONE	Alex Davion

BIANCA	Mary Ure
MARIA	Ann Beach

The Times headline was 'Drama Handicapped by Wilde's Bejewelled Verse'. Robert Shaw and Mary Ure brought to the play the same sort of quiet, ferocious quality they had brought to Middleton and Rowley's *The Changeling* at the Royal Court Theatre in 1961.

1981 *Eine Florentinische Tragodie*: Alexander Zemlinsky's opera at State Opera, Hamburg.

Director	Adolf Dresen
Designer	Margit Bardy

The production transferred to the Edinburgh Festival in a double bill with *The Birthday of the Infanta.*

1984 Little Theatre, London.

Director	Edgar K Bruce
GUIDO	Alexander John
SIMONE	Edgar K Bruce
BIANCA	Joy Roston
MARIA	Camilla Pyemont

1985 *Eine Florentinische Tragodie*: Alexander Zemlinsky's opera at the Royal Opera House, London.

Translator	Edward Downes
Conductor	Colin Davis
Director	Adolf Dresen
Designer	Margit Bardy
GUIDO	Kim Begley
SIMONE	Edward Crafts
BIANCA	Claire Powell

Adolf Dresen and Margit Bardy updated the opera to *fin de siècle* Klimt. It was difficult to reconcile what was being sung with what what was being seen. A tatty and murky production had extra problems. Guillermo Sarabia , who was to have sung Simone, died just before the opening night. Kim Begley then went down with laryngitis and had to mime Guido on stage while Kenneth Reigel sang from the orchestra pit. The critics dismissed Wilde's play as 'an overheated Renaissance drama' and 'a load of the purest hokum'.

> The laboured sadomasochism of *A Florentine Tragedy* is also Wilde at his most turgid and tedious.
>
> *Sunday Times*

> Tasteless junk albeit of very superior orchestra manufacture.
>
> Max Loppert *Financial Times*

1990 Edmonton, Canada.

Director	Martin Millerchip
GUIDO	Stephen Makaj
SIMONE	Tony Eyamie
BIANCA	Anna Valine

La Sainte Courtesane (1894)

or The Woman Covered With Jewels

Characters:
FIRST MAN
SECOND MAN
MYRRHINA
HONORIUS, A HERMIT

Scene:
A valley in Thebaid.

La Sainte Courtesane is only a fragment and it is written in the ornate style of *Salomé*. Wilde began it in 1894 and tried to finish it when he came out of prison but failed.

In the first scene Myrrhina, a prostitute, attempts to seduce a beautiful young Hermit, who is blind. 'I will,' she says, 'smear your body with myrrh and pour spikenard on your hair. I will clothe you in hyacinth and put honey in your mouth.'

By the second scene she has been converted to Christianity and he has regained his sight and is off to Alexandria to 'taste of the seven sins'.

1945 *La Sainte Courtesane* was reconstructed by Juillot de Saix from the reminiscences of Wilde's friends, and performed on French radio under the title of *Myrrhina* with Maria Cesares (star of Marcel Carné's *Les Enfants du Paradis* and Jean Cocteau's *Orphée*) as Myrrhina and Maurice Escande as Honorius.

Mr and Mrs Daventry (1900)

A domestic tragedy by Frank Harris

Based on a scenario by Oscar Wilde.

1990 Premiere: Royalty Theatre, London.

SIR GEORGE LANGHAM	Berte Thomas
MR DAVENTRY	Frederick Kerr
MR ASHURST	Gerald du Maurier
WILLIAM	Howard Sturge
KEANE	George Arliss
GERMAN WAITER	Albert Gran
LADY HALLINGDON	Beryl Faber
LADY SOLWAY	Elisabeth Kirby
LADY LANGHAM	Elinor Molyneux
MRS DAVENTRY	Mrs Patrick Campbell
MRS WILLIE POWELL	Winifred Fraser
MRS BUXTON	Frances Ivor
MRS TOWNSEND	Helen Boucher

In August 1894 Wilde wrote a letter to George Alexander outlining the plot for a play about a husband who encouraged his wife to flirt so that he could carry on with his own affairs. She left him for another man. The husband begged the lover to give her up, but she had no desire to return to him. A duel was arranged. The wife told her husband that she was carrying her lover's child and that she hoped he would be the one to die. The husband killed himself before the duel could take place.

Wilde made it clear in the letter that he did not want any self-sacrifice and any renunciation in his play. He wanted the sheer passion of love to dominate everything.

After his release from prison Wilde was always short of money and regularly raised £100 by selling options on the scenario to actresses and managers.

Frank Harris suggested they should write the play together. Wilde would write the first act and Harris would write the other four. But Wilde no longer had the desire to write. 'I don't think I shall ever write again,' he said. 'Something is killed in me.' In the end Harris wrote all five acts. Wilde did not tell him he had sold the option many times over.

Mr and Mrs Daventry opened to bad notices. Clement Scott, theatre critic of the *Daily Telegraph,* described it as 'the drama of the dustbin'. A B Walkley, writing in *The Times*, said, 'It goes as near to indecency as anything we remember on the stage. So also does the dialogue.'

The bad notices made no difference to the box office, no doubt because the critics dealt at great length on the play's sexual content. The production ran for over 100 performances.

Many people believed that Wilde was the author and that Harris had merely lent his name so that *Mr and Mrs Daventry* could be produced.

I made art a philosophy and philosophy an art. I altered the minds of men and the colour of things. There was nothing I said or did that did not make people wonder.

Oscar Wilde

NOVELS AND TALES

Oscar Wilde in 1893.
Drawing: Phil May.

The Canterville Ghost (1887)

A Hylo-Idealistic Romance

The Plot

Sir Simon de Canterville murdered his wife in 1575. Three hundred years later he is an old ghost of terrible aspect, with long grey fell hair and eyes as red as burning coals. His garments are of antique cut, soiled and ragged, and from his wrists hang heavy manacles and rusty gyves.

Canterville is an egotistical ham of the old school of acting, celebrated for his remarkable impersonations and demoniac laughter. His most famous Oscar-winning roles are Ruben the Strangled Babe, Gaunt Gideon the Blood-Sucker, Reckless Rupert the Headless Earl, and Jonas the Corpse-Snatcher.

His repertoire of rattling chains, ghostly moans, hollow groans (through keyholes) and vanishing tricks, however, do not impress the new tenants of Canterville Hall, an American family by the name of Otis, whom he fails miserably to terrify. Instead, they terrify him. As he himself is forced to admit, 'Never in a brilliant and uninterrupted career of three hundred years had he been so grossly insulted.'

His efforts to assert his dignity and social position are pathetic. He oils his chains and goes round the castle making certain he is neither heard nor seen. Finally, his nerve is completely shattered at the slightest noise. He becomes a lonely and melancholic recluse who longs to die.

The Ghost is befriended by Virginia Otis, a little girl of fifteen with a sweet Puritan gravity, who, filled with pity, weeps for his sins and prays for his soul.

The Canterville Ghost was inspired by Wilde's American tour. 'We have really everything in common with America nowadays,' he observed, 'except, of course, language.'

First published by *The Court and Society Review* in February 1887, it is much more of a fairy story than a ghost story, and like all Wilde's fairy stories, it has a strong Christian message.

1927 German opera: *Bily Pan*
English title: *The Gentleman in White*

Premiere: Breslau.

Music	Jaroslav Kricka
Libretto	Jan Lowen-Bach-Budin

1932 *Bily Pan* was revived in Vienna.

1933 Czech opera: *Spuk in Schloss*
A new version of *Bily Pan*.

Premiere: Prague.

Music	Jaroslav Kricka
Libretto	Max Brod

1943 American film.

Director	Jules Dassin
Screenplay	Edwin Harvey Blum

SIR SIMON	Charles Laughton
GHOST	Charles Laughton
CUFFY WILLIAMS	Robert Young
LADY JESSICA	Margaret O'Brien
SERGEN BENSON	William Gargan
LORD CANTERVILLE	Reginald Owen
BIG HARRY	'Rags' Ragland
MRS UMNEY	Una O'Connor
SIR VALENTINE	Donald Stuart
MRS POLVERDINE	Elisabeth Risdon
LIEUTENANT KANE	Frank Faylen
MR POTTS	Lumsden Hare

METROPOLUS	Mike Mazurki
HECTOR	William Moss
EDDIE	Bobby Readick
BUGSY MCDOUGLE	Marc Cramer
JORDAN	William Tannen
DE CANTERVILLE	Peter Lawford

Jules Dassin's film (a very free adaptation) did not have the style of René Clair's recently released *The Ghost Goes West*.

The story began in 1604 with Sir Simon running away from a duel and his father walling him up alive in an alcove. His soul could only be released by a brave deed performed by a kinsman in his name. But, in the centuries that followed, the Cantervilles bred only cowards and the Ghost despaired of ever being saved.

In World War Two a platoon of American rangers were billeted at the castle. One of the soldiers (Robert Young) turned out to be a kinsman, and he dashed over to France to kill a few Nazis, but when his buddy got shot, he suddenly turned coward. Fortunately, on his return to England, a bomb (a nice big block-buster) arrived by parachute. With the help of his jeep, he dragged it to a nearby ravine before it could kill anybody (like the scriptwriter, for instance).

The Ghost should have been a good role for Charles Laughton, but rewritten it gave him few opportunities. He appeared with a noose round his head and was greeted with machine-gun fire. He appeared headless and the GIs chased him up the chimney.

Laughton, who looked like a camp Billy Bunter in doublet and hose, turned in a tired and sleepy performance. 'Shall I prance about like a saucy antelope?' he asked, hand on hip. 'It's absurd asking me to behave myself. I must rattle my chains.'

James Agee described Laughton's performance as 'mock-pansy, mock-Shakespearian'. Laughton was far more juvenile than six-year-old Margaret O'Brien who was cast as the demure little lady who owned the castle and walked off with the film.

> As the reluctant ghost, Charles Laughton achieves not a characterisation but a self-caricature.
>
> *Daily Telegraph*

> Charles Laughton plays the howling horror with evident relish, and there is a nice piece of work from little Margaret O'Brien, who escapes the fearful prettiness of the film child.
>
> *Manchester Guardian*

1949 American television.
Presented by the Actors Studio.

Adaptor	Robert Anderson
Director	Fred Carr
GHOST	Edward Ashley
CAST	Wendy Barrie
	Ruth Matteson
	John Shay
	Clifford Tatum
	Joan Lozer
	Mark Connelly

Direction by Fred Carr mixed all the production elements neatly and carried off the supernatural effects with well-planned video tricks – superimposition, montages, easel settings and a stand-in for the ghost.

Bril *Variety*

1950 American television.

Director	Norman Felton
GHOST	Cecil Parker
VIRGINIA	Margaret O'Brien
MOTHER	Valerie Cossart
FATHER	Maurice Manson
CLAIRE	Allison Prescott
RONALD	Lex Richards
MRS UMNEY	Phoebe Mackay

Parker was superb as the ghost. The excellent performances of the stars did not extend to the supporting company. Direction likewise lacked pace and failed to accentuate the necessary mood.

Variety

1951 American television.

Adaptors	Brewster Morgan Arthur St Claire
Director	Frank Wisbar
VIRGINIA	Lois Hall
GHOST	Reginald Sheffied
LORD CANTERVILLE	Lester Matthews
CAST	Bruce Lester Ivor James Tommy Mann Gillian Blake

The drama produced by Bing Crosby Enterprises mainly succeeded in being dismal and little else. Print was somewhat fuzzy and lacked clarity.

Gilb *Variety*

1953 American television.

Director	Ralph Nelson
GHOST	Edward Everett Horton

1962 British television.

Adaptor	Elaine Morgan
Director	Stuart Burge
LADY BRACKENDALE	Patricia Raine
LADY DUMBLETON	Fabia Drake
LORD CHEVIOT	Basil Henson
MRS UMNEY	Fay Compton
MRS OTIS	Ruth Dunning
HIRAM OTIS	Derek Francis
JACKSON OTIS	Peter Taylor
JEFFERSON OTIS	Laurie Heath
WASHINGTON OTIS	Iain Gregory
VIRGINIA OTIS	Samantha Eggar

DUKE OF CHESHIRE	Oliver Fox
GHOST	Bernard Cribbins

Bernard Cribbins has little else to do but act the guinea pig for television camera trickery.

Daily Telegraph

1962 Premiere of Heinrich Sutermeister's opera on Swiss television.

1966 British television.

Adaptor	Giles Cooper
Director	Kim Mills

GHOST	Bruce Forsyth
MRS UMNEY	Doris Rogers
PORSON	John Falconer
LORD CANTERVILLE	David Stoll
HIRAM OTIS	David Bauer
MRS OTIS	Libby Morris
VIRGINIA	Angela Thorne
STAR	Colin Pilditch
STRIPE	Darryl Read
DUKE OF CHESHIRE	Robert Mill
HECATE	Eleanor Bron

The verbal wit was overlaid by the pantomime-style production, with Bruce Forsyth giving a heavily overacted comic performance in the title role. However, the acting of Miss Eleanor Bron, a suitably imposing Hecate, and of Miss Angela Thorne did give one genuine pleasure.

The Times

1966 American television.

Adaptor	Hubbell Robinson
Music	Jerry Bock
	Elmer Bernstein

Lyrics	Sheldon Harmick
Director	John Robbins
GHOST	Michael Redgrave
LORD CANTERVILLE	Michael Redgrave
AMBASSADOR OTIS	Douglas Fairbanks, Jr
MRS OTIS	Natalie Schaefer
VIRGINIA	Tippy Walker
MARK OTIS	David Charkham
MATTHEW OTIS	Mark Colleano
DUKE OF CHESHIRE	Peter Noone
THE CONSTABLE	Frankie Howerd
THE BUTLER	George Curzon
THE HOUSEKEEPER	Madge Brindley

The script was a modern update, which had very little to do with Wilde. Sir Simon had killed his wife because she did not want to go to the theatre with him. Her refusal would have been totally understandable if the play on offer had been anything like this poorly staged production.

The songs were feeble interpolations, under-rehearsed and put over in an amateur manner. The running gag was a series of commercial jingles for such things as removing bloodstains from the floor and for oiling rattling chains. The one possibility for a good laugh (the boys dressing up as ghosts and giving Sir Simon the fright of his death) was merely reported. 'Vengeance shall be mine!' sang Sir Simon. Wilde, no doubt, would have said something stronger.

1969 Czechoslovakia. Premiere of Miloslav Duchac's musical.

1973 Asolo Theatre Festival Children's Theatre, Florida, USA.

Adaptors	Robert Strane
	Barbara Reid McIntyre
Director	Richard Hopkins
CAST	John Henderson
	Christine Smith
	William Turner
	Ellen Bate

1974 Leningrad. Premiere of Alexandre Khaitel's opera.

1974 British television.

Adaptor	Robin Miller
Director	Walter Miller
GHOST	David Niven
HYRAM B OTIS	James Whitmore
MRS OTIS	Audra Lindley
VIRGINIA	Lynne Frederick
MRS UMNEY	Flora Robson
LORD CANTERVILLE	Maurice Evans
STAR	Bobby Doran
STRIPE	Christopher Morris
DUKE OF CHESHIRE	Nicholas Jones
LADY CANTERVILLE	Elizabeth Tyrrell
RECTOR	Ronald Russell
LADY STUTFIELD	Isla Blair

David Niven was interviewed by Stewart Knowles in *TV Times* and said:

> The poor old ghost is great fun. He loves dressing up in all sorts of disguises. He doesn't love being a ghost, of course – he'd much rather go to sleep – but he's a terrific ham. Oh, good lord, yes, I identify with that. I overdo it like mad.

> David Niven has a wail of a time rattling his chains, disappearing in clouds of smoke and conjuring up the banshees . . . The whole thing is a splendid piece of hokum and the marvellous Wilde dialogue is delivered at a great gallop by a near perfect cast which includes Dame Flora Robson in a sparkling supporting role as the housekeeper.
>
> James Murray *Daily Express*

1975 Brazilian film: *O Cacador de Fantasma*

1979 Cambridge Ballet Workshop performed a ballet to music by Geoffrey Wright.

1984 The story was related by Martin Jarvis and directed by Christine Secombe on British television.

1985 Opera by Mervyn Burch.

Premiere: Howell's School, Llandaff , Wales.

Director	Lesley Dunstand
Conductor	Gaynor Howard
GHOST	Sarah O'Connor
VIRGINIA	Alison Steadman
MRS LUCAS-BROWNE	Sarah Jones
MISS FERRIS	Amanda Tucker

A girls' school had moved into Canterville Hall. The Ghost and Hiram Otis had had a sex change. Otis was a headmistress and the twins had been transformed into three little schoolgirls from St Trinian's.

1985 American television.

Adaptor	B W Sandefur
Director	William F Claxton
GHOST	Richard Kiley
VIRGINIA	Jenny Beck
MRS UMNEY	Mary Wickes
LUCY	Shelley Fabares
JOHN	Barry Van Dyke
ROB	Christian Jacobs
WILLIE	Brian Green
MR SMYTHE	Don Knight

The story was updated to the 1980s. The script was terrible, the production had neither style nor taste, and the acting was very bad. Richard Kiley, a wild-haired, wild-eyed, weird-looking dude, mugged away as the Ghost. 'I can't help it,' he said. 'It's my curse.' It wasn't clear whether it was the Ghost or Kiley speaking.

1987 British television.

Adaptors	Sue Grafton Steve Humphrey George Zateslo
Director	Paul Bogart
GHOST	John Gielgud
HARRY	Ted Wass
LUCY	Andrea Marcovicci
JENNIFER	Alyssa Milano
MRS UMNEY	Lila Kaye
HUMMLE UMNEY	Harold Innocent
UNCLE HESKETH	George Baker
AUNT GRETCHEN	Dorothea Phillips
FENTON COOK	Bill Wallis
UNCLE GEORGE	Brian Oulton
AUNT CAROLINE	Deddie Davies
PAUL BLAINE	Spencer Chandler
LADY ELEANOR	Celia Breckon

> I never thought my head would be served up on a silver platter in front of the great British public but I loved it.
>
> John Gielgud, quoted by *Daily Mail*

'I want to go to sleep,' said The Ghost, 'and cannot. I have not slept for three hundred years and I am so tired.' John Gielgud's Sir Simon had more charm and less wit than Wilde's Ghost.

The production was more interested in special effects than style. The story was changed so that only Virginia (now called Jennifer) remained unshaken by the haunting.

> Time to give Sir Simon his richly deserved rest.
>
> *Variety*

1995 Musical by Peter Quilter and Charles Miller.

Premiere: The Old Bull Arts Centre, London.

Director	Steven Dexter
GHOST	Peter Reeves
MR OTIS	Gregory Cross
MRS OTIS	Norma Atallah
VIRGINIA	Josie Walker
TWINS	Dean Lotherington
	John Stefaniuk
HOUSEKEEPER	Linda Hibberd

Thank goodness that Peter Quilter's book and lyrics are crisp, kitsch and pacey enough to make you forget that you're watching a travesty . . . Cynics stay away, but for those with a sweet tooth this is a small but perfectly formed piece of genuine family entertainment.

Paula Webb *Time Out*

1996 American television.

Adaptor	Robert Beneditti
Director	Syd Macartney
GHOST	Patrick Stewart
VIRGINIA OTIS	Neve Campbell
MR UMNEY	Donald Sinden
MRS UMNEY	Joan Sims
LORD CANTERVILLE	Leslie Phillips
MRS OTIS	Cheri Lunghi
HIRAM OTIS	Edward Willey
LORD FRANCIS	Daniel Betts
ADAM OTIS	Ciaran Fitzgerald
WASHINGTON OTIS	Raymond Pickard

There was no comedy, no wit, no irony. The adaptation was surprisingly serious. Patrick Stewart's fierce-looking Ghost was not Wilde's egotistical Ghost. In his doublet and hose, Stewart looked all set to act the villain in some gory Jacobean melodrama.

The Ghost spoke in a phoney Elizabethan language. Most of what he said were straight cribs from Shakespeare's plays. He claimed to have known Shakespeare personally and said that he had created the Ghost in *Hamlet* and acted before Queen Elizabeth I.

He was seen only by the children and he terrified them. Virginia decided that the only way to get her parents to believe in his existence was to get the Ghost to repeat his performance in *Hamlet*. The children thought this a wild idea (wild without the 'e' presumably.)

'One rarely gets the chance to see Shakespeare performed by somebody who actually knew him,' said the young Lord, who remembered when he was a little boy seeing the Ghost playing croquet with his own bones. This delight was denied to television viewers, who did not find out that Sir Simon had murdered his wife until the last reel.

The production ended with Stewart reciting Shakespeare's sonnet, 'O Never say I was false of heart.'

> Stewart projects quiet aplomb and avoids hamminess, no small feat when all his dialogue is in Elizabethan cadences . . . The humourous interaction between ghost and mortals, however, is undercut to a degree by intergenerational tension.
>
> John P McCarthy *Variety*

1997 British television.

Adaptor	Olivia Hetreed
Director	Crispin Reece
GHOST	Ian Richardson
LUCRETIA OTIS	Celia Imrie
HIRAM OTIS	Rolf Saxon
VIRGINIA OTIS	Sarah-Jane Potts
LORD CHESHIRE	James D'Arcy
MRS UMNEY	Edna Dore
MADAME MURIELLE	Pauline Quirke
DAMPIER	Rik Mayall
LORD DUMBLETON	Donald Sinden
DAVENPORT	Ian McNeice
TOM CARTER	Tom Bowles
OTIS TWINS	Nicholas Barker
	Jack Barker

Wilde's story is meant to be about a little girl saving a Ghost's soul through love. The Ghost in Olivia Hetreed's adaptation played a supporting role to the romance of Virginia Otis (no longer a fifteen-year-old) and the Duke of Cheshire (no longer a little boy).

Virginia thought the Duke was as poor as a church mouse and a fortune-hunter, when he was, in fact, one of the richest landowners in Europe. Her silly mother wanted her to marry a pauper, so they decided to meet in the orchard one night and elope. The Ghost, thinking Virginia had come to a secret rendezvous in order to release him from his three hundred-year-old curse, abducted her. 'I didn't mean to spoil things for you,' he apologised.

The Duke later asked Virginia what she and the Ghost had been up to. She replied that she couldn't tell him (a good start to their marriage) but that he had told her the difference between life and death and that love was greater than both. This observation was about as near to Wilde as this ghostly/ghastly travesty got.

Hetreed's script also introduced three exorcists – a fortune- teller, a scientist, and a hell-and-damnation preacher – which resulted in three very unfunny cameos very crudely acted. The preacher (Rik Mayall) was greeted by the Ghost in full drag, looking for all the world like the Virgin Queen (red wig and all) and given a big plonking kiss on the mouth. Hell and damnation, indeed.

The Ghost is a perfect role for a Shakespearian actor and Ian Richardson deserved a better script.

1997 Musical

Premiere: Karlstadt, Sweden, and European tour.

Adaptors	Paul Stebbings
	Phil Smith
Music	Paul Flush
Director	Paul Stebbings

THE DUKE OF CANTERVILLE	Bruno Roubicek
MA OTIS (MOM)	Sarah Gale/Jennifer Tubini
VIRGINIA OTIS	Jaime Araujo/Suzanne David
WASHINGTON OTIS	Justin Webb
GHOST	Justin Webb
CROWS, SPIRITS, GHOULS	Eric Tessier Lavigne

The Happy Prince and Other Tales (1888)

The Happy Prince

The Plot

'Swallow, Swallow, little Swallow,' said the Prince, 'will you not stay with me one night longer?' *The Happy Prince*, the finest of Oscar Wilde's fairy stories, tells of the love of a Swallow for the Prince, a beautiful statue, who is gilded all over with fine gold and has two bright sapphires for eyes. The statue sacrifices every single one of its riches, even his eyes, for the poor people of his city. The Swallow, who had intended to spend the winter in Egypt, carries out all his commissions and does not desert him. When the Swallow dies of cold, the Prince's leaden heart cracks. The Town Councillors melt down the statue.

1908 Liza Lehmann set the story to music.

1914 *The Golden Prince*

Premiere: New York.

Adaptation	David Stevens
Music	Henry Hadley

1950 Puppets: *The Happy Prince*
Presented by the Hogarth Puppets.

Premiere: Institut Français, London.

Directors	Jan Bussell Ann Hogarth

Designs	Lotte Reiniger
Voices	Robert Speaight
	Jan Bussell
	Ann Hogarth
	Sally Bussell
	Jack Whitehead

1951 The Hogarth Puppets performed on British television.

1960 Animated British film directed by Peter Pearce.

1962 American opera in Iowa City, USA.

Music	J William Fisher
Libretto	John Gutman

1965 British opera at Farnham Festival.

Music	Malcolm Williamson
Libretto	Malcolm Williamson
Conductor	Mary Joynes
Director	Douglas Leuchers
THE SWALLOW	Pauline Stevens
THE PRINCE	April Cantelo

The opera, lasting less than an hour, was designed expressly for schoolchildren. It was commissioned by the Master of the Queen's Music and performed in the Parish church by the Farnham Girls' Choir and Farnham Singers.

> There are some effective, musically demanding choruses, one intricate and very telling trio for the anxious seamstress, her sick child and the compassionate statue; and there is a recurrent appeal of the Prince to the Swallow which is a real *trouvaille* of ingeniously harmonised melody.
>
> *The Times*

1968 Romanian film: *Printful Fericit*

1974 Canadian animated film.

Director	Murry Shostak
VOICES	Glynis Johns
	Christopher Plummer

1976 The story was related Alec McCowen and directed by Gordon House on British television.

1978 Malcolm Williamson's opera was revived at Farnham Festival.

Music	Malcolm Williamson
Libretto	Malcolm Williamson
Director	Douglas Leuchars
Conductor	Mary Joynes
THE PRINCE	Morys Davies
THE MAYOR	Andrew Stevens
THE SWALLOW	Jacqueline Berry
SEAMSTRESS	Kathleen Harding
HER SON	Nicholas Dayen
RICH GIRL	Katy Long
AUTHOR	Peter Terry
MATCHGIRL	Elizabeth Wakefield
ANGELS	Margaret Daniels
	Shirley Wort
	Dorothy Andrews
	Shirley Winton Bayston
CHORUS	Farnham Girls' Choir and Farnham Singers

1992 British musical at Buxton Opera House.

Music	Sue Casson
Conductor	Chris Brannick

Director	Tom Blackmore
THE PRINCE	John Heriman
THE SWALLOW	Mina Anwar/Valerie Weyland
CHORUS	Andrew Bolton
PANDORA	Sue Casson

. . . enchanting musical, wordy, witty score . . . The finest numbers are the lulling 'Twilight City' and the beautiful 'Swallow's Lament' and the superb 'The Crowd Scene'.

Andrew St George *Financial Times*

1993 Sue Casson's musical was revived at the Old Fire Station, Oxford, and the George Theatre, Richmond, North Yorkshire.

1994 British film directed by Kaori Ito at John Moore's University.

The Remarkable Rocket

The Plot

A very conceited firework fails to go off and is thrown on a fire where its fizz is seen by nobody.

1960 Premiere of Don Gillies's ballet, to music by Maurice Surdin, performed by National Ballet of Canada.

1975 Canadian animated film.

Director	Gerald Potterton
Voice	Graham Stark

The Selfish Giant

The Plot

A giant puts up a wall to stop the children playing in his garden. He then finds that nothing grows and it is always winter. One day the children creep back in and the garden blossoms. The giant takes a special interest in a young boy who grows up to be Jesus Christ.

1931 The story was set to music by Liza Lehmann and premiered at the Duke of York's Theatre, London, in a triple bill with Wilde's *Salomé* and August Strindberg's *The Stronger*.

1952 *The Giant Garden*

Premiere of Sherman Krane's opera in New York.

1955 American television.

Producer	Harry Herrmann
Narrator	Basil Rathbone
CAST	George Mathews
	Mia Slavenska

1965 Cleveland, USA. Premiere of Raymond W White's opera.

1968 A ballet to music by Penelope Thwaite was directed by Nancy Ruthven and performed by the Chelsea Ballet Club at Cripplegate Theatre, London.

1972 Canadian film directed by Peter Sander and set to music by Ron Goodwin.

1973 British film directed by V H McGrath.

1980 Edinburgh. Premiere of Peter Naylor's opera at Queen's Hall.

The Nightingale and the Rose

The Plot

The Nightingale, pressing her heart against the thorns of a white rose, gives her life so that a shallow young student can give 'the reddest rose in the world' to an ungrateful young woman, who rejects him and his flower. The student angrily throws the rose into the gutter and a cartwheel runs over it.

1927 Ballet by Anton Dolin.

Premiere: Coliseum, London.

Music	H Fraser-Simson
NIGHTINGALE	Vera Nemchinova
STUDENT	Anton Dolin
MAIDEN	Margaret Craske
RIVAL	Rupert Doone
GUESTS	Joyce Berry
	Doris Sonn
	Ailine Phillips
	Mary Crew
	F Ashton
	Webster

The ballet was described as a romantic fantasy and Wilde was given no acknowledgement.

> At times it is a trifle confused, and without the printed synopsis the story might be difficult to follow, but the dancing of the two principals is brilliant in the extreme. The miming of some of the others left much to be desired.
>
> *Dancing Times*

1935 Anton Dolin's ballet was revived at the Duke of York's Theatre, London.

NIGHTINGALE	Alicia Markova
STUDENT	Anton Dolin
MAIDEN	Wendy Toye
RIVAL	Guy Massey
GUESTS	Travis Kemp
	Natasha Gregorova
	Phyllis Stickland
	Eileen Baker
	Vera Lavrova
	Molly Bergmayr
	Beryl Rigby
	Joan Kent
	Teddy Haskell
	Robert Doorning
	Norman Waller
	John Thorp
	Toni Repetto

This time, as a result of Vyvyan Holland's intervention, Oscar Wilde was credited.

> This exquisite, tragic trifle supplies Markova, as a self-immolating nightingale, with a part in which her extreme grace of technique is made incandescent by pathos. She danced it with a tensity remarkable even in her.
>
> *The Times*

1938 Riga, Latvia. Premiere of Osvalds Lemanis's ballet to music by Janis Kalnins.

1940 New York. Premiere of a ballet to George Lessner's music.

1950 Italy. Premiere of Renzo Bossi's opera *L'Usignuolo e la Rosa*

1953 Revue sketch: *Nightingale Bring Me a Rose*

Premiere: Imperial Theatre, New York.

Music	Henry Sullivan
Lyric	John Murray Anderson

SINGER	James Jewell
STORY-TELLER	Celia Lipton
STUDENT	Dean Crane
PRINCE	Gerard Leavitt
COQUETTE	Margot Myers
NIGHTINGALE	Nanci Crompton

Nightingale Bring Me a Rose was performed in *John Murray's Almanac*, a revue starring Hermione Gingold, Billy de Wolfe and Harry Belafonte. Only two critics mentioned it and they dismissed it as 'a most pretentious number' and 'more embarrassing than touching'.

1959 Ballet: *Venus Flower*

Premiere: Wyndham's Theatre, London.

Choreographer	Faith Worth
Music	Béla Bartók

NIGHTINGALE	Deanne Bergsma

> The dancing consisted of exactly the sort of classroom *enchaînements* and droopy mime that one would expect to find associated with such a story . . . Fortunately the dancing of Deanne Bergsma was so good that at times she distracted attention from the faults of the ballet.
>
> Fernau Hall *Ballet Today*

1967 Czech film: *Slavik a Ruze*

Director	Josef Kabart
Music	Julius Kalas

1971 Premiere of G Burne's ballet, to music by H Partisch, in Cape Town, South Africa.

1973 Chester, Pennsylvania. Premiere of Margaret Garwood's opera.

1976 The story was related by Alec McCowen and directed by Gordon House on British television.

1978 Lion Theatre Company, New York.

Play by Richard Holm, directed by Kathy Arlt.

1979 Premiere of Thomas Newman and David Madden's musical, directed by Michael Lessac, at the John F Kennedy Centre.

1994 Musical by Elena Firsova.

Premiere: Almeida Theatre, London.

Conductor	David Parry
Director	Caroline Gawn
NIGHTINGALE	Carol Smith
STUDENT	Philip Sheffield
GIRL	Rachael Hallawell

The text included three poems by Christina Rossetti. The story rambled and the director was hard-pressed to know what to do with a chorus of green-faced, thorny-gloved roses. The major disappointment was Elena Firsova's score. 'Not so rosy,' said the *Guardian*.

> Her heavy post-Schoenbergian expressionistic style does not sit comfortably with Wilde's beautiful pre-Raphaelite tale and the simple, poignant story is turned by the music into an oppressive psycho-drama in which even the nightingale emerges as a gruesome character.
>
> Alexander Wauge *Evening Standard*

> All through the piece there is a deadly earnestness which – coupled with the endless rhapsodizing and pallidity – makes for a rather long, wan hour and a half.
>
> Paul Griffiths *Times Literary Supplement*

The Birthday of the Infanta (1889)

The Plot

A dwarf, who has been brought up in the forest, has a huge misshapen head, a hunched back and crooked legs. He is so absurd, so uncouth, so clumsy that even the flowers curl up in disgust; only the birds and lizards actually like him. He is brought to the Spanish court to dance for the Infanta's twelfth birthday, and is a great success.

Completely unconscious of his grotesque appearance, he presumes everybody is laughing with him, rather than at him. He becomes infatuated with the Infanta, a proud, disdainful little girl, and wants to present her with a rose. Just as he is about to do so, he catches sight of himself in a mirror. At first, having never seen a mirror, he thinks a horribly ugly person is mocking him by imitating his every action. When he realises he is looking at himself, he dies of a broken heart.

The Birthday of the Little Princess (its original title) was first published in *Paris Illustré* on 30 March 1889 simultaneously in French and English. It was reprinted as *The Birthday of the Infanta* in *A House of Pomegranates* in 1891 and was dedicated to Wilde's wife, Constance. The story was inspired by Velásquez's *Las Meninas.*

The first two adaptations were ballets.

1909 Vienna. Premiere of a ballet to music by Franz Schreker.

1913 Brockhaus. Premiere of *The Dwarf and the Infanta*, a ballet to music by Bernhard Sekles.

1916 Stuart Walker's Portmanteau Theatre, New York.

PAGE	Edgar Stehli
INFANTA	Nancy Winston
DUCHESS	Judith Lowry
FANTASTIC	Gregory Kelly
CHAMBERLAIN	McKay Morris
COUNT	Robert Cook

The Birthday of the Infanta played in a double bill with *Gammer Gurton's Needle* and was chiefly notable for a striking setting designed by Mrs John W Alexander.

> Gregory Kelly conveys poignantly the heartache of this little tragedy . . . The people of the play move about as though they had just stepped down from some fine, mislaid Velásquez canvas.
>
> *New York Times*

1918 Budapest. Premiere of O Zobische's ballet, choreographed to music by Miklos Radnai.

1922 Opera: *Der Zwerg*

Premiere: Opera House, Cologne.

Music	Alexander Zemlinsky
Libretto	Georg Klaren
Conductor	Otto Klemperer

Alexander Zemlinsky, who had been described by his mistress, Alma Mahler, as 'a horrid little gnome, undersized, chinless, toothless', identified very much with this cruel, little drama. The Dwarf's moment of self-recognition is most movingly scored. But Zemlinsky does not stop there, as Wilde did, but goes on to score the Infanta's rejection. The music, rich, passionate and disturbing, clearly comes out of his own rejection by Mahler.

Alban Berg admired 'the wonderful flow of glorious melody'. The score was highly praised for its 'compelling atmosphere, resourceful character portrayal and yearning melodic intensity'. There were many musicians who thought it a masterpiece. The stumbling block to its success (with the public at any rate) was that Georg Klaren's libretto took far too many liberties with Wilde's story.

1932 Ballet: *The Infanta's Birthday*
Presented by the Camargo Society.

Premiere: Adelphi Theatre, London.

Choreography	Penelope Spencer
Music	Elizabeth Lutyens
Designer	Rex Whistler
Conductor	Constant Lambert
THE INFANTA	Wendy Toye
THE DWARF	Hedley Briggs

Wendy Toye was sixteen years old.

> The costumes by Mr Rex Whistler were of the high fantastic order. All the elements worked well together, but the interest of the story topples over from the Infanta to the dwarf who dies of a broken heart, so that the vicious climax which the ballet needs cannot come. As a substitute we are given an ensemble of all the characters passing in procession.
>
> *The Times*

1941 Chicago. Premiere of a ballet choreographed by John Alden Carpenter. The Dwarf was danced by Adolph Bolm.

1941 Ballet: *On the Rose*. Music by Otaker Zitek.

1944 Premiere of Mario Castelnuovo-Tedesco's opera.

1947 Ballet: *Rose Rouge*

Premiere: Opéra Comique, Paris.

Choreography	Jean-Jacques Etcheverry
Music	Pierre Auclert

INFANTA	Lucienne Berggren
DWARF	Michel Rayne

1949 American television.

CAST	Gene Reynold
	Frank Wilcox
	Gloria Holden

1949 Ballet: *Court de Diamant*
Presented by Grand Ballet de Monte Carlo at the Paris Opera.

Choreography	David Lichine
Music	Jean Hubeau

INFANTA	Tamara Toumanova
DWARF	Georges Skibine

The work is overlong but Lichine and Hubeau have so caught the bitter-sweet atmosphere of Wilde's story that judicious cutting would transform it into a minor masterpiece.

Dancing Times

1951 Ballet: *Die Weisse Rose*

Premiere: Berlin.

Choreography	Jens Keith
Music	Wolfgang Fortner

1959 Ballet: *The Scarf*

Premiere: Jacob's Pillow Dance Festival, Massachusetts.

Choreography	Peter Van Dijak
Music	Ivan Kogan Semenoff

PRINCESS	Tania Karina
HUNCHBACK	Oleg Sabline
PRINCE	Gayle Young
FOLLOWER	Hlenka Devon

1962 Ballet: *The Infanta's Birthday*

Premiere: Belgrade.
Transferred: Edinburgh Festival.

Choreography	Dmitrije Parlic
Music	Wolfgang Fortner
INFANTA	Visnja Djordjevic
DWARF	Rit Parnel
DWARF (as he imagines himself)	Borivoje Mladenovic

Parlic's choreography adds but little to the ballet. It conveys little of the Spanish atmosphere, and even less of the vapid irony characteristic of Wilde's short story. Even the Spanish-style divertissement in the first scene seemed totally devoid of excitement, and the dances alloted to the Dwarf, performed here by a girl, are choreographically too vague for the dancer to mould them into a characterisation.

Clive Barnes *Dance and Dancers*

1971 Ballet.

Premiere: Johannesburg.

Choreography	Gary Burne
Music	Harry Patch
INFANTA	Phyllis Spira
DWARF	Gary Burne
INQUISITOR	Guy Spear

By a clever reversal of the Oscar Wildean characters it is the members of the court who are the grotesques. The dwarf who is the real misshapen being only because he lacks the elaborate trappings of court convention . . . Phyllis Spira displays a flawless technique plus great depth and range of emotional expression in her creation of the Infanta.

June Schneider *Dance News*

1980 Ballet: *Die Weisse Rose*

Premiere: Stadttheater, Basel.

Choreography	Heinz Spoerli
Music	Wolfgang Fortner

1980 Ballet: *Geburtstag der Infantin*

Premiere: Nationaltheater, Mannheim.

Choreography	Joachim Gerster
Music	Maurice Ravel

1981 British film: *Black and Silver*, directed, scripted, edited and photographed by William and Marilyn Raban.

The Rabans described their film as 'an oneiric fantasy in pursuit of reflections and duplicates,' based on Velásquez's *Las Meninas* and Oscar Wilde's story based on the painting. Marilyn Raban played both the Dwarf and the Infanta. The first part was set on a shingle beach. The second part was the painting itself, with the camera replacing the painter.

> For the initiated, the film is a clever visual elaboration of a theatrical text; but for any one else it remained, I suppose, nothing more than a decorative trinket.
>
> Chris Auty *City Limits*

1981 Opera.

Premiere: Hamburg State Opera.

Music	Alexander Zemlinsky
Conductor	Gerd Albrecht
Director	Adolf Dresen
Designer	Margit Bardy

Gerd Albrecht, Adolf Dresen and Margit Bardy, unhappy with Georg Klaren's libretto, went back to the original story to produce their own libretto. They also reverted to Wilde's title. Kenneth Riegel sang the Dwarf.

1981 *Der Zwerg*: Zemlinsky's opera transferred to the Edinburgh Festival.

1985 *Der Zwerg*: Zemlinsky's opera transferred to the Royal Opera House, London, in a translation by Edward Downes.

Conductor	Colin Davis
THE DWARF	Kenneth Riegel
THE INFANTA	Celina Lindsley
GHITA	Isobel Buchanan
MAJOR DOMO	Stafford Dean
THREE MAIDS	Judith Howarth
	Linda Kitchen
	Gillian Knight

Director and designer, surprisingly, did not go to Velásquez for their inspiration and reproduce the sombre black-and-silver splendour of the Spanish Court; instead the opera was played out in a white, light, airy, Edwardian nursery.

Kenneth Riegel, literally on his knees for well over an hour, was both grotesque and pathetic. The actual moment of recognition was heart-rending. His performance, musically and dramatically, was a *tour de force*, one of the finest performances on any stage in 1985, either opera or theatre.

The production played in tandem with Zemlinsky's opera of *A Florentine Tragedy*, which opened the programme.

> No serious operagoer should think of missing *Infanta*; the discerning might consider arriving at the interval.
>
> Max Loppert *Financial Times*

The Picture of Dorian Gray (1890)

> The moment I saw you I knew you were unconscious of what you might be. I felt I must tell you. Beauty fades, limbs fail, senses rot. Youth. There's nothing like it.
>
> Lord Henry Wotton

The Plot

Dorian Gray, a young man of extraordinary personal beauty, a golden youth with crisp gold hair, is seduced by Lord Henry Wotton, a cynical dandy, who represents (so he says) all the sins that Dorian hasn't the courage to commit. Dorian sells his soul for the gift of eternal youth and indulges his passion for pleasure and sin. Thirty years of debauchery, inevitably, leaves its mark. The conceit, however, is that the debauchery and degradation are visible only on the picture, painted by his friend, Basil Hallward, who idolises him and is murdered by him. He remains eternally young and the portrait becomes the emblem of his conscience, a monstrous and loathsome thing, to be locked away in the attic and bear the burden of his shame.

> Basil Hallward is what I think I am. Lord Henry is what the world thinks me. Dorian is what I would like to be in other ages, perhaps.
>
> Oscar Wilde

Lord Henry Wotton has all the best epigrams, many of which Wilde would repeat in his plays 'You would sacrifice anybody, Harry,' says Hallward, 'for the sake of an epigram. No one talks so wonderfully as you do.'

'He was,' Wilde wrote, 'brilliant, fantastic, irresponsible. He charmed the listeners out of themselves.'

In describing Wotton, Wilde was, of course, describing himself: 'He played with the idea, and grew wilful; tossed it into the air and transformed it; let it escape and recaptured it; made it iridescent with fancy, and winged it with paradox.'

The Picture of Dorian Gray first appeared in *Lippincott's Monthly Magazine* in America in 1890. The novel never reveals the nature of Dorian's hold over his male friends, though there were few who couldn't guess.

Publishers didn't want to publish it in book form. Booksellers didn't want to stock it. Editors didn't want to review it. One editor thought it was a matter for the Criminal Investigation department rather than the critic. Those who did review it damned it as 'esoteric prurience', malodorous putrefaction', and said it was 'suitable reading for outlawed noblemen and perverted telegraph boys'. The last comment was a direct reference to the Cleveland Street male-brothel scandal of 1889.

The novel in its original magazine form did Wilde immeasurable harm and was used against him during the first trial. 'There is no such thing as a moral or an immoral book,' he had declared in his Preface. 'Books are well written or badly written. That is all.' If this is so, how comes it then, that Dorian is corrupted by a book? (The book, though never named in the novel, was, as Wilde was forced to admit in court, J J Huysmans's *À Rebours*.)

1910 Temple Theatre, Detroit.

Adaptor/director	Edwards Davis
LORD HENRY WOTTON	Edwards Davis
DORIAN GRAY	Adele Blood

Edwards Davis, a former minister of the Church, sang 'Drink For Ever'. Adele Blood was his wife.

1910 Danish film: *Dorian Grays Portræt*

Director	Axel Strom
CAST	Henrik Malberg
	Clara Pontoppidan
	Valdemar Psilander

1913 American film.

Director	Phillips Smalley
DORIAN GRAY	Wallace Reid
CAST	Lois Weber
	Phillips Smalley

1913 Vaudeville Theatre, London.

Adaptor	G Constant Lounsbery
Director	Monsieur Lou-Tellegen
LORD HENRY WOTTON	Franklin Dyall
BASIL HALLWARD	Arthur Scott Craven
DORIAN GRAY	Monsieur Lou-Tellegen
SIBYL	Julia James
MRS VANE	Molly Hamley Clifford/Edith Parker
JAMES VANE	Edmund Goulding
VICTOR	André Cernay
ALAN CAMPBELL	Charles Kenyon/Stanley Roberts
MR ISSACS	Ivan Berlyn
PARKER	Stanley Roberts

His [Lou-Tellegen's] beautiful face, pure Greek in outline, and his tall, graceful figure lend themselves admirably to the part and his accent is so slight that after the first few minutes it becomes unnoticeable.

Era

Mr Dyall looked the right sort of man and spoke in the right sort of way, and it was no fault of his that his part was ineffective, absurd, nul. Lord Henry's *mots* were simply lost in the theatre. How so tame and so harmless a Mephistopheles could ruin the soul of Faust-Dorian, or anybody's soul – was a puzzle . . . No doubt M. Lou-Tellegen has a face and figure which many people admire. On the other hand, many people – well, won't.

The Times

1915 Russian silent film: *Portret Doriana Greya*

Director	Vsevolod Meyerhold
Co-Director	Mikhail Doronin

LORD HENRY WOTTON	Vsevolod Meyerhold
DORIAN GRAY	Varvara Yanova
CAST	P Belova
	G Enriton

The striking compositions, the dramatic lighting and the use of silhouette led many critics to feel that had the film been released abroad when it was made it would have surpassed the reputation of Robert Wiene's *Das Kabinett des Dr Caligari* (1919).

Vsevolod Meyerhold delivered a lecture in 1918 at the Studio of Cinematic Art of the Skobelev Committee. The translation is by Edward Braun and published in *Meyerhold on Theatre* (Methuen, 1969):

> The director and the cameraman [Alexander Levitsky] were in conflict. Both are to blame for the faults resulting from this conflict: once they disagreed the finished product was bound to be less than perfect. They disagreed over whose responsibility it was to light the film . . . [Varvara Yanova] understands the art of the theatre, but her acting in this film is full of faults: in places she overacts and her characterisation lacks subtlety.

1916 British silent film.

Director	Fred W Durrant
Screenplay	Rowland Talbot

LORD HENRY WOTTON	Jack Jordan
BASIL HALLWARD	Sydney Bland
DORIAN GRAY	Henry Victor
SIBYL	Pat O'Malley
JAMES VANE	Douglas Cox
LADY MARCHMONT	Dorothy Fane
SATAN	A B Imeson

1917 German silent film: *Das Bildnis des Dorian Gray*

Director	Richard Oswald
DORIAN GRAY	Bernd Aldor
CAST	Lea Lara
	Ernst Ludwig
	Lupu Pick
	Ernst Pittschau
	Andreas Van Horn

1918 Hungarian silent film.

LORD HENRY WOTTON	Bela Lugosi
DORIAN GRAY	Norbert Dan

1928 Chanin's Baltimore Theatre, New York.

Adaptor	David Thorne
Director	Augustus Thorne
SATAN	Wallis Clark
SERAPH	Burton Mallory
VOICE OF GOD	Lionel Adams
LORD HENRY WOTTON	Wallis Clark
BASIL HALLWARD	Lionel Adams
DORIAN GRAY	Howard Cull
LORD GEORGE FERMOR	Ray L Royce
DUCHESS OF HARLEY	Helen Holmes
SIBYL VANE	Adele Ronson
JAMES VANE	Will Marsh

Dorian Gray's soul was dissected by Satan, Seraph and the Voice of God. 'It was,' said Gilbert Gabriel in the *New York Sun*, 'an awful evening'.

> [David Thorne] makes Mr Gray a pink and dewy youth to the end . . . James is called in by the butler, looks upon Dorian at rest on the couch and pumps the narcissus through the heart with one well-directed bullet.
>
> Whitney Bolton *New York Daily Tribune*

> His [Howard Cull's] incessantly quivering chin and clucking sobs suggested a Schubert chorus man trying to make up his mind to have a good cry rather than an Adonis of splendid endowments made distraught by the devil.
>
> *New York Graphic*

> The acting, simply and frankly, is pretty terrible.
>
> Leonard Hall *New York World-Telegram*

1930 Opera: *Dorian Gray*

Premiere: Aussig, Czechoslovakia.

Music	Karl Flick-Steger
DORIAN	Christian Hans Stief
SIBYL	Barbara Reitzer

1936 *Dorian Gray*

Premiere: Comedy Theatre, New York.

Adaptor	Jeron Criswell
Director	Edwin O'Hanlon
LORD HENRY WOTTON	Oscar Sterling
BASIL HALLWARD	Robert Carlyle
DORIAN GRAY	David Windsor
SIBYL VANE	Winifred Q Fothergill
LADY FERMOR	Vera Hurst
JAMES VANE	Clement O'Leghlen
HETTY	Flora Sheffiel
ALAN CAMPBELL	Malcolm Softan
PARKER	Leslie King

'More of a calamity than a play,' said the *Brooklyn Daily Eagle*. 'Sets a new low for mediocrity,' said the *New York World-Telegraph*. 'An evening of unintentional merriment,' said the *New York Daily News*. 'Possessed of all the flavor, as dramatic fare, of a cold pork chop,' said the *New York Herald-Tribune*.

> This fabulous creation was entrusted to the talents of David Windsor and came over the footlights with all the sinister implications of last New Year's Eve confetti.
>
> Richard Manson *New York Evening Post*

1936 *The Life and Loves of Dorian Gray*

Premiere: Comedy Theatre, New York.

Adaptor	Cecil Clarke
Director	Edwin O'Hanlon
LORD HENRY WOTTON	Henry Schact
BASIL HALLWARD	Frederic Albee
DORIAN GRAY	Thomas Kennedy
SIBYL DANE	Doris Reed
LADY FERROLL	Stella Dean Alda
JAMES DANE	Bruce Bancroft
FLORA	Vera Patten
ALAN CAMERON	John B Culbertson
MEADOWS	Eric Tarbet

To have one bad play about Dorian Gray at the Comedy Theatre may be regarded as a misfortune. To have two looks like carelessness. Thomas Kennedy took over the leading role at twenty-four hours' notice.

> It is not much more than an album of over-familiar epigrams recited by characters who stubbornly refuse to come to life.
>
> *New York America*

> Thomas Kennedy is as wrong as wrong can be as Dorian Gray. And that's a man-sized compliment.
>
> Robert Cartland *New York World-Telegram*

1943 Robert Helpmann worked with Michael Benthall on a projected ballet production but it was abandoned when the music by Clifton Parker proved unsatisfactory.

1945 Gate Theatre, Dublin.

Director	Hilton Edwards
LORD HENRY WOTTON	Micheál Mac Liammóir
BASIL HALLWARD	Christopher Casson
DORIAN GRAY	Robert Lawson
SIBYL VANE	Betty Chancellor

Unfortunately this novel does not lend itself well to dramatisation. I think Wilde had that in mind when he talked of writing something 'as beautiful as a Persian carpet and as unreal'. We have the unreality in the light, frothy, epigrammatic, and hedonistic philosophy of Lord Henry but that philosophy which can be expressed with such superb wit will not stand the cold reality of putting it into action.

D S *Irish Independent*

Micheál Mac Liammóir's Lord Henry Wotton is an evocative performance in which the spirit of the novelist's time is transmitted with deftness and grace. One expects, perhaps, just a little more of the touch sinister, so to speak.

Gabriel Fallon *Standard* (Eire)

1945 American film.

Director	Albert Lewin
Screenplay	Albert Lewin
Photography	Harry Stradling
Set decorator	Edwin B Willis
LORD HENRY WOTTON	George Sanders
DORIAN GRAY	Hurd Hatfield
GLADYS HALLWARD	Donna Reed
SIBYL VANE	Angela Lansbury
DAVID STONE	Peter Lawford
BASIL HALLWARD	Lowell Gilmore
JAMES VANE	Richard Fraser
ALLEN CAMPBELL	Douglas Walton
ADRIAN SINGLETON	Morton Lowry

SIR ROBERT BENTLEY	Miles Mander
MRS VANE	Lydia Bilbrook
LADY AGATHA	Mary Forbes
SIR THOMAS	Robert Greig
DUCHESS	Moyna MacGill
MALVOLIO JONES, Chairman	Billy Bevan
YOUNG FRENCH WOMAN	Renie Carson
KATE	Lillian Bond
BALINESE DANCER	Devi Dja

> I got involved with making the picture exquisite. I really went to town on every set-up. When you have two thousand set-ups in a picture, it can take rather long. I was even careful about the table linen and the cutlery and whatever was on the wall. All the upholstery was built for me. I decided everything was going to be black and white because of the good and evil symbolism. I packed it full of symbols.
>
> Albert Lewin quoted by Bernard Rosenberg and Harry Silverstein in *The Real Tinsel* (Macmillan, 1970)

The symbols included a butterfly trapped in formaldehyde and a bronze statue of an Egyptian cat. The twenty-seven-year-old Hurd Hatfield was an inscrutable Dorian. It was like watching a silent-film performance. His pallid, doleful, smooth, youthful, chiselled good looks were so glacially cold, so immobile, he might have been made of marble. There was a total lack of facial animation. There was no charm, just callousness. Dorian's perversion was suggested by the fact that he admired the drawings of Aubrey Beardsley and read Oscar Wilde! His only good impulse was his love for Gladys, Basil Hallward's niece, a character who did not appear in Wilde.

Lord Henry Wotton (described, by Basil Hallward, as 'an unmitigated cad') was the sort of role George Sanders had played many times in his career. 'I was beastly but I was never coarse,' said the actor. 'I was a high-class sort of heel.' Sanders's Lord Henry was a bearded Satan in a top hat, a man of sharp intelligence, who read Baudelaire's *Fleurs du Mal* while travelling in a hansom. Elegant and dangerous, he carried a cane and clipped his epigrams.

Wotton was one of Sanders's best performances, fit to rank alongside his De Witt, the theatre critic in *All About Eve*, and it was a role with which he identified. 'The only horrible thing in the world is ennui,' says Lord Henry. In his suicide letter, Sanders wrote in 1972, 'Dear World, I am leaving it because I am bored.' Sibyl Vane was no longer a Shakespearian actress but a Cockney artiste who sang 'Goodbye Little Yellow Bird' in a seedy Victorian music hall. It wasn't Sibyl's singing which disgusted Dorian, but her willingness to lose her virginity.

Albert Lewin avoided censorship by leaving Dorian's unspeakable crimes to the cinemagoer's imagination. The most explicit scene was the one in which Dorian blackmailed Allen Campbell by threatening to tell his wife.

The climax introduced a vulgar burst of colour. Dorian's diseased and rotting soul was seen in all its lurid moral leprosy. ('It's hideous enough to make a stoic quake,' wrote Kate Cameron in the *Daily News.*) The portrait was painted by Ivan Le Lorraine Albright, an American artist, well known for his skill in depicting the compulsively horrible.

Harry Stradling's sharp, deep-focus camerawork and wide-angled lens (revolutionary in its day), won an 'Oscar' for best black-and-white photography. Edwin B Willis's elegant, varnished interiors had real class and also won an 'Oscar' nomination. Angela Lansbury won an 'Oscar' nomination for her performance as Sibyl Vane.

> There seems to be no justification – even financial – for subjecting the American movie public to a barrage of aged and excruciating Briticisms and effete epigrams from a buried age . . . As a nicely and expensively executed exercise in literature appreciation via film, *The Picture of Dorian Gray* is well worth seeing – then rush right home and take a nice, clean-smelling Lifebuoy shower.
>
> John T McManus

> George Sanders in the role of Lord Henry, the cynic who corrupts Dorian's mind, gives the only commendable performance. He is brittle and dandified, at least, and drops the smooth and catty little *bons mots* of Mr Wilde with amusing aplomb. But Hurd Hatfield, yielding plainly to direction, is incredibly stiff as Dorian Gray, and walks through the film with a vapid and mask-like expression on his face.
>
> Bosley Crowther *New York Times*

> The film holds you in constant expectation of its saying something, although in the end it says practically nothing.
>
> C A Lejeune *Observer*

Respectful, earnest, and, I'm afraid, dead.

James Agee *Nation*

1947 Germany. Premiere of Hans Schaeuble's opera.

1947 Q Theatre, Kew, London.

Adaptor	Constance Cox
Director	Jack de Leon
BASIL HALLWARD	Arthur Young
PARKER	Allen Montgomery
LORD HENRY WOTTON	Barry Morse
LADY GWENDOLEN WOTTON	Lesley Brook
DORIAN GRAY	Vernon Greeves
LADY NARBOROUGH	Violet Fairbrother
ADRIAN SINGLETON	Grey Balke
ALAN CAMPBELL	Robert Sansom
FRANCIS	Ronald Price
MR ISSACS	Frederick Shiller
MRS VANE	Barbara Brandon
JAMES VANE	Joseph O'Connor
SIBYL	Josephine Stuart
VICTOR	Geoffrey Wardwell
WOMAN	Ellen Pollock
HELEN HALLWARD	Josephine Stuart

An admirable characterisation comes from Barry Morse as the Mephistophelean Lord Henry Wotton. The manner in which he spreads his vile doctrines to the innocent young man with an air of suave indifference and an attractive sense of cynical humour is excellently conveyed and his contribution is of great value to the play's success.

Stage

1952 Barcelona. Premiere of a ballet by Jean Marais in collaboration with Ned Rorem.

1953 American television.

Director	Mort Abrahams
BASIL HALLWARD	Joseph Anthony
LORD HENRY WOTTON	Peter Fernandez
DORIAN GRAY	John Newland
SIBYL VANE	Natalie Norwich

1955 Augsburg. Premiere of Bico Van Larsky's ballet, to music by Alexander Scriabin.

1961 West German television: *Das Bildnis des Dorian Gray*

1961 British television.

Adaptor	John Bethune
Director	Charles Jarrott
LORD HENRY WOTTON	Dennis Price
BASIL HALLWARD	John Bailey
DORIAN GRAY	Jeremy Brett
SIBYL VANE	Jill Ireland
FRANCIS	J Leslie Frith
IAN CAMPBELL	Basil Dignam
PARKER	Roger Williams
CALL BOY	Paul Cole
ROMEO	Bernard Dudley
WAITER	Raymond Barry
VICTOR	Victor Zander

The production showed the portrait in various stages of degeneration, but there was no hint of perversion in Jeremy Brett's performance.

> Dennis Price's Lord Henry, starting rather cold like asparagus vinaigrette to suit a hot day, kept it cool and was unflustered by the docking, which must have hurt terribly, of some of the best epigrams . . . Jeremy Brett was little the worse for a dash of South American gigolo.
>
> Maurice Richardson, *Observer*

1961 American television.

Director	Paul Bogart
LORD HENRY WOTTON	George C Scott
BASIL HALLWARD	Louis Hayward
DORIAN GRAY	John Fraser
SIBYL VANE	Susan Oliver
PAMELA	Margaret Phillips
FELICIA	Carrie Nye
ALAN CAMPBELL	Norman Bowler
JAMES VANE	Robert Walker

John Fraser as Dorian Gray brought a physical handsomeness to his role and for the most part suggested the corruptness in his soul . . . George C Scott proved to be an engaging villain, as Lord Henry Wotton, cynical, unscrupulous, hedonistic, decadent and witty.

Variety

1963 Showboat Theatre, New York.

Adaptor and director	Andy Milligan
LORD HENRY WOTTON	Jay Robinson
BASIL HALLWARD	Madison Arnold
PARKER	David Cole
DORIAN GRAY	T J Escott
LORD FERMOR	Ira Rubin
LADY WOTTON	Ricki Olshan
SIBYL	Trisha Mortimer
MRS VANE	Fredi Dundee
JAMES VANE	Ben Greer
WAITER	Roy Wilson
VICTOR	Carl Hoyer
ALLAN CAMPBELL	Gerald Rome
LADY NARBOROUGH	Veronica Radburn
ADRIAN SINGLETON	Mike J McGovern
DUCHESS OF MONMOUTH	Barbara Caruso

Aristocratic English mannerisms were too often confused with effeminacy in American casts.

Gene Palatsky *Newark Evening News*

T J Escott is simply a clod . . . Jay Robinson was nothing short of a parody of panhandling down-and-out Shakespearian.

Martin Gottfried *Women's Wear Daily*

To prevent the possibility of some unwary theatregoer inadvertently buying a ticket to this disaster, why doesn't someone rope off the theatre?

Jay Carr *New York Post*

1966 Ballet by Vaslav Orlikowsky.

Premiere: Basel.

Music	Max Lang
LORD HENRY WOTTON	Palle Jacobsen
DORIAN GRAY	Alfredo Köllner

Handsome Palle Jacobsen as Lord Henry is made unintentionally to strike a wrong note from the very beginning by moving possibly like a Prince Siegfried in turn-of-the-century costumes. Since Jacobsen, due to his natural handsomeness, cannot help but outshine Dorian (Alfredo Köllner) he seems doubly miscast.

Dr Wilfried Hofmann *Ballet Today*

1967 It was announced that Ray Milland would appear in a musical version of *The Picture of Dorian Gray* in New York, directed by Donald McKayle. The production never materialised.

1967 Palace Theatre, Watford.

Adaptors	Walter Hartley David Pamely
Director	Giles Havergal
Designer	Philip Prowse

LORD HENRY WOTTON	William Simons
DORIAN GRAY	Christopher Gable
SIBYL VANE	Ros Drinkwater

The Royal Ballet dancer Christopher Gable made his acting début as Dorian.

> [Christopher Gable] takes the stage with stylish, measured strides; and communicates by one or two simple gestures: clenched fists or the anguished pout of the lips. The part, of course, is hardly a genuine character study, but then it was a cruel part to choose for one's very first.
>
> *The Times*

> Christopher Gable's personal magnetism scores a considerable triumph and his physical tributes are exactly right for the part. Vocally, he is not impressive. At present the emotion of the acting obviously means more to him than the words which he speaks without a great deal of expression.
>
> Peter Hepple *Stage*

1969 *Dorian Grayn Muotokuva*

Premiere of a ballet to music by Tauno Marttinen.

1970 West German/Italian film: *Das Bildnis des Dorian Gray*
Italian title: *Il Dio Chiamato Dorian*
American title: *The Secret of Dorian Gray*
Also known as: *Dorian Gray*

Director	Massimo Dallamano
Screenplay	Massimo Dallamano
	Marcel Coscia
	Günter Ebert

LORD HENRY WOTTON	Herbert Lom
BASIL HALLWARD	Richard Todd
DORIAN GRAY	Helmut Berger
SIBYL	Marie Liljedahl
JAMES VANE	Stewart Black

GWENDOLEN	Margaret Lee
ALICE	Maria Rohm
ADRIENNE	Beryl Cunningham
MRS RUXTON	Isa Miranda
ESTHER	Eleanora Rossi Drago
ALAN	Renato Romano

This tawdry adaptation was uncertain whether to play Wilde straight or send him up. The film opened with the murder of Basil Hallward, thus spoiling one of the novel's major surprises.

Lord Henry Wotton and his sexually voracious sister, Gwendolen, fancied Dorian, who loved Sibyl, an actress, who was quite unlike Wilde's innocent. Dorian and Sibyl visited a transvestite stripclub, made love in the empty theatre, and then quarrelled. Dorian went to bed with Gwendolen. Sibyl committed suicide. Dorian became the playboy of an older woman.

Wotton lost most of his epigrams and Dorian, in the American dubbed version, was liable to say things like 'Just forget it!'

> Director Massimo Dallamano's attempts at creating an atmosphere of evil, horror and perversion are frequently ludicrous to the point of provoking laughter.
>
> Rick *Variety*

> Perhaps the soul of Oscar Wilde has a sense of humour. Let's hope so for the sake of the people involved . . . For if he hasn't there'll be hell to pay beyond. Todd attempts a straight and serious performance as the artist but he is spitting in the wind.
>
> John Goff *Hollywood Reporter*

> It is the usual dreary exploitation stuff . . . Helmut Berger and Richard Todd seem to be vying with each other for the distinction of the most embarrassing performance. Richard Todd, though given fewer histrionic opportunities, wins by a canter.
>
> Tom Milne *Month Film Bulletin*

> He [Helmut Berger] is more bland beast than perfumed exquisite and swaggers his way through impersonating a stoned member of the younger generation for several generations.
>
> Thomas Quinn Curtis *International Herald Tribune*

1972 Ballet: *Double Exposure*
A ballet by Joe Layton.

Premiere: City Centre, New York.

Choreographer	Joe Layton
Music	Alexander Scriabin
Electronic Music	Henri Pousseur
DORIAN	Paul Sutherland/ Dermot Burke/Dennis Wayne
THE LEADER	Gary Chryst
GROUPIES	Rebecca Wright
	Sue Lloyd
	Donna Cowem
COUPLE	Nancy Robinson
	Robert Talmage
YOUNG BOY	Russell Sultzbach
DORIAN at 11	Robert Thomas

Paul Sutherland, Dermot Burke and Dennis Wayne alternated the leading role. The ballet began in a photographer's studio with the photographer telling Dorian to strip to his underpants.

> Dorian Gray was heralded as trendy, with-it, and daring. In reality, it was dull . . . That such a lurid tale should be dull is because little of the movement has any intrinsic interest. The mimetic movements are purely functional – one almost expects to hear dialogue spoken along with them – while the dance movements rarely attain anything beyond acrobatic tricksiness . . . Layton's characters are never more than pasteboard.
>
> Jack Anderson *Dance Magazine*

> What is deplorable is that a work of art – not a major thing but a novel of value and repute – has been vulgarised by people to provide a new frisson and a cheap thrill. It leaves a nasty taste in the mind. I felt extremely sorry for the dancers, especially Dennis Wayne who gave a magnificent performance technically as Dorian and within the dramatic limitations of Mr Layton's fairy-butch conception of Dorian, also acted with exceptional power.
>
> Clive Barnes *New York Times*

1973 American television movie.

Director	Glenn Jordan
Screenplay	John Tomerlin
DORIAN GRAY	Shane Briant
LORD HENRY WOTTON	Nigel Davenport
BASIL HALLWARD	Charles Aidman
FELICIA	Fionnula Flanagan
BEATRICE	Linda Kelsey
SIBYL VANE	Vanessa Howard
ALAN CAMPBELL	John Karlen
MADAME DE FERROL	Dixie Marquis
VICTOR	Brenda Dillon

1973 Amsterdam. Premiere of Hans Cox's opera *Graenskibutzen.*

1974 San Franciso. Premiere of Shela Xoregos's ballet, to music by Janice Giteck.

1975 Greenwich Theatre, London.

Adaptor	John Osborne
Director	Clive Donner
LORD HENRY WOTTON	Anton Rodgers
BASIL HALLWARD	John McEnery
DORIAN GRAY	Michael Kitchen
LORD FERMOR	Kenneth Benda
LADY AGATHA	Kitty Fitzgerald
DUCHESS OF HARLEY	Anne Blake
SIR THOMAS BURDON	Lloyd Lamble
SIBYL	Angharad Rees
MRS VANE	Jean Heywood
JAMES VANE	Paul Kelly
VICTOR	Michael Deacon
MR HUBBARD	Lloyd Lamble
FRANCIS	Kenneth Benda

ALAN CAMPBELL	Michael Deacon
DUCHESS OF MONMOUTH	Angharad Rees
FOOTMEN/POLICEMEN	John Daniell
	Iain Roberts

John Osborne's 'moral entertainment' was a hollow piece of Grand Guignol. Clive Donner's sluggish production lacked style and Michael Kitchen's Dorian lacked physical magnetism.

> Mr Rodgers is amusing but he is not evil. Michael Kitchen is not equal either to the innocence or to the corruption of Dorian Gray, and there is no electric alarm in his performance. He delivers Mr Osborne's big sermon as if it bored him.
>
> *Sunday Times*

> For my money only John McEnery as Basil Hallward is playing the text Osborne has written, creating a memorable portrait of a spindly, straw-haired, preoccupied artist endowed with a sense of doom.
>
> Michael Billington *Guardian*

1976 British television.

Adaptor	John Osborne
Director	John Gorrie
LORD HENRY WOTTON	John Gielgud
BASIL HALLWARD	Jeremy Brett
DORIAN GRAY	Peter Firth
LORD FERMOR	Mark Dignam
DUCHESS OF HARLEY	Nan Munro
LADY AGATHA	Gwen Ffrangcon-Davies
MR ERSKINE	Michael Barrington
SIBYL VANE	Judi Bowker
MRS VANE	Gillian Raine
JAMES VANE	Nicholas Ball
VICTOR	Lawrence Davidson
MR HUBBARD	Reginald Barratt
FRANCIS	Paul Greenhalgh
ALAN CAMPBELL	Nicholas Clay

Peter Firth's Dorian (a golden, pre-Raphaelite youth) was not helped by a creamy-white suit and a hat which made him look like a female equestrian. Never for one minute an aristocrat, Firth came across as the sort of common lad Wilde might have picked up while feasting with panthers. Neither his performance nor the production suggested any moral degeneration.

John Gielgud as Lord Henry wore an auburn wig and was trimly bearded and moustached. The epigrams tripped effortlessly off his tongue. 'One should never make one's début with a scandal,' he observed. 'One should keep that in reserve to give an interest to one's old age.'

Gielgud was more frivolous, more capricious, more seductive, less intellectual than George Sanders had been in 1945. 'I love acting,' said Lord Henry to his reflection in the mirror. 'So much more real than real life.' (The line is not to be found in Wilde.) The final shots showed him as an aged and rouged devil, perfect casting for Aschenbach in Thomas Mann's *Death in Venice*.

The problem the production faced was how explicit to be about the homosexuality. Lord Henry made a move to kiss Dorian's hand, a move which was rejected by Dorian. The most explicit scene was Dorian's blackmail of his former lover, Alan Campbell. The scene would have been more explicit had John Gorrie, the director, been allowed to play the scene in bed. But it was pointed out to him by the producers that, were such a scene included, there would be no sales in America. The actors, fully clothed, sat in chairs, head to head, and played the scene as if they were in bed.

Nicholas Clay, as Campbell, was absolutely true to Wilde's description: 'very stern and rather pale, his pallor being intensified by his coal-black hair and dark eyebrows.'

> Gielgud's patrician voice delivered each remark like a small dinner-table aria.
>
> Sylvia Clayton *Daily Telegraph*

> In the last scene with Dorian (a fine performance by Peter Firth) Gielgud looked like an elderly satyr, a masterpiece of make-up and carefully contrived despair.
>
> Ronald Higham *Evening News*

1977 French television: *Portrait de Dorian Gray*

Director	Pierre Boutron
LORD HENRY WOTTON	Raymond Gerome
BASIL HALLWARD	Denis Manuel
DORIAN GRAY	Patrice Alexsandre
SIBYL VANE	Marie-Hélène Breillat
CAST	Bernard Allouf
	Anne-Marie Fijal

Patrice Alexsandre bears little resemblance to Wilde's dilettante . . . Realism and the fantastic, so harmoniously blended in the original, are here ill-matched sparring partners. The superimposed artificiality holds the narrative in chains and smothers its original thrill.

International Herald Tribune

1977 *Mr Dorian Gray, Sir*
or *Prof Chen-Tung's Magic Lantern Horror Show*
by Charles McDonough and Christopher Pumpkin.

Premiere: Van Dam Theatre, New York.

Director	J Perry McDonald
DORIAN	Alan Coates

Director J Perry McDonald has a keen eye for exposing the sexual and psychological undertones of Wildean drama but he is not able to infuse a satisfactory amount of colour and energy into his production.

Alan L Gunsberg *Show Business*

1978 American film: *Take Off*

Director	Armand Weston
Screenplay	Armand Weston
	Daria Price

The story began in the 1920s with Darrin Blue (Wade Nichols) making love to an older woman (Georgina Spelvin). Their love-making was recorded on film by a chauffeur, Max (George Spenser). Darrin prayed the film would age and that he would remain forever young. *Take Off* then went on to parody various cinema genres: the gangster movie of the 1930s, the *film noir* of the 1940s and the road movies of the 1950s.

> Starting out as a straight sexploiter with an excruciating line in smart wisecracks, *Take Off* soon becomes mercifully sidetracked into a welter of what one might charitably call film-buff jokes. The mercy is shortlived, however, since the humour is juvenile.
>
> Tom Milne *Monthly Film Bulletin*

1983 American television: *The Sins of Dorian Gray*

Director	Tony Maylam
Screenplay	Ken August
	Peter Lawrence
DORIAN GRAY	Belinda Bauer
HENRY LORD	Anthony Perkins
CAST	Joseph Bottoms
	Olga Karlatos

Dorian was a woman (Belinda Bauer) who became a top model working for a giant cosmetics company owned by Henry Lord (Anthony Perkins). Her true age was visible only on a screentest, which she viewed from time to time. She gave up a life of murder in order to work in a missionary hospital in Africa. Ten years later she found that her self-sacrifice had made no difference whatsoever and she was still ugly. So she killed herself.

> Tony Maylam's direction sustains an effective aura of gothic glamour enhanced by a haunting simplistic theme song and classy costumes for the wicked heroine by Albert Nipon.
>
> Gail Williams *Hollywood Reporter*

> Although totally ridiculous, *The Sins of Dorian Gray* has its rewards for collectors of the bizarre.
>
> John J O'Connor *New York Times*

1984 West German film.
Dorian Gray im Spiegel der Boulevardpresse
English title: *The Mirror Image of Dorian Gray in the Yellow Press*

Director	Ulricke Ottinger

Frau Dr Mabuse (Seyrig Delphine), head of an international press cartel, creates an androgynous Dorian Gray for her own political reasons and sends him/her out into the world under cover of the yellow press to be seduced, exploited and then destroyed. Dorian was played by a well-known cover girl, Yeruschka Von Lehndorf. The film owed more to J J Huysmans's *À Rebours* than it did to Wilde.

1984 Kiel. Premiere of Heinz Weitz's ballet, to music by John Longstaff.

1985 Musical: *Dorian*

Premiere: City College, Los Angeles.

Book, music and lyrics	Randy Bowers.
Director	Randy Bowers
DORIAN	Grant Matthews
LORD HENRY WOTTON	Marvyn Byrkett
BASIL HALLWARD	Jay Willict
MAGGIE	Melody Archer

Randy Bowers also painted the portrait.

1987 Ballet.

Premiere: Royal Ballet Company at Sadler's Wells.

Choreographer	Derek Deane
Music	Carl Davis
Conductor	Carl Davis
DORIAN GRAY	Peter Jacobsson
BASIL HALLWARD	Nicholas Millington

LORD HENRY WOTTON	Desmond Kelly
LADY HENRY WOTTON	Galina Samsova
THE DUCHESS	Chenca Williams
THE YOUNG LORD	Russell Maliphant
SIBYL VANE	Samira Saidi
MRS VANE	Anita Landa

Pimps, whores, sailors, urchins, transvestites, and party guests were played by members of the company.

> All art is at once surface and symbol. Those who go beneath the surface do so at their peril. Those who read the symbol do so at their peril.
>
> Oscar Wilde's Preface to *The Picture of Dorian Gray*

> Deane may claim that you do not need Wilde's exotic prose but without Wilde it becomes the most lurid melodrama, risible in its indulgence in would-be shocking theatrical effects.
>
> Mary Clarke *Guardian*

> Dance fails signally to explore the motives and the hectic energy of the tale, and Mr Deane (who is a musically sensitive creator) finds no help at all in the saccharin Lisztian pastiche confected by Carl Davis . . . A large cast rampage in period dress, looking for all the world like players in some dire Hollywood costume extravaganza of the 1940s. Led by Peter Jacobsson as Dorian, the dancers behave badly, mumming and cavorting as artists and derelicts; none of them convince us that what they are presenting is more than a lurid charade.
>
> Clement Crisp *Financial Times*

> You have to admire the dancers . . . They must know what rubbish it is, yet they act if they are taking part in a real ballet.
>
> John Percival *The Times*

1988 Ballet by Saeko Ichinohe.

Premiere: Louisville.

Choregrapher	Sacko Ichinoche
Music	Ivana Themmen
DORIAN	Clark Reid
PORTRAIT	Kenneth Braso
LORD HENRY WOTTON	Michael Hauser

1990 *Dorian Gray – The Musical*

Premiere: Rock Theatre, Budapest.

Music	Mátyás Várkonyi
Book	Gunar Braunke, Janos Ács, Duncan Shiels
Director and conductor	Miklós-Gábor Kerényi

1990 American musical: *Dorian Gray*

Premiere: Cubiculo Theatre, New York.

Book and lyrics	Joseph Bravaco
Music	Robert Cioffi
Director	Joseph Bravaco
LORD HENRY WOTTON	Gary Reed
DORIAN GRAY	Doug Welty
BASIL HALLWARD	Stephen Newport
SIBYL VANE	Margaret Wehrle
JAMES VANE	Michael Griffo

The cast were chosen for their singing ability rather than their personal appearance or histrionic talent. Dorian sang 'If I Were the Picture' and Lord Henry sang 'A Love That Dare Not Speak'.

> The heavy-handed book lacks wit, style and subtlety. The hopelessly underwritten characters have no sense of the period in which the story happens to be set. And the over-italicised references to The Love That Dare Not Speak Its Name seem

lascivious and distasteful when the social constraints of the novel are inexplicably ignored and abandoned.

Brian Bradley *Backstage*

1990 American musical: *Dorian Gray*

Premiere: Saval Theatre, New York.

Book	Nan Barcan
Music	Michael Rubell
Lyrics	Nan Barcan
	Michael Rubell
Director	Robert Petito
LORD HENRY WOTTON	Hank Schob
DORIAN GRAY	William Broderick
BASIL HALLWARD	Joel Briel
SIBYL VANE	Kyle Waters
LADY VICTORIA	Paula Newman
JAMES VANE	Dan Frank

1990 Odyssey Theatre, New York.

Adaptors	Mary Wolford
	Andrew Arnault
Music	Barbary Benary
Director	Mary Wolford
LORD HENRY WOTTON	Mark Tankersley
BASIL HALLWARD	Robert Laconi
DORIAN GRAY	John Wuchte
SIBYL VANE	Barbara Svoboda

It's too bad someone decided to show the portrait. Described by Lord Henry as 'the finest portrait of modern times', we see a flat-faced likeness to Wuchte, with strange eyes and huge white hands. And when the picture begins to suffer for its model's sins, it winds up as a weird day-glo mishmash. Alarming it is, but perhaps not in the way Wilde envisioned.

Wendy Brandes *The Villager*

1991 Palace Theatre, Watford.

Adaptor	John Osborne
Director	Lou Stein

LORD HENRY WOTTON	Peter Woodward
BASIL HALLWARD	Peter Bourke
DORIAN GRAY	Ben Walden
LORD FERMOR	John Arnatt
LADY AGATHA	Toni Kanal
SIR THOMAS BURDON	Jon Rumney
SIBYL	Candida Gubbins
MRS VANE	Toni Kanal
JAMES VANE	Jason Calder
VICTOR	John Rumney
MR HUBBARD	Jason Calder
FRANCIS	John Arnatt
ALAN CAMPBELL	Michael Burrell
DUCHESS OF MONMOUTH	Candida Gubbins
CONSTABLE	Michael Burrell

A sleepy, inept revival with a bland, wooden performance in the central role. The portrait remained with its back to the audience.

1993 Citizens' Theatre, Glasgow.

Adaptor, Director, Designer	Philip Prowse

LORD HENRY WOTTON	Rupert Everett
BASIL HALLWARD	Gerrard McArthur
DORIAN GRAY	Henry Ian Cusick
LADY HARRY	Jill Spurrier
SIBYL	Andrea Hart
MRS VANE	Ellen Sheean
JAMES VANE	Andrew Joseph
MR ISSACS	Derwent Watson
ALAN CAMPBELL	Matthew Whittle

Philip Prowse's production, all corruption and decay, was characteristically high camp and visually superb. Dorian lived on from the 1890s right through to the London Blitz of World War Two. The portrait of him was naked and enclosed in a triptych of mirrors.

> The evening is dominated by the ageless Rupert Everett as the ageing Lord Henry Wotton, scattering epigrams like a moralistic fly-spray, preaching the gospel of experimentation and licentiousness and witnessing the tragic dénouement from a wheelchair, transformed by his own decadence into a crumbling dowager plugged into a saline drip and plastered in death-defying make-up and glittering jewellery.
>
> Michael Coveney *Observer*

> Everett speaks in a strangulated voice that seems to have exhausted itself in the effort to clamber through his larynx. Very dandyish, and in reply to Dorian's talk of duty his 'Ah' carries a wealth of jaundiced experience.
>
> Jeremy Kingston *The Times*

1993 Barons Court Theatre, London.

Adaptor	Ronald Selwyn Phillips
Director	Simon Guiver
BASIL HALLWARD	Jonathan Broxholm
LORD HENRY WOTTON	Michael John Wade
DORIAN GRAY	Christian Toba
SIBYL VANE	Joanne Sergent
JAMES VANE	Corin Mellinger
ALAN CAMPBELL	Daniel McKenna
HETTY CAMPBELL	Joanne Sergent

1994 *The Innocence of Dorian Gray*
Devised by Andrew O'Callaghan and Alistair K Daniels.

Premiere: Hen and Chickens, London.

DORIAN	Andrew O'Callaghan
ALL OTHER ROLES	Alistair K Daniels

O'Callaghan and Daniels, members of the Counter Weight Physical Theatre, in white T-shirts and jeans, performed a truncated version of Wilde's text which ended in violent sex, simulated buggery, and male rape.

> As a narrative the performance tends to come across as a well-rehearsed reading rather than a genuine drama, and the acting sits rather heavily alongside their self-conscious attempts to use masks or intersect physical imagery within the story.
>
> Roger Foss *What's On*

1994 Musical: *Dorian Gray*

Premiere: Judith Anderson Theatre, New York.

Book	Allan Reiser Don Price
Lyrics	Allan Reiser
Music	Gary David Levinson
Director	Don Price
BASIL HALLWARD	Michael J Curran
LORD HENRY WOTTON	David Edwards
DORIAN GRAY	Craig Rubano
SIBYL VANE	Leslie Esser
MRS VANE	Marion Markham
DUCHESS OF MONMOUTH	Janet Aldrich

1994 Battersea Arts Centre, London.

Presented by Show of Hands, an integrated hearing and deaf theatre group.

Adaptor	Guy Wilson
Director	Michael Dray
CAST	Craig S Cremin Frank Essery Neil Fox Edward McCabe Dietrich Nanton

1994 Opera by Hans Cox.

Premiere: Opera House, Amsterdam.

Director	Charles Hamilton
Designer	Erich Kondrak
Conductor	Jochem Slothouwer
DORIAN GRAY	David Knutson
LORD HENRY WOTTON	Timothy Nolen
BASIL HALLWARD	Lieuwe Visser
SIBYL VANE	Anne Haenen

1994 Barons Court Theatre, London.

Adaptor	Ronald Selwyn Phillips
Director	Doug Rollins
BASIL HALLWARD	Gavin Miller
LORD HENRY WOTTON	Doug Rollins
DORIAN GRAY	Christian Deal
SIBYL VANE	Rebecca Couper
JAMES VANE	Darren Spencer
ALAN CAMPBELL	James Baker
HETTY CAMPBELL	Rebecca Couper

Deconstruction Theatre Company don't so much take apart an otherwise beguiling allegory as butcher it entirely.

Patrick Marmion *What's On*

1994 Lyric, Hammersmith, London.

Adaptor	Neil Bartlett
Composer	Nicolas Bloomfield
Directors	Neil Bartlett
	Leah Hausman
ADA LEVERSON	Maria Aitken
THE BOY	Benedick Bates
DORIAN GRAY	Benedick Bates
REGGIE TURNER	Betty Bourne

LORD HENRY WOTTON	Betty Bourne
ROBBIE ROSS	Tim Piggott-Smith
BASIL HALLWARD	Tim Piggott-Smith
THE MAID	Joanna Riding
SIDNEY MAVOR	Paul Shaw

> It seemed to me that the very words of *The Picture of Dorian Gray* are as knowing of Wilde and his fate as the fatal picture of Dorian. Frozen in a moment of time, but yet always changing in their significance, they haunt him. They lead him, just as they lead Dorian, to, and then beyond, the end of the century.
>
> Neil Bartlett (programme note)

Neil Bartlett's conceit was a reunion at the Savoy Hotel in the 1920s. The script, drawn from the first edition and other texts, was a mixture of narrative, biography and musical commentary. A chamber orchestra sat on a balcony above the actors. Dorian was played by a guardsman. Guardsmen were well known to supplement their incomes by offering 'a bit of scarlet' to any gentleman who might require the service. The portrait was represented by a mirror.

> But for the most part they simply read and act out chunks of the novel in a style that veers between the camp and the wooden.
>
> Charles Spencer *Daily Telegraph*

> The result is neither confusing enough to be incomprehensible, nor original enough to be entertaining.
>
> John Peter *Sunday Times*

> The result is low camp and no frisson.
>
> Michael Coveney *Observer*

1995 Gate Theatre, Dublin.

Adaptor	Gavin Kostick
Director	Alan Stanford

DORIAN GRAY	William Oxborrow
LORD HENRY WOTTON	Stephen Brennan
BASIL HALLWARD	Robert O'Mahoney

PARKER	David O'Brien
LORD FERMOR	Tom Hickey
SIBYL VANE	Jennifer O'Dea
JAMES VANE	Simon O'Gorman
VICTOR	David Heap
REFLECTION	Sinead O'Carroll
THE DUCHESS OF MONMOUTH	Dana Bledsoe
ALAN CAMPBELL	Des Cave

Alan Stanford's atmospheric and stylish production was faithful to the original, turning the purple passages into dialogue. Bruno Schwengl's set was dominated by a huge, empty frame within which a dancer appeared at regular intervals to mime and mirror Dorian's rot. In the mirror Dorian could see not only himself but his victims as well. David Nowlan in the *Irish Times* found the adaptation 'unsatisfying as a piece of theatre'.

> When the play strives for camp, it succeeds admirably and when the melodrama is deconstructed and played for laughs it's a very enjoyable piece of work. But when it tries to capture the atmosphere of evil it is purely risible.
>
> *In Dublin*

> The ludicrously good-looking William Oxborrow is a real discovery in the title role. All cheekbones and floppy hair, he has the cold, androgynous quality of David Bowie in his prime, though there is no mistaking the sulky petulance beneath the beauty, or his final exhausted despair.
>
> Charles Spencer *Daily Telegraph*

1995 *Dorian Gray –The Musical*: British premiere of Mátyás Várkonyi's musical, at Bloomsbury Theatre , London.

Director/conductor	Miklós-Gábor Kerényi
LORD HENRY WOTTON	Hal Fowler
BASIL HALLWARD	Sándor Sasvári
DORIAN GRAY	Atila Csengeri
SIBYL	Eszter Bíró
MRS VANE	Anikó Nagy

JAMES VANE	Tamás Földes
MR ISSACS	Pal Makrai
BRITANNIA	Claire Moore

Mátyás Várkonyi mixed romantic opera and rock to present an unabashed gay reading of the text. The painting spoke and sang.

> The music was monotonous and highly derivative. The lyrics are sometimes frankly risible, as with Dorian's outburst after Basil's death: 'I have gone one dreadful step too far. I can no longer abide my Shangri-La.'
>
> James Inverne *Plays and Players*

> *Dorian Gray – A Musical* is really best forgotten.
>
> *Stage*

1996 Opera by Lowell Liebermann.

Premiere: Opera House, Monte Carlo.

Co-production with Opera Pacific of Costa Mesa, California.

Libretto	Lowell Lieberman John Cox
Director	John Cox
Designer	Stephen Brimson Lewis
Conductor	Steuart Bedford

DORIAN GRAY	Jeffrey Lentz
LORD HENRY WOTTON	John Hancock
BASIL HALLWARD	Gregory Reinhart
SIBYL VANE	Korliss Uecker
JAMES VANE	Ron Baker
THE WHORE	Vivian Tierney
LORD GEOFFREY	Stephen Chaundy
GAMEKEEPER	Bryan Jones

Lowell Libermann, in a programme note, wrote:

> The entire opera is based on a twelve-note row which is used not serially, but tonally. It is first heard at the beginning of the opera in pizzicato cellos and bases. It is harmonised as Dorian's theme,

and then as the painting's theme. As the painting disintegrates and becomes corrupted, so does the theme.

The almost uninterrupted melodic flow makes it easy for the audience to grasp most of the text while the orchestra usually underlines the dialogue in pointed fashion. Without being in the least pejorative the music was often reminiscent of film music of the highest quality.

Joel Kasow *Opera*

1996 Musical: *Dorian Gray*
Judith Anderson Theatre, New York.

Book	Allan Reiser
	Don Price
Lyrics	Allan Reiser
Music	Gary David Levinson
Director	Don Price

BASIL HALLWARD	Tom Rocco
LORD HENRY WOTTON	Chris Weikee
DORIAN GRAY	Brian Duguay
SIBYL VANE	Laura Stanczyk
MRS VANE	Gerrianne Raphael
DUCHESS OF MONMOUTH	Mary Setrakia

1997 Barons Court Theatre, London.

Adaptor	Robert Selwyn Phillips
Director	Simon Guiver

BASIL HALLWARD	Dan Fineman
LORD HENRY WOTTON	Keith Spur
DORIAN GRAY	Christian Deal
SIBYL VANE	Julia Russell
JAMES VANE	Gregor Hunt
ALAN CAMPBELL	William Finkenrath
HETTY CAMPBELL	Julia Russell

'It's not good for one's morals to see bad acting,' said Oscar Wilde. Simon Guiver's production went no further than stripping Dorian to his underpants. Christian Deal's Spanish accent hinted at a decadence which his performance never developed; emotionally and vocally, he remained on the same note throughout. Keith Spurr made heavy weather of Wotton's epigrams.

1997 Musical: *Dorian Gray*
A musical by David Reeves.

Premiere: Arts Theatre, London.

Books, music and lyrics	David Reeves
Director	Mehmet Ergen
DORIAN GRAY	Marcello Walton
LORD HENRY WOTTON	Nicholas Pound
BASIL HALLWARD	Mark Huggins
SIBYL VANE	Joyce Springe

A flat, fatuous piece of writing with no subtlety, depth or wit whatsoever. Marcello Walton as Dorian has a handsome profile and gamely strikes attitudes, but this doesn't quite cut the mustard somehow.

Sarah Hemming *Financial Times*

As chaste as a pair of knee-length bathing drawers.

Kate Stratton *Time Out*

It takes a certain ingenuity to turn a 19th-century literary masterpiece into a musical Penny Dreadful. Mehmet Ergen's production makes it look like a piece of cake.

James Christopher *The Times*

1999 Opera by Lowell Libermann

Revival: The Florentine Opera Company, Milwaukee, Wisconsin.

Director	Linda Brovsky
Designers	Stephen Brimson Lewis
	Jon Morrell
Conductor	Steuart Bedford
DORIAN GRAY	Mark Thomsen
LORD HENRY WOOTON	John Hancock
BASIL HALLWARD	Kelly Anderson
SIBYL VANE	Erie Mills
JAMES VANE	Kristopher Irmiter
THE WHORE	Nancy Shade
LORD GEOFFREY	Brandon Jovanovich
GAMEKEEPER	Matthew Potterton

The score draws heavily on idioms of the last century – mostly the tonal ones, from Mahler to Minimalism – but the synthesis is generally persuasive on its own terms . . . After being bogged down in faux Strauss and in a banal clamor when the portrait is discovered it reveals Dorian's ravaged character late in the first act, the momentum and imagination of the opening pick up again in the second and carry breathlessly to the conclusion. Mr Libermann's handling of the orchestra is masterly, summoning great power at times without in most cases swamping the voices.

James R Oestreich *The New York Times*

Stage director Linda Brovsky enforced an exaggerated, Victorian-melodrama sort of acting that played up the penny-dreadful aspect of the book. At first I thought some of the humor generated by the style was unintentional. By the end, it was clear Brovsky knew exactly what she was doing and that it was entirely appropriate.

Tom Strini *Wilwaukee Journal Sentinel*

In terms of acting, tenor Mark Thomsen was an impressive Dorian Gray, but his voice sounded occasionally strained.

Wynne Delacoma *Chicago Sun-Times*

1999 One-man-show

Premiere: The Attic Theatre, Wimbledon, London.

Adaptor and actor	Keith Drinkel

Keith Drinkel, wearing an open-necked shirt and black trousers, merely told the story and made no attempt to create either the period or the decadence; nor did he differentiate vocally between the characters. The performance remained a feat of memory, no more. Nobody would have guessed that the novel played a significant part in Wilde's downfall.

Lord Arthur Savile's Crime (1891)

A Study of Duty

The Plot

Septimus Podgers, a professional palm reader, reads Lord Arthur Savile's hand and sees murder written there. Lord Arthur, who is engaged to be married, feels he has a duty to his fiancée to get the murder out of the way before the wedding. He senses that to marry her, 'with the doom of murder hanging over his head, would be a betrayal like that of Judas, a sin worse than any the Borgia had ever dreamed of.'

Arthur decides to poison a dear old lady, Lady Clementina Beauchamp, a second cousin, who 'hated doctors but loved medicine'. Unfortunately, she dies of natural causes before she can take the poison. Arthur postpones his marriage.

He then determines to blow up his uncle, the Dean of Chichester, and to this end buys a small exploding French clock from Herr Winckelkopf, an anarchist and conspirator, who confesses he does not work for money. 'I live entirely for my art,' he says. The clock fails to go off.

Walking home one night, wondering if it would not be better to break off his engagement, he bumps into Podgers by Cleopatra's Needle and, in a flash of inspiration, flings him into the Thames. Everybody presumes Podgers committed suicide.

Oscar Wilde always said murder was a mistake because one should never do anything that one couldn't talk about at the dinner table.

Lord Arthur Savile's Crime was first published in 1891. Interestingly, the following year, on the second night of *A Woman of No Importance*, the society palmist Cheiro (Count Louis Hamon) read Wilde's hand and predicted he would go into exile in his fortieth year.

None of the attempts to stage Wilde's short story has been successful. All have suffered from trying to stretch a short story to three acts. What it needs, and never gets, is the elegance and ironic detachment director Robert Hamer and actor Dennis Price brought to the 1949 British film, *Kind Hearts and Coronets*.

The first two adaptations were in the silent cinema: the Hungarian *Lidercnyomas* in 1920, and the French *Le Crime de Lord Arthur Savile*, directed by Réné Hervil in 1922.

1943 American film: *Flesh and Fantasy*

Director	Julien Duvivier
Screenplay	Ernest Pascal
	Samuel Hoffenstein
	Ellis St Joseph
MARSHALL TAYLOR	Edward G Robinson
PODGERS	Thomas Mitchell
ROWENA	Anna Lee
LADY PAMELA HARDWICK	Dame May Whitty
THE GREAT GASPAR	Charles Boyer
DEAN OF NORFOLK	C Aubrey Smith

Flesh and Fantasy was a portmanteau film in three parts. The second episode, *For All We Know*, was based on Wilde's story and was the best. A London lawyer (Edward G Robinson), having been thwarted in two murders, killed off the palmist (Thomas Mitchell). Pursued by the police, he dashed through a circus and was run over and killed by a truck. Neither Wilde nor London were recognisable.

> It sounds pretty grim – and it is much grimmer than Wilde's version – but with Mr Robinson's other self, cynical, derisive, persuasive, looming up in mirrors, shop windows and all over the place, it is extremely amusing.
>
> Elspeth Grant *Daily Sketch*

Nine years later two stage adaptations opened in London within a week of each other. The first was at the Royal Court. The second was at the Arts Theatre. There was talk of a third play but nobody was surprised when it failed to materialise.

1952 Royal Court Theatre Club, London.

Adaptor	Constance Cox
Director	Jack Hulbert
BAINES	Peter Haddon
LORD ARTHUR SAVILE	Claude Hulbert
SIBYL MERTON	Jean Lodge
THE DEAN OF PADDINGTON	Raymond Rollett
LADY WINDERMERE	Marie Ney
LADY CLEMENTINA BEAUCHAMP	Jean Cadell
LADY JULIA MORTON	Violet Fairbrother
MR PODGERS	John Garley
NELLIE	Jill Hulbert
HERR WINCKELKOPF	Milo Sperber

Constance Cox's plodding adaptation was nearer to a Ben Travers farce than a Wilde comedy. Claude Hulbert played Lord Arthur as if he were a dimwitted relation of Bertie Wooster.

> The foolishness of the whole enterprise is sharply underlined by the setting and costumes of David de Bethel, which are right on the [Cecil] Beaton track and at least twice as elegant as anything Miss Cox has given her actors to say.
>
> *Evening Standard*

> The second act rises to a nice crescendo of frustrated assassination; the third adds rather too much and less effectively to the story.
>
> *Observer*

1952 Arts Theatre Club, London.

Adaptors	Basil Dawson
	St John Clowes
Director	Stephen Murray

LORD SURBITON	Robert Andrews
DEAN OF COLCHESTER	Noel Iliff
LADY CLEMENTINA BEAUCHAMP	Margaret Halstan
LORD ARTHUR SAVILE	David Markham
MISS SIBYL MERTON	Christine Finn
MISS FLORA PERCY	Charlotte Mitchell
BAKER	Walter Hudd
LADY CONISTON	Adrianne Allen
MR PODGERS	Richard Goolden
MR PESTLE	Ivor Barnard
BUTTON	Arthur Hambling/Campbell Singer
HERR WINCKELKOPF	Howard Goorney

The Arts Theatre Club production was preferable to the Royal Court production in that it was more recognisably Wildean. The dialogue had a lighter touch. The direction and acting were more stylish. But the joke still did not last for a whole evening.

David Markham's Lord Arthur was rightly not a silly ass, but a serious, pale-faced young man. Walter Hudd got the best notices:

> His [Walter Hudd's] voice is dulcet, his bearing impeccable, his timing accurate, his tact superlative. It is a joy to watch his eyes as the poisoned tea-cup makes its round in the last act.
>
> *Sketch*

> The evening is ruled for me by Walter Hudd's butler who pours the poison with a more discrete dignity than anyone in Belgrave Square or out. He treads on air.
>
> J C Trewin *Observer*

1955 American television: *A Promise to Murder*

Director	Allen Reisner
Adaptor	John A Kneubuhl

RANDY TOWNSEND	Louis Hayward
MR VOORHEES	Peter Lorre
LADY BERTHA WETHERBY	Ann Harding

The production, a modern update of Wilde, was part of CBS's *Climax* series with Louis Hayward and Peter Lorre in the Lord Arthur and Mr Podgers roles.

Lorre was never better than as the evil weird plotter; Hayward registered strongly as the tormented young man.

Variety

1958 West German television: *My Lord Weiss Sich zu Helfen*

1958 American television.

Script	Francis Cockrell
Director	Robert Stevens
Executive Producer	Alfred Hitchcock
LORD ARTHUR SAVILE	Ronald Howard
MR PODGERS	Sebastian Cabot
SIBYL MORTON	Rosemary Harris
LADY WINDERMERE	Gladys Cooper
MRS MORTON	Mary Forbes
MR MORTON	Melville Cooper
DUCHESS OF PAISLEY	Lily Kemble-Cooper
SIR THOMAS	Kendrix Huxman
LADY MARVEL	Hilda Plowright
CHEMIST	Frederick Worlock
LADY CLEMENTINA	Doris Lloyd
COUNT ROUVALOFF	Alex Davion

1960 British television.

Adaptors	Constance Cox
	Gerald Savory
Director	Alan Cooke
LORD ARTHUR SAVILE	Terry-Thomas
BAINES	Robert Coote
HERR WINCKELKOPF	Eric Pohlmann
DEAN OF PADDINGTON	Ernest Thesiger
SIBYL	June Thorburn
LADY JULIA	Ambrosine Phillpotts
MR PODGERS	Arthur Lowe
LADY CLEMENTINA BEAUCHAMP	Nora Nicholson

UNCLE JASPER	Kynaston Reeves
MR PESTLE	Michael Hitchman

Terry-Thomas, gap-toothed, moustached, monocled, brainless, was hardly the Lord Arthur of the novel and it was quite absurd to hear Aunt Clementina describe him as 'such a sweet, innocent boy'. Terry-Thomas looked as if he were playing the role he always played: a middle-aged cad.

The script had a deadening effect on Wilde, relying on such unfunny farcical devices as a demonstration of smothering by pillow and actors falling down the stairs off-screen.

There was a good moment when Arthur considered killing the Prime Minister and 'gaining the gratitude of the whole nation'. Better still was the funeral reception for Aunt Clementina and his discovery that she had not eaten the poisoned chocolate. He passed the chocolate box round the assembled company, and pressed his granite-faced future mother-in-law (Ambrosine Phillpotts) to take one.

The casting of Nora Nicholson and Ernest Thesiger as aunt and Dean was promising but the actors were given nothing to do. Eric Pohlmann, as the President of the Royal Society of Anarchists, had more to do, but didn't do it well enough. Robert Coote, who had scored a hit as Colonel Pickering in *My Fair Lady*, was very disappointing as the butler.

> Terry-Thomas gave quite a stylish performance, round and cool, free from any trace of goatishness. Ernest Thesiger and Kynaston Reeves as the Dean and Uncle Jasper were a gerontophile's double dream of quavering eld. The only trouble was that it went on a bit too long. Fifty minutes would have been plenty.
>
> Michael Richardson *Observer*

> George Haslam's sets were some of the most inventive and intriguing seen on TV for some time; he captured completely the bizarre, semi-Gothnic [sic] atmosphere – Alan Cooke's direction made the best of the material. Chief disappointment was Terry-Thomas himself, who gave a fumbling, intermittently funny performance, but never within a couple of blocks of the urbanity and polish necessary to bring it off.
>
> Otta *Variety*

1966 British television.

Script	Philip Mackie Hugh Leonard
Director	David Boisseau
LORD ARTHUR SAVILE	Robert Morris
MR PODGERS	John Cater
SIBYL MERTON	Celistine Randall
THRUPP	Jack Austen
LADY CLEMENTINA	Marie Lohr
WINCKELKOPF	Jack Woolgar

The play was included in the Granada television series, *The Liars*, which drew on a number of short stories by famous authors. The stories were linked by four 'liars' (Nyree Dawn Porter, Ian Ogilvy, Mervyn Blake and Richard Porter) who pretended the stories had happened to them.

1967 West German television: *Mylord Weiss Sich zu Helfen*

1967 *A Murder of No Importance*
A comedy by Basil Dawson.

Arts Theatre, Cambridge, and tour.

Director	Toby Robertson
LORD SURBITON	Hugh Latimer
THE DEAN OF COLCHESTER	Charles Carson
LADY CLEMENTINA BEAUCHAMP	Viola Keats
LORD ARTHUR SAVILE	Basil Hoskins
MISS SIBYL MERTON	Marty Cruickshank
MISS FLORA PERCY	Janet Hargreaves
BAKER	James Cairncross
LADY CONISTON	Heather Chasen
MR PODGERS	Michael Rothwell
MR PESTLE	Stanley Lebor
SGT BUTTON	Rowland Davies
HERR WINCKELKOPF	Howard Goorney/Donald Bisset
FOOTMAN	Stephen Batiste

Basil Dawson's adaptation (a rewrite of his 1952 play) added so many of his own epigrams that the genuine Wilde began to seem as bad as the imitation. None of the cast knew how to handle the pastiche wit.

The second act farce failed to build and was bungled by the stage management. The funniest moment was Arthur's momentary righteous indignation that his intended victims were thwarting him.

> This is delicious nonsense superbly accessorised, and performed with the highest polish.
>
> *Guardian*

> The result is extremely funny drawing room Grand Guignol, generously (if incongruously garnished) with epigrams from the original story and elsewhere . . . James Cairncross, unrecognisable, as the all-possessive butler, surveys and directs the goings-on with arrogant, gloomy self-effacement.
>
> *The Times*

1971 Italy. Premiere of G Ferrari's opera *Lord Savile* in Catania.

1972 Sadler's Wells, London.

Adaptor	Constance Cox
Director	John Downing
BAINES	Mervyn Johns
LORD ARTHUR SAVILE	Peter Greene
SIBYL MERTON	Kate O'Mara
THE DEAN OF PADDINGTON	Jack Hulbert
LADY WINDERMERE	Daphne Anderson
LADY CLEMENTINA BEAUCHAMP	Elsie Randolph
LADY JULIA MERTON	Rose Hill
MR PODGERS	McDonald Hobley
NELLIE	Diane Raynor
HERR WINCKELKOPF	Bill Kerr

> The humour of the original story comes from Wilde's straight-faced, unquestioning acceptance of the morality – indeed, the

necessity – of the enterprise. This rather daring attitude is reduced in the play to mere absurdity and frivolity.

Sunday Telegraph

High comedy lines – stolen from Wilde's plays – jostle uncomfortably with low, farcical buiness, crude double-takes and routine horse-play.

John Barber *Daily Telegraph*

It is left to Jack Hulbert as an exuberantly senile Dean of Paddington to provide a splendid character performance, quiet in detail and ideal in scale.

Nicholas de Jongh *Guardian*

1973 Dublin.

Adaptor	Constance Cox
Director	Ann Myler
BAINES	John McKelvey
LORD ARTHUR SAVILE	Paul Murphy
SIBYL MERTON	Liz Davies
THE DEAN OF PADDINGTON	Edward Byrne
LADY WINDERMERE	Yvonne Cooper
LADY CLEMENTINA BEAUCHAMP	Cathleen Delaney
LADY JULIA MERTON	Rachel Burrows
MR PODGERS	Derek Young
NELLIE	Marian Richardson
HERR WINCKELKOPF	Liam Sweeney

1975 West German television: *15 Schritte Distanz*

1980 Arts Theatre, Cambridge, and tour.

Adaptor	Constance Cox
Director	Clifford Williams

BAINES	Patrick Carghill
LORD ARTHUR SAVILE	John Quentin
SIBYL MERTON	Mel Martin
THE DEAN OF PADDINGTON	Anthony Quayle
LADY WINDERMERE	Honor Blackman
LADY CLEMENTINA BEAUCHAMP	Margaret Rawlings
LADY JULIA MERTON	Barbara Murray
MR PODGERS	Paul Hardwick
NELLIE	Judi Goldman
HERR WINCKELKOPF	Ken Wynne

Patrick Carghill's marvellous gentleman's gentleman . . . John Quentin's brainless charm . . . Anthony Quayle's inspired doddering buffoonery . . . triumph for all concerned.

Eric Braun *Plays and Players*

1982 Royal Exchange, Manchester.

Adaptor	Constance Cox
Director	Eric Thompson

BAINES	Barry Foster
LORD ARTHUR SAVILE	Alan Parnaby
SIBYL MERTON	Kika Mirylees
THE DEAN OF PADDINGTON	Trevor Baxter
LADY WINDERMERE	Rosalind Knight
LADY CLEMENTINA BEAUCHAMP	Gwen Nelson
LADY JULIA MERTON	Patsy Byrne
MR PODGERS	John Tordoff
NELLIE	Elizabeth Watts
HERR WINCKELKOPF	Harry Landis

Eric Thompson's production camped everything up. Alan Parnaby played Lord Arthur for a silly ass in the Wodehouse manner.

Evening dominated by Barry Foster's drily whimsical Baines, a bit of a Jeeves to his foolish employer dispensing wisdom (not infallibly) and cynicism and prompting Nellie, the maid (Elizabeth Watts), to remark 'How beautiful you talk – better than a lantern lecture.'

Country Life

1984 The story was related by Martin Jarvis and directed by Christine Secombe on British television.

1991 Russian television: *Prestuplenie Lorda Artura*

Director	Alexander Orlov
CAST	Sergei Vinogradov
	Alexander Filippenko
	Olga Folstetskaya
	Alla Budnitskaya
	Yevgeni Vesnik
	Svetlana Nemolyayeva
	Alla A Kazanskaya
	Igor Yasulovich
	Alexei Yasulovich

1994 Barons Court Theatre, London.

Adaptor	Ronald Selwyn Phillips
Director	Doug Rollins
LORD ARTHUR SAVILE	Christian Deal
SIBYL MERTON	Janne Jarman
THE DEAN OF PADDINGTON	Stuart Rayner
LADY WINDERMERE	Carole Street
LADY CLEMENTINA BEAUCHAMP	Maggie Bourgein
SEPTIMUS PODGERS	Robert Gill
HERR WINCKELKOPF	Stuart Rayner
SMEDLEY, a maid	Maggie Bourgein

Rayner delights in Winckelkopf's disguises, shifting nervously about the stage as if terrified that someone in the audience will reveal his true identity.

Louise Stafford Charles *What's On*

1994 John Houseman Studios, New York.

Director	David Seatter
BAINES	Alan Gilbert
LORD ARTHUR SAVILE	Kevin Connell
SIBYL MERTON	Carol Pasquantonio
THE DEAN OF WINCHESTER	David Seatter
LADY CLEMENTINA BEAUCHAMP	Joanna Brown

1997 Barons Court Theatre, London.

Adaptor/director	Ronald Selwyn Phillips
LORD ARTHUR SAVILE	Christian Deal
SIBYL MERTON	Amber Edlin
THE DEAN OF PADDINGTON	Ian McKillop
LADY WINDERMERE	Poppy Hill
LADY CLEMENTINA BEAUCHAMP	Linda Clark
SEPTIMUS PODGERS	Edward Simpson
HERR WINCKELKOPF	Ian McKillop
SMEDLEY, a maid	Linda Clark

Ronald Selwyn Phillips's version, a complete rewrite, was a complete travesty. There is so much ironic wit on the printed page. None of it appeared on the stage. There was no horror, either. The only horror at the Barons Court Theatre was the acting. Since Christian Deal was hopelessly miscast as Lord Arthur, Podgers emerged the leading character. Edward Simpson fitted Wilde's description perfectly. He had the palmist's bright, beady eyes, his flat, flabby face and his sickly feeble smile. All that was missing were the great gold-rimmed spectacles.

The Fisherman and His Soul (1891)

The Plot

A fisherman gets rid of his soul so that he can marry a mermaid, but when he and his soul are reunited the mermaid dies and he is drowned.

1912 Theatre production in Russia.

1920 Savoy Theatre, Pasadena, California, USA.

Director	Cloyd Dalzell

1963 American film: *The Shadow and the Sea*

Director	Charles Guggenheim
CAST	Anthony Pompeii Terry Karmel Dionizio de Azevedo

> The mythical parts are superbly realised, but the more realistic scenes in the tawdry port are quite unbelievable and clash with the magic of the earlier scenes. Even so it is well worth seeing even in this dubbed version, because of the breathtaking scenery used, and because of the charm and grace of the main characters.
>
> *Film News*

1979 The Little Angel Marionette Theatre, London.

Premiere: International Puppet Festival.

The production was presented with dialogue in English, German or French. It has been regularly revived and toured.

The Star-Child (1891)

The Plot

A woodlander sees a star falling to earth, He discovers a sleeping baby, who grows up to be a selfish, arrogant and cruel boy and it isn't until he mends his ways that a leper and a beggar woman are transformed into a king and queen and he discovers that he is their son.

1976 The story was related by Alec McCowen and directed by Gordon House on British television.

1988 Teodor Berenson directed a three-dimensional animated-clay film in America. The characters were built by Lindsay Van Blerck and Philip Marcus.

Sphinx Without a Secret (1894)

The Sphinx is Lady Alroy, 'a Giaconda in sables', who has such a mania for mystery and such a passion for secrecy that she creates an enigma where there is none.

1984 The story was related by Martin Jarvis and directed by Christine Secombe on British television.

Anthologies

1973 *An Evening of Oscar Wilde*

Premiere: Playhouse Theatre, Vancouver, Canada.

The programme included *The Happy Prince*, letters, poems, and *The Nightingale and the Rose.*

1975 *Wildeflowers*
Conceived and directed by William Koch.

Premiere: Joseph Jefferson Theatre, New York.

The programme was adapted from the stories of Wilde.

1976 British television: *Oscar Wilde Stories*

The stories, related by Alec McCowen and directed by Gordon House, included *The Happy Prince*, *The Star Child* and *The Nightingale and the Rose.*

1984 British television: *Stories by Oscar Wilde*
The stories, related by Martin Jarvis and directed by Christine Secombe, included *Sphinx Without a Secret, Lord Arthur Savile's Crime* and *The Canterville Ghost.*

All critics can be bought; judging by their appearance, they can't be very expensive.

Oscar Wilde

OTHER WORKS

Oscar Wilde in St. Peter's Square, Rome, in the spring 1900.
This snapshot was probably taken with his own camera.

The Critic as Artist (1891)

1971 Premiere: The Open Space Theatre, London.

Adaptor/director	Charles Marowitz
GILBERT	Timothy Vest
ERNEST	Peter Davies

When a work of art is finished it has, as it were, an independent life of its own, and may deliver a message far other than that which was put into its lips to say.

Oscar Wilde

Wilde's conversation piece was first published as an essay in his book, *Intentions.* The surprising thing about Charles Marowitz's adaptation was that it worked as a play. What on paper is merely an intellectual discussion on Art and Life became a series of sexual manoeuvres in which an older man tried to seduce a younger man by sheer force of intellect.

The audience (who had been handed a green carnation on entering the theatre) watched the actors through gauze. It was as if they, too, were in the drawing-room with the actors, eavesdropping. The action was a battle of words, a battle between unequals, intellectually and sexually. The characters may have been called Gilbert and Ernest but they were obviously Wilde and a gauche young man he was browbeating into his bed. Those who liked the play said it was articulate. Those who didn't said it was waffle.

Timothy West, in a green smoking jacket, was very convincing as a self-sufficient, self-conscious, condescending old queen whose egoism and petulance were finally rather pathetic. Peter Davies, as the young man on the defensive, ever anxious to impress the older man with *his* intellect, was a good foil.

The dialogue, virtually lifted verbatim from the essay, was very civilised. Who would have guessed that Wilde would have defended the critics so persuasively? But it was the things that were going on under the dialogue – the sexual ploys and the hint of *fin de siècle* decadence – which gave the epigrams and paradoxes their theatrical edge.

> Timothy West makes a marvellous effete, languid, sparkling figure.
>
> *Evening Standard*

De Profundis (1897)

De Profundis is the name given to the letter Wilde wrote to Lord Alfred Douglas in his last months in prison. 'I do not defend my conduct,' he wrote. 'I explain it.'

The letter would not have survived if Robert Ross, to whom it had been entrusted, had not taken the precaution of making a copy before forwarding it to Douglas. As Wilde predicted, Douglas destroyed his copy.

Extracts from *De Profundis* were published by Ross in 1905. A slightly longer version was published in 1908. Neither edition contained any mention of Douglas. In 1909 Ross presented Wilde's original manuscript to the British Museum on the condition that nobody would see it for fifty years. In 1949 the 'first complete and accurate version' was published. It was found to be neither complete nor accurate. In 1962 Rupert Hart-Davis edited and published *The Letters of Oscar Wilde* and for the first time readers could read what Wilde had actually written in *De Profundis* without excisions and in the order he had written it.

1990 Choral work by Robert Walker.

Premiere: Winchester Cathedral.

Conductor	David Hill
BARITONE	David Wilson Johnson
CHORUS	Wayneflete Singers
ORCHESTRA	Bournemouth Symphony Orchestra

Robert Walker was commissioned to write a choral work which could be coupled with Edward Elgar' s *The Dream of Gerontius*. He started with the spoken word: Wilde's description of his degradation at Clapham Junction when for half an hour he stood in convict clothes surrounded by a jeering mob. But as the work progressed, he deliberately selected passages that avoided personalising Wilde's painful story to make the subject more and more universal.

1997 The Chelsea Centre and Moving Theatre, London.

Editor	Merlin Holland
Actor	Corin Redgrave

Merlin Holland, Wilde's grandson, introducing the performance, said that he believed the letter, which had been written in anger and remorse, and in arrogance and humility, had saved Wilde's sanity. The script concentrated on those parts which dealt with Douglas's appalling behaviour.

Wilde accused Douglas of bankrupting him by his extravagance and absolutely ruining his art by stopping him from writing, yet at the same time he never ceased to blame himself for allowing a degrading relationship to continue.

Corin Redgrave (who looked nothing like Wilde) was dressed in prison uniform. There was a patch of blue sky behind him, a reference to a recurring line in *The Ballad of Reading Goal.* There were just a hint of an Irish accent and no histrionics. Redgrave had learned the text by heart, but his delivery was so understated that he might as well have been reading the letter on radio as performing it in a theatre.

1997 American film.

Director	Lawrence Brose
CAST	Agnes de Garron
	Aleksandra Mark Miller
	Leon Ko
	The Radical Faeries
	Keisha Lorraine
	Ken Cooper
	Tom Chomont

1998 Revival of Robert Walker's choral work, at Royal Festival Hall.

Conductor	David Hill
BARITONE	David Wilson Johnson
CHORUS	The Bach Choir
ORCHESTRA	Bournemouth Symphony Orchestra

All too often the music seems ancillary to the words, sweetly generalised rather than rising to the heights of Wilde's visionary passion and bitterness. However, the performance from the Bach Choir was full of feeling with exemplary clarity of enunciation.

Stephen Joseph *Independent*

The Ballad of Reading Gaol (1898)

The ballad was written in France after Wilde's release from prison and published in February 1898. His name did not appear on the title page, only his cell number, C 3 3. The feelings he expresses in this extract complement the sentiments in the letters he wrote to the *Daily Chronicle* on prison reform.

I know not whether Laws be right,
  Or whether Laws be wrong;
All that we know who lie in gaol
  Is that the wall is strong;
And that each day is like a year,
  A year whose days are long.

But this I know, that every Law
  That men hath made for Man,
Since first Man took his brother's life,
  And the sad world began,
But straws the wheat and saves the chaff
  With a most evil fan.

This too I know – and wise it were
  If each could know the same –
That every prison that men build
  Is built with bricks of shame,
And bound with bars lest Christ should see
  How men their brothers maim.

With bars they blur the gracious moon,
  And blind the goodly sun;
And they do well to hide their Hell,
  For in it things are done

That Son of God nor son of Man
  Ever should look upon!

1912 Robert Ross edited *The Ballad* and Arnold Daly acted it at the Harris Theatre, New York.

1920 *Kerker-Ballade* was set to music by Henri Zagwijn.

1924 *Ballade de la Geôle de Reading* was set to music by Jacques Ibert.

1933 Richard Miller, the young hero of Eugene O'Neill's *Ah, Wilderness* quotes from *The Ballad.* Miller was created by Elisha Cook, Jr, in New York and by Cyril Cusack in Dublin and London.

1937 *The Ballad* was performed by the Wayfarer's Civic Repertory Theatre, San Francisco.

1947 Jean-Jacques Etchevery choreographed a ballet to music by Jacques Ibert at Opéra-Comique, Paris.

1961 Vladek Scheybal appeared in *Man of Rope*, a fourteen-minute 16mm film directed by Michael Elster for BFI Experimental Film/Oxford University Labour Club. The screenplay was by Michael Elster and Laszlo Marton.

1963 George C Scott appeared in *The Brazen Bell*, an American film directed by James Sheldon, in which he was cast as a schoolmaster, who gave an impassioned reading of *The Ballad* to distract two convicts who were holding the school to hostage.

1974 The BBC played a tape of Oscar Wilde reading the last three stanzas of *The Ballad*, which it was purported he had made when he visited the American stand at the Paris Exhibition in 1900. The authenticity of the recording was doubted.

1979 Robert Tanitch directed a production at Christopher Wren School, Hammersmith, London.

1983 Robert Stephens read *The Ballad* at the Royal National Theatre, London.

1988 Richard Kwietniowski directed a British film, which 'attempted to provide a modern-day visual interpretation of Oscar Wilde's testimonial at Reading Gaol.'

1992 Mark Burgess dramatised and performed *Oscar Wilde and The Ballad of Reading Gaol* at the Brighton Festival and then on tour. The director was Ian Rimington.

1994 A one-off concert reading was staged at the Lyric Theatre, Hammersmith, London, and broadcast on BBC Radio 3. The cast included Bette Bourne, Stephen Fry, Ian McKellen, Malcolm Sinclair, Neil Tennant, Tom Wakefield and Stephen Whinnery. Neil Bartlett directed and hosted the production, which was in aid of Stonewall.

1998 Shaw Festival, Niagara-on-the-Lake, Ontario, Canada. Neil Munro directed a staged reading of *The Ballad of Oscar Wilde*, an adaptation of *The Ballad of Reading Gaol*, interspersed with extracts from the transcripts of the trials. Neil Barclay played Oscar Wilde.

ACKNOWLEDGEMENTS

I should like to begin by expressing my appreciation to my publisher, Michael Earley, and my editors, Liz Hornby and David Salmo.

I am grateful to Merlin Holland, Oscar Wilde's grandson, for his assistance and also for his permission to reproduce photographs from his private collection.

I should like to thank Madeleine Boughton at Abbey Theatre, Dublin, Ireland; Marie Rooney and Dorothea Melvin at Gate Theatre, Dublin, Ireland; Odette Yazbeck and Dawn Pustelnik at Shaw Festival, Niagara-on-the-Lake, Ontario, Canada; Dina Croce at Trinity Rep, Rhode Island, Washington, USA; Dan Petry at The Florentine Opera Company, Milwaukee, Wisconsin, USA; Ralph Weeks at The Pasdanena Playhouse, California, USA; Daisy Kaiser and Margaret Mooney at Citadel, Edmonton, Canada; Richie Keaster and Ryan Levett at Bill Kenwright Ltd; the press office at Palace Theatre, Watford; the press office at the Opera House, Buxton; the press office at The Citizens' Theatre, Glasgow; Pam Langfield at Key Theatre, Peterbrough; Neil Dickens at Turner Entertainment Networks International Ltd; Jennifer Vernor-Miles at The Bach Choir; Sarah-Jane Edwards at Kerwin Millard; Eric Tessier Lavigne at TNT Music Theatre; Tim Croall at Theatre Royal, Plymouth.

I should like to express my appreciation to all the staff at The New York Library for Performing Arts, New York, USA; Jonathan Rosenthal and Rob Scott at The Museum of Television and Radio, New York, USA; R.Russell Maylone at Northwestern University, Illinois, USA; Leslie Steel at Mitchell Library, State Library, New South Wales, Australia; the librarian at Stratford Festival Archive, Stratford, Ontario, Canada; Fiona Meiklejohn at TNL Picture Library, London; the staff at the library of The French Institute, London.

I should like also to thank Daniel Betts, Daniel Figuero, Peter Hirst, Syd McCartney, Charles McDonald and Flint McKinney.

Finally, and certainly not least, I am extremely grateful to all the staff of the Theatre Museum, London; all the staff of Westminster Central Library, London; and all the staff of the British Film Institute reference library and viewing services.

Index

ACTORS WHO HAVE PLAYED OSCAR WILDE

ACTORS WHO HAVE PLAYED LADY BRACKNELL